ENCYCLOPEDIA OF
HUMAN
GEOGRAPHY

GERALD R. PITZL

GREENWOOD PUBLISHING
Westport, Connecticut • London

Library of Congress Cataloging-in-Publication Data

Pitzl, Gerald R.
  Encyclopedia of human geography / Gerald R. Pitzl.
    p. cm.
  Includes bibliographical references (p.).
  ISBN 0–313–32010–1 (alk. paper)
  1. Human geography—Encyclopedias. I. Title.
GF4.P58 2004
304.2′03—dc21   2002041594

British Library Cataloguing-in-Publication Data is available.

Library of Congress Catalog Card Number: 2002041594
ISBN: 0–313–32010–1

First published in 2004

Greenwood Press, 88 Post Road West, Westport, CT 06881
An imprint of Greenwood Publishing Group, Inc.
www.greenwood.com

Printed in the United States of America

∞

The paper used in this book complies with the
Permanent Paper Standard issued by the National
Information Standards Organization (Z39.48–1984).

10 9 8 7 6 5 4 3 2 1

To my wife,
for her encouragement and understanding

Contents

List of Entries

List of Entries by Topic

HUMAN GEOGRAPHY (GENERAL)

ENVIRONMENT

MAPS AND CARTOGRAPHY

NOTABLE INDIVIDUALS IN THE FIELD OF HUMAN GEOGRAPHY

POLITICAL GEOGRAPHY

POPULATION GEOGRAPHY

URBAN GEOGRAPHY

Introduction

Human geography is a broad and fascinating field within the larger discipline of geography. Simply stated, human geography considers all aspects of geography not covered by physical geography except for the more technically based areas, such as cartography and geographic information systems. However, human geography uses maps and other graphics produced in these two areas in research and analysis and incorporates themes in physical geography when doing so will advance the work under way.

The main focus of human geography is, of course, the presence and activities of humans. Themes within human geography reflect a number of perspectives: culture, population, economic activity, spatial behavior, political activity, urbanization, perception of place, and the many and varied ways in which humans interact with one another and with their environment. Studying the dynamic content of human geography is like journeying into the minds of other culture groups, being present as socioeconomic development unfolds in a remote African nation, or cruising the speed-of-light communications systems that make the global economy hum. Human geography is about human activity and it is, therefore, an exciting intellectual and emotional engagement.

Beginning with **absolute location** and ending with **zero population growth (ZPG),** this encyclopedia includes 266 entries covering pertinent models, concepts, and theories used in human geography. In addition, many of the most prominent personalities associated with geography throughout history are introduced. For example, the eminent nineteenth-century scientist Charles Darwin was a member of Britain's esteemed Royal Geographical Society. The Greek scholar Herodotus, who has been called the father of both history and ethnography, wrote extensively about the people and places he visited. The field of geography can claim him as well, because of the profound work he did in describing, and theorizing about, the earth and its physical and human elements.

Each of the entries is followed by at least two suggested readings (book, article, or stable Web site) that may be referred to for additional information.

Some entries contain cross-references, which are identified in **bold.** The entry section is followed by a selected bibliography, comprising current books within the field. Finally, an appendix lists all the entries grouped by topics within human geography.

The entries in the *Encyclopedia of Human Geography* represent only the tip of the iceberg, so to speak, in this expansive and exciting field of study. There are hundreds of prominent personalities who wear the mantle of "geographer," and there are thousands of ideas and concepts awaiting those who would choose to go further in their exploration of human geography. It is hoped that this encyclopedia will be helpful to the student as a companion to an Advanced Placement or college textbook, to the general user who simply wants information on aspects of human geography, or to the researcher who wishes to confirm the understanding of a particular topic.

A

Absolute location. The concept of location identifies one of the basic properties of geography: all places are located on the surface of the earth, and their locations can be unambiguously identified using a number of spatial reference systems. Commonly, the spatial reference system is latitude and longitude. For example, Hanoi, Vietnam, is located at 21 degrees north latitude and 106 degrees east longitude. There can be no confusion about this form of spatial specification: it is an unambiguous reference to Hanoi's location within the latitude-longitude system. The absolute location of Hanoi has been determined. There are other spatial systems that can be used to find absolute location.

Geography is a discipline that deals with all forms of interaction, movement, and spatial variation on the earth's surface. Because it is a spatial discipline, the need for a precise and unambiguous method to pinpoint a place is essential. China's landing on Mischief Reef in the South China Sea in February 1995 drew worldwide attention. If one were not intimately familiar with the location of Mischief Reef, a glance at an atlas would reveal its absolute location to be 10 degrees latitude and 116 degrees east longitude. Further reading of the map would show Mischief Reef to be one of a number of tiny landmasses in the Spratly Islands. Once absolute location is found, a geographer can use another powerful concept to gain greater understanding of the significance of a place. It is often stated that absolute location alone is of limited importance; this is certainly true in the case of Mischief Reef. In fact, the true importance of the place lies in its proximity to countries that surround it. If we refer to Mischief Reef, or any other place, in relation to surrounding places, we have invoked the powerful geographical concept of **relative location.** The geographer's starting point in using relative location analysis, however, must proceed from a consideration of absolute location.

The examples of absolute location given thus far have been of point form. That is, the precise intersection of a set of latitude and longitude lines, which describes a point with no real areal dimension. Clearly, Hanoi and Mischief Reef have area. The validity of the absolute location is, nonetheless, not compromised. Both places are unambiguously located. But what about specifying the absolute location of a place that has an extensive area? For example, Colorado's absolute location would require the designation of the latitude and longitude coordinates for all four of its corners and the specification that the state comprises the area of the polygon enclosed by these points. Clearly, an attempt to use this technique to state the absolute location of an administrative area with irregular boundaries, such as Chile or Japan, would be difficult. Yet the principle is valid; cadastral maps, those that clearly identify the dimensions and areal extent of land for legal purposes such as ownership and transfer of title, are examples of absolute location.

Suggested Readings: George J. Demko, *Why in the World: Adventures in Geography*, New York: Anchor Books/Doubleday, 1992; Tim F. Wood, "Thinking in Geography," *Geography*, vol. 72 (1987).

Accessibility. Geography is a spatial discipline concerned not only with the location of people and places but also, more important, with the manner in which these entities interact. The concept of **connectivity** considers the many pathways (highways, air routes, sea-lanes, e-mail, fax, etc.) that allow interaction between distant points. Accessibility is the concept that determines the efficiency of these pathways. The advent of the telephone dramatically increased the accessibility of users. In recent years, cellular phones further increased this accessibility. No longer is it necessary to be near a permanently installed telephone; a person can be reached virtually anywhere within the service area of the cellular phone. However, cellular circuits can become overloaded at times, and when this occurs, the message "all lines are busy; please try again later" signals that accessibility through this medium is temporarily diminished.

Traveling by automobile from the suburbs of any large city to the **central business district (CBD)** reflects variable accessibility, depending on the time of day. To drive this route during rush hour in the morning would take longer than it would at 8 P.M., for instance. Inclement weather can affect accessibility. Blizzards and severe rainstorms will slow highway traffic, and if a storm is sufficiently severe, airports may be closed. Here, again, accessibility is diminished for a period of time.

Accessibility may be considered in historical context. During the westward movement in the United States, a journey from New York to the Pacific Coast could take months. By contrast, a passenger jet can leave La Guardia airport in New York City and arrive in San Francisco, for instance, in a matter of hours. Improvements in transportation technology "bring places closer together," as the saying goes.

The concept of accessibility in geographical studies has traditionally dealt with determining the efficiency of transportation and communication systems. In recent years, accessibility has also been applied in the social realm. For example, during the era of **apartheid** in South Africa, black South Africans were effectively excluded from access to sectors of the economy and social settings exclusive to whites.

Suggested Readings: Brian Goodall, *The Facts on File Dictionary of Human Geography,* New York: Facts on File, 1987; Ali Rogers et al., *The Student's Companion to Geography,* Cambridge, Mass.: Basil Blackwell, 1992.

Acculturation. Changes in value systems, attitudes, customs, language, and other cultural traits brought about by the contact of dissimilar culture groups make up the process of acculturation. Contact by one culture with another invariably implies **cultural diffusion** in its various forms, the movement of one or more culture groups into the area of another. In most cases, the weaker culture group will adopt a significant array of cultural attributes from the dominant group. It is not uncommon, however, for dominant groups to adopt some cultural traits through the interaction. For example, when the Spanish and the Portuguese occupied regions in Latin America, these dominant groups established towns, introduced their religion, and altered the agricultural systems. In turn, the European occupiers adopted certain aspects of architecture, clothing forms, and other cultural attributes from the indigenous culture groups. Another example of acculturation can be found in the southwestern United States, where ancient architectural styles reflect influences from Spain, Morocco, and various American Indian groups in the region.

In the nineteenth century, following the Meiji Restoration (1868), Japan adopted Western technology and began the development of a global economic system after the European model, an unprecedented action at that time by an Asian nation. Following World War II, during the U.S. occupation of Japan, many Japanese adopted American dress styles, diets, and sports, especially baseball and golf. In turn, the United States adopted, in some measure, certain Japanese foods and ways of thinking. The Japanese adoption of Western foods (milk and meat in particular) has resulted in a gain in the average physical height of the Japanese. These dietary changes have also brought on a higher incidence of certain stomach cancers.

Acculturation usually requires considerable time to be effected; it is not an overnight process. Also, acculturation may be a painful process. If the weaker culture group has been conquered, then the process of acculturation may well be forced and unpleasant.

The second period of **colonialism,** beginning in the nineteenth century, resulted in an abundant number of examples of acculturation. The French encouraged acculturation in their North African colonies with the aim of moving the process toward complete **assimilation.**

Acculturation in the United States is, of course, related to the notion of the **melting pot,** the idea that any and all culture groups migrating to the United States would undergo a complete and unequivocal "Americanization." This outcome has never been realized, and in recent decades there has been an increase in ethnic identity and the desire of many minority groups to retain more of their own cultural traits. Conflict between official governmental aims and the persistence of ethnic identity has surfaced in attempts to make English the official language in some states. Those in favor of this move suggest that language is a key component in cultural makeup and that to avoid making English the official language undermines the process of acculturation. Those against this stance counter that one's native language is essential to retaining ethnic identity and that English can be learned more slowly and as needed. This is a significant controversy, because census results show that 15 percent of American families report that a language other than English is routinely spoken in their homes. *See also* **Ethnicity.**

Suggested Readings: James P. Allen and Eugene Tumer, *We the People: An Atlas of America's Ethnic Diversity*, New York: Macmillan, 1988; Stanley Lieberson and Mary C. Waters, *From Many Strands: Ethnic and Racial Groupings in Contemporary America*, Census Monograph Series, New York: Russell Sage Foundation, 1988.

Acid rain. Areas of high population density and heavy industrial production are the sources of acid rain, a general term covering rainfall that is laden with pollutants. The regions of highest generation of the materials found in acid rain are the Midwest in the United States and the area in Europe of extensive industrial production in eastern Germany. Acid rain forms from the burning of fossil fuels, especially coal, and the release of sulfur dioxide and nitrogen oxide into the atmosphere. These materials are sent aloft and picked up by the prevailing winds and sent hundreds of kilometers into adjacent regions. When these materials mix with water in the atmosphere, a chemical reaction takes place and the new material is deposited as acid rain. In the case of sulfur dioxide (SO_2), the chemical reaction is straightforward: SO_2 (sulfur dioxide) + O (oxygen) + H_2O (water) → H_2SO_4 (weak sulfuric acid). When acid rain falls to earth, it can, over time, cause extensive damage to forests, lakes, soil, and even buildings.

Lake drainage has been extensive in the eastern United States and eastern Canada. Over 20 percent of the lakes in eastern Canada have high levels of toxins attributed to acid rain. Ironically, the source region for the acid rain that plagues the eastern United States and eastern Canada is the American Midwest, where heavy industry and coal-fired power plants emit the pollutants. This is a prime example of a negative environmental outcome of **spatial interaction.**

Levels of acid rain are at their highest in regions of eastern Europe. Large parts of the Bohemian Forest in the Czech Republic have been severely damaged. Consequent loss of forest and vegetative cover has resulted in higher incidence of flooding as rainwater cascades down barren slopes, swelling rivers beyond their capacity.

The Black Triangle in central and eastern Europe, comprising portions of Germany, Poland, the Czech Republic, and Slovakia has, without doubt, the most extreme acid rain damage. Forests, lakes, and soil have been severely affected, and respiratory problems in humans are exceptionally high. People living within the Black Triangle have a life expectancy 10 years lower than that of their parents.

Buildings and monuments have also suffered from the effects of acid rain. The Acropolis in Greece, the Taj Mahal in India, and Cleopatra's Needle in England all show signs of deterioration from acid rain. Acid rain is a classic example of severe environmental degradation.

Suggested Readings: David Waugh, *Geography: An Integrated Approach*, London: Thomas Nelson and Sons, 1990; Alan Wellburn, *Air Pollution and Acid Rain*, 2nd ed., Reading, Mass.: Addison, Wesley, Longman, 1994.

Activity space. Geographers use the term *activity space* to identify the areal extent of a person's regularly visited places during a day. The activity space of an individual is an aspect of human spatial behavior, a key theme in geography. The daily set of activities and the space in which they occur will vary greatly, depending on a number of factors. For instance, the activity space of a preschool child will be limited to perhaps a few rooms in the home and a sojourn into an enclosed yard. As the child enters the school-age years, significant changes will occur in the areal extent of the activity space. The day may begin with a ride on a school bus, followed by several hours of varying activities within the school (class time, exercise, lunch, more classes, and assemblies) before the return trip home.

The extent of activity space for an adult engaged in the work world may be very extensive. It is quite common for a worker to commute as far as 100 miles by automobile or train on a daily basis. Also, hundreds of individuals travel daily, or at least several times a week, by air between the key metropolitan areas of New York, Boston, and Washington. The activity space for most people in the agricultural regions of developing countries is minuscule by comparison. Regardless of societal setting, the activity space of older people may be constricted because of physical infirmity or limited access to transportation.

In the 1960s and 1970s, the Swedish geographer **Torsten Hagerstrand** pioneered the notion of "time geography," providing a technique to diagram and assign duration and direction to each event and movement within an activity space. Also around that time, Alan Pred used activity space analysis in a study of the daily visits and movements of a Boston mercantilist in the nineteenth century. Pred's study included a detailed map of the area in which the mercantilist carried out his daily activities. Pred contended that the study of activity spaces of multiple businessmen in the same area of Boston would be helpful in gaining insights into how the mercantilist operated.

Suggested Readings: Paul Cloke et al., *Approaching Human Geography*, New York: Guilford Press, 1991; Brian Goodall, *The Facts on File Dictionary of Human Geography*, New York: Facts on File, 1987.

Age and sex ratios. *See* **Population pyramid.**

Agglomeration. People and activities tend to concentrate in a location to share facilities and services for mutual benefit. The localization of activities and the centralization of business and manufacturing activities are identified as agglomeration. Clustering of people and activities in this manner maximizes the opportunities for sharing facilities and services and for the easy transfer of commodities, components in manufacturing processes, information of mutual interest and importance, and labor supply.

The advantage of agglomeration to manufacturing activities is especially important in the category of transportation costs. An industry requiring a regular supply of components for its production processes will minimize transport costs to the greatest extent possible. Thus, suppliers of components are at an economic advantage to locate close to the major firm. The importance of locating industrial activities in order to minimize transport costs was strongly advocated early in the twentieth century by the economist Alfred Weber, who developed **Weber's least cost theory.**

One of the best examples of agglomeration in a single industry is automobile manufacturing in the United States. Throughout the twentieth century, Detroit, Michigan, remained the prominent production center for automobiles. The major manufacturers (Ford, Chrysler, General Motors) and others clustered together in this metropolitan area. In addition, thousands of suppliers of components needed in automobile assembly located in or near Detroit to ensure the most efficient and low-cost transfer of components to the assembly points in Detroit. In recent years, the degree of concentration exhibited by Detroit during the heyday of automobile production has decreased. However, the Detroit metropolitan area remains the single most important automobile-manufacturing center in the United States. Another example of agglomeration in manufacturing is the concentration of armament-producing firms in Essen, Germany.

Retail firms, as well, tend to agglomerate, realizing that shoppers will take advantage of the close proximity of several competing stores within walking distance in order to compare products and prices. In this sense, the modern shopping mall with many retailers and food vendors under one roof is quintessential agglomeration.

The location of office complexes within metropolitan areas is another example of agglomeration. It is still true that a great deal of business is conducted face to face. The high-rise skyscrapers found in virtually every well-developed metropolitan center best exemplify the recognized advantage of placing office personnel in the closest possible proximity to others with whom they do business.

The high-technology industry, which emerged with dramatic speed in the late twentieth century, was agglomerated from the beginning. Silicon Valley, near San Jose, California; Route 128 around Boston; and the Research Triangle in Raleigh and Durham, North Carolina, represent only a few of the many clusters of high-technology industries in the United States. Two of the major reasons for the localization of firms in this industry are (1) proximity to major research universities, and (2) the availability of a trained labor force.

Concentration and centralization of industrial and manufacturing activities creates spatial inequities regionally and globally. These points of intense production, known as **growth pole**s, become accumulators of immense wealth and tend to increase economic disadvantages in peripheral locations.

Suggested Readings: Keith Chapman and David Walker, *Industrial Location*, Cambridge, Mass.: Basil Blackwell, 1991; H. P. Watts, *Industrial Geography*, New York: Longman Scientific and Technical/Wiley, 1987.

Agribusiness. Agribusiness generally means the industry that includes the operation of farms, farm equipment, and farm commodities. Monumental changes have occurred in agriculture since the 1950s. New technology has created advanced agricultural implements, more-effective chemical additives, and hybrid crops engineered to produce higher yields in a shorter growing time. A modern-day **agricultural revolution** has been underway for more than 50 years, and it will likely continue.

The farm scene in North America and Europe is marked by increased output of crops per unit area, decreasing farm numbers and increasing farm size, and great specialization in agricultural products. All of these technological inputs, combined with vastly improved surface transportation systems and food-storage facilities, have taken agriculture far beyond the days of the isolated family farm serving only its immediate area. Large-scale agriculture systems exhibit extraordinary areal range, and the industry's **accessibility** to distant markets is steadily increasing.

Agribusiness identifies the vast and dynamic interaction of the farm sector with other technological and business sectors. Briefly, this intricate system includes all aspects of agriculture: implements and machinery; seeds; chemicals; modern farm-management practices; the farms themselves; the crops and animal products that are sent to food-processing plants; and the vast delivery and marketing organizations that produce, package, and distribute the final products. Agribusiness is truly big business. Although only 2 percent of both the U.S. and Canadian workforce is directly involved in the growing of food products, 20 percent of the workforce is engaged throughout the myriad of activities in the agribusiness complex.

The agribusiness system is highly capital intensive and, consequently, it is increasingly costly for farmers to take part in this sophisticated system. Thousands of small farms, unable to compete with the large, specialized, and more financially sound farms, have been forced out of business. Although most farms are still in private hands, other operations in the agribusiness system are based in large corporations.

Suggested Readings: David B. Grigg, *An Introduction to Agricultural Geography*, 2nd ed., New York: Routledge, 1995; Ingolph Vogeler, *The Myth of the Family Farm: Agribusiness Dominance of United States Agriculture*, Boulder, Colo.: Westview Press, 1981.

Agricultural Revolution. The term *Agricultural Revolution* is most frequently associated with pronounced changes and improvements in agriculture in England before and during the **Industrial Revolution** of the late eighteenth century. This revolution has been variously identified as beginning as early as the end of the Middle Ages and extending into the nineteenth century. The Agricultural Revolution both acted as a stimulus to the Industrial Revolution and benefited from a number of its inventions, including advanced agricultural machinery to replace human and animal labor. New approaches to crop rotation; the elimination of the open-field system; the awarding of land to private owners through the Enclosure Acts (such as the Statute of Merton, passed in 1235); the use of fences, walls, and other boundary identifiers; and the expansion of arable land were key factors in this important era. Cities were growing as the Industrial Revolution continued its phenomenal growth, and the agricultural sector was expanding in order to provide necessary food for a growing population.

The name Agricultural Revolution has also been applied to two other periods in human history. The first period of agricultural advancement and innovation occurred between 12,000 and 14,000 years ago, and the process most likely continued for several thousand years over a number of regions. The most significant innovation was the practice of cultivating plants in place rather than migrating to find edible plants in the wild. Cultivation of roots and seeds in place allowed for the subsequent development of a sedentary form of life and permanent settlements. In time, the first significant moves toward urbanization and new governmental forms began to evolve. With the amount of food increasing, the first recognizable **population explosion** occurred.

Another Agricultural Revolution began in earnest in the 1950s. Continued improvements in seed and chemical additives combined with advanced agricultural machinery and computer-based farm management practices continue to bring higher crop yields with less human labor. Remarkable transformations have taken place in the farm section as the era of the traditional family farm gives way to corporate-structured **agribusiness** enterprises. Advances in agriculture have been most pronounced in the developed countries, but an important exception is the **Green Revolution,** which brought great increases in grain production to the countries of South Asia.

Suggested Readings: William H. Bender, "How Much Food Will We Need in the 21st Century?" *Environment*, vol. 39 (1997); I. Seidl and C. A. Tisdell, "Carrying Capacity Reconsidered: From Malthus' Population Theory to Culture Carrying Capacity," *Ecological Economics*, vol. 31 (1999).

Apartheid. Apartheid, which means "apartness," was an official policy in South Africa from 1948 until its demise in 1991. It stipulated the strict separation of the nation's four racial groups: whites, Asians, "colored" (people who were racially mixed), and black. Each group had separate legal status. The apartheid policy was enacted at a time when other African countries were gaining independence from colonial-era rulers and blacks were assuming leadership positions. The National Party in South Africa, controlled by white South Africans, known as Afrikaners, took the opposite position and enacted a policy that was unambiguously white supremacist.

Blacks were discriminated against in public transportation, theaters, parks, education, and the workplace. Within the cities of South Africa, particular areas were designated for residential, economic, and social activities strictly along racial lines. The main impetus for the apartheid policy was to ensure white supremacy and to control the black population, which represented 75 percent of the people in South Africa.

The official position of the government of South Africa was that separation would ensure that whites would not be in a position to dominate blacks. In order to further this position, the government established 10 "homeland" areas designated for occupation by the leading black national groups. The ultimate aim of the government was for these homelands to become independent sovereign states. It was clear from the beginning, however, that the homelands did not have the necessary economic, social, and political structures to ever become separate countries. The homelands were located in the poorest areas of South Africa and those least accessible to points of employment in cities outside the homelands.

The apartheid system was by its very nature repressive to blacks in South Africa. As such, the government was under pressure to end the policy from the beginning of apartheid through the 1980s. In 1977, the United States adopted the Sullivan Principles in an effort to increase opportunities for black Africans. By doing so, the United States hoped to influence South Africa to set aside its apartheid policy. By 1989, a number of sanctions had been placed on South Africa. Even neighboring African countries, including Zimbabwe, were expressing their opposition to South Africa's apartheid policy. However, Zimbabwe's response was tempered somewhat, because it relied on South Africa's ports for its import and export activity.

The United States also enacted sanctions to eliminate bank loans to South Africa, discontinue the purchase of Krugerrands (the South African currency), and to discourage the purchase of stocks from companies that did business in South Africa.

Throughout the early 1990s, internal rebellion by blacks was frequent and vocal. Finally, in 1991, South African president Frederick W. DeKlerk repealed all legislation authorizing apartheid. During the previous year, DeKlerk had released Nelson Mandela, African National Congress leader, who had been in prison for 26 years. Mandela eventually was elected president of South Africa. Apartheid laws are gone, but the effects of this policy will be felt in South Africa for years to come.

Suggested Readings: Anthony Lemon, ed., *The Geography of Change in South Africa*, Chichester, England: Wiley, 1995; Ali Mazrui, *The Africans: A Triple Heritage*, Boston: Little, Brown, 1986.

Aquaculture. Aquaculture, the practice of raising and harvesting fish and other water produce, has been practiced for thousands of years, especially in Asia. Breeding of some fish has occurred for more than 200 years. In recent years, however, a more sophisticated form of aquaculture is being conducted in many regions of the world. Aquaculturists are increasing the production of animal protein and some edible plants in controlled and isolated environments in order to increase yields. Aquaculture is an important response to continually expanding food needs in the world. Lakes, ponds, canals, and coastal bays are the settings for this efficient and low-cost method of producing edible marine life. Fish grow more rapidly in these controlled situations, where food sources are regular and predators are not a concern.

Fish production globally comes from three primary sources: inland lakes and rivers, comprising about 7 percent of total production; marine sources, by far the greatest contributor, at 78 percent; and aquaculture from both inland and marine containments, totaling 15 percent. The variety of fish produced through aquaculture is impressive. Trout hatcheries are especially abundant; shrimp breeding is expanding along coastal locations; and extensive crayfish, catfish, and oyster operations are found especially in the southeastern United States.

Recently, large-scale, mechanized aquaculture "farms" have been developed. These giant operations are similar in scale and financial structure to **agribusiness** concerns found in the farming sector. It is not surprising to see the scale of operation increase in aquaculture. First, world food demand continues to increase. Second, overfishing in ocean waters is fast depleting once-abundant schools of fish, and yields are decreasing. Third, the potential for growth in aquaculture is very high as the market for seafood continues to expand. Regional reliance on fish in diets varies a great deal, and only about 2 percent of all food consumed globally comes from that source. The coastal regions of Asia are the clear leaders in fish consumption, and their production of this product through aquaculture is high. Production of shellfish through aquaculture along the coastal zone from India through Southeast Asia to China and Japan accounts for 80 percent of the world's total.

Suggested Readings: Tom Dyson, *Population and Food: Global Trends and Future Prospects*, New York: Routledge, 1996; Hal Kane, "Growing Fish in Fields," *World Watch*, vol. 6 (1993).

Aristotle (384–322 B.C.). Student of the great Greek philosopher Plato, teacher of the Macedonian king Alexander the Great, and one of the giants in Greek thought, Aristotle conceived of the world as striving toward a state of perfection. His was a teleological view, one based on the belief that the universe was planned by a higher power and was being constructed as time passed according to a grand plan. His view on this matter differed from that of Plato, his schoolmaster, who contended that the world was degrading from perfection.

Aristotle is important in early geography because he dealt with the earth and its components. He taught that the best way to develop and test a theory was through direct observation. In proposing this approach, Aristotle formally introduced the inductive procedure of investigation: proceed from the detailed and directly observable phenomena toward higher-level generalization and theory. Plato, taking the opposite approach, proposed beginning an analysis with a theory derived from deduction and then working toward the particular.

Aristotle agreed with Plato that the earth was spherical. Aristotle's conclusion in this regard reflected his strong belief in direct observation. He noted the curved surface of the shadow that covered the moon during an eclipse. Aristotle also determined that the altitude above the horizon for stars would increase as the observer moved north. If the earth were flat, no change would occur.

Aristotle was incorrect about one important feature of the earth: he contended that the earth was stationary in the universe and that all other celestial bodies revolved around it. This idea was taken up by **Ptolemy** (ca. A.D. 100–ca. 170) and persisted as a false theory until Copernicus (1473–1543) correctly proposed a sun-centered solar system and Galileo (1564–1642) proved the correctness of Copernican ideas.

Aristotle concurred with the earlier prominent scholar, Empedocles (490–430 B.C.), who stated that all matter was composed of four basic substances: air, fire, earth, and water. Aristotle added a fifth substance, the "aether," which he contended did not occur on earth but made up the celestial bodies. Although these early notions were later refuted, Aristotle's conclusion that the basic substances combined and modified to create new matter implied the important principle of process, or change over time. Aristotle used only logic to support his theories. He gave no thought to setting up controlled experiments. This is surprising, given his strong position on direct observation to both build and test theories.

Aristotle believed in the early notions of the latitudinal zonation of the earth. In this model, the zone nearest the equator was too hot for human occupancy and was named the Torrid Zone. Seafarers carefully avoided sailing too far south toward the equator for fear that they would literally burn up from the heat of the sun. To the north of the inhabited region of the earth was the Frigid Zone, again uninhabitable because of severely low temperatures. Between them was the *ecumene,* or temperate zone, the inhabitable region. Aristotle also speculated that a southern temperate zone existed but that it was inaccessible because of the Torrid Zone.

This zonal climatic theory persisted for centuries. In the thirteenth century A.D., the German scholar Albertus Magnus (1193–1280) took Aristotle's idea about the Torrid Zone and suggested that if humans entered it, their skin would turn black. He then further postulated that following a move back to the temperate zone, the skin would return to its original light color. The climatic zone theory is an early example of **environmental determinism.**

Suggested Readings: George Kish, *A Source Book in Geography*, Cambridge, Mass.: Harvard University Press, 1978; Geoffrey J. Martin and Preston E. James, *All Possible Worlds: A History of Geographical Ideas*, 3rd ed., New York: John Wiley & Sons, 1993.

Arithmetic density. *See* **Population density.**

Asian Tigers. *Asian Tigers* refers to South Korea, Taiwan, Hong Kong, and Singapore, each of which made dramatic advances in economic growth in the late twentieth century. The amazing success of Japan, rising from its defeat after World War II to its preeminent position as a leading global economic power only a few decades later, was the model for the success of the Asian Tigers. All four of these states benefited from highly skilled and educated workforces, depended on export sales of primarily high-value-added products, and could boast of high-level entrepreneurial leadership. The four original Tigers are now, in a way, reduced to three with the return, in 1997, of Hong Kong to Chinese control. The ultimate fate of Taiwan is in doubt; China considers Taiwan to be one of its provinces and in time it may well revert to China's control. Both South Korea and Taiwan were occupied by Japan early in the twentieth century and were released following the end of World War II.

South Korea was forced to develop an industrial base following the division of the Korean Peninsula at the 38th parallel. This rather arbitrary splitting of the country left virtually all industry in the north, leaving the south with the major agricultural region. By the 1970s, with heavy inputs of aid from the United States, South Korea was on the road to becoming an industrial power in East Asia. Iron and steel, automobiles, and shipbuilding became well established in burgeoning urban centers. Only two decades earlier, South Korea had primarily an agriculturally based economy. Textile manufacturing expanded throughout the growth period, and in the 1990s, South Korea was developing a high-technology industry.

Taiwan became the home of the Kuomintang government following its ouster from the Chinese mainland in 1949. As China followed Mao Tse Tung—who emerged as leader of the Chinese Communist Party (CCP) in 1935—into the era of communism, Taiwan immediately moved toward the establishment of an industrial base. The island had a well-established and commercially productive agricultural sector, which proved to be an important economic stimulus to the newly developing industrial thrust. Taiwan began to develop high-technology industries in the 1980s and 1990s.

Hong Kong, a British colony for 99 years until its return to China in 1997, is one of the world's most important trading centers. Long famous for its textile and clothing businesses, Hong Kong has expanded its economic base to include the manufacture of electronics, a global financial sector, and a thriving tourism industry. Under the Basic Law, established following Hong Kong's return to Chinese control, the city is allowed to operate as a free-trade center until 2047. Some experts doubt whether the Chinese leadership will allow Hong Kong to retain this status for that length of time, and Hong Kong's long-term status in China is unclear.

Singapore, like Hong Kong, is a **city-state.** Its strategic location astride the Malacca Strait has guaranteed its primacy as a world-class import-export center for many years. Singapore is an established and vibrant trading center and in recent years has begun the manufacture of high-technology equipment and computer parts. Both Hong Kong and Singapore are considered entrepôt states, or intermediary centers of trade, because of their roles at intermediary points facilitating trade between foreign countries.

All four of the Asian Tigers have established a clear global reach. Although Hong Kong's future is somewhat in doubt and that of Taiwan is similarly unclear, it is true that all four, along with Japan and China—as members of the **Pacific Rim economic region**—are the key economic centers of East Asia.

Suggested Readings: Barbara Weightman, *Dragons and Tigers: A Geography of South, East, and Southeast Asia,* New York: John Wiley & Sons, 2002; World Bank, *The East Asian Miracle,* New York: Oxford University Press, 1993.

Assimilation. The concept of assimilation addresses the theoretical completion of the **acculturation** process. Two forms of assimilation have been identified: (1) cultural or behavioral assimilation, which is essentially the acculturation part of the process; and (2) structural assimilation, the acceptance by the entering culture of the value system of the host group, the uniting of the ethnic aspects of the two groups, and the incorporation of the new group within the occupational structure of the host. Two of the important indicators of the degree to which assimilation has progressed are rates of intermarriage and the degree of areal segregation of new groups, especially as evidenced in urban areas.

It is clear that the assimilation process is an extension of acculturation. And like acculturation, the process will show varying degrees of completion. Even the early European immigrants to the United States have retained particular cultural traits decades after entering the country and experiencing the process leading to assimilation. The presence of Irish restaurants, Italian markets, and German social clubs are examples of original cultural attributes expressed long after the essential aspects of assimilation have been completed.

During the period of **colonialism** that followed the discovery of the Western Hemisphere by Europeans in 1492, a form of selective assimilation was practiced. For example, the Portuguese developed a type of social hierarchy; those in their colonies choosing to attain Portuguese citizenship were allowed to assimilate, whereas those not in that category were relegated to a lesser social status and lower-level jobs.

The completion of a process of assimilation may reverse. As assimilated culture group members gain better jobs and better social situations, cultural differences may again be more apparent. When a reversal of the assimilation process occurs, the situation may well become violent. Examples of reversals include the demands, demonstrations, and forceful actions by several nationalities following the demise of the Soviet Union in 1989. Movements for independence started throughout the region.

Reversals may occur through significant changes in the location of places of employment. For example, when the automobile production facilities in Detroit, Michigan, were moved to the suburbs in the 1960s and 1970s, workers in the city, most of whom were African American, found that their **accessibility** to the new plants was taken away. In this case, an important aspect of structural assimilation, incorporation within the work setting of the host, was virtually eliminated. When assimilation does not occur, or is seriously reversed, the host (country, metropolitan area, neighborhood) may experience serious problems.

Suggested Readings: James P. Allen and Eugene Turner, "Spatial Patterns of Immigrant Assimilation," *Professional Geographer,* vol. 48 (1996); Alejandro Portes and Ruben J. Rumbaut, *Immigrant America,* 2nd ed., Berkeley: University of California Press, 1996.

B

Balkanization. Balkanization is the division of a region or country into smaller administrative units, usually along ethnic lines. The term derives from a region in southern Europe originally composed of five countries—Albania, Bulgaria, Hungary, Romania, and Yugoslavia—created by the Allied powers following World War I from the Austro-Hungarian Empire and the Ottoman Empire. The five countries became known collectively as the Balkans (or Balkan States), the name of a regional mountain range and peninsula. The region comprising the old empires had a long-standing history of strife among adherents of different religions, who came into close contact with one another. Christians and Muslims competed, as did Catholics and Orthodox groups and Serbs and Kosovars.

The Balkans held together through most of the remaining decades of the twentieth century. However, in the early 1990s, following the demise of the Soviet Union, several regional groups within Yugoslavia broke away, and four new countries were formed: Bosnia and Herzegovina, Croatia, Macedonia, and Slovenia. Once the breakup took place, ethnic strife quickly followed, as conflict raged over boundary disputes among the new countries. Conflict occurred again in the late 1990s in Kosovo between Serbs and Kosovars, who are ethnic Albanian Muslims. Strife and tension continued into the twenty-first century. The region experienced balkanization twice in the twentieth century.

Balkanization has also occurred in Africa. In some ways, the **apartheid** policy of creating 10 new homelands to isolate the leading black cultural groups in South Africa was a form of balkanization. However, the Nigerian experience in this regard is especially pertinent. Nigeria was a British colony until it achieved independence in 1960. At that time, the country had three major regions and an extremely diverse population comprising 300 ethnic groups. Nigeria is also a major producer of petroleum, and competition among many of the ethnic groups for a share in oil revenues created tensions throughout the country. Nigeria experienced considerable ethnic strife and a major civil war that killed millions in the 1960s. Balkanization occurred over the years from 1967 through 1991 in four restructuring phases, which resulted in the eventual creation of 30 district states. Along with this tenfold increase in administrative units has come regional demands for autonomy and the polarization of ethnic tensions. Once deemed to be the country in Africa with the greatest promise for future success, Nigeria today faces an uncertain future.

Suggested Readings: David Hooson, *Geography and National Identity*, London: Oxford University Press, 1994; Alan Best and Harm de Blij, *African Survey*, New York: John Wiley & Sons, 1977.

Basic and nonbasic industries. The economic base of an urban area includes its basic industries, those providing goods and services to areas outside its center, and its nonbasic industries—activities directed to maintaining the internal health and viability of the area, such as housing, medical and dental services, schools, shopping, entertainment, and so forth. The ratio between the two gives an indication (although never completely accurate) of their relationship. As a city increases in size, the nonbasic sector will grow at a higher rate than the basic sector.

To understand this variance, consider the city of San Jose, California, the earliest of the major computer-technology centers. Clearly, the major employment sector in San Jose is the computer field, which grew dramatically in the last quarter of the twentieth century. Also, virtually all workers in the computer field were producing for a market outside San Jose. With growth in the basic sector, the nonbasic sector grew at a higher rate, because the increased number of workers providing necessary services in San Jose would also require these same nonbasic services. As a general rule, for every 100 basic workers added to the economy, about 200 additional nonbasic workers are needed. In addition to the new workers, their families are added to the total number of people comprising the population. Clearly, an increase in the number of basic industry workers will create a sizable growth in total population; the measure of this increase has been referred to as the **multiplier effect.** But what happens to the basic-to-nonbasic ratio in times of industry decline? Consider the San Jose example again. In 2000–2001, the technology industry was hard hit by a national economic slowdown. Thousands of computer-related jobs in San Jose were lost, and the basic sector was diminished in size. The nonbasic sector, in this case, did not suffer nearly the same loss. The main reason for this difference lies in the fact that discharged workers do not, as a rule, immediately pull up stakes and leave an area. They stay, along with their families, and continue to rely on the nonbasic sector as they seek other employment.

Suggested Readings: Paul L. Knox, *Urbanization: An Introduction to Urban Geography,* Englewood Cliffs, N.J.: Prentice Hall, 1994; Allan J. Scott, *Metropolis: From the Division of Labor to Urban Form,* Berkeley: University of California Press, 1988.

Behavioral geography. Behavioral geography, in which geographers attempt to explain individual spatial patterns of behavior through studying varied thought processes, began in the 1960s and emerged from the era of the **Quantitative Revolution** in geography. The term *behavioral geography* comes in part from behavioralism, a set of concepts found widely in the social and behavioral sciences. The Quantitative Revolution focused primarily on the optimizing of spatial behavior through the theoretical activities of an entity named "economic man." The focus of investigation centered on aggregate behavior and rational and logical outcomes. There was no consideration of the thought processes of individuals involved in the spatial outcomes under investigation. Behavioral geography, on the other hand, views the thoughts and perceptions of individuals as valid in attempts to explain their spatial patterns of behavior.

When the emphasis shifted to the study of individuals and their approaches to decision making about their environment, the focus of geographical investigation began to consider the mental processes that guided those decisions. Studies emerged that reported individual preferences for residential location, which were then aggregated and recorded as a **mental map.** Other works looked into the question of the perception of **natural hazards.** An extensive literature began to accumulate, attempting to explain why people chose to live in known hazardous areas. Why, for instance, do millions of people choose to live on or near the San Andreas fault in California, a known hazardous region? Why would people choose to live in the hurricane zone on the American southeast coast?

Studies began to appear that looked at **migration** in a different way. In the new approach, the emphasis was on the reasons behind the decision to migrate, an emphasis again on the thought processes involved. The vast and expansive field of **diffusion** emerged from behavioral geography. Diffusion studies have become an exceptionally important subfield in geography. Diffusion deals with the movement of people, goods, and ideas across space; a **diffusion barrier,** as the name implies, may well be encountered, which might stop or slow the process. Behavioral geography gave rise, as well, to studies of individual **activity space,** the study of which can help to explain complex questions in social, political, and economic processes.

Suggested Readings: R. G. Golledge and R. J. Stimson, *Decision Making and Spatial Behavior: A Geographical Perspective,* New York: Guilford Press, 1996; D. J. Walmsley and G. J. Lewis, eds., *People and Environment: Behavioral Approaches to Human Geography,* 2nd ed., New York: John Wiley & Sons, 1993.

Bid-rent curve. In an urban setting, it is generally true that the highest land values will be found near the city center, or **central business district.** Land values away from the city center will decline. Land value and distance from the city center is expressed in a relationship called the bid-rent curve. The shape of the curve is usually convex, indicating rapid declines in land value in zones just outside city center and lower declines in land value farther away from the city center, as the curve flattens.

In a generalized model of the location of functional zones in a city, the city center will have the highest values; a commercial and office zone is found next, then an industrial zone, and finally a broad residential zone. It follows that **population density** will be highest toward the center because of the high cost of land. Conversely, the residential zones, with their lower land costs, will allow a homeowner to purchase a relatively large plat of land for a homesite. It would be cost prohibitive for the homeowner to purchase the same land area near the city center.

The advantages of locating a business closer to the city center are lower transportation costs and increased **accessibility** to activities at the center. This accessibility advantage is gained through the higher cost for land. For a residential location, the requirement for optimal accessibility to the city center is much lower than it is for a business that requires frequent contact with the center throughout the workweek. The general rules expressed in the bid-rent curve are (1) transport costs are lower nearer the city center and increase away from the city center, (2) land costs are higher near the center and diminish with distance outward, and (3) any location along a line from city center to city boundary reflects the acceptance of a specific degree of accessibility to the center.

The bid-rent curve idea is found in **von Thunen's land use model,** the classic study of agricultural land use in concentric zones around a single market center, which was published in 1829 but was not used by American geographers until the mid-twentieth century.

Suggested Readings: Brian Goodall, *The Facts on File Dictionary of Human Geography*, New York: Facts on File, 1987; David T. Herbert and Colin J. Thomas, *Cities in Space, City as Place*, New York: John Wiley & Sons, 1997.

Biotechnology. *See* **Green Revolution.**

Blockbusting and redlining. In 1954, the legal decision rendered in *Brown v. Board of Education* (Topeka, Kansas) stated that separate schools for whites and blacks were unconstitutional. Even though the individual schools may have had all the needed facilities and staff to provide a sound education, the notion of separate but equal was struck down. The U.S. Supreme Court ruled in 1955 that schools be desegregated with all due haste. In many U.S. cities, whites fled the cities to the less socially mixed suburbs. This so-called white flight was encouraged and hastened by blockbusting, an effort by realtors to convince whites living on the edges of the expanding black housing areas to sell their homes, usually at prices lower than fair market value. Whites were convinced that if they stayed, their property values would decrease once blacks moved into their neighborhoods. Realtors then sold the properties to blacks at prices higher than market value. The practice of blockbusting added to the levels of tension and hostility between blacks and whites.

The now illegal practice of redlining worked to disallow deteriorating inner city neighborhoods from receiving mortgage money to make necessary improvements. Redlining occurred when banks identified areas within the inner city that, in their view, presented too high a risk of financial loss to receive funding. The result of this practice was to further the decline of structures within the redlined areas and to drive up prices in other areas. Redlining began in the United States and spread to other countries, including England. The Community Reinvestment Act (1977) now requires banks to show that inner-city neighborhoods within their area have received a proportionate share of loans. The practice of redlining, although illegal, may still be practiced in some form; laws against this activity are difficult to enforce.

Suggested Readings: Mark Goodwin, *Reshaping the City*, London: Edward Arnold, 1998; Philip Kivell, *Land and the City: Patterns and Processes of Urban Change*, London: Routledge, 1993.

Boundary. The term *boundary* is used extensively in geography. At the international level, boundaries are the lines that separate countries. Boundaries provide the spatial expression of a country and clearly identify its areal extent as a sovereign state. International boundaries are powerful designators. Within the boundary of a country, there exists a unique set of cultural, economic, social, and political attributes. International law demands that boundaries are recognized by outsiders as barriers to arbitrary entry. Crossing an international border is done only under certain prescribed conditions and at specific border crossing points.

Boundaries are found at all political levels: countries, states, metropolitan centers, cities, towns, and hamlets. The actual boundary may follow a natural occurrence, such as a mountain range, river, or lake. This form of demarcation has its problems, however. Lakes can change shape in times of drought or heavy rainfall; mountainous borders may be difficult to follow due to the complexity of the rock formations; and rivers may change course during periods of high water. For example, the boundary between Illinois and Missouri changed due to severe flooding of the Mississippi River in the 1990s.

Boundaries may be geometric in origin, following particular latitude or longitude lines. A number of states in the western United States follow geometric lines. The same is true of many of the African countries created during the time of **colonialism.** Arbitrary boundaries were established by occupying European powers, which paid no attention to the boundaries long used by the indigenous culture groups.

Further classification of boundaries is used, especially in **political geography.** An antecedent boundary is one drawn before significant settlement has occurred. The boundary between the United States and Canada from midcontinent westward was drawn in anticipation of the western movement of people in both countries. A subsequent boundary is one drawn following significant settlement. The splitting of Korea at the 38th parallel for administrative purposes following World War II was intended to be temporary. However, as a result of the Korean War, two countries common in culture emerged as sovereign states. This division continued into the twenty-first century and is likely to remain for many years because of the diametrically opposed political regimes of each country.

On occasion, boundary disputes may occur between countries. Some of these disputes are long standing. For example, Japan and Russia have yet to sign a peace treaty ending their involvement in World War II. This difficult situation exists because of Russia's occupation of four islands north of Hokkaido, Japan's northernmost main island. Russia considers these islands to be spoils of war. Japan, however, contends that the islands should be returned to it because of earlier treaties. This boundary dispute has lasted over five decades and is not expected to be completely resolved in the foreseeable future.

Suggested Readings: Andrew Boyd, *An Atlas of World Affairs*, 10th ed., New York: Routledge, 1998; Clive H. Scholfield, ed., *Global Boundaries*, World Boundaries Series, vol. 1, London: Routledge, 1994.

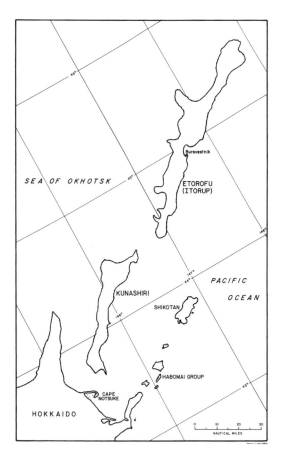

A map showing boundaries of the former Soviet Union's Northern Territories. *Source: Naval War College Review.* Autumn 1991.

Break-of-bulk point. Break-of-bulk point refers to the place at which cargo is transferred from one form of transportation to another. For example, Cleveland, Ohio, is a break-of-bulk point where taconite ore loaded aboard Great Lakes boats is transferred to railroad cars for further shipment to regional steel mills. Large industrial cities are the major break-of-bulk points because of the great volumes of commodities destined either for their own manufacturing processes or for further shipment to other centers.

Seaports are break-of-bulk points where oceangoing vessels berth and their cargo is transferred to trucks or railroad cars. River traffic will reach a break-of-bulk point at a waterfall, where cargo on the boats must be off-loaded for further shipment by truck or rail.

During the colonial period in the United States, a series of break-of-bulk points were developed on the eastern seaboard from New York to Georgia. Many rivers flow out of the Appalachian Mountains across the crystalline rock of the Piedmont Plateau and then over falls onto the coastal plane. Boats from the coast could move upriver as far as the falls. There, loading and transshipment by land vehicles occurred. Dozens of these break-of-bulk points grew up along what became known as the **fall line.**

Break-of-bulk points are of historical importance because they generated the growth of settlements. The unloading of cargo from one form of transportation and the reloading onto another may take days. During this process, workers need all of the services provided by the nonbasic business sector—lodging, food, perhaps medical and dental care, and retail stores. As the break-of-bulk business increases, so will the service sector. Thousands of settlements have grown up around break-of-bulk points.

Suggested Readings: Dean M. Hanink, *Principles and Applications of Economic Geography*, New York: John Wiley & Sons, 1997; James W. Harrington and Barney Warf, *Industrial Location: Principles and Practice*, New York: Routledge, 1995.

Buffer state and buffer zone. A buffer state is an independent country that lies between two larger and more powerful countries that are, in many cases, antagonistic toward one another. The presence of a buffer state can help to lessen the potential for direct conflict between the larger states. For years Mongolia has served as a buffer state between Russia and China. These two giant countries have at times been allies, but for most of their history a great deal of tension has existed between them.

Nepal, a relatively remote country high in the mountainous terrain of South Asia, is a buffer state between India and China, two countries that have frequently been at odds with each other. Nepal's role as a buffer state between these two larger countries is unique—China and India rank first and second in the world in population. Together, their population exceeds 2.4 billion, more than one-third of the world's population.

At various times through history, Taiwan and Korea have acted as buffers between longtime antagonists Japan and China. For nearly 40 years of the twentieth century, both Taiwan and Korea were occupied by Japan. When a buffer state falls under the control of one of the larger antagonists, its status changes to that of a satellite state. As such, it is no longer acting to discourage or deter possible conflict between the two larger entities but has been joined to one of them.

When more than one buffer state lies between two larger and competing countries, a buffer zone exists. The function of the buffer zone is exactly the same—to deter potential conflict between the larger and more powerful contending countries. In Africa, a cluster of European colonial entities served as a buffer zone separating black nationalist countries in the northern part of the continent from South Africa, a white-controlled country. In the mid-twentieth

21

century, this buffer zone ceased to exist as countries within the zone gained independence from colonial rule.

Probably the best known buffer zone comprised the eastern European tier of countries located between the old Soviet Union and western Europe and emerged following World War II. With the rapid withdrawal of U.S., British, and French forces following the liberation of Europe, the Soviets quickly began to exert their influence in eastern Europe. Overnight a true buffer zone came into being as a postwar adversarial relationship developed between western European countries (and the United States) and the Soviet Union. Within a few short years, the eastern European buffer zone was transformed into a tier of Soviet satellite states, as each became inextricably tied to the Soviet Union. This arrangement, too, saw its end in 1990 with the demise of the Soviet Union and its splintering into 15 new sovereign states.

Suggested Readings: Saul B. Cohen, "Global Geopolitical Change in the Post–Cold War Era," *Annals of the Association of American Geographers*, vol. 81 (1991); John R. Short, *An Introduction to Political Geography*, 2nd ed., New York: Routledge, 1993.

C

Carrying capacity. Carrying capacity may be generally defined as the level of use of a resource short of that resource's deterioration. How many head of cattle can graze on an area of grassland and not deteriorate the vegetative cover for the following year? What is the maximum yield of a particular agricultural product on a particular farmstead? How heavily can a transportation system be used before its efficiency begins to decline? What is the ideal number of visitors to a national park in a tourist season? What is the maximum tonnage of fish that may be taken from an ocean fishing ground without depleting the resource for the next season?

In the grazing example, if too many cattle graze for a season, grasses may be unable to fully regenerate the following year. If this happens, fewer cattle can be supported, and the resource (the land and its grasses) has then exceeded its carrying capacity. The transportation system example speaks to the real-world situation in Russia, where the rolling stock on the Trans-Siberian Railroad has been overused for years and is badly in need of maintenance and, in some cases, replacement. Carrying capacity of that important rail line has been severely strained, and many experts believe that it is only a matter of time before the system slows dramatically.

Carrying capacity is a relative term. That is, a cropland area may be producing at maximum levels without causing undue harm to the soil. With the addition of a new fertilizer, for instance, yields may increase significantly. If this occurs, and the soil remains healthy, a new and higher-level carrying capacity has been set. Improvements in agricultural technology through the introduction of new seeds, advanced fertilizers, and improved machinery have greatly improved yields over time. A continual increase in carrying capacities is one important outcome of advanced farming systems and a good measure of the success of the twentieth-century **Agricultural Revolution.**

In agriculture, carrying capacities have increased throughout history. Hunter-gatherer societies subsisted on whatever edible food products they could find, and the carrying capacity of most areas was exceedingly low. Consequently, the early hunter-gatherer groups were constantly on the move to find food. The modern world faces a new set of problems in terms of food availability. In some regions of the world, population growth has put severe pressures on the land, and food shortages have frequently occurred. Some demographics suggest that expansion of productive capacity in agriculture cannot continue indefinitely. Two questions seem to emerge most frequently in this regard: Is there a fixed upper level of carrying capacity that the earth can support given continuing population increase? Will new technological breakthroughs occur in time to avert crisis?

There are regions of the world where carrying capacity has already been greatly exceeded. One of these is the Sub-Saharan region of Africa. Increased numbers of people and cattle have led to serious declines in farming and grazing areas. Unable to apply the latest technology, these areas experience perennial shortfalls in productivity. With population continuing to increase, more regions may suffer a similar fate in the future.

Suggested Readings: John Bongaarts, "Population Pressure and the Food Supply System in the Developing World," *Population and Development Review,* vol. 22 (1996); Joel E. Cohen, *How Many People Can the Earth Support?,* New York: W. W. Norton, 1995.

Cartogram. A cartogram is a map transformation in which the administrative units (countries, states, counties, etc.) have been either enlarged or reduced in map area to graphically reflect their numerical share in the topic presented. For instance, in a cartogram of population for each country in the world, countries with the highest population, such as India and China, would be largest in size to reflect their share of world population. Those countries with very low populations would be the most diminished in size. The graphic results can be very dramatic. For example, Canada, whose land area is comparable to that of China, would be greatly diminished in a cartogram of population because it has only about 26 million people as opposed to China's 1.3 billion. Japan, on the other hand, although its land area is about that of Montana, would appear much larger on a cartogram of population because of its dense population of 135 million.

Cartograms are effective in providing graphic presentation of data at a glance. The observer can get an immediate interpretation of the topic mapped and the representation of each country or state in that data set. In the production of a cartogram, the map attribute of scale is lost as each administrative unit is represented in a transformed manner. However, continuity (the spatial arrangement of each administrative unit) is maintained to the greatest extent possible.

Cartograms of economic themes can be equally revealing. For instance, on a cartogram showing **gross national product** per capita, the developed countries in the Northern Hemisphere would be large, reflecting their high values. Conversely, Africa would be greatly diminished relative to the rest of the world, a reflection of its low values in this economic measure.

Suggested Readings: Mark Monmonier, *Drawing the Line: Tales of Maps and Cartocontroversy*, New York: Henry Holt, 1995; Arthur H. Robinson et al., *Elements of Cartography*, 6th ed., New York: John Wiley & Sons, 1995.

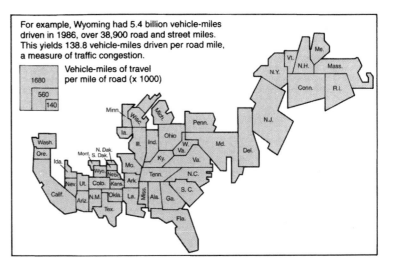

Relative traffic congestion. A typical value-by-area cartogram with states drawn in proportion to the number of vehicle-miles driven per road mile. *Source:* J. Fellmann and A. Getis, *Human Geography: Landscapes of Human Activities,* updated ed. Reproduced by permission of The McGraw-Hill Companies.

Cartography. Cartography is a discipline that has worked over centuries to advance both the scientific and artistic aspects of making maps. Scan the pages of virtually any geography book, and a profusion of maps will be found. Geography and maps are inextricably connected. Because geography is a spatial discipline that deals with places and interactions, the discipline needs a graphic medium to record and exhibit these spatial properties. Maps provide that medium.

Cartography, like geography, has enjoyed a long and colorful history. Some of the earliest maps in existence date to ancient times. Throughout history, maps have evolved to meet the needs of explorers and analysts of the spatial tradition. Cartographers have created thousands of different map types to meet as many needs.

One of the most famous of all maps is the Mercator projection, a map developed by Flemish cartographer Gerardus Mercator in 1569 to assist explorers on long oceanic journeys out of site of familiar coastlines. The Mercator projection is used even today as a general reference map of the world, a purpose for which it was not designed. Like all maps, the Mercator provides a distorted representation of the earth's land and water areas. Distortion on a Mercator is extreme. On this map, Greenland appears to be larger than South America, and the Eurasian landmass, greatly enlarged, seems to almost dwarf the continent of Africa. The distortion comes from two factors: (1) the lines of longitude (meridians) are parallel to each other rather than converging toward the poles as they do on a globe; and (2) the latitude lines become progressively more widely spaced moving from the equator to the poles. These two cartographic features, created for navigation in the age of exploration, present a very distorted view of the earth and its major features.

Cartography has benefited over the years from a number of technological advances. With the advent of aviation, space flight, and aerial photography, new breakthroughs in mapmaking resulted. The high-speed computer provided cartography with an incredibly powerful analytic tool used in mapmaking to store volumes of data and to generate and display detailed maps in seconds.

Cartography as a modern discipline has national and regional organizations, holds professional meetings devoted to the sharing of cartographic research and advancements, and publishes professional journals. Despite its individuality as a discipline, however, its product—maps—are so closely associated with geography that cartography appears for all practical purposes to be a part of the discipline of geography. Courses in cartography are taught in college geography programs. Cartography laboratories, now replete with high-speed-graphics computers, are found in geography departments, and fully trained cartographers are members of the faculties of nearly all college geography departments.

Suggested Readings: John Campbell, *Map Use and Analysis*, 3rd ed., Dubuque, Iowa: WCB/McGraw-Hill, 1998; Arthur H. Robinson et al., *Elements of Cartography*, 6th ed., New York: John Wiley & Sons, 1995.

Census. A census is an official governmental count of such characteristics as population, housing, agriculture, or manufacturing. In the United States, population and housing censuses are taken every decade, in years ending in zero. Census taking for agriculture and manufacturing occurs every five years. By far the most widely known census is that of population. In addition to the numbers of people tabulated, information is gathered on a variety of demographic, economic, and social characteristics of the population. This enormous assemblage of population data is extremely important in **human geography.** The population census is the most important single source of information available about the populace.

Not only are the data of value, but the manner in which the data are collected is ideally configured for the geographer. All population data are tabulated by census tract, an areal unit representing approximately 5,000 people that is closely aligned with existing neighborhoods. The actual size of a census tract will vary considerably: tracts in the high-density central city may be only a few square blocks, reflecting the greater number of people per unit area. Conversely, suburban districts will be larger in size. Data accumulated by census tract are ideally configured for the compilation of **choropleth map**s.

Geographers study census tract data on education, income, age, ethnicity, and a host of other categories to better understand the demographic complexities of a place. Politicians, for instance, would be interested in census tract data that could lead to predictions about voting behavior.

The U.S. Constitution directed that the census be conducted so that apportionment of seats in the House of Representatives could be accomplished. If the enumeration for a region is significantly lower than that of the previous census, a state may lose seats in the House of Representatives. Likewise, an increase in population could result in a state's gaining one or more seats. Reapportionment is an extremely important outcome of the population census. Strong criticism has resulted when areas in central cities have allegedly been undercounted due to higher numbers of transients, homeless, and generally less accessible people. In such situations, statistical estimating has been suggested. This approach has met with resistance by those who point out that the U.S. Constitution requires that the population census be accomplished with a 100 percent physical count. This issue will no doubt remain controversial as each census year approaches.

Suggested Readings: The Census Bureau Home Page, www.census.gov; State Census Data Centers, www.census.gov/sdc/www; Arthur Haupt and Thomas Kane, *Population Handbook*, 4th ed., Population Reference Bureau, 1997.

Central business district. Traditionally, the term *central business district* (CBD) was used to mean the downtown area of American cities. The CBD is the core of an urban area and the center of commercial activity, civic life, and entertainment. The role of the CBD is still generally strong, but its preeminence of earlier decades has faded to some degree with the growth of suburbs and the decentralization and dispersal of some core activities.

The CBD is important in urban history. It marked the first permanent developed area of a settlement, and its location was usually decided by a significant **site** factor, such as a landing point on a navigable river, location on a railroad line, or key location on a seacoast. CBD growth and a focus on transportation have gone hand in hand with the growth of American cities. If a city had railroad lines, the station or depot was invariably in the downtown area. Internal public transportation systems, such as streetcars and buses, converged on the CBD from all quadrants to provide service to employees of downtown businesses. In its heyday the CBD was a major employment complex during the day and an entertainment center in the evening.

The CBD contained the highest-value land and the highest density of activities (*see* **Bid-rent curve**). Since land was costly, tall skyscrapers emerged; and these structures allowed for maximum **accessibility** for business workers in their daily activities.

All of the classic models of urban structure contain a well-defined CBD. As urban areas expanded in size and new transportation systems allowed businesses to locate farther from the center without sacrificing accessibility to it, the traditional function of the CBD began to change. In some cities, areas in the CBD became neglected and the infrastructure began to deteriorate. In some of the worst cases, abandoned buildings and slum areas began to appear as business and personal tax bases moved out of the CBD. Concerted efforts have been ongoing in most American cities to upgrade the CBD and to enhance its economic well-being. Previously run-down neighborhoods are experiencing **gentrification** as investment money is directed toward restoration and renewal of residential blocks. Businesses that may have previously fled to **suburbia** are being enticed to again locate within the CBD. No single rebuilding formula will fit all CBDs, but it is clear that virtually all urban areas want to develop and maintain a viable, if somewhat functionally modified, CBD.

Suggested Readings: Larry R. Ford, *Cities and Buildings: Skyscrapers, Skid Rows, and Suburbs,* Baltimore: Johns Hopkins University Press, 1994; Mark Goodwin, *Reshaping the City,* London: Edward Arnold, 1998.

Centrifugal/centripetal forces. The terms *centrifugal* and *centripetal forces,* when taken from the physical sciences and applied to geography, refer to forces that tend to disintegrate (centrifugal) or bind together (centripetal) a spatial unit. These terms were first used to identify forces that produced change in urban areas.

Centrifugal forces compel businesses and population segments to leave the urban center and relocate to the suburban fringe. A number of reasons may be associated with this movement, including crowding and traffic congestion near the center of cities as both population and business activity expand within a limited area. Another factor may be the need for a larger storage facility as a manufacturer increases production. If there is no opportunity to expand in the city center, businesses move to the suburban fringe. As American cities began to experience infrastructural decay, an increase in crime, and generally poorer services in the post–World War II era, many business concerns chose to relocate in the suburban areas. By 1960, for instance, more manufacturing was located in the suburbs than in the city centers.

Centripetal forces, on the other hand, tend to draw people to the center of a city. The downtown area appeals to people and businesses that value the important attribute of **accessibility** and will benefit from the close proximity of other activities. Businesses that operate best in the business skyscraper, for instance, will be drawn to the center of viable, strong cities. Many service functions—such as restaurants, hotels, cultural centers, and government offices—will locate where they can best serve the needs of people and businesses in the city center.

These counteracting forces have also been applied to sovereign states. Centrifugal forces are divisive in their power to pull states apart. For example, the Soviet Union fractured into 15 new countries following its demise in 1991. Within the new Russia, a number of ethnic groups have made overtures toward becoming independent sovereign states. At one point in the early 1990s, all of Siberia was intent on detaching from Russia. A number of other regions have seen similar occurrences. Among them are the former Yugoslavia (*see* **Balkanization**) and Czechoslovakia.

At the **nation-state** level, centripetal forces work to hold the country together. Strong national traditions that are accepted by the people can be a binding factor. A single language and a unified set of beliefs are other cohesive factors. A strong education system can work to reinforce the building nature of a nation-state and inform its youth.

Suggested Readings: Brian Goodall, *The Facts on File Dictionary of Human Geography,* New York: Facts on File, 1987; David Hooson, ed., *Geography and National Identity,* London: Basil Blackwell, 1994.

Choropleth map. The choropleth map, which shows distributions by area, is one of the most frequently used maps in geography. The word *choropleth* derives from the Greek roots *choro* (area) and *pleth* (value). The choropleth map uses symbols to represent values for administrative units such as countries, states, counties, and census districts. As such, it is a map that can effectively be used to report area values at virtually any **scale,** from global to local.

For example, a choropleth map showing the percentage of manufacturing workers in each state in the United States would have a single, uniform symbol (e.g., color, gray tone, etc.) for each state. The symbols are assigned to the range of values, lowest to highest, in a selected number of intervals, using one of several statistical methods. Both the number of intervals and the symbols are chosen to achieve the truest cartographic representation of the numerical data range and configuration.

Since the choropleth map uses an average number (i.e., percent of manufacturing employees in our example) to represent the entire state, there would be no basis on which a viewer of the map could validly infer that one part of the state or another had higher or lower values, although this would surely be true. In order to gain perspective on any state's internal distribution of values, a choropleth map based on county averages would be required. Taking this notion another step, detailed information about the distribution of values within a county would require a choropleth map of census districts within that county. Each of these examples specifies a change in scale, and such changes suggest certain implicit limitations in the choropleth map.

A choropleth map showing a global pattern would have a uniform symbol for each country. The advantage here is wide global coverage; the disadvantage is that every country is represented by only one symbol and no detailed information can be shown. At a local level (country, for example) a great deal of detailed information is provided, but the area presented is greatly limited. With these limitations of choropleth maps in mind, the geographer must decide the scale of investigation (and the detail of the map) that is appropriate for the analysis underway.

Suggested Readings: Borden C. Dent, *Cartography: Thematic Map Design,* Dubuque, Iowa: Wm. C. Brown Publishers, 1996; Alan M. MacEachren, *How Maps Work,* New York: Guilford Press, 1995.

Christaller's central place theory. Walter Christaller (1896–1969), a German economic geographer, wrote his dissertation in 1933 on the subject of urban settlements and the roles they play in providing goods and services to their surrounding nonurban region. Christaller was the first geographer to fully develop this notion; others had done preliminary work on the idea but not to any significant degree. Christaller used the term *central place* to designate these urban settlements. He set out to build a theory to explain regularities noted in the size and spacing of urban settlements in southern Germany. Central places tended to be spaced apart one from the other so that each had a monopoly on providing goods and services to their local area. In addition, all central places were part of a system of counterparts that spread across the wider area. Also, larger central places controlled a more extensive area and small ones a lesser area. With this last inclusion in the theory, Christaller introduced the idea of hierarchical levels, each with an areal spread dependent on its size.

Walter Christaller. *Source:* Library of Congress.

To truly develop a theory from his original empirical observations, Christaller used an approach remarkably similar to the one developed in **von Thunen's land use model,** which was published in 1826. Christaller, like von Thunen, proposed a uniform plain, a central place that provided basic goods and services, and a population in the nonurban area that was evenly spread out on the plain and uniform in its characteristics. Each central place provided products and services that had their own threshold, or necessary numbers of consumers, to support the businesses. Also, each of the goods and services provided in the central place reflected a maximum range, the distance traveled by nonurban residents to procure the goods and services.

The resulting spatial configuration of the central place system was one of complementary and contiguous regions, with each region in the shape of a hexagon. A central place was located in each of the hexagons, and smaller central places were found along the edges of the hexagons, each of which was smaller in size with its own region of influence.

Christaller's dissertation on central places did not become part of geography's conceptual mainstream until the 1960s, when the **Quantitative Revolution** in the discipline was in full swing. Christaller's ideas were especially welcomed at that time by a group of geographers at the University of Washington, who used his central place theory as a basis for a number of quantitative and statistical approaches to geography. Christaller's central place theory is an important component in geography today, and an extensive body of literature on central places has evolved in the decades since the 1960s.

Suggested Readings: Walter Christaller, *Central Places in Southern Germany,* trans. C. W. Baskin, Englewood Cliffs, N.J.: Prentice Hall, 1966; Leslie J. King, *Central Place Theory,* Newbury Park, Calif.: Sage, 1984.

City-state. The term *city-state* refers to any state that is principally composed of a city and a limited hinterland, or service area. City-states represent the earliest form of states. Following the first **Agricultural Revolution,** some 12,000 years ago, city-states began to form in South Asia, the Middle East, and Latin America. Centers for these emerging urban strongholds were found in Mesopotamia, the Nile Valley, and in the regions of the Inca and Aztec culture groups in Latin America.

These centers usually contained a relatively dense concentration of people in a limited area surrounded by a protective wall. The region immediately adjacent to the walled city housed farmers, craftsmen, and merchants closely bound to the city. The city-state, in time, evolved into the sovereign state we know today as population increased, economic activity expanded, more urban places were established, and the political reach of the major city extended great distances.

In the modern era, two major centers in Asia are recognized as true city-states: Hong Kong and Singapore, both former British colonies. Until its return to the political control of China, Hong Kong functioned as a true city-state. With its strategic location on the coast of China and with immediate access to the major Chinese industrial center of Kuangtung Province, Hong Kong thrived as a global financial, trade, and shipping center. One of the original Asian economic powerhouses, known as the **Asian Tigers,** Hong Kong has a future that is somewhat clouded now that it has again come under Chinese political control.

Singapore continues to thrive as a strong economic center strategically located on global air transportation routes and important sea-lanes of commerce through the Strait of Malacca. Singapore is an island city-state with an area of only 620 square kilometers. Despite its size, Singapore is an extremely important transshipment center and financial leader. English is the primary language, a plus for global business, and the population is 70 percent ethnic Chinese, many with strong business connections throughout East and Southeast Asia. Singapore's port is first rate, and the city-state has become a leader in handling containerized cargo.

Suggested Readings: Thomas R. Leinback and Richard Ulack, eds., *Southeast Asia: Development and Diversity,* Upper Saddle River, N.J.: Prentice Hall, 2000; Martin Perry et al., *Singapore: A Developmental City State,* New York: John Wiley & Sons, 1997.

Cold war. World War II ended in 1945, but the prospects for a true and lasting peace were short lived. With the quick withdrawal of Allied forces from Western Europe following the surrender of Germany, the Soviet Union (USSR) quickly brought the neighboring Eastern European countries under its control. The subsequent threat of a Soviet takeover of Germany prompted the United States and other Western European countries to unite to prevent such a move. The Truman Doctrine was enacted in 1947, committing the United States to a number of military alliances around the world. At the same time, the Soviet

Union continued to solidify its hold on Eastern Europe. The two major antagonists in this era of tension were the United States and the Soviet Union. Each was supported by a cadre of countries sympathetic to the political stance of one of the emerging superpowers.

In this era the model of first, second, and third worlds evolved. The first world included the United States and its cohort of supporters, the Western European countries, Canada, Japan, Australia, and New Zealand. The second world was composed of the Soviet Union, its Eastern European satellites, and China. The third world included all the rest of the world, primarily the poorest countries.

For the next 40 years the so-called cold war persisted. It was marked by a clear, bipolar power balance between the United States and the Soviet Union. Both competed for economic growth, military might, and influence over other countries. Although direct conflict between the two antagonists was averted, there were numerous proxy wars and skirmishes around the world that certainly involved the superpowers. Direct military involvement on the part of the superpowers happened on a number of occasions. The Soviet Union interceded in Hungary (1956) and Afghanistan (1979–89). The United States was engaged directly in the Korean War (1950–53), the Dominican Republic (1965), Granada (1983), and Panama (1983). Its most significant military engagement began as a small-scale military assistance commitment in South Vietnam in 1954 following the withdrawal of the French from military activity in Vietnam during that year. The Vietnam War escalated through the 1960s and early 1970s into an extremely serious and protracted war of attrition. The United States finally withdrew from Vietnam in 1975, ending an era of great military controversy and domestic unrest. The Soviet Union experienced its own extended military engagement when it invaded Afghanistan in 1979 in order to defend the national government it had helped to establish. Soviet troops finally withdrew from Afghan soil 10 years later.

Without doubt the United States and the Soviet Union came closest to direct conflict during the Cuban missile crisis in 1962. War was averted when the Soviets agreed to dismantle missile installations in Cuba that were well within range of striking a large portion of the eastern United States.

The cold war brought with it the notion of containment, a plan to deter the advance of communism by containing it within the borders of the Soviet Union. The domino theory also emerged in this period. A corollary to containment, the domino theory postulated that if, for instance, one Southeast Asian country fell to communism, then others would fall in sequence, like a row of dominoes.

Each of the superpowers enacted programs during the cold war to bolster its position. The United States set up the Marshall Plan in 1948 to assist in the rebuilding of shattered European economies. The Soviet Union responded with the Council for Mutual Economic Assistance (COMECON), aimed at consolidating the economies of its Eastern European satellites. The United States and its allies formed the **North Atlantic Treaty Organization** (NATO). The Soviet Union responded with the creation of the Warsaw Pact. Other countries in the Warsaw Pact included Albania, Bulgaria, Czechoslovakia, East Germany, Hungary, Poland, and Romania. Both of these organizations formalized the military integration of each side.

With the fall of the Soviet Union in 1991, COMECON was disbanded, NATO began to change in structure, and the cold war was over. With the end of the bipolar balance of power and the emergence of the United States as the only superpower, the global geopolitical situation clearly began changing. It has even been proposed that Russia become a NATO member because the new threats to global peace may well emanate from regions to the south, especially the Middle East.

Suggested Readings: Saul B. Cohen, "Global Political Change in the Post–Cold War Era," *Annals of the Association of American Geographers,* vol. 81 (1991); Jan Nijman, "The Limits of Superpower: The United States and the Soviet Union since World War II," *Annals of the Association of American Geographers,* vol. 82 (1992).

Colonialism. The term *colonialism* refers to the exercise of control by a developed state over an underdeveloped state or region. Although the historical incidence of colonialism is most widely associated with dominance exerted by European countries, the process is not exclusive to them. Russia, Japan, and the United States have also engaged in colonialism. Two major periods in colonialism have been identified.

The first period followed the European discovery of the land in the Western Hemisphere in 1492. Two years later, the Treaty of Tordesillas (1494) divided new land areas between Spain and Portugal. The dividing line was drawn along a meridian 1,800 kilometers west of the Cape Verde Islands. Spain was the great benefactor of this decision, receiving claim to all of North America and all of South America except the eastern position, which became Portuguese Brazil.

The second major wave of colonialism occurred in the late nineteenth century. In 1884, the Berlin Conference convened to decide which regions in Africa would be occupied by which European countries. The "carving up of Africa," as it has been called, eventually brought an unprecedented degree of change to Africa south of the Sahara Desert. The impact of this era is felt even today. France and Britain collectively occupied the largest area of Africa (about 70 percent of colonial territory). Portugal, Belgium, Italy, and Spain also colonized Africa.

The primary incentive for colonialism was economic gain. In the case of Latin America, vast amounts of gold and silver were shipped back to fill the coffers on the Iberian Peninsula. Another incentive was to spread Christianity. The colonial experience brought enormous changes to the indigenous culture groups (*see* **Acculturation**).

Although the colonial era had some positive outcomes, the experience for the indigenous culture groups was decidedly negative. Perhaps the most serious outcome was the economic exploitation of the colonies by the occupying countries. Some have suggested that the form of global **economic geography** developed during the colonial era heavily favored the industrial countries and played havoc with the colonies. The economic system put in place was called **mercantilism.** In this system, the colony provided raw materials and foodstuffs to the colonizer, which in turn produced finished goods with a high-value-added component. In short, the colony received very little compensation for the raw materials, and the colonizer made the largest profits through manufacture. In addition, the colony was not allowed to make items that were made by the colonizer. The colonial era brought about a system of uneven **economic development** that worked to the immense advantage of the colonizers. The **core-periphery model** of economic development had its start in the colonial era.

By the middle of the twentieth century, most colonies had received their independence. But their developmental problems are far from over. One of the legacies of the colonial era was the minimal degree of internal development that was accomplished. Incomplete road networks, underdeveloped agricultural regions, and inadequate physical infrastructural systems were left to the colonies when independence was gained. With little capital and experienced leadership, colonies were faced with the ominous task of completing the basic building of their countries at very high costs. In many former colonies, the task of completing regional development is still far from completed.

Suggested Readings: Samuel Aryeetey-Attoh, ed., *Geography of Sub-Saharan Africa,* Upper Saddle River, N.J.: Prentice Hall, 1997; Peter J. Taylor, *Political Geography: World Economy, Nation-State and Locality,* 3rd ed., New York: John Wiley & Sons, 1993.

Commercial Revolution. The great European voyages of exploration and discovery beginning in the fifteenth century changed the world. The era of the great sailing ships coursing the world's oceans eventually connected all continents and opened up an era of unprecedented economic exchange that has continued to the present. The 100 years from 1650 to 1750 mark the era of the Commercial Revolution, a time when European connections had been made in virtually every part of the world. This time period, running concurrently with the second **Agricultural Revolution** and occurring just before the **Industrial Revolution,** was marked by an extraordinary increase in the exchange of goods worldwide. Agricultural products from South Asia, spices from East Asia, and sugarcane from the Caribbean made their way to Europe, the global headquarters for marketing of commercial products.

The Commercial Revolution came about because of technological advancements in shipbuilding and a particularly significant breakthrough in the art of marine navigation. New ships of the era were larger, stronger, and capable of weathering long and often stormy transoceanic voyages. Their large cargo capacities ensured profitable returns on acquired commodities.

Toward the end of the Commercial Revolution a breakthrough in navigation was made that greatly expanded global maritime outreach. This advancement was the perfection of timepieces accurate enough to be used in the precise measurement of longitude at sea. John Harrison (1693–1776), a clock maker from Yorkshire, England, invented the timepiece, a marine chronometer, which was called H5. Before this breakthrough, navigators had the ability to accurately measure latitude (from observations of the sun at noon and the north star, Polaris, in the Northern Hemisphere) but precise longitude determination was not possible. With this advancement, the era of global outreach was significantly enhanced.

Suggested Readings: Rondo Cameron, *A Concise Economic History of the World: From Paleolithic Times to the Present*, New York: Oxford University Press, 1997; Dava Sobel, *Longitude: The True Story of a Lone Genius Who Solved the Greatest Scientific Problem of His Time*, New York: Walker & Co., 1995.

Comparative advantage. The concept of comparative advantage states that an area will specialize in the production of items for which it has the greatest economic advantage over other areas. Countries and regions in a free-market system will specialize in the production of particular goods when it is to their economic advantage to do so. The economic advantage in this sense derives from two measures, the ratio of advantage and the ratio of disadvantage. These two measures determine comparative advantage. For example, assume that region X produces tractors at 60 percent of the cost of producing tractors in region Y. Assume as well that region X produces calculators at 80 percent of the cost of producing calculators in region Y. With this basic information at hand, and noting that each region can, if it chooses, produce both tractors and calculators for local consumption and not engage in trade, region X will specialize in tractors because of a greater ratio of advantage, and region Y will produce calculators because of a lesser ratio of disadvantage. Both regions have derived a comparative advantage in this simple example: region X can produce tractors more efficiently and region Y can produce calculators more efficiently.

Obviously, the economic landscape is much more complex than this example suggests. A region may have an advantage in resource base that ultimately will favor it for specialization in particular goods. There may be a particularly valuable labor supply in a region that would provide it a significant advantage over other regions. Access to markets and lower costs of transportation and other production inputs could also provide advantages to one region over others in the production of particular goods. On occasion, firms will relocate to take advantage of lower labor costs, lower taxes, and greater resource availability.

Regions have also shifted to the production of other goods when price structures have changed. For example, for most of the twentieth century, western Europe chose to produce manufactured goods and to import large quantities of grains from other regions. But when grain prices grew dramatically following surges in crude oil costs in the 1970s, western Europe shifted some of its productive efforts to the raising of grains for local consumption rather than continue to pay the inflated prices on the global market. Shifts of this type are indicators of the dynamic and ever-changing global economic system.

Suggested Readings: Bela Balassa, "The Changing Pattern of Comparative Advantage of Manufactured Goods," *Review of Economics and Statistics*, May 1979; Edward E. Leamer, *Sources of International Comparative Advantage: Theory and Evidence*, Cambridge, Mass.: MIT Press, 1984.

Concentric zone model. In the mid-1920s, sociologist Ernest W. Burgess developed the concentric zone model, a theoretical model of urban structure based on his studies of Chicago. The model assumed a circular urban place that included five functional zones in a concentric circle design (compare with **Christaller's central place theory** and **von Thunen's land use model**). At the center of the model was the **central business district** (CBD) with its own financial, office, entertainment, and cultural sectors. Land in the CBD was the highest in value (*see* **Bid-rent curve**). The second zone was one of transition. Within this zone were found wholesaling and warehousing businesses, light industry, and a mix of occupied and deteriorating residential housing. Zones one and two, Burgess suggested, identified the dynamic aspect of city growth. As Chicago grew in population and number of economic functions, pressure was exerted outward from the center to expand each zone into the next. The CBD and the transition zone, according to Burgess, were always expanding. Adding to this dynamic change was the movement of immigrant groups from the transition zone outward to areas of better housing, only to have their vacated spaces filled by newly arrived immigrants.

Primarily blue-collar workers who traveled by public transportation into the transition zone for employment occupied the third zone. More-affluent middle-class residents who worked primarily in the CBD occupied the fourth zone. The final zone in Burgess's model was the suburban. This zone contained high-value residential sections for persons who worked in management positions, especially within the CBD.

Chicago was of particular importance to Burgess because of the way it grew following the great fire of 1871. The city developed a socially segregated urban structure in the decades following that tragedy. Social patterning reflected a need for low-cost housing for blue-collar workers as economic growth in the city expanded. The new industries initially located in the transition zone near the blue-collar housing zone. However, it was not necessary that housing be located within walking distance of the industries because of the new streetcar system, which provided workers with efficient and low-cost access to the workplace. Real estate speculation increased in the suburbs as wealth began to accumulate for business owners and managers.

Burgess's zones came to be known as "rings of rising affluence" within a dynamic model in which the inner zones encroached on the outer.

Suggested Readings: Sue Hanson, *The Geography of Urban Transportation*, 2nd ed., New York: Guilford Press, 1995; Philip Kivell, *Land and the City: Patterns and Processes of Urban Change*, London: Routledge, 1993.

Connectivity. *Connectivity* is a term applied to all of the possible ways in which people and places are connected. In going to work or school, an individual will take the most efficient course and conveyance to reach a destination. For the high school student this may involve a short walk across an open field in a rural area or a several-mile ride on a school bus in the city. Workers may drive to the office or take the bus or streetcar. People who are going to be late for work or school use the telephone to alert someone of their delayed arrival. People can easily speak with relatives in another state or order something from a catalog by telephone or through e-mail. The gasoline used in cars and buses originated as crude oil, probably shipped by tanker from a distant country. The speaker at the civic center flew by international airliner from Europe, took a taxicab to the presentation and then was driven to a hotel for a night's stay before taking an Amtrak train to the next engagement.

It follows that there is a direct relationship between the degree of connectivity across space and resultant measures of **accessibility,** a companion concept. During the **Quantitative Revolution** numerical measures of connectivity were developed. The purpose of these measures was to determine the efficiency of a set of places. For instance, two points (nodes) connected by one line (vertice) would be less efficient than having the two points connected by two lines. Imagine the points to represent two hamlets in a rural area. Connectivity measurement would suggest that two roads connecting the hamlets would result in a more efficient connection. A number of indices of connectivity were derived to measure the efficiency of spatial networks during this era. *See also* **Network.**

Suggested Readings: John C. Lowe and S. Moryadas, *The Geography of Movement*, Boston: Houghton Mifflin, 1975; Tim F. Wood, "Thinking in Geography," *Geography*, vol. 72 (1987).

Conservation. *See* **Environmental awareness.**

Contagion diffusion. *See* **Expansion diffusion.**

Conurbation. Conurbation is the joining together of large urban centers so that their edges create a continuous developed area. There are a number of these giant urban complexes in the world. The most prominent is the highly urbanized corridor in the northeastern United States, the conurbation named **Megalopolis** by the French geographer Jean Gottmann, in a study in the 1950s.

There are two more conurbations of great size in the United States. One extends from Chicago along the Great Lakes to Pittsburgh, lying in the center of the great North American manufacturing belt and straddling the major transportation corridor connecting the East with the Midwest. The other lies along the West Coast and runs from San Francisco to San Diego. From the 1970s to the end of the twentieth century, the West Coast conurbation grew the fastest of the three, a reflection of generally higher population growth in the western (and southern) United States during that period. The three major U.S. conurbations have been named Boswash (Boston to Washington, D.C.), Chipitts (Chicago to Pittsburgh), and Sansan (San Francisco to San Diego).

A number of conurbations are found in other parts of the world. The east–west corridor between Tokyo and the industrial region on northern Kyushu, Japan, contains a densely packed set of major cities. A part of the corridor follows the ancient Tokaido Road, an important transportation link in centuries past. Canada's Main Street from the Ontario Peninsula through Montreal and Quebec City is another. In England, conurbations are found in the north linking the industrial cities of Manchester and Sheffield, and in the highly urbanized London area. The Ruhr region of Germany is another conurbation linking a number of industrial cities.

Urban growth is continuing throughout the world. It is expected that existing conurbations will gradually increase in size and new ones will begin to emerge.

Suggested Readings: Martin P. Brockerhoff, "An Urbanizing World," *Population Bulletin*, vol. 55 (2000); Stanley D. Brunn and Jack F. Williams, *Cities of the World: World Regional Urban Development*, 2nd ed., New York: HarperCollins, 1993.

Core-periphery model. The spatial structure of an economic system that includes unequal development is the basis of the core-periphery model. The core region consists of countries holding the greatest economic power. These countries have accumulated the most wealth and have attained the highest levels of affluence. They are the most productive economically and traditionally are the most innovative. Countries on the periphery, on the other hand, lack these positive measures of development. They have for the most part been suppliers of raw materials, commodities, and brainpower to the core. The core-periphery model reflects a regionalism that got its start in the first era of **colonialism,** became reinforced in the **Industrial Revolution,** and continues to the present era of **globalization.** Core-periphery interactions are marked by a trade relationship that favors the core and results in a decidedly uneven economic development. The core consists of the highly developed countries (HDC) and the periphery consists of the lesser-developed countries (LDC).

The model is most closely related with the economist John Friedmann, who initially wrote about it in the 1960s. Friedmann saw the core-periphery relationship as one of four major stages in the historical development of the global economic system. His stages included: (1) a preindustrial society; (2) core-periphery relationships; (3) the dispersal of some economic activity (and a minimal level of control) to the periphery; and (4) the spatial integration of the global economic system, resulting in greater interdependency between member countries in both the core and the periphery.

The core-periphery model is found in **Wallerstein's world-system analysis,** developed by American social scientist Immanuel Wallerstein in the 1960s and 1970s, whose work has become a mainstay in economic and political geography.

The core-periphery model has accurately reflected basic global economic relationships since the advent of **colonialism.** This is true despite great changes in specific economic forms and activities over time. For instance, in recent years the core has shifted its economic focus more toward high-technology industries, global finance, and other service-related efforts. In turn, their historic high reliance on the production of basic commodities, like steel and the manufacture of tangible goods, has declined relatively. Some of these activities have been taken up by countries in the periphery. Yet, the basic economic inequity that has historically identified the core and the periphery persists.

Although the core-periphery model is most associated with global economic relations, it applies as well at the regional level. For instance, the industrial success of the highly urbanized U.S. eastern seaboard (core) is due, at least in part, to the transfer of coal from the Appalachian region (periphery), with little heed to the associated negative social and environmental consequences in the Appalachian Mountains.

Suggested Readings: David S. Landes, *The Wealth and Poverty of Nations: Why Some Are So Rich and Some Are So Poor,* New York: W. W. Norton, 1998; Philip W. Porter and Eric S. Sheppard, *A World of Difference: Society, Nature, Development,* New York: Guilford Press, 1998.

Counterurbanization. Counterurbanization refers to a shift in population movement from urban to rural areas. In the 1970s and 1980s in the United States, the steady influx of people from rural areas into cities began to reverse. During that period more people moved from metropolitan areas and beyond **suburbia** to small towns and rural settings than those moving to cities.

There were a number of reasons for this shift. Among them were the search for a slower pace of life and an opportunity to experience a farm setting, although most did not intend to earn a living through farming. Many people in the counterurbanization movement were retired and had achieved a high enough level of affluence to change residential location. Improved transportation and communication systems also made it easier for people to relocate to the rural areas and still be connected to the city. For example, with the advent of **telecommuting,** many employees worked from home via computers and rarely traveled to the office. The counterurbanization movement slowed in the late 1980s. Interest again peaked in urban renewal projects and the **gentrification** of older and deteriorated urban neighborhoods.

A number of European countries experienced counterurbanization during the same time period. As in the United States, the movement tended to slow in the 1980s for essentially the same reasons.

Suggested Readings: A. G. Champion, *Counterurbanization: The Changing Pace and Nature of Population Deconcentration,* London: Edward Arnold, 1989; Patricia Gober, "Americans on the Move," *Population Bulletin,* vol. 48 (1993).

Crude birthrate. A common measure of fertility, the crude birthrate (CBR) is based on the annual number of live births per thousand population. For example, the western African country of Benin in 1998 had approximately 270,000 live births and a total population of 6 million. Benin's crude birthrate is determined in the following manner:

$$CBR = \frac{270,000 \times 1,000}{6,000,000} = 45$$

Its crude birthrate is stated as "45 births per 1,000 population." The CBR is termed crude because total population is used in the calculation, and this number therefore includes males and those females who cannot give birth. More-refined and age-specific birthrate calculations are used by demographers.

CBR measures are used to determine specific regional differences in birthrate within a country. For example, the Soviet Union, before its demise, had widely ranging birthrates among its republics. Birthrates in the predominantly Slavic republics (Russia, Ukraine, Byelorussia, etc.) were much lower than in the Central Asian republics, where Muslim culture groups lived. The higher rates reflected customs and traditions emphasizing larger family-size expectations.

CBR measures vary widely around the world. Countries in western Africa have CBRs ranging from the mid-40s to over 50. Western European countries, on the other hand, have CBR values that average about 11. Generally, it is true that CBRs are lower in developed countries than are those in the developing world. The CBR for the world in the year 2000 was approximately 22 per thousand.

Individual countries have instituted population policies at times. For instance, in 1979, China started its famous "one child per family" plan. Concerned with its burgeoning total population and wanting to cut back on population growth, China tried hard to convince its people of the merits of this stringent approach. There was a great deal of resistance to the plan, and the rates of feminine infanticide rose dramatically. In China, male offspring are highly desired. If the one child born was a female, in many cases she was put to death. Such brutal outcomes eventually led to the effective end of the one-child policy in the mid-1980s. CBR is one of the two population measures, along with **crude death rate,** used in the calculation of **demographic transition,** another powerful indicator of a country's population history.

Suggested Readings: Arthur Haupt and Thomas Kane, *Population Handbook*, 4th ed., Washington, D.C.: Population Reference Bureau, 1997; several world links are found at the Web site for the Centers for Disease Control and Prevention, www.cdc.gov/nchswww.

Crude death rate. The crude death rate (CDR) is a measure of mortality within a population. CDR is based on the annual number of deaths per thousand population. For example, the western African country of Benin in 1998 had approximately 84,000 deaths in its total population of 6 million. Benin's crude death rate is determined in the following manner:

$$\text{CDR} = \frac{84{,}000 \times 1{,}000}{6{,}000{,}000} = 14$$

It is stated as "14 deaths per 1,000 population." The crude death rate is termed crude because the total population is used in the expression. As such, age-specific death rate measures are used to gain precise estimates. Usually, these measures consider five-year age groups and use the same basic formula. So, for the five-year cohort 55–59, the death rate would be considerably higher than the rate for the 25–29 age group. Death rate measures are used to study differences regionally and to compare urban and rural variability. Death rate measures also illustrate that women have longer life spans than men and that occupational types can be related to higher or lower death rates. Women in the developing world are much more likely to die in childbirth than in other regions of the world.

Since the end of World War II, death rates have been declining all over the world. This is due in large part to the spread of technology and medical care, which have brought a generally healthier environment to all world regions, and to significant declines in the **infant mortality rate.** It may be surprising to note that death rates in the developed and less-developed regions are essentially comparable. In fact, in some years the death rate for developed regions may be higher. This is due to the much higher average ages in the developed regions and the higher death rates associated with advanced age. Despite generally lower death rates globally, there are still significant differences noted regionally. Western African CDRs average about 16 per thousand. Some European countries have seen periods of several years in which CDRs have exceeded CBRs, which results in a negative **rate of natural increase.** Crude death rate is used, along with **crude birthrate,** in the determination of **demographic transition,** an indicator of the historical changes in a country's population.

Suggested Readings: Arthur Haupt and Thomas Kane, *Population Handbook,* 4th ed., Washington, D.C.: Population Reference Bureau, 1997; several world population links are found at www.cdc.gov/nchswww.

Cultural convergence. Cultural convergence occurs when an attribute of one culture group is adopted by another. Countries in the developed world have remarkably similar technological bases and economic structures. Even similar cultural traits are shared; one example is Japan's adoption of golf and baseball from the United States. These outcomes are the result of cultural convergence and occur because of instantaneous communication systems and high-speed transportation links connecting these countries (*see* **Accessibility**). All of the countries in the developed world are equipped with the latest in computer technology, modern industrial capability, and advanced marketing mechanisms to ensure their economic success.

Cultural convergence is evident at the global level in the vast belt of manufacturing regions that reaches from North America through Europe to East

Asia. The economic activities within this highly productive belt have developed industries and business systems to gain the greatest economic advantage. This is the core region in the **core-periphery model,** the spatial structure of an economic system that includes unequal development. As communication and transportation systems spread to other regions of the world, cultural convergence acts to spread some economic aspects of the core outward. For example, a number of countries in Latin America, Africa, and Asia are producing crude steel and taking part in industrial and manufacturing activities as the globalization of economic activity expands. However, a significant development gap persists between the core and the periphery. Countries in the periphery do not, as a rule, have the wealth to develop the complete set of economic attributes seen in the core. As such, there are limits to the effectiveness of cultural convergence in closing the core-periphery gap.

Suggested Readings: Brian Berry et al., *The Global Economy in Transition*, Upper Saddle River, N.J.: Prentice Hall, 1997; John Dickenson, *Geography of the Third World*, 2nd ed., New York: Routledge, 1996.

Cultural diffusion. *See* **Diffusion.**

Cultural ecology. Perhaps the most basic and enduring theme in the development of geographic thought has been the consideration of human interaction with the physical environment, which is called cultural ecology. Examples of this focus are found in the earliest of Greek writings. The ancient Greek historian **Herodotus,** for instance, expressed concern about soil erosion in Athens resulting from the expansion of agriculture. The English geographer **Halford J. Mackinder** proposed in 1887 that geography become the science whose main function is the study of human interaction with the local environment. The term *cultural ecology,* proposed by geographer Harlan Barrows in the 1940s, addresses this important interplay and sets it in the modern era. Barrows noted that human responses to the environment reflect the specific composition of the culture group involved. Cultures steeped in technological expertise and advanced engineering capabilities will be able to exert much greater influence on their environment than culture groups without these powerful attributes.

In addition to the broad confines of human environment interaction embraced by cultural ecology, the concept also includes consideration of **environmental perception** and use of the environment. The latter focus has been the subject of controversy on many occasions, especially in high-technology cultures. Environmental modifications can have both positive and negative outcomes. The transformation of the North American interior basis to vast agricultural fields has provided much-needed food worldwide; yet, vast amounts of topsoil are lost every year to erosion and precipitation runoff. Dams created to develop hydroelectric power and water reserves for irrigation have also flooded great expanses of scenic grandeur and, in the Pacific Northwest, upset the annual migration of salmon upriver to their breeding areas.

Cultural ecology is opposite to the concept of **environmental determinism,** an uncompromising notion in geography early in the twentieth century. It does include many of the notions found in **Paul Vidal de la Blache**'s concept of **possibilism.**

Suggested Readings: Andrew Goudie, *The Earth Transformed: An Introduction to Human Impacts on the Environment*, Oxford, U.K.: Blackwell, 1997; Robert M. Netting, *Cultural Ecology*, 2nd ed., Prospect Heights, Ill.: Waveland Press, 1996.

Cultural geography. A systematic subfield of **human geography,** cultural geography deals with spatial variations in language, economic systems, governmental forms, relation, perceptions of environment, and a myriad of other cultural expressions. Cultural geography uses a synthesizing approach through studying the close relationship between culture and the physical environment (*see* **Cultural ecology**). Cultural geographers believe that aspects of a culture cannot be fully understood without reference to the environment in which it is found. As such, cultural geographers include terrain analysis, climate, vegetation, soil, and animal life because these factors have an impact on, and help to explain, cultural patterns.

Cultural geography had its formal origins with **Carl Sauer,** a twentieth-century American geographer who emphasized direct field observation of cultural responses to the environment as imprinted on the landscape. For example, food preferences reflect a cultural relationship to the environment. In southern China the environment allows for double-cropping of rice, but in northern China wheat prevails as the primary grain. Settlement patterns, building types, and building materials also interest the cultural geographer, especially the way these attributes differ among culture groups. For example, the **township and range system** of land division extensively used in the United States differs radically from the **long lot system** used by the French.

Suggested Readings: William Norton, *Explorations in the Understanding of Landscape: A Cultural Geography*, Westport, Conn.: Greenwood Press, 1989; Web site for the Cultural Geography Specialty Group, Association of American Geographers, www.geocities.com/Athens/5802/cgsg.html.

Cultural integration. The basic tenet of both **cultural ecology** and **cultural geography** is the integration of cultural elements and the physical environment in which that culture is found. This holistic view of human–environment interaction is an enduring and basic theme in geography. Cultural integration deals with another holistic approach: the contention that culture itself is an integrated and synthesized dynamic whole. Further, culture operates as a system: a change in one aspect of a culture will bring about changes in other aspects of the culture and, to a certain degree, in the culture itself. The concept of cultural integration addresses these complex dynamics.

For example, two dissimilar culture groups are found along the border between the United States and Mexico. It is not surprising to find that differences exist in agricultural practices and the kinds of food products grown in each country. Yet, with greater interaction between these two countries, the foods of each have found their way into the cultural domain of the other. The interaction is so intense in recent decades that a new **region** has developed along the 1,300-mile border, a region that is truly a combination of both cultures. Even the unofficial language spoken there, "Spanglish," attests to the change.

Industrial development in Japan, begun in earnest following the Meiji Restoration in 1868 and reconstituted after the end of World War II in 1945, brought far-reaching changes in Japan's culture. Its global reach in the economic realm, highlighted by the production of high-value-added goods ranging from cameras and computers to automobiles and giant crude oil tankers, brought Japan into virtually every region of the world.

Cultural integration is also apparent in the realm of language. For example, English has supplanted French as the language of diplomacy throughout the world. All countries, it seems, are insisting that their citizenry become versed in English. As a result, the United States has deemphasized the need for its citizens to become bilingual.

During the recent conflict in Afghanistan following the destruction of the World Trade Centers and damage to the Pentagon, a hurried call went out from the federal government for speakers of Arabic to help in translation and communication work. It was clear that there were simply too few such linguists in the United States. Further, within weeks following the military engagement, colleges and universities were reporting greatly increased student demand for courses on Middle Eastern languages and culture.

Suggested Readings: Kenneth E. Foote et al., *Re-reading Cultural Geography*, Austin: University of Texas Press, 1994; various issues of *Ekumene: A Geographical Journal of Environment, Culture, Meaning*, first published in 1994.

Cultural landscape. Tokyo Tower, the Chicago skyline, a Wisconsin dairy farm, the market center in Timbuktu, and an Inuit igloo all have one thing in common: each one is part of a cultural landscape. Wherever a culture group has modified its environmental setting, a cultural landscape results. These physical manifestations of human presence have been an important area of investigation within **cultural geography.**

Examples of cultural landscapes are endless and of great variety. The practice of terracing in Asian countries to maximize agricultural production on lands with high gradient is a particularly dramatic example of cultural landscape. Equally impressive, though quite different, are the vast and expansive wheat fields in the great plains of the United States and Canada. This region has been characterized as the breadbasket to the world. Yet, during the westward movement in the nineteenth century, it was a region initially avoided for agricultural pursuits. Called the Great American Desert by early explorers, the region did not become important until the steel plow was invented, an agricultural implement strong enough to break through the hard surface of the soil and open it for agriculture.

The creation of cultural landscapes can take time. In Europe, over several centuries, the gradual clearing of the forests for agriculture resulted in an expansive cultural landscape. Intensive agricultural activity along the lower Nile River in Egypt presents a cultural landscape in stark contrast to both the European plain and the interior basin in North America. A cultural landscape is also produced when a transportation line is built. Countries in the developed world have dense networks of surface transportation, such as railroads and interstate and local highways. Places in the developing world are much less efficiently connected because of a paucity of surface links. Both are, nonetheless, examples of cultural landscapes.

The New York City skyline is perhaps the most famous urban image in the world. On September 11, 2001, that skyline was tragically altered. Within weeks, bombing commenced on military targets throughout Afghanistan. In each place, the cultural landscape was radically changed. The massive destruction of Hiroshima and Nagasaki, Japan, in August 1945, during World War II, are two pointed examples of horrific change in the cultural landscape.

Suggested Readings: Andrew Goudie, *The Human Impact on the Natural Environment*, New York: Blackwell, 1999; I. G. Simmons, *Changing the Face of the Earth: Culture, Environment, History*, 2nd ed., Cambridge, Mass.: Blackwell, 1995.

Culture hearth. Culture hearths were the areas in which agriculture and technology originated. By the end of the Neolithic period (New Stone Age), which spanned the period from 8000 to 3500 B.C., a number of highly productive and well-organized centers of culture had emerged. **Urbanization** had begun; agricultural activities, reflective of each physical setting, were well established; and distinct holistic **cultural integration** was established. In time, many of the technological and cultural attributes developed in these culture hearths began to diffuse outward and were incorporated by other groups of people. These centers of civilization provided an important impetus to the growth and spread of cultural traits throughout the world over time.

The culture hearths were similar in their organization and activities but not identical. Common to all of them, however, was a well-developed agricultural system. It is generally accepted that a viable urban system could not have emerged without the presence of a sound agricultural base.

Major culture hearths began in Middle America, the Andes Mountains, West Africa, the Near East, Mesopotamia, the Indus Valley, North China, and Southeast Asia. Three of the culture hearths emerged before 10,000 B.C.: those in the Near East, the Nile Valley, and Europe. The latest arrival was that of the Indus Valley, about 3500 B.C. Ironically, this culture hearth did not last beyond 1500 B.C. Its cities were abandoned as a result of a severe decline in the agricultural sector. Climate research indicates the presence of a long-term drought in the Indus Valley that led to the demise of this center. The culture hearth in

East Asia, on the other hand, holds the record for having the longest uninterrupted history of agricultural activity. Emerging about 7000 B.C. with the cultivation of rice and other crops, East Asian agriculture continues to this day and is central to one of China's most populous regions. The culture hearth began at the junction of the Huang and Wei Rivers in northern China. In time, the region expanded to include the North China plain on both sides of the lower third of the Huang. Very fertile soils coming from both alluvial deposits and wind-borne loess from the northwestern deserts have made this region exceptionally productive. One-fifth of the population of China lives there.

Suggested Readings: Rick Gore, "The Most Ancient Americans," *National Geographic* 192 (October 1997): 92–99; Richard S. McLeish, *The Origins of Agriculture and Settled Life*, Norman: University of Oklahoma Press, 1991.

Darwin, Charles (1809–1882). Widely recognized as the primary advocate of evolution, English naturalist Charles Darwin proved to have a profound influence on geography as well. Darwin sought explanations for the immense diversity found in organic life on earth. His research centered on identifying the processes of change in nature that ultimately produced organic change.

Darwin was influenced by work on population by English economist **Thomas Robert Malthus** a half century earlier. Malthus contended that a true struggle for existence would result from rapid growth of human population and the inability of agriculturalists to provide food in volume sufficient to satisfy rising demand. Darwin considered Malthus's notion of struggle for existence as a key concept in his evolving search for the processes of natural selection, a cornerstone of evolutionary theory.

German naturalist **Alexander von Humboldt** (1769–1859) and his writings on the tropical regions also influenced Darwin. Von

Charles Darwin. *Source:* National Library of Medicine.

Humboldt's descriptions of varied plant and animal life provided further evidence for Darwin to support his work on organic diversity. Darwin's own travels to the Galápagos Islands in the South Pacific further convinced him that his theory of evolution through natural selection was correct.

In 1859, Darwin published his highly influential book, *The Origin of Species*, a work that had a profound influence in virtually every sector of Western society. In the field of geography, Darwin's ideas were applied to landforms and the cycle of erosion, which brought about change through time; to soils, where the idea of transformation from young to mature farms was advanced; and to societal settings, where the notion of survival of the fittest eventually resulted in the concept of **environmental determinism.**

Darwin was made a Fellow of the Royal Geographical Society in England in 1838. This honor was primarily in recognition of his extensive travels; at that early date his eventual contributions to the discipline of geography were not yet apparent.

Suggested Readings: P. T. Bowler, *Evolution: The History of an Idea,* Berkeley: University of California Press, 1984; D. R. Stoddart, "Darwin's Impact on Geography," *Annals of the Association of American Geographers,* vol. 56 (1966).

Davis, William Morris (1850–1934). Considered by many in the field to be the father of geography in the United States, William Morris Davis was first appointed to the Department of Geology and Geography at Harvard University in 1878. He became professor of physical geography in 1890 at Harvard. Davis became a prominent scholar of geomorphology, the study of surface features on the earth and how they were formed.

Davis is especially remembered for his use of an organic analogy to describe the erosion cycle in a landscape: a river valley, for instance, will change from a stage of youth to one of maturity and finally old age. Davis had a profound influence on British geomorphology, although his organic analogy to landscape change was rejected by Russian geographers.

Davis was a keen observer of the landscape, and his fieldwork, especially his detailed ink drawings of surface features, was first rate. He provided the basis of physical geography in the United States and Britain that held until the 1940s.

Geographic content, Davis claimed, was to be found in the relationship between physical geography (the control-

William Morris Davis. *Source:* CORBIS.

ling agent) and human responses. In this view, Davis was linked to the concept presented earlier by the nineteenth-century English naturalist **Charles Darwin,** and he was attempting to develop a conceptual base to include humans within the landscape instead of separate from it. A number of prominent geographers of the time took issue with this view, and it is ironic that an eventual split between physical geography and **human geography** occurred as a result of this disagreement.

In 1889, Davis adopted his erosion cycle model for use by teachers in elementary and secondary schools. Davis was also instrumental in the formation of the Association of American Geographers, the most influential professional society in the discipline. He formed the group in 1904 and the following year was elected to the first of three terms as its president.

Suggested Readings: Geoffrey J. Martin and Preston E. James, *All Possible Worlds: A History of Geographical Ideas*, 3rd ed., New York: John Wiley & Sons, 1993; Tim Unwin, *The Place of Geography*, New York: John Wiley & Sons, 1992.

Deforestation. The great continental forests on earth are fast disappearing. The practice of deforestation, or large-scale clearing of trees, has greatly reduced forest cover in all major regions. For more than 3,000 years humans have cut down stands of trees to create farmland and to use the wood for building materials and fuel. Virtually all the European region was cleared of forests over a 1,000-year period. In recent years forests have given way to expanding metropolitan areas, roads and railroad corridors, and varied industrial activities.

Removal of forest cover leads to erosion and the loss of fertile topsoil. Erosion is particularly serious when it occurs at high elevations. Runoff of added materials can cause flooding at lower levels. For example, Seoul, South Korea, experienced rapid population increases during the early 1960s. The mountains near Seoul were stripped of their forest cover primarily for fuel for cooking and heating. The result was mud slides that inundated the city during the rainy season. The problem was serious enough to force the South Korean government to limit the number of people moving into the city and to begin a reforestation program in the affected region.

In China, the removal of large sections of the bamboo forests has led to a serious decline in the number of giant pandas. The panda is now an endangered species.

Environmental destruction from deforestation is not new. By the time of the collapse of the Roman Empire (ca. A.D. 476), some previously productive agricultural areas had become useless as a result of deforestation and subsequent erosion.

Much later, rapid clearing of the vast white-pine forests in the United States during the nineteenth and early twentieth centuries was especially devastating. From Maine to Minnesota, clear-cutting of the tall pines continued until the forests were essentially gone. Significant conservation efforts were not begun until the forestry industry was operating in the far western states of Washington, Oregon, and California. At risk in recent years are the old-growth stands of redwood in the western United States. Environmentalists suggest that the old-growth forests, with their 1,000-year-old trees, could be completely eliminated during the twenty-first century.

The most-dramatic losses through deforestation are occurring in the equatorial regions. The vast tropical rain forests of Asia, Africa, and Latin America have been cleared at alarming rates in recent decades. More than half the tropical rain forest cover has been eliminated; the African stands have diminished by more than 70 percent. Forests are being cleared to create grazing and agricultural land.

A number of concerns have been raised as a result of the demise of the tropical rain forests. First, the great forests act as absorbers of carbon in the atmosphere and emitters of oxygen. As trees are cut down, the important carbon-oxygen exchange is upset. Second, significant climatic changes are possible through declines in the amount of moisture originating in the tropical rain forests and carried to higher latitudes through atmospheric circulation. Third, the loss of the tropical rain forest results in the extinction of plants with potentially valuable medicinal properties. It is estimated that 60,000 plant varieties in the tropical rain forests will be lost by the middle of the twenty-first century.

Suggested Readings: David A. Castillon, *Conservation of Natural Resources: A Management Approach*, 2nd ed., Dubuque, Iowa: Wm. C. Brown, 1997; Kenton Miller and Laura Tangley, *Trees of Life: Saving Tropical Forests and Their Biological Wealth*, Washington, D.C.: World Resources Institute, 1991.

Deindustrialization. During the second half of the twentieth century, urban industrialized regions saw manufacturing jobs decline in great numbers and older, outmoded industrial plants taken out of production. This process is known as deindustrialization and is explained by a number of factors. Among them are increasing labor and energy costs in the industrialized countries, more-efficient plants in other regions, the reduction of transportation costs that allows basic commodities such as crude steel to be shipped from other countries, and the rise of transnational corporations that have established manufacturing plants in the developing world.

Manufacturing jobs lost through deindustrialization have been replaced by jobs in the service sector. Old steel mills and foundries have given way to research parks, shopping centers, and office buildings. This transformation in job profiles brought concomitant problems. Workers in industry and manufacturing were generally well paid, and the transition to lower-paid entry-level jobs in the service sector produced great hardship. For example, a skilled steelworker would not be prepared to immediately step into a position requiring extensive training in computer maintenance. Yet, the transition to a predominantly service sector economy is continuing and is irreversible. By the year

2000, only 20 percent of all jobs in the United States were in manufacturing and extractive industries, whereas in 1850 these two categories had accounted for nearly 85 percent of U.S. jobs. The United States, Canada, western Europe, Japan, and Australia have seen a dramatic shift from primary reliance on manufacturing to a service-sector economic base. This transition, in which industrialization is a key factor, has produced in those countries a **postindustrial economy.**

Suggested Readings: P. W. Daniels, *The Global Economy in Transition,* White Plains, N.Y.: Longman, 1996; Ron Martin and Robert Rowthorn, eds., *The Geography of Deindustrialization,* Dobbs Ferry, N.Y.: Sheridan House, 1986.

Demographic transition. The demographic transition model uses **crude birthrate** and **crude death rate** to illustrate changes in the historical trends of population for a country or region. The model was first used for England and Wales over the period 1750–1950. During this 200-year period, the population doubled.

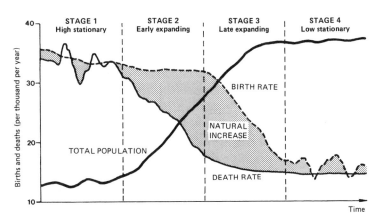

Demographic transition. *Source:* Brian Goodall, *The Penguin Dictionary of Human Geography* (Penguin Books, 1987). Copyright Brian Goodall, 1987. Reproduced by permission of Penguin Books Ltd.

The general model of demographic transition is divided into four stages. In Stage 1, both the crude birthrate and the crude death rate are high in value (nearly 40 per 1,000) and fluctuating. High birthrates were offset by high death rates. This stage was prevalent throughout history until about the mid-1800s, when Stage 2 became the norm.

Stage 2 in the model occurs when death rates drop well below birthrates. Significant and steady declines in the death rate occurred during the **Industrial Revolution,** which began in the late 1800s, through advances in medical technology. Birthrates in Stage 2 either remain high or decline less rapidly than death rates. With birthrates high and death rates declining, the difference between the two widens. The difference, stated as a percentage, is the **rate of natural increase.** It is clear that the higher the rate of natural increase, the greater the overall increase in total population (except for gains or losses due to migration).

In Stage 3, both the birth- and death rates are declining. The explanation for lowering birthrates is not as straightforward as that for declining death rates. Initially in Stage 3, birthrates remain high, indicative of social traditions that favor large families, but this growth gradually slows. For example, as the Industrial Revolution continued, more families moved into cities, where housing was less amenable to large families. In time the urban lifestyle brought changes, and family size declined from earlier higher numbers seen in rural areas. During Stage 3, population growth continues but not as rapidly as it did in Stage 2.

Stage 4 is entered when birth- and death rates are again close in value. Population growth rates are very low or even show slight declines. Some European countries have, in fact, entered what could be a new stage in the demographic transition: death rates have exceeded birthrates for short periods of time. The European countries were the first to complete the demographic transition, and the average longevity of their people continues to increase. An older population will have more deaths and fewer births. Russia, for example, experienced unusually high death rates through the late 1980s into the first years of the twenty-first century. Russia is the first industrialized country to have what appears to be a steady increase in death rates.

Countries in the developed world are alone in completing the demographic transition. The developing world is still seeing high rates of natural increase because most countries are still in either Stage 2 or Stage 3 of the demographic transition. As long as death rates are significantly lower than birthrates in the highly populated developing world, the so-called **population explosion** will continue.

Suggested Readings: Joseph A. McFalls Jr., "Population: A Lively Introduction," *Population Bulletin*, vol. 53, no. 3 (1998); Jennifer D. Mitchell, "Before the Next Doubling," *World Watch*, January–February 1998, 20–27.

Density gradient. Density gradient is the rate at which any land use or function declines with increasing distance from a center point. **Von Thunen's land use model,** developed in the early 1800s by German economist Johann Heinrich von Thunen, illustrates the density gradient notion: activities at and near the center of the isolated state are intensive and densely packed; with increasing distance from the center, activities become more extensive and reflect lower densities.

Cities in the early twentieth century had high densities of population near the center. Densities declined with distance from the center. The suburban fringe had the lowest densities of population.

The density gradient is a spatial model of **distance decay,** the concept that any process will decline in intensity with increasing distance from a center. In recent decades there have been changes in density gradients within urban areas. With the increase of suburbanization and improved transportation from urban centers to the suburbs, greater numbers of people have moved to the fringes. With increases in suburban population have come declines in the number of people living near urban centers. This is partly due to the abandonment of old apartment buildings and the relocation of business activities to the suburbs. As a result of these changes, the density gradient has become more shallow.

Suggested Readings: Paul L. Knox, ed., *The Restless Urban Landscape*, Englewood Cliffs, N.J.: Prentice Hall, 1993; William C. Wheaton, "Land Use and Density in Cities with Congestion," *Journal of Urban Economics*, vol. 43 (1998).

Dependency ratio. The cohort identified as active workers in any country is generally taken to be those aged 15–64. Individuals younger or older than the worker group are considered dependent on them. The dependency ratio indicates the relationship between these two groups.

The **population pyramid** for any country provides a graphic glimpse of its dependency ratio. For instance, a developing country will have a large percentage of its population in the 0–14 age group and a small number of people over 64 years of age. On the other hand, a developed country having completed the **demographic transition** will have a smaller percentage of its population in the 0–14 group and a large and growing number of people age 65 and above. In both cases, the workforce, those aged 15–64, will provide for the younger and older members of the population.

Japan provides a good example of problems faced by a country that has completed the demographic transition and has seen increases in both life expectancy and average age of the population. In 1970, the population 65 years and older in Japan was 8 percent, whereas the population of those younger than 15 was 22 percent. By 2000, those 65 and above accounted for 20 percent of the population, and the under-15 cohort was 17 percent.

The resulting dependency ratios reveal significant changes over that 30-year period. The mathematical form of the expression is as follows:

$$\frac{(\text{Percent under 15}) + (\text{Percent over 64})}{\text{Percent in workforce}} * 100 = \text{dependency ratio}$$

for 1970 in Japan:

$$\frac{22 + 8}{70} = .43 * 100 = 43$$

for 2000 in Japan:

$$\frac{17 + 20}{63} = .59 * 100 = 59$$

The resulting figures indicate that every 100 workers supported 43 others in 1970 and 59 others in 2000. The increase in the number to be supported in

2000 is attributed to the much larger population aged 65 and above. Note that the percentage under age 15 declined from 1970 to 2000.

An aging population will require adjustment in health care, retirement options, and possibly will result in shortages in the workforce. In developing countries that have not completed the demographic transition, the biggest burden is caring for those in the 0–14 age group. It is expected that this age cohort will slowly decline in overall percentage as policies are enacted to curtail high population growth.

Suggested Readings: Lester R. Brown et al., *Beyond Malthus: Nineteen Dimensions of the Population Challenge*, New York: W. W. Norton, 1999; United Nations Population Fund, *The State of World Population*, United Nations, annual.

Dependency theory. Dependency theory contends that colonial entities established during the period of **colonialism**—from about 1500 to 1800 in the Western Hemisphere and during the late 1800s in Africa—remained dependent on the developed world even after gaining their independence and becoming sovereign states. During the period of colonialism, an imbalance emerged in which European occupiers gained a supreme economic advantage over their colonies, which supplied raw materials and commodities for European manufacturers. The period of colonialism marked the beginning of the core-periphery relationship that currently exists.

Dependency theory advocates suggest that the basis for the dependence is the system of inequitable trade relationships that favor the developed countries. In the absence of the European powers that dictated the trade arrangements during colonial rule, **transnational corporation**s have entered the newly formed countries to continue the pattern of economic imbalances.

Dependency theory is related to **Wallerstein's world-system analysis,** developed by American social scientist Immanuel Wallerstein in the 1960s and 1970s, which states, in part, that the core countries are the drivers of the global economic system and the periphery supports the core by providing raw materials, commodities, labor supply, and a market for goods and services emanating from the core. In the **core-periphery model,** any economic gain made by the periphery is offset by greater gains for the core. In short, the system is self-perpetuating, and the economic gap between the core and the periphery will continue to widen.

The somber reality of the dependency theory with its attendant core-periphery basis can be compared with the more optimistic (although greatly discredited) model of economic development proposed by American economic historian **Walter W. Rostow** in 1960. Rostow suggested that all developing countries would proceed through five stages of economic development, from traditional society to an age of mass consumption. Economic development experience in the developing world since Rostow's writings has not proven to follow his model.

Suggested Readings: Richard Peet, *Theories of Development*, New York: Guilford Press, 1999; The World Bank, *The World Development Report*, New York: Oxford University Press, annual.

Desertification. The degradation of semiarid lands through either climate change or increasing human use (or both) is termed desertification. All continents lying in the desert latitudinal belts, 30 degrees north and 30 degrees south of the equator, have been affected by desert advance.

Of particular significance in this regard is the semiarid region of the Sahel, bordering the southern margin of the Sahara Desert in Africa. From 1980 onward, desert conditions have moved into the Sahel at a rate of advance averaging four miles per year. Actual advance of the desert has varied in individual years. When rainfall is higher, the advance will be slowed or even temporarily reversed. However, the long-term trend in the Sahel strongly suggests continued desertification. Much of the natural vegetation has been cleared for agriculture and the grazing of animals. Trees have been felled for fuel wood and building materials. Grazing has been particularly hard on the land because of the severe packing of the soil by animal hooves. Rain falling on hardened and packed soil will not soak into the ground but instead flows to lower elevations. The resulting soil is drier and less able to support new plant growth, and the subsurface water table is lowered, making well water less accessible.

Population pressures have exacerbated desertification in the Sahel. Increases in population have led to more demands on the land for grazing and agriculture. Environmental experts predict that more than 40 percent of Africa's non-desert land will be lost to desertification if present trends continue.

Suggested Readings: Mick Hulme and Mick Kelly, "Desertification and Climate Change," *Environment,* vol. 35 (1993); Nick Middleton and David Thomas, *World Atlas of Desertification,* 2nd ed., United Nations Development Programme, London: Edward Arnold, 1997.

Devolution. Devolution, as applied to sovereign states, is the granting of powers, and possibly autonomy, to subgroups within the states. Most of the sovereign states in the world include a number of distinct ethnic groups within their individual borders. This multicultural characteristic does not usually constitute a threat to the unified integrity of the country. But at times, and for particular reasons, pressures may be exerted by one or more of the internal ethnic groups as they destabilize the system and demand greater recognition. The most extreme demand is to separate from the country and become a separate sovereign state. Such centrifugal, or separating, forces are found in a number of world centers.

Quebec's separatist movement over the past several years is a pointed example of devolution. The predominately French-speaking Quebecois seem determined to separate from English Canada because of purported inequitable treatment by the national government. The fact that Quebec is home to virtually all of Canada's French speakers gives added strength to the devolution effort. If the French were spread about the whole of Canada, the movement could not have been nearly as effective.

A number of moves toward devolution are occurring in European countries. Northern Ireland, Scotland, and Wales are trying to break free from the rule of Great Britain. The Basques and Catalans in Spain have initiated efforts leading to separation. In Belgium, the Flemish and Walloon culture groups have spoken out, demanding greater recognition.

In the 1990s Czechoslovakia was peacefully divided into the Czech Republic and Slovakia, new sovereign states. The 1990s also witnessed turmoil as Yugoslavia disintegrated and several new countries emerged. Yugoslavia was held together before its devolution by the strong hand of Marshal Josip Tito and the country's position as a satellite of the Soviet Union. With the death of Tito in 1980 and the demise of the Soviet Union in 1991, the voices of ethnic identity became stronger, and significant separatist movements—some extremely violent—emerged in force.

Suggested Readings: Brian W. Blouet, "The Political Geography of Europe: 1900–2000," *Journal of Geography*, vol. 95 (1996); Allan M. Williams, *The European Community: The Contradiction of Integration*, 2nd ed., Oxford, U.K.: Basil Blackwell, 1994.

Diffusion. The areal spread of ideas, innovations, substances, practices, enterprises, styles, religions, or organized sports from a point of origin is generally known as diffusion. The study of diffusion in its various forms is an important aspect of **human geography.** One of the pioneers in the field and its principal contributor is **Torsten Hagerstrand,** a twentieth-century Swedish geographer who developed models and quantitative techniques for application in diffusion studies.

There are two general forms of diffusion: **expansion diffusion** and **relocation diffusion.** In expansion diffusion, ideas or substances spread from a point of origin throughout adjacent areas. The spread of hybrid corn from its center in Illinois outward to adjacent corn-growing states is an example of expansion diffusion. Relocation diffusion is exemplified in the move of European religions to North America during the colonial period.

A number of diffusions involved a combination of relocation and expansion forms. For example, Dutch elm disease emanated from a shipment of European wood to Ohio in the 1930s. The wood contained a beetle that would burrow into the bark of elm trees. The tree's defense response was to shut down its own circulation in that place. Eventually its branches would wither and the tree would be removed in order to avoid spreading the disease to other trees. By 1970, Dutch elm disease had spread as far west as Minnesota. The relocation took place in the shipment of wood to Ohio; the expansion took the form of a spread from tree to tree outward from Ohio.

Suggested Readings: Fred B. Kniffen, "Cultural Diffusion and Landscapes: Selection by Fred B. Kniffen," *Geoscience and Man*, vol. 27 (1990); Richard K. Ormrod, "Adaptation and Cultural Diffusion," *Journal of Geography*, vol. 91 (1992).

Diffusion barrier. Any condition that interrupts or prohibits the **diffusion** process is considered a diffusion barrier. Barriers are found in the physical environment. For example, the diffusion of wheat growing in the Great Plains eventually met physical barriers in Canada (where temperatures were too low), the Rocky Mountains, and the arid Southwest. The spread of the boll weevil through the cotton fields in the southeastern United States halted at the edge of the cotton-growing region.

Diffusion barriers can also be cultural in nature. An innovation or idea that is spreading may encounter a culture group that does not accept it. Nonacceptance of the innovation or idea has been characterized as an absorbing barrier. That is, instead of accepting the innovation or idea and allowing the diffusion process to continue, the innovation or idea is said to have been absorbed or, in a sense, lost to further diffusion, at least in the area of absorption.

The concept of friction of distance (*see* **Distance decay**) is also considered to be a form of diffusion barrier. It is generally true that distance itself can deter or delay the transfer of ideas, people, substances, and so forth, and the greater the distance, the lower will be the degree of transfer. For example, several hundred years passed before the process of papermaking made its way from China to Europe.

Suggested Readings: Lawrence A. Brown, *Innovation Diffusion: A New Perspective*, New York: Methuen, 1981; R. J. Johnston et al., *The Dictionary of Human Geography*, Oxford, U.K.: Basil Blackwell, 2000.

Distance decay. The concept of distance decay states that spatial interaction will diminish with increased distance. For example, people will operate primarily within their daily **activity space** and will travel outside that area much less frequently. For a family living in St. Louis, a trip to visit relatives in Denver will certainly not occur weekly or perhaps even monthly. This diminishment of spatial interaction has a very practical basis: extensive trips take more time and are costly. The trip from St. Louis to Denver, for instance, would have to be planned carefully in order to adjust the normal sequence of daily and weekly activities (school and work schedules) within the family's activity space.

The models developed by nineteenth-century German economist Johann Heinrich von Thunen and twentieth-century German economic geographer Walter Christaller both consider the effect of distance on spatial interaction. Work by geographers during the **Quantitative Revolution** focused closely on the effects of distance. Models were developed to quantify the degree of spatial interaction between places as distance increased. Practical outcomes of these studies include estimations of migration patterns from one area to another and traffic flows between urban areas, as well as predictions of shopping activity at competing centers. *See also* **Von Thunen's land use model** and **Christaller's central place theory.**

Suggested Readings: Paul Boyle and Keith Halfacre, *Migration into Rural Areas: Theories and Issues*, London: John Wiley & Sons, 1998; W. Tobler, "A Computer Movie," *Economic Geography*, vol. 46 (1970).

Double-cropping. A common agricultural practice in the warmer Asian regions, double-cropping is the growing of two crops on the same land within the same year. In southern China and on the island of Kyushu in Japan, double-cropping of paddy rice is common. Not only must the temperature be warm enough throughout the two growing periods, but sufficient water is necessary for paddy growth.

The normal practice involves the planting of seedbeds early in the spring and then the transplanting of the new rice shoots into the paddies at the optimum time. The work is labor intensive, because each new rice shoot must be carefully extracted from the seedbed and planted in the paddy by hand. Before the first rice crop is harvested, the second seedbed is planted. Following the harvesting of the first paddy crop, the second is quickly planted in time to ensure maturing of the rice before the end of the growing season in November. The Chinese and the Japanese are recognized world leaders in double-cropping agricultural techniques.

In regions where temperatures are suitable for double-cropping but water availability is not sufficient for a second paddy rice crop, other grains, such as wheat and barley, are planted. In Iraq, a flood-control depression between the Tigris and the Euphrates Rivers provides water for double-cropping in years when the two rivers have swelled with excess water. Water is released in late summer from the catchment basin, allowing flow to agricultural fields for a second crop.

Double-cropping is an indication that (1) population numbers are high, and (2) there is not enough agricultural land to produce sufficient food in one crop. Both China and Japan fit this description. Less than 15 percent of total land area in both countries is ideally suitable for agriculture, and the **population density** of each country is high.

Suggested Readings: Gregory G. Knapp, *Chinese Landscapes: The Village as Place*, Honolulu: University of Hawaii Press, 1992; Michael Smitka, *Agricultural Growth and Japanese Economic Development*, New York: Guilford Press, 1998.

Doubling time. The **rate of natural increase** (RNI) for any area for which population data are available (state, country, region, world) can be used to determine the time necessary for that population to double, which is known as doubling time. Very close approximations are possible using a simple arithmetic operation: doubling time in years is equal to the integer value 70 divided by the RNI. For example, a 1 percent RNI results in a doubling of the population in 70 years (70/1). A 2 percent RNI yields a doubling in 35 years (70/2). A doubling in 140 years will result from an RNI of 0.5 percent.

A glance at the RNIs for countries in the developing world helps to explain why their populations are growing so rapidly. RNIs of 3.0 percent or higher are not uncommon. Countries in Africa, the Middle East, and most of Latin America will most certainly double in the next 20–25 years. On the other hand, countries in North America, Europe, and Japan, have completed the **demographic transition,** and their populations are aging. As such, their RNIs are below 1 percent and their doubling times are in the hundreds of years. In fact, some European countries have negative RNIs. For instance, in 1998 Russia's RNI was –0.5 percent, meaning that its population (not including net migration) was declining. In cases of this type, it is clear that doubling time is not applicable.

Consider a country with a high RNI and a large population. In 1998, India's RNI was 1.9 percent, and its population was close to 990 million. The doubling time for India is 70/1.9 = 37 years. So, if the RNI stays constant until 2035, India's population will swell to 1,980 million. Another doubling to 3,960 million would occur in 2970. Is this likely to happen? Most assuredly not. Doubling time is an indicator of population growth but must not be used to estimate the future population of a country. The main reason for this is the fact that RNIs are predicted to decline steadily in future years, a trend that began in 1963, when world RNI was 2.2 percent. Since then, world RNI has gradually come down to about 1.3 percent and is expected to further decline.

Suggested Readings: Alene Gelbard and Mary M. Kent, "World Population Beyond Six Billion," *Population Bulletin*, vol. 54 (1999); Nathan Kayfitz and Wilhelm Flinger, *World Population Growth and Aging: Demographic Trends in the Late 20th Century*, Chicago: University of Chicago Press, 1991.

E

Economic development. In a general sense, the term *economic development* refers to the processes involved in the growth and refinement of an economic system of any form. In **economic geography** and development studies, the term has a more specific meaning and applies to regional economic systems, their particular attributes, and how they interact at the global level.

There are many ways of characterizing economic development in any country or region. Some of these characteristics are measures of national production, per capita income, attributes of the labor force, and energy consumption. In addition, the degree of interval regional development, the diversity of its economic structure, and the levels of technology within the system may determine the strength of an economic system. Other aspects of an economic system include the percentage of the workforce engaged in agriculture, the degree of urbanization in the country or region, and the level of industrial development.

These characteristics, and others, when accumulated for any country will determine its level of economic development. Countries have been placed in the broad categories of "developed" and "developing." In the developed category are the United States, Canada, western European countries, Japan, Australia, and New Zealand. These countries have completed the **demographic transition,** have become highly urbanized, and are leading industrial and high-technology centers. Countries in the developing world have a higher percentage of their workforce in agriculture, are not heavily industrialized, and have lower levels of urbanization. The developing countries that were occupied by European powers during colonization did not experience full regional development, and many are still struggling to accomplish this important goal.

The developed-developing theme is the outcome of the core-periphery relationship established centuries ago. The **North-South** line demarcating the developed and developing worlds was introduced in 1980 as a means of distinguishing the affluent northern countries from the poorer southern countries.

Suggested Readings: United Nations Development Programme, *Human Development Report*, United Nations, annual; www.odc.org, Web site for the Overseas Development Council, a private internation research group with information on economic development.

Economic geography. As the **Industrial Revolution** continued to strengthen the economic systems in Europe and the United States in the late 1800s, a series of books and articles appeared on the theme of commercial geography. These early research efforts in what would become economic geography aimed at determining the location of usable resources and understanding the details of productive processes globally.

Early in the twentieth century, advocates of the two disciplines—economics and geography—began asking questions that involved the conceptual bases of the other: geographers were entertaining notions raised in economics, and economists began to consider the spatial element and the ways this context effected economics. Economic geography was one of the first subdisciplines to emerge in geography. Since that time, economic geography has further split into a number of subspecialties: agricultural geography, industrial geography, and even welfare geography.

Economic geography followed closely the major conceptual shifts that occurred over time within the discipline. When the shift was made to more-analytical and process-oriented geographical analyses, economic geography incorporated, and in some cases generated, these new approaches. For example, economic geographers began to ask why particular economic activities were located where they were. Studies of industrial locations incorporated themes from economics within the spatial context in order to better understand the patterns of economic activity found in the landscape. Further refinements occurred during the **Quantitative Revolution** in the form of regional science and location theory.

Economic geographers have studied regions of concentrated economic activities. Well-known examples are the manufacturing belt in the United States and Canada, the Fertile Triangle in the Russian Federation, and the Ruhr industrial corridor in Germany.

Suggested Readings: Dean M. Hanink, *Principles and Applications of Economic Geography*, New York: John Wiley & Sons, 1997; Edward J. Malecki, "The Geography of High Technology," *Focus*, vol. 35 (1985).

Ecosystem. The living earth comprises tens of thousands of ecological units operating in a self-contained and self-regulating manner. These ecosystems, as they are called, have achieved the ideal balance in their local topographical and climatic situations. Ecosystems will maintain themselves over time and will change and adapt to reflect alterations in larger systems influencing them. For instance, in recent years the average air temperatures over the Arctic Ocean have gradually increased. This change in temperature has resulted in the diminishment of average ice thickness on the ocean surface.

Ecosystems are also characterized as self-regulating, and their components interact. In the Arctic Ocean example, the ecosystem will regulate itself to reflect the higher average temperatures and thinning ice conditions. The ice diminishment is the result of a form of interaction with the altered conditions in the ecosystem.

Research suggests that the warming of the polar regions is the result of human activity. Increased carbon dioxide in the atmosphere from industrial and automotive emissions is creating a **greenhouse effect,** a general warming of the atmosphere enveloping the planet. This is just one example of many that illustrate how human activity alters ecosystems. Some alterations are minor and others are quite destructive. The recent dramatic changes in the Florida Everglades ecosystem are a case in point. For a number of years, water from the Everglades has been diverted for agricultural activities southeast of Lake Okeechobee, Florida, and the extensive urban settlements along Florida's Atlantic Coast. Diversion of water from the Everglades has altered its conditions greatly; it is no longer a "river of grass," as it was once known. As a result of water diminishment in the Everglades, other natural entities have been affected. Among them are the saw grass, woody vegetation, and animal life that had found a niche in the Everglades.

With world population continuing to increase and economic activity expanding, as it must, there will be more alterations to ecosystems in the future.

Suggested Readings: Robert G. Bailey, *Ecoregions: The Ecosystem Geography of the Oceans and Continents*, New York: Springer Verlag, 1998; Web site of the North American Association of Environmental Education (NAAEE), www.eelink.net. (The focus of EE-Link is environmental education; it is aimed at teachers of K–12 students.)

Ecumene. The word *ecumene*, from the Greek, means "to inhabit." Ecumene is a term used in contemporary geography to identify that part of the earth's surface that is permanently settled. A quick view of a world map of population density will reveal the uneven distribution of people on the earth's surface. Some areas are densely populated, and others are essentially devoid of significant numbers of people. Over time, the area of the ecumene has expanded. When the major **culture hearth**s emerged, the settled areas on earth were limited. With population increase and **migration** of people to other areas, the ecumene began to expand. At the time of the Roman Empire, the known ecumene included parts of Europe, North Africa, the Middle East and areas in Asia. In time, more of the European area received permanent settlers. With the opening of the Western Hemisphere to settlement during the age of exploration, the ecumene further expanded, adding European peoples to the native peoples who had long resided on the American continents.

In modern times, the ecumene is at its largest to date. Settlement has expanded into regions where human habitation was previously impossible. For example, many desert areas are now settled and productive, primarily through advances in technology that have brought industry and irrigation agriculture to hyperarid regions.

Despite expansions of this type, there remain vast areas that are not suitable for permanent settlement. These areas include much of the Arctic and Antarctica, vast areas of northern North America and Siberia, the expansive deserts associated with the belts of high atmospheric pressure at 30 degrees north and south of the equator, and several tropical rain forest regions straddling the equator. These areas are not suitable for permanent settlement because they are too cold, too dry, or too wet. Yet, with future advances in technology, some areas now outside the ecumene could be settled. As world population continues to increase and technological breakthroughs continue to be made, expansion of the ecumene is likely.

Suggested Readings: Gareth Lewis, "Changing Places in a Rural World: The Population Turnaround in Perspective," *Geography: Journal of the Geographical Association,* vol. 85 (2000); Brian K. Roberts, *Landscapes of Settlement,* London: Routledge, 1996.

Edge city. In his 1991 book *Edge Cities: Life on the Frontier,* journalist Joel Garreau introduced the idea of the edge city, an urban complex of varied activities and functions that develops in a suburban residential setting. Over the past 20 years, edge cities (also called suburban downtowns and urban villages) have sprung up along the transportation beltways circling most metropolitan areas in North America.

Once the home of commuters traveling to the inner city for work and shopping, **suburbia** has added manufacturing centers, office parks, shopping malls, medical centers, and entertainment complexes in clusters along limited-access transportation corridors encircling the metropolitan area.

Edge cities tend to be as self-sufficient as possible, containing the functions and services that were once found only in the inner city. **Accessibility** is a key attribute of edge cities. With improved transportation corridors and advanced communication systems made available in recent years, a location distant from the inner city does not pose a disadvantage for successful business operations. Commuting to and from the edge city is marked by travel along beltways and segments of interstate highway systems.

Garreau characterized edge cities as having more jobs than bedrooms, suggesting the importance of their place in the metropolitan economic system. An early precursor of the emerging economic importance of areas on the urban periphery was evident in the 1960 **census,** which pointed out that for the first time in U.S. history, more manufacturing jobs were located in suburbia than in the inner city. Another of Garreau's characteristics was the perception that edge cities had an identity that did not apply to suburbia before their development.

Edge cities are not without their own internal problems, however. Problems of **urban sprawl** and traffic congestion are becoming more apparent as metropolitan areas, and their edge cities, continue to grow.

Suggested Readings: Joel Garreau, *Edge Cities: Life on the Frontier*, New York: Doubleday, 1991; Susan Hanson, *The Geography of Urban Transportation*, 2nd ed., New York: Guilford Press, 1995.

Electoral geography. On the evening of U.S. national elections, all the major television networks illustrate the voting results on a large map of the United States. As each state's election returns come in, the map is changed to reflect the voting outcome. This event is one example of electoral geography, a discipline that looks at the spatial aspects of voting behavior. Experts in **political geography** can use voting results to analyze election outcomes and determine why people in particular areas vote as they do.

There are a number of major attributes that are considered when voting patterns are scrutinized. Among them are ethnic background, income levels, religious affiliation, education levels, and predictable regional differences. The latter attribute points to some perennial strongholds of political party preference in the United States. For instance, the western Mountain states and the Great Plains states lean strongly to the Republican side, whereas the northeastern states vote predominately Democratic.

Another aspect of electoral geography is the study of proportional representation in government. The House of Representatives, for instance, has 435 seats established to ensure proportional representation based on population. The states largest in population will have the greatest number of representatives. (A balancing factor in national government is seen in the way Senate membership is established: two senators represent each state, a system not based on population.)

Following each **census,** states may be required to redraw their congressional districts to adjust to population gains or declines. Congressional redistricting efforts are

THE GERRY-MANDER. (Boston, 1811.)

The original gerrymander map.

very complex and gain the attention of political geographers. Some resulting congressional districts are extraordinarily odd in shape and extent. These unusual outcomes usually result from attempts to ensure that minority members of the populace gain fair representation.

There is historical precedent for unusually shaped districts. In 1812, Governor Eldridge Gerry of Massachusetts authorized the creation of a district that some in government said resembled a salamander. One pundit took the word *salamander* and changed it to *gerrymander*, incorporating the governor's last name. Since that time, the term *gerrymandering* has been used to refer to the creation of districts for specific purposes.

Suggested Readings: R. J. Johnston et al., *Development in Electoral Geography*, New York: Routledge, 1990; John O'Loughlin, "The Identification and Evaluation of Racial Gerrymandering," *Annals of the Association of American Geographers*, vol. 72 (1982).

Enclave and exclave. An enclave is territory of a state within and surrounded by a different state. For example, Lesotho is an enclave within South Africa and is an independent entity. San Marino and the Vatican City are enclaves within Italy. An enclave may also be correctly referred to as an exclave. Cueta and Melilla are small enclaves in Morocco. These two places are also considered exclaves of Spain, because in reality they belong to Spain. Interestingly, there is a small enclave on the southeast coast of the Island of Newfoundland in Canada that belongs to France. Saint Pierre and Miquelon are exclaves of France and enclaves within Canada.

Before German unification, the city of West Berlin was an enclave within the German Democratic Republic (East Germany). It was also an exclave of West Germany. Following German unification and the uniting of East and West Berlin in 1990, these terms no longer applied.

The presence of an enclave creates a perforated state, one of the five recognized state shapes. Other state shapes include elongated (e.g., Chile), compact (e.g., Zimbabwe), prorupt (e.g., Thailand), and fragmented (e.g., the Philippines). In West Africa, the Gambia exists as a narrow land indentation following the Gambia River into the larger republic of Senegal. The Gambia is referred to as a pene-enclave.

The presence of enclaves and exclaves can be the source of tension in a region. This is especially true if there are differences in value systems, religion, or political orientation between the enclave and the perforated state. A case in point is the turmoil between Nagorno-Karabakh, an enclave within the country of Azerbaijan. Nagorno-Karabakh has a population that is 80 percent Armenian Christian, whereas Azerbaijan is primarily Shiite Muslim. Tensions were high between the two groups for decades, but strong control by the communist regime disallowed any serious uprising. Once the Soviet Union disintegrated in 1991, however, the pressures of nationalism and desires for independence resurfaced and fighting broke out. In 1986, Nagorno-Karabakh demanded to be united with neighboring Armenia, lying only 16 kilometers to the west. It was proposed that a narrow land corridor be established on Azerbaijani land to make the connection. The response of the Azeris was to further suppress the Karabakh Armenians. Fighting broke out in 1988 and in the end, thousands on both sides were killed or became refugees. In time the conflict abated, and both Armenia and Azerbaijan became independent states. Nagorno-Karabakh remains an enclave within Azerbaijan and an exclave of Armenia but is free of Azeris.

Suggested Readings: Alexander B. Murphy, "Territorial Policies in Multiethnic States," *Geographical Review*, vol. 79 (1989); Colin H. Williams, *Linguistic Minorities, Society, and Territory*, Clevendon, U.K.: Multilingual Matters, 1991.

Entrepôt. *See* **Asian Tigers.**

Environmental awareness. Curtailing lumber operations in the Pacific Northwest to save the spotted owl, diverting water in the Rio Grande watershed to ensure the safety of the silvery minnow, and the carefully planned exploration for oil in Colorado's Canyon of the Ancients National Monument are all examples of environmental awareness. Concern about the environment, especially when a form of economic development is involved, has become an important human activity. In the United States, environmental awareness has led to the establishment of the Environmental Protection Agency, an arm of the federal government that aims to protect the environment from neglect and harm. In every community throughout the country, prospective economic development efforts must be preceded by an environmental impact analysis to ensure that the planned installation will not cause avoidable injury to the environment.

Environmental awareness is not new, although the degree of concern about protecting the physical fabric of places is perhaps as great as it has ever been. The ancient Greek historian **Herodotus** expressed concern about the loss of soil in agricultural fields in Greece. The conservation movement in the United States, spearheaded by President Theodore Roosevelt at the turn of the twentieth century, was a monumental effort to preserve natural areas for future generations. The creation of the national park system in the United States is traced to the conservation movement begun by President Roosevelt.

In the 1980s, a dramatic confrontation unfolded between developers and environmentalists over proposed expansion of both hydroelectric power development and water diversion for irrigation from the Tuolumne River in California. The Tuolumne rises in Yosemite National Park and flows west to the Central Valley in California, one of the country's richest agricultural areas. The economic arguments for further development of the Tuolumne were compelling: more hydroelectric generation was needed in the growing urban areas and more water was needed to ensure agricultural expansion. Both of these development efforts would produce more jobs in the growing California economy.

Environmentalists countered with claims that the pristine canyons and majestic scenery of the Tuolumne gorge had a value that would be lost forever if another dam were built. Not only would recreation opportunities be eliminated but also a key area of wilderness would be drowned. The Tuolumne controversy raged for months before finally being resolved in favor of the environmentalists' position. The decision became a precedent for other proposed economic development in the United States. Environmental awareness is under way in many countries throughout the world.

Suggested Readings: Andrew Goudie, *The Earth Transformed: An Introduction to Human Impacts on the Environment*, Oxford, U.K.: Basil Blackwell, 1997; I. G. Simmons, *Changing the Face of the Earth: Culture, Environment, History*, 2nd ed., Oxford, U.K.: Basil Blackwell, 1996.

Environmental determinism. For two decades at the beginning of the twentieth century, the concept of environmental determinism was dominant in American geography, largely through the work of Ellsworth Huntington, a prominent geographer at Yale University. Environmental determinism proclaims that climate and terrain are the dominant forces in determining cultural directions. For example, people in the temperate climates of Europe and North America would have clear, quick minds, an abundance of creativity, and high levels of industry because of the bracing winds and seasonality of the mid-latitudes. On the other hand, individuals in the hot, humid, and seasonally unchanging weather of the tropics would be lethargic and lacking in energy.

Environmental determinism had important conceptual precedents. Prominent geographers such as **Friedrich Ratzel, Halford J. Mackinder,** and **William Morris Davis,** among others, had written convincingly about the role of the physical environment and its influences on human groups. Ratzel, who was German, wrote about the effects of different physical features on the course of human history in the first volume of his work *Anthropogeographie* (1882). Although his second volume in the series, published a few years later, spoke more directly about culture groups, many prominent geographers continued to hold with his pronouncements on the power of the physical environment.

Mackinder, Britain's dominant geographical leader at the end of the nineteenth century, also spoke of the influence of the physical environment on humans. Mackinder, in 1877, was seeking to find a solid role for geography in the expanding universities. He contended that no other discipline dealt with the interface of the natural world and human culture and that geography must take up that challenge. Mackinder further stated that the function of geography was to show how physical causes directed human activity.

In the United States, Davis, in the late 1800s, contended that the core of geography was the relationship between the physical environment and human behavior. Reflective of the thinking at that time, Davis concluded that the physical world controlled human behavior.

Environmental determinism is a concept that eventually was judged to be too rigid. Geographers began to move away from the strict deterministic tenet in this concept. Certainly the environment influences human activity and will have an impact on behavior, but to contend that environmental factors determined human behavior was seen to be too pointed. Environmental determinism gradually gave way to the more flexible and logical concept of **possibilism** in the 1920s.

Suggested Readings: R. J. Johnston et al., *The Dictionary of Human Geography*, 2nd ed., Oxford, U.K.: Basil Blackwell, 1993; David N. Livingston, *The Geographical Tradition*, Cambridge, Mass.: Blackwell, 1994.

Environmental perception. Perceptions of the environment held by individuals and culture groups condition attitudes and influence decisions about those places. How people perceive environments and the images they hold are shaped by the level of knowledge about the place, their experiences, beliefs, value systems, and attitudes. We all view and perceive places through our individual cultural prisms.

A perceptionist contends that people cannot see their physical setting objectively. This view may be traced back to the work of Immanuel Kant, the famous eighteenth-century German philosopher, who wrote that our knowledge of the world is always gained through our perceptions and that all we can really know are the images the mind creates.

Geographers have used the concepts embedded in environmental perception to study human attitudes toward particular attitudes and behaviors. For instance, a significant number of works have been completed that consider perceptions of **natural hazards.** Why do groups choose to live in known hazardous regions? Why would people live in areas that are prone to the destruction caused by floods, hurricanes, tornadoes, volcanic eruptions, earthquakes, and other natural phenomena? Some people believe that religious belief will spare them from harm. Others hold governmental agencies responsible for alerting them to coming hazards. In Western societies it is commonly held that technology will ensure that the hazard will not be harmful.

Environmental perception also comes into play when people migrate. In the United States it is not accidental that **migration** from the northern regions has been predominantly to warm, sunny states such as California, Arizona, and Florida. Migrations can invoke other perceptual bases as well. For example, early residents of the Appalachian Mountains, choosing to migrate as population numbers increased, chose the Ozark and Ouachita Mountains of Missouri, Arkansas, and Oklahoma, which they perceived to be similar to the Appalachians. Some later migrated to the Texas Hill Country.

Suggested Readings: David Lowenthal and Marlyn J. Bowden, *Geographies of the Mind*, New York: Oxford University Press, 1976; Risa Palm, *Natural Hazards*, Baltimore: Johns Hopkins University Press, 1990.

Eratosthenes (272–192 B.C.). Eratosthenes, an important Greek astronomer and geographer, is widely considered the father of **geography** because he was the first to use the term. Literally translated, the word means earth (*geo*) writing (*graphy*); hence, writing about the earth in all its myriad details. Eratosthenes was broadly educated in mathematics, philosophy, philology, and rhetoric. He became chief librarian at the Egyptian Museum in Alexandria in 234 B.C., a position of great prestige.

Eratosthenes is noted for his calculations of the circumference of the earth. His approach to this accomplishment was quite novel at the time. It was common knowledge that at the time of the summer solstice, the sun's reflection could be seen at the bottom of a deep well on an island in the Nile River near Syene (present-day Aswan). The sun at that time would be directly overhead, and this established one part of Eratosthenes' solution. His second observation, made at the same time, noted the length of a shadow from a tower at the Alexandria Museum, directly north of the well. Both the well and the tower were vertical and therefore pointed to the center of the earth. Using the length of the shadow cast from the tower, Eratosthenes was able to measure its angular displacement and, knowing that the distance from the well to the tower was 500 miles, he calculated the circumference of the earth to be 25,000 miles. His calculation proved to be very accurate; the circumference of the earth was later determined with precision instruments to be 24,860 miles.

It is noteworthy that fifteenth-century Italian explorer Christopher Columbus commenced his travels west across the Atlantic Ocean believing the circumference of the earth to be 18,000 miles. He accepted the long-held belief that the circumference measurement made by another Greek scholar, Posidonius, and accepted by the second-century Egyptian mathematician and geographer **Ptolemy,** to be accurate. It was for this reason that Columbus believed he had reached Asia when he landed in the Western Hemisphere.

Eratosthenes also wrote a book about the known world of his time, and he made a world map that included the closely spaced land areas of Europa (what is now Europe) and Libya (northern Africa), surrounded by the waters of Oceanus (a postulated body of water surrounding the known land masses of Europe, Libya, and India).

Suggested Readings: Geoffrey J. Martin and Preston E. James, *All Possible Worlds: A History of Geographical Ideas*, 3rd ed., New York: John Wiley & Sons, 1993; George Sarton, *A History of Science: Ancient Science through the Golden Age of Greece*, Cambridge, Mass.: Harvard University Press, 1964.

Ethnicity. Culture groups are unique in the specific set of attributes that identify them. Each group has its own belief systems and behaviors that distinguish it from other groups. *Ethnicity* is a term that refers to these cultural differences. The word derives from Greek origins and is simply translated as "people" or "nationality."

Ethnicity is expressed spatially. Every culture group has an area that serves as the group's base territory. Because of the spatial expression of ethnicity, the subdiscipline of ethnic geography has developed over time to study these ethnic groupings. Examples of ethnic territory are plentiful (e.g., Japan's four-island complex is its base territory). But humans are mobile, and members of an ethnic group migrate to other regions for a variety of reasons. For instance, a number of Vietnamese and Hmong communities developed outside their country after the Vietnam War ended. Such communities may be classified as exclaves of their country of origin and enclaves within the country of current residence.

In the United States, people of Hispanic origin account for about 12 percent of the total population. In the state of New Mexico, however, Hispanics account for 40 percent of the population. Some counties in New Mexico have upward of 80 percent Hispanic residents. This example points out that ethnic groups tend to stay together in a region to retain their distinctive character.

African Americans still represent a large percentage of the population in the Southern states. This is true despite their significant migration out of the South, especially after World War II. In recent years, as the social setting in the South has become more sympathetic to African Americans, more are migrating to the South. The specter of segregation forced on African Americans in the past has abated. Yet, African Americans and other ethnic groups, in many cases, prefer to stay together in their own spatial settings. The notion of the **melting pot** in the United States has not been realized to the extent originally expected.

Tensions may arise when ethnic groups find themselves living in proximity to one another. The violent uprisings and conflict that scarred the former Yugoslavia are a case in point. The plight of the Kurdish ethnic group in southwestern Asia is particularly distressing. The Kurds are living in parts of several countries and do not have their own sovereign state. As such, they are essentially at the whim of the government ruling those countries and are powerless, with no true homeland of their own.

Suggested Readings: James P. Allen and Eugene Turner, *We the People: An Atlas of America's Ethnic Diversity*, New York: Macmillan, 1988; "Ethnicity and Geography," *GeoJournal*, vol. 30, special issue (1993).

European Union. The European Union (EU), a 15-country supranational organization formed in 1992, represents the culmination of attempts over many years to form an economic union of European states. The basis of the integration is economic solidarity. As the process of uniting unfolded over the years after the 1950s, it became clear that the EU, once formed, would wield considerable political power as well.

The EU is the most powerful supranational organization in the world. Composed of Austria, Belgium, Denmark, Finland, France, Germany, Greece, Ireland, Italy, Luxembourg, The Netherlands, Portugal, Spain, Sweden, and the United Kingdom, the EU gradually emerged in its final configuration from a number of previous organizations. Among these preliminary attempts at integration were the European Economic Community, or Common Market, in 1958, and the European Community, in 1986.

Frustrated by the lack of progress in achieving the hoped-for economic integration, the European leaders passed the Single Europe Act (SEA) in 1986. The purpose of this document was to put in place the mechanisms necessary to eliminate barriers to a unified economic system by the early 1990s. Progress was made in this regard, and the long-anticipated interlocking of the economies of the 15 EU members was achieved in 1992.

The need for a supranational organization linking the European countries was seen as crucial. Twice during the twentieth century, European countries had declared war on one another. The results of both these wars were great devastation and the ruination of the overall economic structure of Europe. There was unanimous agreement among the European policy makers that a union of states would work to avoid a repeat of the kind of conflict seen in the past century.

One of the greatest achievements of the EU has been the creation of a greatly expanded and more efficient internal market. Most borders in the EU are completely open, and there are no tariffs existing between member countries. In addition, economic growth within the member countries has expanded significantly. Economic growth within the EU has also benefited from increased foreign investment.

The advances made in the EU economic structure have not come without some sacrifices. Initially there was a great deal of reluctance on the part of member countries to give up their national currency in favor of the Euro. Europe without its pounds, francs, marks, and lire seemed unimaginable. A nation's currency is, after all, an important attribute of its culture. It appears, however, that this hurdle is successfully passed.

One additional concession required of all member states was the relinquishing of some degree of political control in favor of the EU's governing organization. However, it seemed that a loss of power would be more than compensated by the advantages of membership in the EU.

Ten countries have been invited to join the EU on May 1, 2004: Cyprus (the Greek region), the Czech Republic, Estonia, Latvia, Lithuania, Hungary, Malta, Poland, Slovakia, and Slovenia. Talks are planned with Turkey in 2005.

Suggested Readings: A. H. Dawson, *The Geography of European Integration: A Common European Home?*, New York: John Wiley & Sons, 1993; David Hooson, *Geography and National Identity*, Oxford, U.K.: Basil Blackwell, 1994.

Exclave. *See* **Enclave and exclave.**

Exclusive economic zone. Countries with a coastline on an ocean may claim exclusive use of the water and sea bottom for economic exploitation. This area is called an exclusive economic zone (EEZ). At the turn of the twentieth century, coastal states in the United States began to claim control of the ocean waters within three miles of their land. Their concern was to protect coastal industries and to guarantee their neutrality in times of conflict between adversaries in the region. Following World War I, the League of Nations began to discuss the question of the rights of coastal states to extend their sovereignty seaward from their seacoasts. The League took no formal position at that time.

Interest in extending control of the sea adjacent to the coastline of the United States peaked in 1945 with the Truman Proclamation. As a result of this decree, the U.S. government laid claim to all resources on and above the continental shelf extending from its coastlines. The initial incentive for this claim was the desire to embark on offshore oil exploration. Other countries followed the United States' lead.

In time, nearly all the world's countries having coastlines were claiming sovereignty over adjacent ocean waters. A series of disputes and unjustified claims ensued, and the United Nations (UN) Conference on the Law of the Sea convened to address the complex issue. In 1982, draft legislation was passed in the form of the **UN Convention on the Law of the Sea** (UNCLOS), which proclaimed in part, that coastal states could claim an exclusive economic zone extending up to 200 nautical miles from shore. The country claiming this region had rights to explore, exploit, conserve, and manage the natural resources within the waters and in the seabed. There was an additional provision that extended the claim to 350 miles from the coast if the continental shelf extended that far. Freedom of the high seas was guaranteed for seafarers traveling within the EEZ as long as they did not attempt to acquire resources protected by the proclamation. In 1994, UNCLOS became international law.

Suggested Readings: Gerald H. Blake, *Maritime Boundaries,* New York: Routledge, 1994; M. I. Glassner, *Neptune's Domain: A Political Geography of the Sea,* Boston: Unwin Hyman, 1990.

Expansion diffusion. An idea, innovation, or disease may spread from a center and impact others as it expands outward. Diffusion of this kind is called expansion diffusion. There are three recognized forms of expansion diffusion: hierarchical, contagious, and stimulus.

Hierarchical diffusion occurs when an idea, innovation, or substance is spread from one node or individual to another. If the hierarchy is composed of urban centers, the item may travel up or down the urban hierarchy. Fashions are diffused in this manner and will travel from high-order centers (Paris, New York, and Los Angeles, for instance) to lower-order urban places, and finally to rural areas. The spread of McDonald's restaurants throughout the world occurred through hierarchical diffusion.

Diseases and influenzas have been traced to hierarchical diffusion. In the nineteenth century, cholera moved along the urban hierarchy from origins on the East Coast to lower-order centers in the Midwest. The so-called Asian flu outbreaks common every year in the United States enter through high-order centers and are then diffused throughout the urban hierarchy.

Once established in an urban center, a disease may spread in an ever increasing wavelike pattern outward from the origin. This identifies the second form of expansion diffusion, called contagious diffusion. The concept of **distance decay** applies in contagious diffusion: the shorter the distance the trait travels, the greater its likelihood of finding accepters.

Stimulus diffusion is another process that accommodates the spread of a trait. In stimulus diffusion, a particular idea or innovation may well be rejected, but the underlying idea may be accepted. The herding, rather than hunting, of reindeer in Siberia came about through observation of cattle herding in areas along the Trans-Siberian Railroad. The indigenous Siberians did not want to work with cattle but took the herding idea and applied it to reindeer.

Suggested Readings: Richard Morrill et al., *Spatial Diffusion*, vol. 10, Scientific Geography Series, Newbury Park, Calif.: Sage, 1988; Richard K. Ormrod, "Adaptation and Cultural Diffusion," *Journal of Geography*, vol. 91 (1992).

Extensive agriculture. In **von Thunen's land use model,** developed in the early 1800s by the German economist Johann Heinrich von Thunen, the concentric zone farthest from the market center—and consequently the largest area—is an example of the use of land for extensive agriculture. The area itself is extensive compared to others, and the land is the least costly.

One agricultural product grown extensively is wheat. This grain needs more space to grow; therefore, yields per unit area are low compared to those with corn or rice, which are examples of **intensive agriculture.** Wheat farming involves large costs for harvesting machinery, but since the areas are so extensive, the cost per unit area is relatively low. Although wheat farming is considered to be more machine intensive, its human labor costs are lower. Farms in the wheat belt of the United States and Canada may reach 500 hectares in size.

Another extensive land use is livestock ranching. Free-range grazing of cattle is common in the western United States and some areas of Canada and Mexico. Although these operations are usually found a considerable distance from their markets, they are, nonetheless, accessible to them by surface transportation (i.e., roads, railroads, etc.).

Nomadic herding is a common practice throughout most of the developing world. Like ranching in North America, nomadic herding is an extensive land use practice. The controlled movement of animals to find naturally occurring food sources characterizes nomadic herding. Nomadic herding is practiced extensively in mid-latitude Asian countries, throughout Africa south of the Sahara Desert, and in countries with coastlines on the Arctic Ocean.

Shifting cultivation is another form of extensive agriculture found in the low-latitude regions of the developing world. In this practice, a field is cleared and crops are planted and harvested for a multiyear period. When the soil begins to lose its fertility due to continued use without time for regeneration, the field is abandoned and another area is opened for farming. This process will continue (1) as long as there are new fields to bring into production, or (2) the first field abandoned has regained soil fertility and may again become part of the cycle of land use.

Suggested Readings: Chris Dixon, *Rural Development in the Third World*, New York: Routledge, 1990; William J. Peters and Leon F. Neuerschwander, *Slash and Burn: Farming in the Third World Forests*, Moscow, Idaho: University of Idaho Press, 1988.

F

Fall line. The topography of the eastern United States includes a flat coastal plain that meets a hilly region of hard, crystalline rock called the Piedmont. West of the Piedmont is the ancient and weathered Appalachian Mountains. The interface of the Piedmont and the coastal plain is an important juncture, both physically and historically. A series of waterfalls are found at the juncture of the Piedmont and coastal plain. These points on the river comprise the fall line.

During colonial times, settlement from New York southward was limited primarily to sites on the coastal plain. Although dozens of navigable rivers flowed out of the Piedmont and across the coastal plain, they were navigable only to the interface with the Piedmont. When a river left the Piedmont, it came through rapids and over rock waterfalls before settling on the smooth surface of the plain.

The falls marked the head of navigation on the rivers and disallowed boat traffic beyond that point, prohibiting access to the inland. But they also provided a source of power. In time, a series of settlements began to develop along this line of falls, or fall line, as it came to be known.

Several important functions were established in fall line settlements. Since the falls stopped boat traffic upstream, these sites became **break-of-bulk points**. Any cargo slated for shipment to places upstream beyond the falls had to be unloaded and packed on land vehicles for the next leg of the journey. Of great importance was the power afforded by the waterfalls. Lumber milling and the grinding of grain were two important industries that developed because of waterpower at these settlements. Finally, the settlements themselves began to add all the necessary functions to support these growing activities.

Hotels, repair facilities, general stores, and homes for permanent residents were built.

Many of today's prominent cities had their start as fall line settlements. Among them are Trenton, New Jersey; Philadelphia, Pennsylvania; Wilmington, Delaware; Baltimore, Maryland; Washington, D.C.; and Richmond, Virginia.

Suggested Readings: John Frazer Hart, *The Look of the Land*, Englewood Cliffs, N.J.: Prentice Hall, 1975; Robert D. Mitchell and Paul A. Groves, *North America: The Historical Geography of a Changing Continent*, Savage, Md.: Rowman & Littlefield, 1987.

Feedlot. During the first half of the twentieth century, livestock were fattened and readied for slaughter at a relatively small number of stockyards. Two of the largest were in Chicago, Illinois, and Kansas City, Missouri. In the 1950s, however, commercial livestock operators began to specialize in the slaughter-preparation process. One special operation involved the fattening of livestock at highly mechanized feedlots located close to large metropolitan centers.

Since the 1950s there has been a dramatic increase in the number of feedlots in the Great Plains and western states. A concentration of feedlots exists in a corridor from South Dakota to Texas. Some of the feedlots in West Texas handle as many as one million cattle. Feedlots are also found in significant numbers in Arizona, Utah, Idaho, and Washington.

Dairy farmers also use the feedlot system. Dairy feedlots are also located on the suburban fringe of large cities, allowing quick access to market for milk and other dairy products.

The feedlot system has been characterized as a form of factory farming because it is a large-scale operation, highly mechanized, and technologically advanced. Dairy feedlots, for instance, can handle many more cows than even the largest dairy farm. Feedlots represent another example of **agribusiness** in its most highly developed form.

Suggested Readings: John Fraser Hart, *The Rural Landscape*, Baltimore: Johns Hopkins University Press, 1998; Iain Wallace, "Towards a Geography of Agribusiness," *Progress in Human Geography*, vol. 9 (1985).

Folk and popular culture. Examples of particular cultural attributes—such as music, foods, or dress styles—may be distinguished as being "folk" or "popular." Although the attribute itself may be found in both folk and popular culture, there are significant differences in the way they originate and diffuse.

Folk culture is usually limited to a small area and number of practitioners. The Amish tradition, for instance, dictates the use of horse and carriage for transporting children to school. This form of transportation, representative of folk culture, is in stark contrast to the widespread and ubiquitous yellow school buses used since the 1950s in the United States to transport students. The advent of the school bus represents attributes of popular culture: the transportation form is widespread, and it diffused quickly from its points of origin.

Folk culture is also represented by building and fence types that remain at or near their centers of origin. The yurt house in China, the pueblo building style in the southwestern United States, Quebec cottages, and post-and-rail fencing all exemplify folk culture.

Folk music originated at a number of localized points primarily in the rural areas of the South and the Appalachian Mountains. Their spread to other regions was limited in distance and was normally the result of **relocation diffusion,** the spread of a characteristic through migration.

Aspects of popular culture, on the other hand, if accepted by others, will diffuse rapidly and may expand globally in a short time. The appearance of McDonald's restaurants in virtually every major city worldwide is a classic example of hierarchical diffusion (see **Expansion diffusion**). The spread of pizza parlors in North America and then to other countries is another example of a wide diffusion of popular culture.

Japan has accepted a number of attributes of U.S. popular culture. Among these are baseball and golf, two popular sports introduced into Japan during the U.S. military occupation following World War II. Soccer represents another example of popular culture that has achieved worldwide acceptance—it has become the most popular sport on the globe.

Any number of additional examples of popular culture can be given. Among these are blue jeans, a clothing style that spread worldwide from origins in the United States; the popularity and global acceptance of musicians such as Elvis Presley, the Beatles, and the Rolling Stones; and Western dress styles. It is becoming more common in Asian and African countries for Western business suits to replace traditional clothing styles. Replacement of traditional attributes of culture by the acceptance of substitutes through widespread diffusion has been seen as a threat to the existence of local folk cultures. The decline in popularity of locally produced soft drinks in China following the introduction of Coca-Cola and Pepsi Cola is a case in point.

Suggested Readings: George O. Carney, *The Sounds of People and Places: Readings in the Geography of American Folk and Popular Music*, 3rd ed., Lanham, Md.: Rowman & Littlefield, 1994; Paul Oliver, *The House across the World*, Austin: University of Texas Press, 1987.

Footloose industry. A manufacturing activity that is free to locate where it wants to and whose transportation costs are a minor element in total product cost is said to be footloose in its choice of a site to establish its place of business. In like manner, a footloose industry is not required to locate near its raw material source or a power site.

Examples of footloose industries in **economic geography** include electronics manufacture, manufacturing operations that assemble component parts, high-technology equipment, manufacture requiring high levels of information inputs and brainpower, and some forms of food processing.

The manufacture of electronic equipment, for instance, involves the production of highly valuable items that are usually lightweight. As such, transport costs do not become a factor in location, either for the procurement of raw materials or for shipment to market centers. Electronic equipment manufacture will not be tied to a power site, because electricity can be accessed virtually anywhere in the developed world.

Despite the locational advantages enjoyed by footloose industries, they will, nonetheless, choose to locate within areas of the greatest potential profit. Thus, a location within a few miles of its market will be favored over one that is 50 or 100 miles away.

Some industries are inseparable from their markets, such as bakeries, newspaper publishing firms, and producers of dairy products. These will be found in or near towns and cities because their sole purpose is to provide their products with near immediacy. These operations are called ubiquitous industries, a close relative of the footloose form.

Suggested Readings: Keith Chapman and David Walker, *Industrial Location*, 2nd ed., Cambridge, Mass.: Basil Blackwell, 1991; James O. Wheeler et al., *Economic Geography*, 3rd ed., New York: John Wiley & Sons, 1998.

Fordist. The pioneering American automobile manufacturer Henry Ford (1863–1947) was instrumental in revolutionizing the manner in which his vehicles were produced. Beginning in the post–World War I years, Ford applied the assembly line process to the manufacture of automobiles and succeeded in producing vehicles that were priced within the budget of most American families and could easily be repaired because of interchangeable parts. Ford's effort and ingenuity resulted in the mass production of automobiles for a growing mass market. Ford's ideas on manufacturing were so influential throughout the North American industrial system that the term *Fordist* was used to identify the process.

Ford's assembly line process was soon applied throughout the manufacturing sector. Assembly line operations sprung up throughout the great North American manufacturing belt, producing washing machines, refrigerators, and a myriad of consumer goods. Ford's manufacturing system ended the days of small-scale, isolated, and relatively inefficient operations. In their place was the single large manufacturing center in which each worker on the assembly line had one or two tasks to perform on the automobile or refrigerator moving along the line. Corporate ownership of large plants allowed for greater economies of scale, and the costs per unit produced were greatly lowered.

The assembly line operation was the first of many innovations that occurred in the period from 1920 to the 1970s. Others included the building of an efficient highway system to augment the limited reach of fixed railroad lines. The highway system was greatly enhanced beginning in the mid-1950s with the initiation of the interstate, limited-access roads.

Commerce and industry advanced as well with the growth of a fully integrated airline system designed for the fast delivery of lightweight industrial items, mail, and passengers. Finally, communication improvements were realized with the wide-scale incorporation of radio (1920s) and television (1950s).

Without the Fordist system, the economic progress enjoyed throughout the century could not have occurred as quickly.

Suggested Readings: David R. Meyer, "Emergence of the American Manufacturing Belt: An Interpretation," *Journal of Historical Geography*, vol. 9 (1983); James M. Rubinstein, *The Changing U.S. Auto Industry*, New York: Routledge, 1992.

Formal (uniform) region. *See* **Region.**

Forward thrust capital city. On occasion a state government will relocate its capital city. The reasons for such a move vary, from concern for national security, to a desire to alert the state of government intentions to expand settlement beyond a frontier, or to a need to stimulate economic development. A city of this type is called a forward thrust capital city.

Brasilia, an interior city, was named capital of Brazil following the transfer of state government from Rio de Janeiro in 1960. Brasilia is an ultramodern city literally carved out of the tropical rain forest. Since the time of Portuguese settlement during the first era of **colonialism,** from about 1500 to 1800, coastal locations have predominated. The Brazilian government moved the capital to Brasilia to signal its intention to develop its remote western regions.

Brazilian governmental officials believed that Brasilia would attract migrants from Rio de Janeiro, São Paulo, and other coastal centers. This migration was not realized to the degree expected. In fact, something of a reverse move took place. Residents of small settlements in the interior moved to Brasilia and then continued to migrate to the very coastal cities the government hoped would be the source of migrants to Brasilia and the interior.

Nigeria's new capital of Abuja, so named in 1991, is located very near the center of the country. In this case, the government wanted to develop the northern region of the country, which was essentially ignored during the colonial era. There is also the desire to locate the seat of government equidistant from the Muslim north and the Christian south in the hope of avoiding conflicts in the future. Finally, the old capital of Lagos, a true **primate city** and premier administrative point during the colonial era, is extremely crowded. Moving the capital and its associated government functions and workers, it is hoped, will alleviate some of the pressures within this burgeoning urban center.

Pakistan's transfer of its capital from Karachi to Islamabad in the 1960s was an attempt to focus government attention on the historical center of the country. Pakistan's **culture hearth** is located in the northern part of the country. There is another reason for this move: the governmental center would be closer to Kashmir, a province whose ownership is disputed with neighboring India. By locating closer to Kashmir, any threats emanating from that region could be noted and a response initiated.

Suggested Readings: John Agnew, *Political Geography: A Reader*, New York: John Wiley & Sons, 1996; Peter M. Slowe, *Geography and Political Power: The Geography of Nations and States*, London: Routledge, 1990.

Friction of distance. *See* **Distance decay.**

Frontier. A frontier is a zone or area separating states. Frontiers are demarcated areas, whereas boundaries are lines. The frontier area is usually sparsely populated, and its presence marks the limit of state administration and control.

With the discovery and occupation of nearly all of the world's land areas, frontiers have been replaced by boundaries. A few frontiers still remain, however. Antarctica contains a number of frontier zones separating states that have administrative responsibilities. Saudi Arabia has frontier with Qatar, Oman, Yemen, and the United Arab Emirates. Within these areas, nomadic herding activities operate freely. The Saudis have a small frontier zone along part of their border with Iraq. Military personnel have manned this so-called neutral zone on both sides, and in 1990 this became an unofficial boundary.

The boundary between Russia and China has all of the attributes of a frontier, even though the line separating the two countries is unambiguously clear. Nonetheless, the area is sparsely populated, remote from the major concentrations of population and economic activity, and has been the site of border disputes and military skirmishes for years. In this sense, it is a frontierlike area.

The frontier played a large role in the westward expansion of the United States. The first true frontier in the United States lay along the **fall line,** the series of waterfalls that stopped navigation on rivers flowing from the Piedmont onto the coastal plain. As settlement moved west, the frontier moved with it, and regions previously not under governmental control became occupied territories.

The American historian Frederick Jackson Turner (1861–1932) eloquently stated the theme of the frontier and what it means in American history. The real meaning of much of American history, Turner contended, could be gained only through understanding the frontier experience. The westward movement molded a truly American character and developed a new, non-European settler, according to Turner.

Turner's frontier thesis had a profound influence on historical thinking for generations and is still revered as a seminal work on the American experience. The eminent nineteenth-century German geographer **Friedrich Ratzel** considered Turner's thesis to be an important theory supporting his own notions comparing the state to an organism that must grow and change. **Carl Sauer,** one of the most prominent twentieth-century American geographers, however, took issue with Turner's thesis, considering it simplistic and inaccurate.

Suggested Readings: David Hooson, *Geography and National Identity,* Oxford, U.K.: Basil Blackwell, 1994; J. R. V. Prescott, *Political Frontiers and Boundaries,* Winchester, Mass.: Allen & Unwin, 1990.

G

Gender. A considerable amount of research in recent years has centered on the spatial aspects of gender differences. The major outcome of this research in **cultural geography** is the realization that women in every society are not treated as positively as men. A great measure of gender inequality may be found in all culture groups.

One demographic fact does favor women: worldwide, and to varying degrees, women live longer. Women's longevity has been at least partially explained by their comparative restraint from physically harmful practices, such as smoking and abuse of alcohol and drugs. Some experts have suggested that women's longevity may also be traced to an innate ability to better handle stress. This contention, if true, may dissipate as more women—especially in developed countries—gain full-time employment while continuing to be the primary homemaker.

There are a number of ways in which women are treated inequitably. It is universally true that wage rates for women are, on average, significantly lower than for men. This is true even though the job has the same degree of difficulty and responsibility. Also, there are far fewer women in the highest levels of business and industry. Women climbing the corporate ladder will eventually hit what has been called a "glass ceiling" that bars them from rising higher in the corporate hierarchy.

It is also true in the United States that women are not present in national government to the same degree as men, even though the country's population is approximately equal in the number of males and females.

Inequities between men and women are found in the developed countries, but they are far more prevalent in the developing world. Illiteracy rates are much higher among women in developing countries. Young girls may trace this fact to the lower number of school years attended. The traditional view of the role of girls and women is that they should work in the home.

It has also been shown that women and children fare much worse in refugee camps. Death and disease rates are much higher than for men living under the same conditions.

In Saudi Arabia, many restrictions are placed on women. For instance, women's clothing must adhere to government-dictated standards, and women are not allowed to drive automobiles. Under the Taliban regime in Afghanistan, women suffered greatly. They were not allowed to work outside the home or obtain formal education, and they were ordered to wear a *burkha,* a garment that completely covered them from head to foot. A mesh fabric partially covering the face allowed them to see the outside.

Most cultures in the developing world favor the birth of male children. As such, it is not uncommon for female fetuses to be aborted in the hope that a subsequent pregnancy will bring a boy. In China, the one-child family became national policy in 1979. Negative incentives dissuaded most Chinese couples from having more than one child. If a female baby was born, it was often put to death because if the couple were to have only one child, they preferred it to be a boy. Widespread infanticide began in the early 1980s and continued into the 1990s but then declined as the one-child policy was not prosecuted as strongly. Female infanticide is a stunning example of the favoritism afforded the male gender.

Suggested Readings: Susan Hanson and Geraldine Pratt, *Gender, Work, and Space*, New York: Routledge, 1995; Daphne Spain, *Gendered Spaces*, Chapel Hill: University of North Carolina Press, 1992.

General Agreement on Tariffs and Trade. Twenty-three countries passed the General Agreement on Tariffs and Trade (GATT) in 1948. GATT was an attempt to stabilize and organize a reasonable and workable tariff system covering international trade. Under GATT, tariffs were initially reduced on more than 40,000 items regularly traded.

The rules under which GATT operated brought a measure of common sense into the world-trading arena. The major rules imparted by GATT included the following:

1. If one state reduced tariffs against another, then the second was required to lower its tariffs.

2. Preferential trade arrangements that favored one state more than others could not be established. This rule created the "most favored nation" policy, which stated that every country must be treated with equal fairness.

3. Existing nontariff barriers were to be replaced with tariffs. Visible tariffs could be open to inspection and would be easier to reduce if necessary.

4. Developing countries received favorable trade treatment under special provisions in GATT.

GATT members met on a regular basis to monitor trade and tariff activities and to settle any disputes that arose.

GATT worked well through the 1970s as world trade increased and tariffs were reduced. However, in the 1980s GATT became less effective. GATT was set up primarily to regulate tariffs on manufactured goods. It was not set up to work with trade in agricultural products nor could its mechanisms handle negotiations involving international trading in the service sector. Both of these areas of the global economy were increasing in importance as manufacturing was stabilizing, or declining in some regions.

GATT members continued to meet through the 1980s to work on a vastly revised document that would bring it effectively into the changed global economy. By this time, GATT membership included nearly all of the trading nations in the world. In December 1994, a new GATT document was signed that further reduced tariffs and changed a number of rules dealing with world trade. The new GATT document also created the World Trade Organization (WTO), which was empowered to enforce the new trade regulations. WTO also has the power to assess penalties against countries that violate the new rules on trade.

Suggested Readings: John H. Dunning, "What's Wrong—and Right—with Trade Theory?" *International Trade Journal* (summer 1995); Michael E. Porter, *The Competitive Advantage of Nations*, New York: Free Press, 1990.

Gentrification. Beginning in the 1970s, run-down dwellings in low-income neighborhoods in U.S. inner cities became targets for restoration and upgrading, called gentrification. The refurbished apartments and single-family houses were made available primarily to middle-class families and individuals who wanted to live closer to jobs in the central cities. In many ways the gentrification movement marked the first significant reversal of the move to the outlying areas of **suburbia.** Ironically, the same concept of **accessibility** that explained the suburban phenomenon, in this case improved **transportation systems,** is applied to gentrification: proximity to jobs, primarily in the expanding service sector in the city centers.

Upgrading deteriorating but structurally sound buildings in the inner city has some positive sides. First is the added attractiveness of the newly refurbished neighborhood. Second is the increase in the city's tax base as higher-income residents occupy improved housing. Third is the additional development of restaurants, urban mini-malls, and other services, which add to the economic base of the inner city.

There are negative outcomes, as well, from gentrification. Removing low-rent housing displaces people who cannot afford to purchase a home or pay the higher rent associated with an upgraded apartment complex. Gentrification also breaks the filtering process in which older, obsolete housing, when vacated, is made available (filtered down) to people of lesser means. When this cycle is broken, those who would have found a residence have fewer choices.

Added to the problem of housing for low-income people was the precipitous decline in the 1980s in federal money for building subsidized housing. More than $30 billion was allotted for these projects in 1980; by the early 1990s the amount available declined to less than $9 billion. The decline in new subsidized housing has led, in part, to a great increase in the number of homeless people in the United States. In 2000, the homeless population was estimated to be over 3.5 million.

Some researchers have attributed the homeless problem to gentrification. This is true to a limited extent, but gentrification was never a major factor in urban migration. In fact, the movement was limited to select neighborhoods close to the central city that had an inventory of run-down but structurally sound buildings. Further, gentrification movements were most evident in the eastern seaboard cities of **Megalopolis,** and they have not been as extensive in other regions.

Suggested Readings: Daniel J. Hammel and Elvin K. Wyly, "A Model for Identifying Gentrified Areas with Census Data," *Urban Geography*, vol. 17 (1996); Paul L. Knox, *The Restless Urban Landscape*, Englewood Cliffs, N.J.: Prentice Hall, 1993.

Geographic information systems. One of the most powerful new methodologies in geography developed in the past 25 years is geographic information systems (GIS). GIS is a comprehensive, complex, and integrated set of computer programs that handles all aspects of data acquisition, management, and display. The computer has revolutionized mapmaking and data storage; GIS has refined this powerful electronic medium and elevated it to a higher scientific plane. In fact, GIS is sometimes referred to as "geographic information science."

A GIS will handle the access of spatial data—either digitally acquired or optically scanned—its storage, organization, quantification and statistical analysis, and display of resulting maps and graphics. None of these individual processes are new to the field of computer **cartography.** Before the development of GIS, however, each represented a single step in the process. With GIS, all of the operations are contained in a single package.

GIS uses a process called information layering, the storage of spatial information in separate packages that can be displayed on a computer graphics screen either individually or in layers.

Suppose a firm wants to select the ideal location for a new shopping mall on the fringes of a metropolitan area. The mall will attract thousands of people on a daily basis, so **accessibility** by private automobile and public transportation is essential. The new mall must be located in an area not already containing a comparable retail operation. The new location must have sufficient electrical power, gas lines, sewer connections, and water supply to support the daily operation of the mall. Data on all of these requirements and many more can be accessed, stored, analyzed, and graphically displayed using a GIS.

Some of the layers in a GIS used to locate the shopping mall might display base mapping (roads, developed areas, physical contour lines, existing malls, and other basic spatial information), zoned areas, current land ownership, and existing utilities (gas, electric, water, and sewers). The GIS can then be used to display and print a series of maps that will be useful in choosing the best location for the new mall.

GIS is widely used as a powerful spatial analysis tool in geography and other disciplines, and just as extensively in business, industry, and government.

Suggested Readings: Mark Monmonier, "Raster Data for the Layman: Just What Is GIS?" *Mercator's World,* vol. 1 (1996); GEOSOURCE, at www.geo.ed.ac.uk, has a listing of GIS-related sites maintained by the University of Edinburgh.

Geography. The word *geography* derives from the Greek words *ge* (earth) and *graphein* (to write). Literally translated, geography means "writing about the earth." **Eratosthenes,** a prominent Greek scholar, was the first to use the word *geography,* in the third century B.C. However, studies that could be characterized as being geographic in nature had been documented for at least five millennia before Eratosthenes' day.

In the preface to his *Source Book in Geography* (1978), George Kish includes the following statement about geography:

> Geography is as old as man's first search for a bit of soil to dig for plantings, for a path that leads to water, for a trail to a place where hard rock for arrowheads may be found. Geography is as new as man's search for ways to relieve urban congestion, to establish well-marked international boundaries, to describe and analyze vegetation patterns in remote parts of the earth. (p. ix)

Geography and its practice have been around as long as humans have inhabited the earth.

Preston E. James and Geoffrey J. Martin include in their work *All Possible Worlds: A History of Geographical Ideas* (1993) a useful method for tracing the origins and continuation of geography through time. James and Martin suggest that five types of questions identify geographical analysis, and that these types can be found throughout human history. They include generic questions about the content of earth space. For example, what kinds of land and water features are located in particular areas? What are their inherent characteristics? How are they identified and named? Next are questions that help to explain how particular features on the earth's surface developed. For instance, the ancient Greek historian **Herodotus** speculated on the processes involved in the creation of the Nile River delta. In many cases, these early speculations proved to be false, but it was still important to ask process questions: what is the sequence of events, both physical and cultural, that explains a landscape?

James and Martin also suggest that theoretical questions of a geographical nature have been asked throughout time. Geographers, like other disciplinarians, attempt to derive concepts and theories to better understand their work.

Christaller's central place theory, developed by twentieth-century German economic geographer Walter Christaller, is an example.

James and Martin's next question concerns geographic methodologies developed over time. What techniques and instruments were derived that helped investigators in their work? In recent decades, the advent of the computer, with its capacity to store and manipulate data, has greatly advanced geographic analyses. Advances in satellite imagery and computer graphics have also revolutionized the fields of **cartography** and geography.

Finally, James and Martin identify remedial questions as being important in geographical studies over time. For example, Herodotus expressed concern over the loss of topsoil through erosion in ancient Greece, a concern that is applicable to modern times.

In 1964, William D. Pattison, an influential advocate of geographic education, presented his four traditions of geography in an article in the *Journal of Geography.* Pattison said that geography derived from an earth-science tradition wherein the research emphasis was on noting and studying the physical features comprising the earth's surface. Second, Pattison contended that geography had a human-environment tradition. There is abundant evidence of this tradition dating to the time of the notable geographers **Halford J. Mackinder, Friedrich Ratzel,** and **William Morris Davis,** all of whom worked to develop a base for geography in the newly configured universities of the late nineteenth and early twentieth centuries. Their aim was to codify geography as the discipline that studied the spatial aspects of the union of nature and culture (human–environment interactions).

Pattison's first tradition, earth science, sets the physical world stage for the second tradition, in which humans are introduced. Studies can then be launched to note the ways in which humans interact with their environment. Pattison takes the process ahead to a third tradition: area studies. Geographers refer to area studies as regions. The East Asian **region,** for instance, will be markedly different from that of North America, even though some environmental elements are similar. The differences are attributable to the varied human responses to their environment by each culture group. Finally, Pattison identified the spatial tradition, which, many geographers contend, is intrinsic to the previous three.

Geography is a bridging discipline. That is, it has its roots in all four of the major divisions of knowledge: the physical or natural sciences, the biological sciences, the social sciences, and the humanities. As such, geography has been categorized as an integrating and synthesizing discipline.

Consider Yi-Fu Tuan's pointed definition: geography is the study of the earth as the home of people. Within this brief statement is a working premise for understanding geography. Tuan, who developed **humanistic geography** in the early 1970s, includes references to the physical world and the human domain. The important aspect of their relationship is embodied in the word *home*. Geography, then, is the interplay of the physical world, or environment, and its human occupants. Geography is the physical world and the cultural world, considered as one. Any attempted separation of the discipline into physical geography and **human geography,** for instance, is for convenience only.

Suggested Readings: Peter R. Gould, *Becoming a Geographer (Space, Place, and Society)*, Syracuse, N.Y.: Syracuse University Press, 1999; National Research Council, *Rediscovering Geography: New Relevance for Science and Society*, Washington, D.C.: National Academy Press, 1997; Tim F. Wood, "Thinking in Geography," *Geography*, vol. 72 (1987).

Geopolitics. Geopolitics is a branch of **political geography** that deals with the strategic aspects of states. Included within the purview of geopolitics are spatial relationships that have implications for military defense, national security, the protection of national interests, and any other situation that may have an impact on the sovereignty of the state.

Geopolitics emerged in the early twentieth century in the context of European political alignments. One of its early exponents was **Halford J. Mackinder,** the prominent British geographer, in his "heartland" theory. Mackinder contended that the age of sea power was ending and that the large landmasses would exert the greatest degree of political control in the future. His theory, briefly stated, suggested that control of eastern Europe would mean control of the heartland (the immense interior of Eurasia), which, in turn, would lead to control of the world island (the entirety of Eurasia). Controlling the world island, according to Mackinder's theory, would lead to world domination.

Geopoliticians in Germany invoked the nineteenth-century German geographer **Friedrich Ratzel**'s organic state analogy to justify German territorial expansion into adjacent European countries.

Mackinder's basic theme later had a great influence not only on other geopoliticians but on state government as well. With the rise of the powerful Soviet Union following World War II, the United States developed a policy of containment to keep the Soviets within their Eurasian-landed area and not allow expansion to adjacent countries.

U.S. involvement in Vietnam, beginning immediately after the extrication of the French in 1954 and ending with U.S. withdrawal in 1975, proceeded on the containment premise. Associated with containment was the domino theory, the belief that if communism expanded into adjacent regions, the fall of one country would quickly lead to the fall of others, in a pattern like falling dominoes.

With the demise of the Soviet Union in 1991 and radical changes occurring worldwide, it is certain that new regional political alignments will call for new geopolitical strategies. For instance, membership in the **North Atlantic Treaty Organization** (NATO), one of the supranational organizations put into place to contain the Soviet Union and its satellite states, has been extended to some of the very states it once contained. Even Russia has, at times, been mentioned for potential membership in NATO. Justification for these changes came from the perception of threat to countries in the Northern Hemisphere from regional blocs forming in the developing world and in the Middle East.

Suggested Readings: Saul B. Cohen, "Global Geopolitical Change in the Post–Cold War Era," *Annals of the Association of American Geographers,* vol. 81 (1991); John O'Loughlin, *Dictionary of Geopolitics,* Westport, Conn.: Greenwood Press, 1994.

Gerrymandering. *See* **Electoral geography.**

Global warming. *See* **Greenhouse effect.**

Globalization. Globalization is the spread of economic activities from a home country to other regions of the world and the establishment of fully integrated industrial and service organizations beyond home country borders. Primarily an economic process, globalization has grown to such enormous proportions that it has powerfully influenced social and political realms worldwide.

The principal actors in the globalization process are large **transnational corporation**s (TNCs), most of which have headquarters in the United States, Europe, or Japan, and have offices and production facilities in other regions of the world. TNCs have become dominant in the economic and political systems within the countries where they operate. In many cases, their monetary income exceeds the total **gross national product** of the host country.

A firm in the developed world gets its start in the globalization process by expanding the export of its products. Once overseas expansion has proved to be profitable, the firm may choose to set up manufacturing operations in another country. One of the prime incentives for firms to do this is the vastly lower wage rates to be found overseas. For example, Polaroid Corporation has established operations in China. Nike, with headquarters in the United States, manufactures all sport clothing in overseas locations.

The final stage in a firm's transition to globalization is perceptual: the firm begins to identify itself in global terms. In this sense, Boeing is a major player in the global economy. One of the recent aircraft it produced was assembled at the firm's headquarters in Seattle, Washington, with major components coming from manufacturing plants in 14 different countries, including the completely assembled fuselage, which was shipped from Japan.

The globalization process proceeds effectively for a number of reasons. First, lower transportation costs allow components and parts to be sent longer distances. It is commonplace in today's global economy to see computer parts sent from Southeast Asia to assembly points in the United States or Japan. Second, communication by e-mail, fax, satellite transmission, and fiber optics is instantaneous. These modes of communicating account for the globalization of service sector economies as well. Banking, finance, and telecommunication operations have become almost as ubiquitous as bakeries in every urban center. Third, governmental intervention in the global economic process is minimal.

For all of its inherent efficiencies, globalization has not escaped criticism. Globalization, it is claimed, works to increase economic inequities already existing between core and periphery (*see* **Wallerstein's world-system analysis**). Many experts consider the presence of TNCs in a developing country as a form of **neocolonialism,** in which an entity exploits the host country without compensating it fairly. Others suggest that the global economy has made the sovereign state system obsolete because host countries are essentially powerless over the operations of the TNCs.

Suggested Readings: Peter Dicken, *Global Shift: The Internalization of Economic Activity*, 3rd ed., New York: Guilford Press, 1992; Kenichi Ohmae, "The Rise of the Region State," *Foreign Affairs*, spring 1993.

Gottmann, Jean. *See* **Megalopolis.**

Gravity model. The concept of **distance decay** states that interaction between two places decreases as the distance between them increases. For instance, it is highly likely that we would attend a motion picture at a theater that is one mile from us rather than travel a greater distance for the same purpose. The gravity model, derived from Newtonian physics, expands on the distance decay concept and adds quantitative measures.

Newton's law of gravity, developed by the seventeenth-century English physicist and mathematician Sir Isaac Newton, states that any two bodies attract one another with a force equal to the product of their masses divided by the square of the distance separating them. Geographers have borrowed this law and applied it to migration flows, the attraction of various-sized cities, commodity flows, and studies of journey-to-work distances. For example, the interaction between two urban places may be quantitatively determined by a formula using the population of each place and the distance between them:

$$I = \frac{P1P2}{D2}$$

where I is the measure of interaction, P1 and P2 are the populations of each place, and D is the distance separating them. If one place is larger than the other, the gravitation law states that its attraction will be greater than that of the smaller place. Also, if the distance between the two is greater, a generally lower measure of attraction will result.

Formulas have also been developed to determine the attraction breaking point between two places. That is, a person located precisely on the attraction breaking point between two places can choose either, provided the place has the service or item needed. If one place is larger and as a result has greater attraction, the breaking point will be farther from that place and closer to the smaller place. The use of population in the formula suggests that the place with a larger number of people will have a larger number and variety of functions.

As such, its reach will be greater. For instance, consider Chicago and Peoria, Illinois. Someone wanting to purchase a Tiffany-cut diamond ring after shopping at several jewelers would mostly likely go to Chicago.

Studies using the gravity model reached their peak during the **Quantitative Revolution** in geography. Since that time, the model has continued to be applied, especially in migration and transportation studies. Important refinements have been made to the model that allow estimates of interactions involving more than two places. These so-called potential models use the same basic principle as the gravity model, calculating population sizes and distances between all places in the study area.

Suggested Readings: John M. Lowe and Ashish Sen, "Gravity Model Applications in Health Planning: Analysis of an Urban Hospital Market," *Journal of Regional Science,* vol. 36 (1996); Si-Il Mun, "Transport Network and System of Cities," *Journal of Urban Economics,* vol. 42 (1997).

Green belt. The allocation of a green belt, a land sector surrounding a major city within which development is strictly limited, was first proposed in Europe during the early twentieth century. In the interwar years in London, new and improved transportation systems allowed for expansion beyond the city limits. The response of the government was to create a green belt of approximately 30 kilometers encircling the city. Within this green belt, there were to be no large-scale development projects. The land was to be used only for farming, recreation, and the maintenance of open space.

The decision to create a green belt around London also prevented the city from getting too large and experiencing **urban sprawl,** a problem that plagues cities in the United States. In 1947, the British passed the Town and Country Planning Act, which dictated that all major cities establish green belts similar to the one surrounding London.

In time, a number of other European cities enacted green belt legislation. For example, cities in Germany's densely settled Ruhr industrial corridor have created green belts to limit the negative impact of power plants and manufacturing complexes and to avoid the development of suburbs. Tokyo, Japan, also developed plans for a green belt surrounding the city. However, growth following the end of World War II quickly overtook the plan, and little evidence of open space can be found anywhere in the vast Tokyo metropolitan area.

European cities have successfully avoided the kind of urban sprawl found in most cities in the United States by creating green belts. Yet, growth has not stopped. High-density development has taken place beyond the green belts in the rural areas.

Suggested Readings: D. Burtenshow et al., *The European City: A Western Perspective,* New York: John Wiley & Sons, 1991; Hugh Clout, *Europe's Cities in the Late Twentieth Century,* Utrecht: Royal Dutch Geographical Society, 1994.

Green Revolution. New strains of rice and wheat were developed in the 1950s for the purpose of increasing the yields of those crops. The rice hybrids, introduced first in the Philippines, were enormously successful in a number of regions. The resulting Green Revolution, as it is called, spread rapidly through India, where yields of rice doubled in the 1960s.

The new rice hybrids require ample amounts of chemical fertilizer, regular use of pesticides, and substantial amounts of water to ensure maximum plant growth. Conditions in the well-watered Ganges River Valley in northern India are ideal for the new rice.

Other regions of southern and southeastern Asia also benefited from the Green Revolution. However, many areas were not positively affected for several reasons. There were a few places that opted not to use the new hybrid seeds. Other areas did not have sufficient water available to support the process. But the major reason for the limited effectiveness of the Green Revolution was cost. The use of the hybrid rice involves considerable outlays of money for fertilizer, pesticides, and water. Unfortunately, many regions in the developing world do not have the monetary resources to afford the new hybrid process. It is a cruel irony that countries most needing to increase grain yields cannot take advantage of an agricultural process that was, from its inception, developed for them. Only about 2 percent of African agricultural activity involves use of Green Revolution hybrid seeds.

Another criticism of the Green Revolution centers on environmental degradation. Pesticides and fertilizers used in the rice-growing process remain in the soil and, in time, rob it of its fertility. This is not unique to the Green Revolution. Agriculturalists in the developed world have been aware of the seriousness of soil degradation from pesticides and fertilizers for decades.

The Consultative Group on International Agriculture Research (CGIAR), a Washington, D.C., organization established as a monitoring agency for the Green Revolution, tracks progress in agriculture with the help of 13 research stations around the world. The CGIAR is working to eradicate the negative aspects attributed to the Green Revolution and to ensure that more agriculturists in the developing world will be able to take part in the process.

Suggested Readings: Edward C. Wolf, *Worldwatch Paper #73: Beyond the Green Revolution: New Approaches for Third World Agriculture*, Washington, D.C.: Worldwatch Institute, October 1986; Food and Agriculture Organization of the United Nations Web site, www.fao.org.

Greenhouse effect. Carbon dioxide, water vapor, methane, and chlorofluorocarbons (CFCs) in the atmosphere absorb incoming shortwave radiation from the sun. In time, the shortwave radiation is transformed into long-wave radiation, or sensible heat. In the early twentieth century, the gradual accumulation of higher volumes of the noted substances in the atmosphere is causing a measurable rise in average global temperature. Because the process is similar to that in a greenhouse, the term *greenhouse effect* has been applied. In a greenhouse, shortwave solar rays penetrate the glass and are absorbed by materials inside the greenhouse. The shortwave inputs change to long waves and radiate heat. The glass in the greenhouse traps the heat inside. Another example of the greenhouse effect is found in an automobile parked in the sun with its windows closed. After a few hours, the inside of the car will be much warmer than outside.

Concern has been raised that increasing accumulations of carbon dioxide, the leading absorber of shortwave radiation, will have damaging effects globally. The phenomenon of global warming is believed to be responsible for climatic change, the melting of the Antarctic ice cap, and the diminishment of Arctic sea ice. In addition, a gradual increase in sea level has been attributed to the melting of high-latitude ice and the thermal expansion of seawater as it warms. Proponents of the greenhouse effect and global warming theories contend that atmospheric conditions are in place to ensure global temperature increases throughout the twenty-first century.

Another process that has increased the amount of carbon dioxide in the atmosphere is **deforestation.** This happens in two ways. First, a cleared forest can no longer act as a carbon sink. That is, because trees are very effective absorbers of carbon dioxide, every tree that is eliminated reduces the amount of carbon dioxide that can be absorbed from the atmosphere. Second, many of the trees felled in a deforestation project are burned, releasing carbon dioxide.

Carbon dioxide and other greenhouse gases have been accumulating in the atmosphere since the beginning of the **Industrial Revolution,** in the late eighteenth century. Over time, as the industrialization process has increased its output, more greenhouse gases have been added. With the industrialization of developing countries increasing every year, the volume of greenhouse gases sent into the atmosphere will certainly expand.

The United Nations Environmental Programme predicts that by the year 2025, the total carbon dioxide emissions from the developing world will equal the output from the developed world. In the 1980s, the ratio of these outputs was 80 percent from the developed world and 20 percent from the developing world.

Concern about global warming brought representatives from 171 countries to the Kyoto (Japan) Climate Change Summit in 1997 to deal with this important environmental problem. The major outcome of the meeting was the **Kyoto Protocol,** a plan to reduce greenhouse gas emissions into the twenty-first century. Although every developed country was required to reduce emissions by a specified amount, the developing countries were not required to do so. The search continues for a viable global plan to effectively reduce greenhouse gas emissions.

Suggested Readings: William P. Cunningham and Barbara W. Saigo, *Environmental Science: A Global Concern,* 4th ed., Dubuque, Iowa: Wm. C. Brown, 1997; Ian D. Whyte, *Climatic Change and Human Society,* New York: John Wiley & Sons, 1996.

Gross national product/Gross domestic product. Gross national product (GNP) and gross domestic product (GDP) are measures of economic systems. GDP is the total value of goods and services produced within a country and usually reported on a yearly basis. GNP, a measure seen more frequently in **economic geography,** is GDP plus income from labor and capital accrued from other countries minus payments to those working abroad. Both measures are routinely converted to a per capita form that yields a more meaningful figure. Both measures may be adjusted, as well, to reflect the purchasing power of the currency in a particular country.

One glance at a table of values of GNP/cap (per capita) for countries and regions of the world reveals some astounding inequities. First, more than 80 percent of GNP/cap is held by only 20 percent of the world's population, living in the rich countries in the developed world. The range in value of GNP/cap is also indicative of the extraordinary differences in wealth. The United States' GNP/cap in the late 1990s was more than $28,000. Several countries in Sub-Saharan Africa during that same time period had GNP/cap values of less than $400. These figures are a clear indication of the development gap, the difference between the core (the urban-industrialized countries) and the periphery (the less-developed countries): Indications over past decades point to an increase in the development gap. It appears that the old adage "The rich get richer and the poor get poorer," is generally accurate.

Inequities in GNP/cap are also found within countries. For instance, the GNP/cap in the highly urbanized **Megalopolis** of the northeastern United States is significantly higher than in the southern states of the Mississippi River delta. Some of the highest internal disparities are found in oil-producing countries in the Middle East. A small percentage of individuals at the top of the system have exceedingly high incomes, whereas most of the populace has very little.

GNP/cap in combination with other economic and social measures can be equally revealing. For instance, there is a positive relationship between GNP/cap and energy consumption by country. Higher energy consumption is an attribute of the affluent developed countries where GNP/cap is also high. Conversely, countries with low GNP/cap will not have the means to purchase energy for productive purposes. A negative relationship is found in a comparison of GNP/cap and percentage of workforce in agriculture. In this case, high GNP/cap relates to low percentages of workers in agriculture. Yet, agricultural production in developed countries is the highest in the world. This is due to inputs of mechanization and high technology, affordable only in countries with a substantial GNP/cap.

Both GDP and GNP, and their per capita forms, are widely used as measures of development. They are, however, most accurate as measures in the developed countries, where data on virtually every aspect of the economy is available and measured. Such levels of accuracy are not generally achieved in most developing countries. Also, GDP and GNP do not account for capital generated in the so-called **informal sector** (businesses that operate outside the governmental structure) in the developing world, and in some of these countries the informal sector may represent a higher overall monetary value than the formal, measurable sector.

Suggested Readings: Brian J. Berry et al., *The Global Economy in Transition*, Upper Saddle River, N.J.: Prentice Hall, 1997; P. R. Gregory and R. C. Stuart, *Comparative Economic Systems*, Boston: Houghton Mifflin, 1995.

Growth pole. The concept of the growth pole was devised by the French scholar Francois Perroux in the 1950s. The term is associated with economic development and refers to a center of extraordinary industrial growth focused on a particularly dynamic single firm leading in growth. The firm in the center is referred to as a propulsive industry, the clear leader in that industrial sector.

The economic situation afforded by a growth pole results in (1) the accumulation of positive factors of production, including entrepreneurial leadership, skilled labor, and abundant capital, and (2) economic growth at the expense of the **hinterland,** or service area, from which it draws its positive growth factors.

In theory, the vast accumulation of wealth in the growth pole will gradually be dispersed throughout the larger region. It is suggested that the positive attribute of this spread effect, as it is called, will take over 20 years. For this reason, such scholars as Swedish economist and sociologist Gunnar Myrdal (1898–1987) have insisted that government intervention is necessary to ensure that the redistribution of growth pole wealth to the outlying areas be legislated and regulated.

The growth pole concept can operate on any geographical scale. For instance, a single successful industrial plant in a small town can attract the positive economic factors of production in the same manner as giant firms like General Motors and IBM. The growth pole theme applies to regional levels as well. The Ruhr industrial district in Germany can be considered a growth pole. Also, Japan's highly industrialized Inland Sea corridor from Tokyo west to the steelmaking complexes in northern Kyushu is an important growth pole. **Megalopolis,** the extensive metropolitan area of the northeastern United States, is another. All of these regions are comprised of perhaps hundreds of individual firms (propulsive industries) that are in themselves growth poles.

Finally, the growth pole concept operates at the global level in the **core-periphery model** of economic development. The core, in this sense, takes on the role of a vast accumulator of capital, labor, and in fact, all the positive economic factors of production needed to maintain its growth. This is one of the premises of **Wallerstein's world-system analysis,** developed by social scientist Immanuel Wallerstein.

Suggested Readings: Peter Dicken, *Global Shift: Transforming the World Economy*, New York: Guilford Press, 1998; Tim Unwin, *Atlas of World Development*, New York: John Wiley & Sons, 1995.

H

Hagerstrand, Torsten (1916–). Torsten Hagerstrand is the most prominent geographer in **diffusion** studies. His contributions to this important area of **human geography** laid the foundation for decades of work in diffusion that followed. Hagerstrand's doctoral dissertation, "Innovation Diffusion as a Spatial Process," completed at the University of Lund, Sweden, in 1953, is a classic study in the field.

The work is particularly important in diffusion studies because of his inclusion of mathematical and statistical models that provided a sound basis for making predictions. Perhaps its greatest importance is Hagerstrand's insistence that diffusion studies emphasize process, the sequence of events that clearly identify the key steps occurring in space and time that help to explain an outcome. That is, if an innovation begins at Point A and is later noted at Point B, what is the sequence of occurrences that explain this diffusion? Process is an important approach in **geography,** and it has precedent in studies of the

Torsten Hagerstrand. *Source:* Courtesy of Torsten Hagerstrand.

earth's surface all the way back to the ancient Greek historian **Herodotus** and other significant contributors to the discipline.

Hagerstrand's dissertation was translated into English in 1967 at the height of the **Quantitative Revolution.** The work became an important document in American and British geography because of its use of mathematical and statistical models. His subsequent work on location theory incorporated the process approach that marked his diffusion studies.

Hagerstrand also pioneered the field of time geography. In the 1960s he identified and mapped the spatial behavior of individuals in their daily travels through space and time. He also contributed meaningfully to the fields of **urban geography** and quantitative **cartography.** Hagerstrand correctly pointed out that individuals are more likely to be an accepter of an innovation if they are closer to its origin. This idea relates to the established concept of **distance decay,** important in understanding aspects of **spatial interaction.**

Suggested Readings: Richard Morrill, *Spatial Diffusion*, vol. 10, Scientific Geography Series, Newbury Park, Calif.: Sage, 1988; Richard K. Ormrod, "Local Context and Innovation Diffusion in a Well-Connected World," *Economic Geography*, vol. 66 (1990).

Heartland theory. *See* **Geopolitics** and **Mackinder, Halford J.**

Herodotus (484–ca. 425 B.C.). Herodotus, a Greek, was, like most early thinkers, a universal scholar—one who observed, commented on, and theorized about all activities in view. He described places and people in the known world of his time. He was a field researcher and traveled extensively in the region of the Mediterranean.

Herodotus has been called the father of both history and ethnography (the study of cultural traits of people). Geographers claim him as one of their own because he asked geographical questions and engaged in research that was clearly within the purview of the discipline. Sound in his thinking, Herodotus believed that geography provided the physical background for historical events and that the geography of a place changed through time. Ideas of this form are key components in contemporary **historical geography.**

Herodotus may well be considered the father of environmental awareness. He wrote of his concern about soil loss in the agricultural fields of Greece at an early time. His concern was that **soil erosion** from wind and runoff following rainfall would gradually decrease soil fertility for future agricultural use. This is, of course, an important environmental concern in the modern era.

Herodotus speculated on the development of the Nile River delta. He theorized that winter winds from Europe forced the sun to retreat southward. As the sun moved south, it pulled the Nile waters with it. In the summer, the winds shifted and the sun again moved northward and the water in the Nile River swelled to its annual high point. With the water came particulate matter that was eventually deposited and extended the delta farther into the Mediterranean Sea. In time, Herodotus was proven wrong; his was a false theory. But it is nonetheless important, because it exemplified a process explanation, an approach that is very powerful in geographical analysis.

Suggested Readings: George Kish, *A Source Book in Geography*, Cambridge, Mass.: Harvard University Press, 1978; Geoffrey J. Martin and Preston E. James, *All Possible Worlds: A History of Geographical Ideas*, 3rd ed., New York: John Wiley & Sons, 1993.

Hierarchical diffusion. *See* **Expansion diffusion.**

Highly developed countries. *See* **Core-periphery model.**

High-tech corridors. The high-technology industries have tended to locate in well-defined concentrations in areas that come to be known as high-tech corridors. Extensive research and development departments manned by scientists, communications experts, engineers, and skilled technicians support these companies. The high-technology sector of the economy includes firms that specialize in the production of electronic components, computers and peripheral equipment, communications equipment, biotechnology products, and some pharmaceuticals. From the listing of industry types, it is clear that the high-technology industrial sector is found almost exclusively in the developed world. However, many components used in high-technology industries, such as computer chips, are produced in the developing world. Despite this fact, it is the high-technology firms in the core that derive the greatest profit from the sale of their finished product.

In the computer and electronics fields, a number of regional concentrations have been established in the United States. The favored location for these high-tech corridors is close to research universities and sources of skilled labor and away from areas where unionization is strong. Also, high-tech industries want locations that have a good quality of life and the availability of venture capital to launch and support their dynamic business.

Some of the high-tech corridors in the United States include Silicon Valley near San Jose, California; Silicon Forest near Seattle, Washington; the North Carolina Research Triangle Park complex in the Raleigh-Durham-Chapel Hill area, and Route 128 circling Boston. High-tech centers have also developed in Canada, in British Columbia and near the cities of Toronto and Ottawa. High-tech corridors are found in a number of European locations and in Japan. There is also an important high-tech corridor near Bangalor, India.

Highly concentrated, these corridors have been characterized as techno-poles, centers containing propulsive industries that are exceptionally successful and are leaders in their fields. The techno-pole identifier is analogous to the notion of the **growth pole,** long a part of the conceptual base of **economic geography.**

Suggested Readings: Judith Alfrey and Catherine Clark, *The Landscape of Industry*, London: Routledge, 1993; Sharon Kellerman, *Telecommunications and Geography*, New York: John Wiley & Sons, 1993.

Hinterland. The original meaning of the word *hinterland* was associated with coastal locations and specified the service area landward of a port. *Hinterland* is a German word that translates as "behind *(hinter)* land." The use of the term has expanded to cover the service area of virtually any settlement.

The notion of the hinterland is implicitly a part of both **von Thunen's land use model** and **Christaller's central place theory.** The areas adjacent to the central places in both works are characterized as hinterlands, or spheres of influence, of the central places. Other terms that refer to a hinterland are *tributary region* and *trade area.* In **urban geography,** the term *hinterland,* in most cases, has been replaced with the more contemporary term *urban field.* It may be noted, as well, that the term *nodal region* is similar in concept to hinterland.

In von Thunen's model, developed in the early 1800s by German economist Johann Heinrich von Thunen, the hinterland included concentric zones surrounding the market center. The center provided all goods and services needed in the hinterland and, in turn, was the market for all commodities produced in the hinterland. Von Thunen's model provides the most straightforward example of the center–hinterland relationship. Christaller's central place theory, developed by twentieth-century German economic geographer Walter Christaller, adds a new dimension to the hinterland notion. Christaller discussed the functions in an extensive area containing many centers, each with its own hinterland. People living on the boundary between two hinterlands had the option of traveling to either one of the centers for needed goods and services. They could be said to be located near or on the line of indifference between the two centers.

In a metropolitan center such as Paris, London, Tokyo, or Chicago, the hinterland is quite extensive because of their population size and numbers and types of functions. The world's paramount nodal center in terms of functions, corporate headquarters, and financial leadership is New York City. It is not incorrect to say that, depending on functions unique to New York City, its hinterland is the entire world.

The hinterland idea has also been applied to the core-periphery concept. In this context, the core represents the nodal center and the periphery its hinterland. Clearly, use of the term *hinterland* has been greatly extended from its original meaning as the land adjacent to a port.

Suggested Readings: Brian Goodall, *The Facts on File Dictionary of Human Geography,* New York: Facts on File, 1987; J. N. Marshall, *Services and Space: Aspects of Urban and Regional Development,* London: Longman, 1995.

Historical geography. The term *historical geography* has been used in a number of ways in the past and in recent years has come to mean the reconstruction of the geographies of past times. For instance, a geographer may analyze and report on aspects of the current industrial geography of Chicago, identifying industry types and noting their location, number of employees, product line, markets, and a host of other potential topics.

If the study was focused on the industrial geography of Chicago in 1900, the geographer could do essentially the same kind of study, ask essentially the same questions, and prepare a written work reflective of the analysis. There are two major differences in the two studies: (1) the 1900 research could not be done in person, so to speak, because time has passed and there is no opportunity to visit industrial sites and observe their operation firsthand; and (2) the researcher would have to rely wholly on historical documents, data collections, photographs, plans, drawings, and business records that were preserved. If some of the physical plant was still standing, it would be useful to visit the site; there may be physical evidence of industrial processes long abandoned. For the historical geographer, there is a certain measure of excitement researching the past to create a picture of what a place was like and how it functioned.

Earlier applications of the term *historical geography* were to geography's role in history. **Herodotus,** the eminent ancient Greek scholar, contended that geography provided the physical background for historical events. He also noted that the geography of a place changes through time. This is another example of how the term *historical geography* has been applied. Both of these applications have merit: all historical events occur in places, and the geography of a place— its physical and cultural attributes—changes through time.

In recent years, historical geographers have established close ties with historians and other social scientists. The favored approach to historical geographic studies has been to focus on particular time periods and re-create their geography. This approach produces what is called a cross-sectional view of the place at the selected time. The study of the industrial geography of Chicago in 1900 would be a cross section. This notion may be extended to include a series of cross sections of a place. The researcher may want to gain insights into Chicago's industrial geography before and after World War I, during the Great Depression of the 1930s, following World War II, and at selected periods from the 1950s to the present. Comparison of the cross sections would reveal changes that took place over the century. The research could then continue with questions about how and why the industrial geography changed. Speculations and hypotheses centering on the process of change may validly be entertained.

Historical geography, like **cultural geography,** remained unaffected during the era of the **Quantitative Revolution** in the United States. Although quantitative and statistical techniques could have been applied in a reintroduction of a past geography, there were few studies that did so.

Suggested Readings: Ralph H. Brown, *Historical Geography in the United States*, New York: Harcourt, Brace, & World, 1948; R. J. Johnston et al., *The Dictionary of Human Geography*, Oxford, U.K.: Basil Blackwell, 1993.

HIV/AIDS. In 1981, it was firmly established that a new and deadly virus had established itself within the human community. The virus that causes AIDS is the human immunodeficiency virus (HIV), and the disease produced by the virus is called acquired immunodeficiency syndrome (AIDS). As the names suggest, AIDS destroys the immune system, the disease-fighting centers in the human body. When the immune system is adversely affected, the body is essentially defenseless against other potentially deadly diseases, such as tuberculosis and pneumonia.

HIV/AIDS has reached pandemic proportions since it first came into the human population. More than 20 years after it was first identified, no cure has been found, although certain treatments can lengthen the time before an HIV infection becomes full-blown AIDS.

The AIDS virus is passed from source to recipient in an exchange of bodily fluids. Particularly effective is contact with the blood of an infected individual. As such, high vulnerability to acquiring the virus is associated with engaging in sexual activity with an infected person or receiving a blood transfusion inadvertently containing the virus.

In 2000, best estimates of people infected with HIV/AIDS stood at 50 million worldwide, of whom 10 million were children. In addition, 90 percent of these cases were found in Sub-Saharan African countries. In the recent decade, 2 million deaths per year have been attributed to AIDS. In some developing countries, life expectancy has declined and child mortality rates have increased.

The virus originated in two regions in Sub-Saharan Africa: the Guinea Highlands in West Africa and the East African Lake District. Researchers conclude that the virus was acquired through the practice of injecting monkey blood as an aphrodisiac. Once the virus became established in humans, its **diffusion** was rapid. In Africa, the disease followed transportation routes, and its incidence rates were highest in rapidly growing major cities.

When AIDS first appeared in the United States, two apparently unrelated cohort groups were most affected: gay men and Haitians. Further research shed light on this mystery. In the 1960s, a number of Haitians immigrated to Africa as government workers. When they returned to Haiti, the disease came with them. In the case of gay men, investigations revealed that Europeans visiting Africa brought the virus to England and other places on the continent. From this source, gay men in the United States were eventually infected.

Once established in the United States, the virus spread quickly through gay communities in large cities such as San Francisco and New York. The disease filtered down the urban hierarchy and into the rural areas. By the mid-1990s, every state in the United States reported cases of HIV/AIDS. However, as insidious as the disease is in the United States, its numbers cannot compare with those of Africa. For instance, Botswana and Zimbabwe have the world's highest per capita incidence of HIV/AIDS. HIV/AIDS is also found in Latin America and Asia. Bangkok, Thailand, is experiencing particularly high rates of infection. Researchers had hoped that the pandemic would not reach the vast Asian populations. That hope has been dashed. Even China and India, with a total of 2.3 billion people, are reporting HIV/AIDS infections. China, India, and Thailand began experiencing HIV and AIDS in the 1990s. The disease is rapidly increasing. In December 2002, the incidence of HIV in the Asia-Pacific region reached over 7 million. India has 4 million cases, and China could reach 11 million by 2010.

Especially insidious is the fact that an individual may carry HIV for years before any overt symptoms are noted. This means that an unaware carrier may potentially infect many other people.

Researchers hope that in time a cure for AIDS will be found and that a preventative inoculation can be developed. Short of these breakthroughs, it is certain that millions of people will die of this disease.

Suggested Readings: Ann Hwang, "AIDS Has Arrived in India and China," *World Watch*, January–February 2001; "A Turning Point for AIDS?" *The Economist*, July 15, 2000.

Human Development Index. The United Nations Development Programme developed and first published the Human Development Index (HDI) in 1990. Since its inception, the HDI has become the most used index for comparing countries and regions.

Development scholars had long attempted to derive an objective measure to compare the developed and developing countries. It is well understood that developing countries lag far behind their counterparts in the industrial world in the categories of income, level of affluence, productivity, and a host of other economic and social measures. But the question was continually raised about the correctness of applying measures that clearly fit the developed countries to those in the developing world. For instance, did it make sense to use measures of industrial productivity when making comparisons with a country that had little or no industry?

The HDI uses only four basic variables within the three categories of demography, social ranking, and economic level. The four variables are life expectancy at birth, educational level attained, degree of literacy, and gross domestic product per capita. The highest possible score that a country can attain is 1.000 and the lowest is 0.000. It must be noted that the United Nations has, on occasion, modified the HDI by assigning weightings to each of the variables. As such, the index cannot be said to be completely objective. Yet, it is a very useful measure for comparisons.

In the late 1990s, world HDI was 0.72, whereas the developed countries collectively registered 0.93, considerably higher than the world average. Developing countries, on the other hand, registered 0.63, significantly lower. If HDIs for the countries of Sub-Saharan Africa are averaged, the result is 0.38, far below the figure for all developing countries.

The African country Niger has a low HDI and a population that is expected to double in the next two decades. Life expectancy at birth is 47 years, far below the developing country average of 63 years. Niger's literacy rate is 14 percent, which points to a severe lack of formal education. Only 48 percent of the population has access to safe drinking water. Finally, Niger's **gross national** product (GNP) per capita is about $200. Many other countries are living in similar conditions of deprivation.

HDI values will be watched carefully in the future. Their value in comparisons of countries and regions will indicate to what degree the developing countries are closing the development gap.

Suggested Readings: Development Assistance Committee of the Organisation for Economic Co-operation and Development Web site, www.oecd.org (the goal of this organization is to measure development progress); Allen C. Kelley, "The Human Development Index: 'Handle With Care,'" *Population and Development Review*, vol. 17 (1991); United Nations Development Programme, *Human Development Report*, New York: Oxford University Press, annual.

Human geography. Simply stated, human geography considers all aspects of the greater discipline of **geography** except those concerned directly with physical geography and technical areas, such as **cartography.** In most countries, geography has been split into two basic camps: physical and human. The split occurred at the end of the nineteenth century and during the first few years of the twentieth century. It is ironic that a split of this proportion happened so soon after some of the leaders in geography in the late nineteenth century were convinced that the discipline could find a place in universities if it championed the theme of being the science that studies the interface between nature and culture. Today this intellectual position is referred to as human–environment interaction.

Human geography is a very broad field that includes a varied and diverse range of subdisciplines. Among the many geographies included are agricultural, behavioral, cultural, economic, elective, historical, industrial, political, population, rural, social, and transportation. Within all of these subdisciplines are found three common approaches to research: (1) spatial analysis; (2) the interrelationship of places; and (3) regional synthesis in varying forms.

Essentially, human geographers ask "where" and "why" questions regarding human activities. For instance, where are the major centers of aircraft manufacturing and why are they located there? To what states did African Americans migrate out of the southern United States and why? Human geographers might also consider the global pattern of population density. A glance at a world population map shows three major population concentrations: East Asia, South Asia, and the European littoral, reaching east to the Ural Mountains. These three centers of population contain about one-half of the world's people. The human geographer would ask why these concentrations occurred and what consequences emerge given their presence.

The nineteenth-century German geographer **Friedrich Ratzel** was one of the earliest geographers to write specifically about human geography. Ratzel proposed that culture groups be the topic of systematic study. In his two-volume work, *Anthropogeographie*, Ratzel considered the influence of the physical environment on culture groups (in volume 1, 1882) and then looked more closely at the attributes of the culture groups themselves without considering physical impacts (in volume 2, 1891). Another early exponent of human geography was **Paul Vidal de la Blache,** the noted French scholar. In the early twentieth century, he wrote an important book on the principles of human geography, *Principles of Human Geography* (1922).

Many geographers lament the split that has separated human geography from physical geography. Although the separation is justified as an example of specialization of effort found in every discipline, in geography the split is more significant. Geography is a holistic, synthesizing, and integrating discipline. The examples of the "where" and "why" questions asked by human geographers invariably enter the realm of physical geography with the "where" questions. Further, the "why" question may elicit aspects of physical geography that provide the soundest explanation. A recent move in the discipline suggests the development of an environmental geography that would focus on the interface of physical geography and human geography. Conceptually this would be a return to the ideas of such late-nineteenth-century scholars as **Ratzel, Halford J. Mackinder,** and **William Morris Davis.** It is the geography they envisioned.

Suggested Readings: George J. Demko et al., *Why in the World? Adventures in Geography,* New York: Anchor Books/Doubleday, 1992; R. J. Johnston, *The Nature of Human Geography,* Oxford, U.K.: Basil Blackwell, 1996.

Human Poverty Index. The Human Poverty Index (HPI), published by the United Nations Development Programme, focuses attention on the poorest of people in each country. The HPI is reported as a percentage of the population of any country that are the most deprived of basic human essentials. The index considers longevity, the ability to read and write, and three additional variables that indicate proximity to basic health needs: (1) presence of medical facilities; (2) access to safe drinking water; and (3) the percentage of malnourished children under age five.

When these values are combined, the outcome is in the form of a percentage of the population that exists at the lowest economic levels. Countries in the developed world have low percentages of their population living at substandard levels. Yet, even the richest of countries has some of its people in this unfortunate circumstance. For instance, in 1994 Canada and the United States had HPI percentages of 12.0 and 16.5, respectively. Costa Rica, perhaps the most progressive of all Latin American countries, had an HPI of 4.1 in that same year.

Not surprisingly, some of the highest HPIs are in countries of Sub-Saharan Africa. Index percentages in the 40s and 50s were not uncommon in this region in the late 1990s. Burkina Faso (58), Niger (62), Sierra Leone (58), and Ethiopia (56) were the African countries with the most serious conditions of deprivation.

A cruel irony lies within the deprivation existing in countries that have high percentages of their population living so far below even the most basic levels. The irony is that these countries will experience the greatest population increases in the next 50 years. World population is expected to reach 8.5 billion by 2050, and most of the increases will be within countries in the developing world, which are already heavily taxed to keep up with today's demands.

The African country of Burkina Faso, for example, had a population of 12 million in the late 1990s, and that number was expected to double in 24 years. Its infant mortality rate is 94 per thousand, an indicator of inadequate childbirth delivery systems and poor sanitation conditions. Only 42 percent of the population has access to safe drinking water. Life expectancy at birth is 47 years, compared to 63 years, the average for all developing countries. Burkina Faso is just one of many developing countries living in excessively poor conditions. HPI is a measure that will be monitored regularly in the future to indicate changes in the quality of life in the poorest of countries.

Suggested Readings: David R. Phillips and Yola Verhasselt, *Health and Development,* New York: Routledge, 1994; UNICEF, *The State of the World's Children*, United Nations, annual.

Humanistic geography. The approach of the humanistic geographer is to give center stage to human awareness, human inventiveness, and individual perception of place. Humanistic geography is somewhat connected with early French **human geography,** but it has a closer tie with contemporary **social geography.**

Humanistic geography emerged in the 1970s as a reaction against the mechanistic approaches of the **Quantitative Revolution.** A key question asked by humanistic geographers is "why do people act as they do?" Implicit in this question is a searching for attitudes, perceptions, and awareness in humans that help to explain how they behave, individually and collectively, in the spatial context. An important reversal of emphasis occurred in humanistic geography from the notion of the "spatial confinement of people and societies" to "ones concerned with the human and social construction of space" (Johnston, 1986, p. 208).

Yi-Fu Tuan, an early advocate of humanistic geography, suggested that achieving a more thorough understanding of humans was the main goal of the discipline. Tuan also compared the scientific approach to the study of humans, which paid little attention to the role of human awareness, and the approach of the humanistic geographer, which emphasizes human awareness and links it to spatial activities. Tuan, originally from China, was a longtime geography professor at the University of Minnesota and is now retired.

Humanistic geographical approaches were radically different from that of the accepted geographies of the 1970s. Physical geographers especially were critical of the new forms of explanation offered by humanistic geographers. In the new approach, empirically based hypotheses supported by analysis and objectivity were replaced by subjective conclusions and methodologies that were seen as intellectually suspect.

Humanistic geographers address the role of evaluating human awareness of the environment and consequent activities within it. Most important, humanistic geography emphasizes the importance of the subjective view and the merits of the individual human being existing within spatial bounds.

Suggested Readings: J. N. Entrikin, "Contemporary Humanism in Geography," *Annals of the Association of American Geographers,* vol. 66 (1976); Yi-Fu Tuan, "Humanistic Geography," *Annals of the Association of American Geographers,* vol. 66 (1976).

Hunting and gathering. As the glaciers receded at the end of the Ice Age some 12,000 years ago, small groups of humans began to migrate into newly opened lands. As the temperatures began a slow but steady increase, plant and animal communities expanded onto previously frozen land. The human groups that inhabited these regions are called hunter-gatherers. Fishing may be added to their food-acquiring practices.

The end of the Ice Age marked the end of the Paleolithic period, or Old Stone Age. Tools were rudimentary. Simple stone blades and pointed spearheads were primitive but effective in the hands of the experienced hunter. There was also a proliferation of plants and animals in regions inhabited by small roving bands.

Family groups were necessarily limited in number. Smaller groups had greater mobility in the tracking of migrating animals and the search for seasonally ripening plants. The number of children in these groups was also minimized, because too many dependent children could slow the group in its nearly continuous movement in search of food.

In time, the inventory of tools improved for at least two reasons: (1) group encounters resulted in the sharing of tools developed by each group; and (2) movement into new environments called for the development of tools suitable for that area. There is even evidence that regular trade routes were established before the advent of agriculture about 10,000 years ago. Trading of clothing items, animal skins, flint, and obsidian have been documented in southern Europe. As tool making improved and group contact resulted in the acquisition of commodities and the understanding of new processes and the ability to procure food more efficiently, populations began to increase. It is also thought that groups living in regions with a significant number of lakes were able to establish a quasi-sedentary life style based on fishing augmented by hunting and gathering.

Anthropologists contend that human social systems have evolved through four distinct stages. Hunting and gathering represents the first stage in this sequence. The term *social system* implies the development of a clearly identifiable cultural base, a feature that certainly was present in the hunter-gatherer groups. The remaining three stages in the anthropological model are identified by seminomadic groups engaged in subsistence or slash-and-burn agriculture (*see* **Extensive agriculture**), settled villages based on agriculture or animal herding, and complex social systems that used plows and irrigation techniques in field agricultural systems.

In the contemporary world there are still some culture groups that use the early hunting and gathering methods. Among them are the few remaining Alaskan Inuit that have not settled in villages, the Australian aborigines, and the African Bushmen. These groups represent a very small percentage of total world population.

Suggested Readings: John G. Galaty and Douglas L. Johnson, *The World of Pastoralism: Herding Systems in Comparative Perspective*, New York: Guilford Press, 1990; University of Evansville (Ind.), "Exploring Ancient World Cultures," Web site, http://eawc.evansville.edu.

Hydrologic cycle. The hydrologic cycle tracks the worldwide transfer and transformation of moisture in its various forms (water, water vapor, ice, snow) through the continuing process of evaporation, transpiration, precipitation, soil absorption, and runoff. Globally, the cycle is always in balance, but at the regional level, there may be a deficiency of moisture (more moisture is transferred out of the region than is received) or a surplus (more is retained). Also, short- and long-term atmospheric changes, such as El Niño and La Niña, can alter a region's input of moisture.

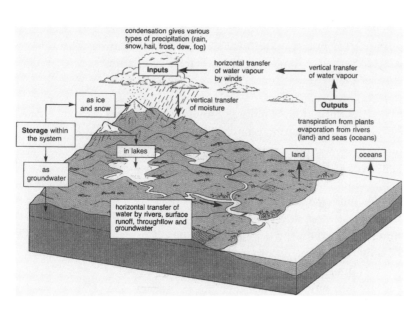

Hydrologic cycle. *Source: Geography: An Integrated Approach*, by David Waugh. Reproduced by permission of Nelson Thornes.

The hydrologic cycle has been characterized as chaotic in its operation. In 1988 the Global Energy and Water Cycle Experiment (GEWEX) was established. GEWEX is part of the World Climate Research Program set up to study climate change. GEWEX and other atmospheric monitoring programs are important sources of information in this era of global warming and unusual weather patterns (*see* **Greenhouse effect**).

A description of the hydrologic cycle begins with the oceans, which contain 97 percent of the earth's water. The oceans are continually evaporating water from their surface. Evaporation also occurs in much lower volumes from land areas and freshwater bodies. Another source of moisture is received from plants through the process of transpiration. Moisture from ocean evaporation accounts for 86 percent of the total; land, freshwater evaporation, and transpiration contribute the remaining 14 percent.

Evaporated moisture is carried aloft and forms as clouds. When the water vapor cools in its ascent, condensation occurs and precipitation begins in the form of rain, sleet, or snowfall. The hydrologic cycle continues with the return of moisture to the surface.

Most of the precipitation (78 percent) returns to the ocean surfaces, primarily in the equatorial and low-latitude belt. The remaining 22 percent falls on land areas, where it can take a number of different directions. Some of the water collects at the surface in lakes, rivers, and wetlands and is eventually used by humans and animals or absorbed by vegetation. Some water filters through to subterranean aquifers and is stored as groundwater. This water may be accessed by wells for human use. Finally, some water returns to the oceans as surface or underground runoff.

The operation of the hydrologic cycle can be affected by human activity. More people making greater demands on existing water supplies can have an impact on groundwater storage. For example, irrigation agriculture in the American Southwest uses large amounts of groundwater, and in some years, the recharge from precipitation is less than the amount taken. The Ogallala Aquifer in the Midwest and Great Plains is a vast underground source of water. Over the years, hundreds of wells bringing water to the surface primarily for agriculture have significantly lowered the level of the aquifer. In time, a serious cutback in agricultural activity might be required.

The demise of the topical rain forests, an important source of transpired moisture, has had a direct effect on the hydrologic cycle. Further clearing of the rain forests could change weather patterns poleward of the equator.

Suggested Readings: William H. Calvin, "The Great Climate Flip-Flop," *Atlantic Monthly*, vol. 281, 1998; Earth Systems Web site, www.earthsystems.org (monitors environmental situations).

I

Imperialism. *See* **Colonialism.**

Industrial inertia. In physics, inertia refers to the tendency of a body to remain at rest unless acted on by some external force. For example, a block of wood will remain in place on the garage floor until someone moves it. In **economic geography** the term *industrial inertia* refers to industrial plants that remain in place even though the original advantages of their site are no longer applicable. There are compelling reasons for an industrial operation to remain in place even though it may be costing more to do so. Among them are the costs to initially build the facility. In addition, the costs to move from the present site to a more optimal location may be too high. An industrial plant has ties to the local area, the labor force, and nearby plants with which it does business. Other external factors advantageous to the present location may also compel management to remain in place. Finally, **agglomeration** factors may be present. The plant may be one of several plants that have located close to each other for mutual advantage. The loss of these positive locational attributes must be weighed against the prospect of moving the plant to gain other advantages.

Inertia is a powerful force in determining whether a plant will remain in place or move. If the plant cannot be moved and the present location has lost its previous advantage, it may be necessary for the operation to shift to other products. The steelmaking industry is a case in point. Since the 1970s, the Japanese steelmaking industry has surpassed that of the United States in product quality and lower price. Many plants in the United States were subsequently closed, and some steel companies diversified into other industries. The historically famous steelmaking city of Pittsburgh, Pennsylvania, was particularly affected in this era. The city shifted its heavy focus on steel to electronics and high technology. Cincinnati, Ohio, also shifted to a more diversified economic structure when its role as a port city for agricultural products declined.

In the automobile industry, the use of robotics on assembly lines downgraded the importance of a local skilled labor force, which had been an important external factor contributing to the inertia of plants. Another innovation working against plant inertia is the so-called on-time distribution system of parts and components used in production. This new system has reduced the need for excessive on-site inventories. Robotics and the on-time distribution system have allowed plants to function more as assembly points and to disperse to more-advantageous locations. Despite these factors, the decision to move an industrial plant must be very compelling. Whenever possible, it is economically more feasible to adapt an operation than to move.

Suggested Readings: Stephan S. Birdsall and John W. Florin, *Regional Landscapes of the United States and Canada*, 4th ed., New York: John Wiley & Sons, 1992; H. D. Watts, *Industrial Geography*, New York: Longman Scientific/Wiley, 1987.

Industrial Revolution. The Industrial Revolution occurred as a long-term transition from small-scale crafts industries to the use of machinery and mass-production techniques. This revolution began in Great Britain about 1750 and lasted for approximately 100 years. During this period, industrial processes changed dramatically, a rural-to-urban shift of population began the era of great cities, and important advances were made in health care, transportation, and agriculture.

The Industrial Revolution was supported by the mechanization of **transportation systems.** James Watt refined the steam engine and made it a more fuel-efficient machine (1778). Watt's invention was crucial to the growth of the Industrial Revolution. His steam engine was used in iron making, to keep the ovens hot. This allowed more iron to be produced, which in turn was used to make the machines that accelerated the Industrial Revolution.

The Industrial Revolution was preceded and supported by advances in agriculture that began in the late seventeenth century. In turn, the Industrial Revolution produced a great number of manufactured items, including the tractor, which revolutionized agriculture (*see* **Agricultural Revolution**).

In the growing cities, the Industrial Revolution provided jobs for workers moving from rural areas. With newfound wealth from the sale of manufactured goods, cities were able to add sewer systems and greatly improve sanitation levels. Medical technology benefited from all of these improvements as well.

The second stage in the **demographic transition** began during the Industrial Revolution. Improvements in sanitation and medical delivery systems in the cities resulted in the steady decline in **crude death rate**s, and total population began to increase.

The new factory system of mass production added significant efficiency to the manufacturing process. As a result, the cost of goods produced was lowered and more people could afford to purchase needed items. Evidence suggests that couples married at earlier ages in Great Britain during the Industrial Revolution, and more children were born in this era.

The Industrial Revolution spread from Great Britain to continental Europe in the nineteenth century and then to Russia and Japan. North America began in earnest to build an industrial base at the end of the nineteenth century. By 1900, the European countries collectively accounted for more than 75 percent of world industrial production. Europe would hold this leadership until the post–World War II period, when the United States and then Japan emerged as the dominant producers. In recent years, industrial expansion has moved to the developing countries. Some of the operations in the developing world are based within **transnational corporation**s.

Suggested Readings: David Gibbs and Michael Healey, "Industrial Geography and the Environment," *Applied Geography*, vol. 17 (1997); Jon Stobart, "Geography and Industrialization, 1701–1760," *Transactions of the Institute of British Geographers*, vol. 21 (1996).

Infant mortality rate. Development researchers pay very close attention to the infant mortality rate (IMR) in regions and countries. The IMR measures the number of deaths per 1,000 live births in the first year of life and is perhaps the best index available of socioeconomic levels. IMR is specified in tables of demographic information as a whole number. For instance, in 1999 the IMR for the world was 57. So, for every 1,000 live births, 57 infants did not reach their first birthday.

The IMR for the developing world in that year was 68, somewhat higher than the world figure. However, the largest difference in IMR is seen in a comparison with the developed world, where the figure was 8 in 1999.

The difference in IMR between these two global regions is striking. The gap in IMR is another indicator of the significant disparities in development that are seen globally. IMR is a key index of development because it is an indicator of the nutrition levels, sanitation systems, medical delivery systems (access to doctors, availability of hospitals, medical stations, medicines, and preventive measures), and housing. IMR is also closely tied to the health and situation of the mother. In many cases, expectant mothers are engaged in manual labor, are malnourished, and do not receive proper prenatal care. Education also plays a part; new parents may not know how to care for a child who contracts an illness that could be easily treated.

IMR varies greatly from country to country. A number of countries, especially in Sub-Saharan Africa, have IMR values surpassing 100. For instance, some of the highest values are found in the West African countries of Gambia (130), Guinea (134), Guinea-Bissau (136), and Sierra Leone (136). In East Africa several countries have IMRs above 100, including Malawi (137) and Mozambique (134).

The lowest IMRs are found in the developed world. Most of the European countries, for instance, have values between 6 and 10. Japan's IMR is the lowest in the world, at 3.7, and is reflective of its high level of development, the availability of first-rate health systems, and a highly educated and dedicated populace. Japan's IMRs do not vary regionally to any significant degree. The same cannot be said for the United States (IMR 7.0), where notable regional disparities are found. Southern states, for instance, have IMRs from 9 to 11, whereas rates in the upper Midwest range from 4 to 6. IMRs are usually lower in cities and higher in rural areas.

A comparison index to IMR is the child mortality rate, which measures the number of deaths per 1,000 children aged one to five. In this age cohort, the highest rates of death are found in the developing countries.

Suggested Readings: W. Henry Mosely and Peter Cowley, "The Challenge of World Health," *Population Bulletin*, vol. 46 (1991); United Nations Children's Fund (UNICEF) Web site, www.unicef.org (includes extensive data on its "Information Statistics" page).

Informal sector. Within the overall economic system in a developing country, a significant number of productive workers are found in what is called the informal sector. The income of these workers is not reported to government officials. As such, the government is unable to levy taxes on it, nor is the income of these workers reported in the country's **gross national product.**

The informal sector is large; perhaps as much as 40 percent of the total labor force in developing countries works in the informal sector. The workers are primarily unskilled women and children. Informal sector jobs include the selling of food and commodities from mobile carts, operating pedicabs, serving as domestic helpers, street trading, and minor maintenance work. There are also categories of illegal work in the informal sector, such as prostitution and trafficking in illicit drugs.

One function in the informal sector that is advantageous to the government is the recycling of waste materials and fashioning of them into useful products. Even though the government does not learn of these workers' incomes and cannot collect tax on their products, the accumulation of waste materials is eliminated through this enterprise. All sorts of usable products are made from discarded automobile tires, glass bottles, and pieces of wood and metal.

The informal sector in developing countries exists for a number of reasons. First, the retail and service economies in the formal sector are inadequately developed to absorb all of the activities found in the informal sector. Second, demand for the products and services of the informal sector dictates that prices remain low. As such, permanent business sites are not affordable. Finally, in many cases the quality of the work or products in the informal sector is low. Nonetheless, the informal sector serves a purpose in the economic structure of these countries, and its goods and services are an important, although essentially immeasurable, part of overall monetary income.

The World Bank has recognized the impact of the informal sector in developing country economies. It provides development assistance to the poorest countries; the World Bank's aim is to help developing countries to attain sustainable economic growth. For more than 20 years, growth strategies and investment in the economic systems in developing countries has targeted the informal sector and noted its importance in providing models of entrepreneurship.

Suggested Readings: John Dickenson, *Geography of the Third World,* 2nd ed., New York: Routledge, 1996; Janet H. Momsen and Vivian Kinnaird, *Different Places, Different Voices: Gender and Development in Africa, Asia, and Latin America,* New York: Routledge, 1993.

Infrastructure. For economic development to take place, there must be mechanisms in place to support business operations. The collective set of mechanisms is called its infrastructure. Adequate transportation systems in the form of roads, railroads, and airports; communication systems; power supplies; water and electricity; and needed services (financing, equipment, personnel, etc.) are representative of the components in an economic infrastructure. Each economic activity should have all of its infrastructural needs in place to facilitate its operation and maximize its profit.

Infrastructural considerations are important in **agglomeration** economies. Industries will find it attractive to locate near similar industries to take advantage of an already established infrastructure. For example, Detroit, Michigan, was for decades the leading automobile manufacturer in the United States. Most of the major automakers were located in and around Detroit, as were hundreds of firms that supplied them with the thousands of parts and components that became part of an automobile. The prominent German economist Alfred Weber (1868–1958) referred to this form of plant clustering as "economies of association": each firm that arrives to join the agglomeration adds to the dynamic of the group.

Economists have long recognized infrastructure as one of the major factors of production, along with physical and human resources, associated industrial knowledge, and capital. If the necessary factors are not present, it is unlikely that the economic activity will be successful. In the case of developing countries following the end of **colonialism** in general, and especially in African countries, infrastructural deficiencies were very pronounced. During the colonial era, the occupying European countries developed the colony only to the extent necessary to extract and export the commodities they desired. There was no attempt at full regional development.

Consequently, the newly independent countries were faced with building the full infrastructure necessary for economic development. This became a nearly impossible task because one of the basic factors of production, capital, was in short supply. The developing countries ran into problems in another way: rapid urbanization following independence flooded cities with more people than could be supported by the urban infrastructure.

Infrastructural problems can haunt even the most developed countries. In the 1960s, Japan launched a plan to decentralize and disperse industry from its densely populated and crowded manufacturing belt along the Inland Sea from Tokyo west to northern Kyushu. In the plan, several new industrial zones were designated; all of them were located outside the major corridor. When the plan was implemented, it became clear that most of the designated areas had inadequate infrastructures to support the planned economic activities. Large capital outlays were necessary to improve the infrastructure of these places before the relocation of economic activities could occur.

Suggested Readings: P. W. Daniels and W. F. Lever, eds., *The Global Economy in Transition,* Harlow, U.K.: Longman, 1996; Anders Malmberg, "Industrial Geography: Agglomeration and Local Milieu," *Progress in Human Geography,* vol. 20 (1996).

Intensive agriculture. In the agricultural sector, any adjustments to increase inputs of labor, capital, fertilizers, pesticides, or technology to increase crop yields are representative of intensive agriculture. This widespread practice takes many forms and is used both in large-scale, technologically advanced **agribusiness** and in subsistence agricultural practices in developing countries.

Intensive agriculture is associated with the **Green Revolution,** which began in Asia in the 1950s and used new strains of rice with added fertilizers, pesticides, and high volumes of water to greatly increase crop yields. Intensive agriculture is also related to the practices of **double-cropping** and intercropping, both used extensively in Asian agriculture. Intercropping is the planting of young shoots between the rows of maturing plants. This gives the new plants more growing time, needed because they will reach maturity late in the season.

Intensive agricultural practices are found throughout South Asia, East Asia, and Southeast Asia. Rice is the primary grain throughout this part of the world, and it is grown in a labor-intensive manner. Paddy rice is grown in seedbeds and then transplanted by hand into the paddy fields. The plants are spaced as closely as possible to one another in order to gain the highest possible yield per unit area. A mark of the intensive agriculturist is to waste no land. Even small plots of a few square meters and long, narrow strips of land between roads and railroad lines come under cultivation.

Countries with large populations and limited land areas suitable for agriculture invariably engage in intensive agricultural methods. China and Japan both fit this description, and their use of agricultural land is markedly intensive.

In Western countries, intensive agricultural practices are applied to fruit and vegetable crops and dairy farming. Large truck farms and chicken and egg producers operate close to major metropolitan areas, providing needed food on a daily basis. Even the **feedlot** system of livestock raising exemplifies intensive agricultural practices by concentrating maximum numbers of livestock on a limited land area close to market.

Globally, intensive agriculture has raised the total amount of food produced in virtually every region. However, increased food production in the developing world has been offset by comparable increases in population. Consequently, food production per capita in these regions has not increased and in some countries has actually gone down.

A new form of intensive agriculture has developed in cities of the developing world. Empty lots, rooftops, and strips of land along roads are being used to grow food. These tiny urban agricultural plots, individually or collectively owned and operated, account for a significant amount of the food produced in developing countries.

As population increases in the future, it is anticipated that intensive agricultural practices will grow in importance throughout the world.

Suggested Readings: William Bender and Margaret Smith, "Population, Food, and Nutrition," *Population Bulletin*, vol. 51 (1997); Pierre R. Crosson and Norman J. Rosenberg, "Strategies for Agriculture," *Scientific American*, vol. 269 (1989).

Intervening opportunity. The concept of intervening opportunity states that the number of movements to, for example, Place A, is dependent on the number of opportunities available at Place A. Further, if similar opportunities become available closer to a consumer's origin, there will be fewer trips to Place A. For example, if Place A is 10 miles away and a shopper regularly buys pizzas from a national franchise there, the shopper will continue to do so unless that same franchise, or one similar to it, opens a store closer to the shopper's home. In this case, the new store is an intervening opportunity, one that will decrease the shopper's number of trips to Place A to buy pizzas.

Intervening opportunity is a concept initially used in the study of **migration.** The same principle applies. Migrants entering California from Mexico may have the goal of reaching Los Angeles to find employment. However, on entering the United States from Tijuana, for instance, some may find work in the San Diego area and never complete their intended trip to Los Angeles, because work in San Diego provided an intervening opportunity. Thousands of young Americans move every year from the rural areas in the Midwest in hopes of finding opportunity in the Chicago metropolitan area. It is not uncommon for many of them to locate in other urban places, such as St. Paul, Minnesota, or Madison, Wisconsin, if they find opportunities similar to those in Chicago.

The intervening opportunity concept has been used extensively in studies of economic activity. Shopping patterns, entertainment centers, and industrial activities have been studied to determine their connections with patrons and other businesses. In the 1950s, geographer Edward L. Ullman published a study in which he combined intervening opportunity within a three-part explanation of movements within an economic system.

Ullman specified that complementarity is necessary before movement can take place. That is, Place A must have a need for a product from Place B. Or, Places A and B each must have a product that the other needs. In these cases, movement can take place. Next, Ullman introduced intervening opportunity. If, for example, Place C is closer to Place A than is Place B, Place C may become the supplier of the needed product, providing the intervening opportunity. If this occurs, complementarity is established between Place A and

Place C. Complementarity still exists between Places A and B, but the degree of movement between the two is lessened.

Finally, Ullman introduced the idea of transferability. Regardless of the presence of complementarity and intervening opportunity in an economic system, movement will not occur unless there are usable transportation systems available to facilitate that movement (*see* **Accessibility**).

There are many variations on this set of concepts. Place A, for instance, may choose to create its own intervening opportunity by setting up its own product supplier in Place D, which is closer to Place A than are Places B and C. Ullman's three-concept model suggests a close relationship with the notion of **agglomeration,** a dominant theme in **economic geography.**

Suggested Readings: Keith Chapman and David Walker, *Industrial Location*, Cambridge, Mass.: Basil Blackwell, 1991; John C. Lowe and S. Moryadas, *The Geography of Movement*, Boston: Houghton Mifflin, 1975.

Irredentism. Irredentism derives from the Italian word *irredentia*, meaning unredeemed, and refers to the control of land under a foreign government when that land is claimed by another country. The claim may be based on cultural and historical connections, or it may occur when a **superimposed boundary** splits a culture group and subjects those outside their original country to the rule of another.

In Italy, the term was originally invoked during the dispute with Austria over the region of South Tyrol. This dispute between Austria and Italy emerged in 1866 and continued until 1971, when a treaty was signed by the adversaries. The Tyroleans have long sought to secede from Italy, and the Austrians have been in support of this move. At the same time, Italy claims South Tyrol. During the years of controversy, the Austrians referred to the area as *terra irredentia*, or land unredeemed.

There are other examples where irredentism has occurred. Before World War II, Adolf Hitler, Nazi Germany's leader, claimed that the Sudetenland, a region in Czechoslovakia with a sizable German population, should be returned to Germany. Hitler moved into the Sudetenland with military forces in 1938 and successfully annexed this region. Hitler also used the irredentia theme in 1939 to justify similar military actions in Poland.

More recently, Somalia claimed a region in eastern Ethiopia, the Ogaden, as their own because a high percentage of the population in that region of Ethiopia is Somali. Warfare between the two countries has broken out in recent years over this territorial dispute. Somalia has a long history of territorial disputes with neighboring countries. The Somali national flag contains five stars, each one representing land claims in Ethiopia, Djibouti, Kenya, and the hoped-for unification of the two major regions by Somalia. All of these claims are based in irredentism.

Suggested Readings: Michael Heffernan, *Twentieth Century Europe: A Political Geography*, New York: John Wiley & Sons, 1997; David Laitin and Said Samatar, *Somalia: Nation in Search of a State*, Boulder, Colo.: Westview Press, 1987.

Isarithmic map. The isarithmic map is one of the most frequently used thematic maps in **geography** and **cartography.** Maps of this type are seen daily in newspapers for reporting temperature and barometric pressure. An isarithmic map contains a number of lines, each of which represents an equal data value. In addition, the lines are assigned values in a uniform sequence. For example, if temperatures are being recorded on an isarithmic map and the low and high readings in the reporting area are 20 degrees and 85 degrees, respectively, isarithmic line values in increments of 10 from 20 to 90 would be suitable.

In the temperature map example, the cartographic process begins by plotting the individual temperatures reported at each weather station. Once this step is completed, the isarithmic lines are placed on the map. A line assigned a value of 30, for instance, would run through every point of that exact value. The 30-line could continue to be plotted between points that are below or above 30 in value. Thus, the 30-line would pass between points reporting 28 and 33. This process would continue until all points in the reporting area were represented in the series of isarithmic lines.

The term *isotherm*, meaning "equal temperature," is used to refer to this line. So, any point on the isotherm labeled 30 is assumed to have that value. Where the isotherm line goes through a point that has that value, it is obviously reporting the exact temperature. However, when the line is placed between two values, such as 29 and 34, it is assumed that a value of 30 exists somewhere between the two values. In this example, the isotherm line would be placed closer to the station reporting 30, and the assumption is that temperatures between 29 and 34 are changing uniformly across the distance between them. This may not be the case, but with the chosen 10-degree interval, a generalized pattern results. If a closer approximation of the temperature pattern is desired, and if sufficient data points are available, a 5-degree isotherm interval could be used. This would double the number of isotherms and provide a more detailed map view of the temperature range.

Isarithmic lines give the map viewer a sense of the shape and configuration of the statistical surface represented. That is, just as a contour map provides a view of the terrain mapped, an isotherm map adds an apparent third dimension to a two-dimensional map. The area itself is represented by a set of x, y horizontal coordinates, and the temperatures add a set of z values, giving an apparent vertical dimension to the array of numbers.

Isarithmic maps are used to report a number of topics, each with its own name. Among them are isochrones, representing lines of equal time; isohyets, reporting lines of equal rainfall; isovel, reporting equal wind velocity, and isagon, reporting equal magnetic declination.

Suggested Readings: Borden C. Dent, *Cartography: Thematic Map Design*, Dubuque, Iowa: Wm. C. Brown, 1996; Alan H. MacEachren, *How Maps Work*, New York: Guilford Press, 1995.

K

Kyoto Protocol. In 1979, the World Meteorological Organization and the United Nations Environmental Programme convened the first World Climate Conference and established the World Climate Program. This meeting recognized climate change to be a serious global problem. A declaration issued at the meeting called on all countries to work toward preventing potentially damaging changes in climate caused by humans. Meetings continued frequently over the next several years to refine the procedure necessary to ensure that human-induced climatic change be reduced.

In 1990, the United Nations completed a draft of its Framework Convention on Climatic Change (UNFCCC). Two years later, 154 countries signed the UNFCCC at the Earth Summit in Rio de Janeiro, Brazil. In this agreement, developed countries committed to reduce greenhouse gas emissions to 1990 levels by the year 2000 and to help developing countries to reduce emissions as well (see **Greenhouse effect**).

Two subsequent meetings, in 1995 and 1996, concluded that the initial UNFCCC commitments were not strong enough and once again affirmed that human influence on global climate change was significant. In November 1997, 171 countries met in Kyoto, Japan, and agreed to legally binding commitments on greenhouse gas emissions. The difficulty in the process is that the agreement would not be enforceable until developed countries, which collectively produce 55 percent of greenhouse gas emissions, ratify it. The document signed at this conference was called the Kyoto Protocol to the UNFCCC. Vice President Al Gore signed the document for the United States.

The fact that the United States signed the Kyoto Protocol did not legally obligate the country to comply with the stipulations in the document. In order for full compliance to occur, the U.S. Senate must ratify it, an action that the Senate was not given the opportunity to consider.

There were two reasons given by President Bill Clinton's administration for not submitting the Kyoto Protocol to the Senate for ratification: (1) the United States needed assurance that its overall economy would not suffer if stipulated emission levels were achieved; and (2) the United States would not agree to lower emissions unless the developing countries were also tasked with reducing emissions.

When George W. Bush became president in 2001, he too chose not to submit the Kyoto Protocol to the Senate for ratification, stating that a different approach to reducing greenhouse gas emissions was needed. The Bush plan, announced early in 2001, essentially placed the responsibility for reducing emissions in the hands of individual industrial companies. With the Kyoto Protocol abandoned, no subsequent global plan to reduce greenhouse gas emissions has been advanced.

Suggested Readings: Jerry Pitzl and Emily Stewart, "The U.S. Position on the Kyoto Protocol—Senate Ratification or Not?" Case 240, Institute for the Study of Diplomacy, 2000; "Changing the Climate of Opinion," *The Economist*, 12 August 2000.

L

Landlocked country. More than 40 of the world's countries do not have at least some territory bordering on an ocean. Fourteen of these countries are on the African continent, a legacy of the era of **colonialism.** During the period of European domination in Africa, which began in the late 1800s, the primary motive of the occupiers was to extract and export minerals and commodities from the interior of Africa to the coasts for shipment to Europe. Roads and railroad lines were installed to facilitate the movement of goods to the coastal cities. When the era of colonialism ended, the newly independent countries were left with the economic **infrastructure** installed by the Europeans. None of the previous colonies realized full regional development, and the lands in the interior of the continent received the least attention. As such, these countries are the poorest in Africa, and their prospects for future development are hampered by not having easy access to the sea.

Landlocked countries are at a commercial and strategic disadvantage. They must rely on agreements with neighboring countries to have access to port facilities, an important factor in international trade. In many cases, unfriendly neighbors have blocked this access. Landlocked countries are also at a disadvantage because they do not have access to the riches of the continental shelf in the offshore zone, which coastal countries claim for economic purposes (see **Exclusive economic zone**).

Without access to the sea, landlocked countries have demanded a share of the wealth found in the ocean's depths and exploited by seacoast countries. Of particular interest was the acquisition of manganese nodules, concentrated clusters of valuable metals mined from the ocean floor by developed countries (see **United Nations Convention on the Law of the Sea**).

Bolivia is the only landlocked country in Latin America. At one time, Bolivia had access to the Pacific Ocean, but it lost that land bridge in a war with Chile.

In many cases, landlocked states have acted as **buffer states** between potential adversaries. During the **cold war,** several landlocked eastern European countries came under control of the Soviet Union and served collectively as a buffer zone adjacent to western Europe and the **North Atlantic Treaty Organization** nations.

The degree of isolation experienced by landlocked states varies. The Czech Republic and Slovakia, two landlocked countries in eastern Europe, have achieved high levels of **accessibility** by road and railroad lines through adjacent countries.

The former Soviet Union was not a completely landlocked country, but its access points to the oceans were limited and distant from its major regions of population and economic activity. The Soviet Union, and the Russian Empire before it, long wanted a warm-water port. When the Soviets invaded Afghanistan in 1979, many experts thought this incursion would lead to further movement into Pakistan and eventually to the establishment of a port on the Indian Ocean. This did not occur, but the sequence of events points out how compelling it is for a country to have access to the sea.

Suggested Readings: John O'Loughlin, *Dictionary of Geopolitics*, Westport, Conn.: Greenwood Press, 1994; Clive H. Scholfield, *Global Boundaries*, vol. 1, World Boundaries Series, London: Routledge, 1994.

Language family. Such individual languages as Mandarin, French, Arabic, and Swahili each belong to a language family that has common roots in an earlier single tongue. Language families vary in size, from Indo-European, spoken by about half the world's population, to such languages as Aborigine and Papuan, with speakers only in the thousands.

The Indo-European language family is believed to have begun in prehistoric eastern Europe and western Ukraine. The speakers of the original root language were hunter-gatherers who later developed animal husbandry and early forms of agriculture. About 2500 B.C., the culture group migrated to a number of locations in Europe and to the Indian subcontinent. Over time, variations in the original root language began to occur, and individual languages in the family developed.

Three of the Indo-European languages—English, Portuguese, and Spanish—were transplanted to the Western Hemisphere during the era of **colonialism,** from about 1500 to 1800, where they are found over an extensive area. The individual languages in a language family are determined by finding words that are similar in composition and have the same meaning. For example, the English word *mother* is *madre* in Spanish, *matka* in Polish, and *meter* in Greek, all closely related versions of the term in languages within the Indo-European family.

Other prominent language families include Sino-Tibetan, Niger-Congo, Dravidian, Afro-Asiatic, Austronesian, and Austro-Asiatic. Two Asian language families have only one language each: Japanese and Korean. These two languages developed independent of the Sino-Tibetan language family found primarily in neighboring China. Japan and Korea are two examples of countries that can truly be classified as **nation-states** due to their uniformity of culture and a language unique to each.

Suggested Readings: Thomas V. Gamkrelidze and V. V. Ivanov, *The Indo-European Language and the Indo-Europeans*, 2 vols., The Hague, Netherlands: Mouton, 1990; Christopher Mosley and R. E. Asher, *Atlas of the World's Languages*, New York: Routledge, 1994.

Lesser-developed country. *See* **Core-periphery model.**

Lingua franca. The term *lingua franca* originated in the Middle Ages and refers to the language used by Arab traders to communicate with the Franks, their European trading partners living along the north coast of the Mediterranean Sea. The term is still used to identify a number of languages that have gained prominence globally and regionally to facilitate communications among dissimilar culture groups.

Language differences can deter the free flow of ideas, the exchange of goods, and the **diffusion** of innovations. To eliminate this barrier to communication, some languages have been used beyond the regions in which they are the native tongue. An example of a regional lingua franca is Swahili, which is used extensively in several countries in East Africa.

English has become the most common lingua franca. Many countries have included English instruction in their education systems. In Russia, there is a great demand for teachers of English in the schools and in the business sector, where the shift to capitalism called for more-direct communication with business counterparts in Europe and the United States. In the former Soviet Union, Russian was the lingua franca in the 15 republics.

A number of lingua francas can be found in other regions. Among them are Hindustan in South Asia, Urdu in Pakistan, and Mandarin in China. More than one billion people, the largest number of speakers of any single language, speak Mandarin. At an earlier time in history, Latin was the lingua franca throughout the Mediterranean area.

A lingua franca has developed along the border of the United States and Mexico. The language is a mixture of Spanish and English called Spanglish, and it includes word combinations from both cultures. A great deal of economic activity is taking place along this border, and Spanglish is enhancing interaction between the two countries.

Suggested Readings: Kenneth Katzner, *The Languages of the World*, New York: Funk & Wagnalls, 1986; Web site for the Summer Institute of Linguistics, www.sil.org (includes the Language Family Index).

Loess. Loess refers to a fine silty material that is wind blown and eventually deposited in thick beds. The material is yellow or buff in color and is very fertile. Some of the world's most productive agricultural regions contain significant amounts of loess. There are extensive loess deposits in the United States, Central Europe, Central Asia, Argentina, and China.

Winds pick up fine particulate material and transport it to areas of deposition. During the deglaciation period, which began 11,000 years ago, ice grinding on rock produced a fine powdery material that was picked up by wind and transplanted to distant locations in what are now the Great Plains of the American Midwest. In this manner, large areas of the Midwest accumulated loess plains. The Loess Plateau in northern China was formed as winds from Mongolia picked up loess soils from the Ordos Desert. This deposit of loess is by far the largest single accumulation in the world. Stretching across thousands of square miles, the loess layers average 20 to 30 meters in depth. In some valleys, loess thickness exceeds 200 meters.

Loess soil compacts very tightly because of the small particle size. In China's Loess Plateau, the Chinese carved extensive cave-like dwellings out of the thick loess layers. These caves served as homes for agriculturists who worked the fertile loess soil. Unfortunately, loess soil is highly prone to erosion, and in one giant flood early in the twentieth century, thousands of Chinese lost their lives as raging waters destroyed the loess dwellings they occupied.

Every year about 1.5 billion tons of soil erodes from the Loess Plateau. The loess is carried away by the major river of northern China, the Hwang He (Yellow River). The Hwang He appears yellow during flood seasons because of the color imparted by the suspended loess particles. About six centimeters of loess soil accumulate every year at the bottom of the Hwang He as it crosses the level North China Plain. Over time, this accumulation has raised the river bottom to a height of 10 meters above the surrounding floodplain. Great levees have been in place for years to contain the elevated river. At times the levees break and a concerted effort is required of all people in the area to fill the gap and contain the river within its channel. The Hwang He has been called China's Sorrow because of this difficult situation.

Suggested Readings: Ian Livingston and Andrew Warren, *Aeolian Geomorphology: An Introduction*, Harlow, U.K.: Addison Wesley Longman, 1996; Songgiao Zhao, *Geography of China: Environment, Resources, Population, and Development*, New York: John Wiley & Sons, 1994.

Long lot system. The settlement pattern marked by long, narrow agricultural lots facing a river or road is found in a number of locations in the United States, western Europe, Argentina, Brazil, and in Quebec, Canada. In North America, the system dates to colonial times, when rivers were the main corridors of transportation. Lots with 130–180-meter fronts on the St. Lawrence River extended as rectangles for several kilometers inland. Each farm had access to river water and transportation.

As population increased in French Canada and available fronts on the river were all claimed, a road was built at the inland terminus of the long lots. Another series of long lots was then extended farther inland to accommodate the expanding agricultural sector. The roads provided access either directly to market centers or to points on the river, where long-distance transportation was available.

The long lot system is still in use in French Canada, although it has experienced some adjustments over the years. Some of the lots, already narrow from the original plan, were further narrowed as heirs to the land divided them along their length. In some cases, the long lots were divided to an extent that limited their usefulness for agriculture.

When the British sent the Acadians of the Canadian Maritime Provinces out of the country in the early nineteenth century, they settled in southern Louisiana. There they established the long lot system of agricultural settlement.

The long lot system is also found in several areas in Texas, especially along the Rio Grande and the Red River. Long lots are located along southward-flowing rivers at the borders of Colorado and New Mexico and in limited areas in Illinois, Indiana, and Wisconsin.

Suggested Readings: David B. Grigg, *An Introduction to Agricultural Geography*, New York: Routledge, 1995; Tom L. McKnight, *Regional Geography of the United States and Canada*, Englewood Cliffs, N.J.: Prentice Hall, 1992.

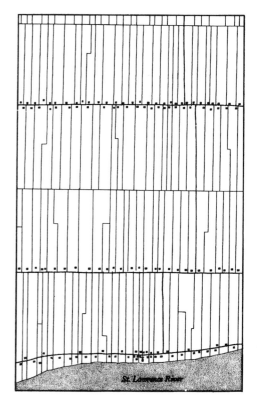

Long lot system. *Source: Canada before Confederation: A Study in Historical Geography,* by R. Cole Harris and John Warkentin. Copyright 1974 by Oxford University Press, Inc. Used by permission of Oxford University Press.

M

Mackinder, Halford J. (1861–1947). The British geographer Halford J. Mackinder was one of geography's most important advocates in the late nineteenth century. During this time, geographers were formulating the focus of the discipline so it might be included in the new university systems. Mackinder, along with German geographer **Friedrich Ratzel,** American geographer **William Morris Davis,** and others, was convinced that geography should be the science that studies the interface between nature and culture, an early reference to the important contemporary theme of human–environment interaction.

If it seems strange that geography would seek to identify itself intellectually at that late date, it is pertinent to note that the great era of exploration was ending; most land and sea areas on the earth's surface had been discovered, explored, inventoried, and charted. For many in the discipline, the golden age of geography was closing and a new direction, one that would have a sound intellectual basis suitable for university acceptance, was required.

Halford J. Mackinder. *Source:* Library of Congress.

Mackinder became a reader in geography at Oxford University in 1887, a time when the discipline was firmly establishing itself in higher education. He recommended the establishment of a geographic center at Oxford in 1895; the center came into existence four years later. Mackinder realized the importance of history and geography working together, a theme that is today followed in **historical geography** and in process studies. His recommended approach in this regard was to re-create past geographies, noting how the sequence of changes over time produced current settings.

Mackinder is also prominent in **geopolitics** for his heartland theory. This theory contends that the great Eurasian heartland, the most inaccessible region in the world, is essentially invulnerable from attack by sea powers. The coastlands, however, are vulnerable to attack from both the heartland and attacks from the sea. In his 1919 book, *Democratic Ideas and Reality*, Mackinder succinctly stated his heartland theory (p. 113):

Who rules East Europe commands the Heartland.
Who rules the Heartland commands the World Island;
Who rules the World Island commands the world.

The World Island, in Mackinder's theory, is the combined landmasses of Eurasia and Africa. In the age of sea-power dominance, Mackinder's notions had merit. Everything changed in time, however, with the advent of long-distance aircraft and then the intercontinental ballistic missile. In the modern era, every point on the earth's surface is potentially vulnerable to large-scale attack within minutes. However, one aspect of Mackinder's theory may still hold true if the focus is on actual ground invasion and occupation. The expansive Eurasian landmass in this context remains essentially invulnerable. Nazi German leader Adolf Hitler discovered this in World War II, when he sent German troops into the Soviet Union. French emperor Napoleon Bonaparte learned the same lesson years earlier in his attempt to invade and conquer Russia.

Suggested Readings: Paul Cloke et al., *Approaching Human Geography: An Introduction to Contemporary Theoretical Debates*, London: Guilford Press, 1991; Geoffrey J. Martin and Preston E. James, *All Possible Worlds: A History of Geographical Ideas*, 3rd ed., New York: John Wiley & Sons, 1992.

Malthus, Thomas Robert (1760–1834). Thomas Robert Malthus was an English economist who is renowned for his essay signaling concern about disparities between population increase and food production. His "Essay on the Principle of Populations As It Affects the Further Improvement of Society," published in 1798, was widely read and commented on, both positively and negatively, for years. Malthus contended that human population was increasing geometrically, whereas food supplies necessary to support the growing numbers of people were expanding arithmetically.

Malthus had no way of knowing of the significant number of advances in agricultural technology that were to occur in subsequent years and the new agricultural regions that would be opened. Nor could he have known the degree of population increase that would occur through both the nineteenth and twentieth centuries. Had he known that world population would surpass six billion by 2000, his predictions would have been even more dire.

According to Malthus, there were positive checks on population growth that could be invoked. These included celibacy and postponing marriage so that childbearing would be delayed. Negative checks on population growth were not so pleasant, Malthus warned: war, poverty, pestilence, and famine would result if steps were not taken to curb population growth.

Charles Darwin, the eminent nineteenth-century English naturalist, was keenly aware of Malthus's work. He used some of his findings in developing his famous 1859 book on evolution, *The Origin of Species.*

In the late nineteenth century, concern about population outstripping food production was lessened as new agricultural lands were opened to full production in eastern Europe and the Crimea. Another immense increase in food production was realized when the Midwest agricultural region and the Great Plains wheat belt in the United States and Canada were in full production. This unequaled agricultural heartland came to be known as the breadbasket to the world. Yet, world population continued to grow at high rates, and by the 1950s, Malthusian concerns were again being raised.

A major response to the need for more food was the **Green Revolution,** beginning in the 1950s, an effort to develop higher-yielding strains of rice and wheat. The Green Revolution was particularly successful in India, although the process calling for high inputs of fertilizer, pesticides, and water was quite expensive. Because of the high cost of implementation, many regions, especially in Sub-Saharan Africa, could not afford to grow the new grains. Despite significant increases in food output in recent decades, starvation is still experienced in some regions of the world. Particularly hard hit have been such countries as Somalia and the Sudan, where shortages result from both an inability to produce enough food locally and difficulties in making food available from outside sources. Problems related to distribution are found even within individual countries. In India, for instance, local political situations work against the easy transfer of grains from one part of the country to another.

Recent efforts to invoke strict family planning in fast-growing countries and the fostering of **sustainable development** programs are identified as being neo-Malthusian in concept. These efforts are in place to avert the continuing **population explosion** that characterizes major regions in the developing world.

The basic premise offered by Malthus more than 200 years ago appears to be eminently valid today. The race between population growth and food production, it seems, will continue well into the future.

Suggested Readings: J. Dupaquier and A. Fauve-Chamoux, *Malthus Past and Present*, New York: Academic Press, 1983; Robert W. McColl and Youguan Kou, "Feeding China's Millions," *Geographical Review*, vol. 80 (1990).

Maquiladoras. The region along the United States–Mexico border has grown steadily in recent decades. The economic engine driving this growth is the 2,500 factories, or maquiladoras, first established in 1965 and greatly expanded since the 1980s. The term *maquiladora* derives from the Spanish word *maquilar*, which means to receive a payment for the milling of corn. The maquiladora program was established by the Mexican government in hopes of employing displaced agricultural workers when the earlier bracero program, in which millions of Mexican farm laborers worked in U.S. fields, terminated.

Originally called the Border Industrialization Program, the maquiladora plan provided subsidized land and tax breaks to U.S. firms if they would locate across the border in Mexico and employ Mexican workers. In addition, all the goods produced in the maquiladoras would be shipped tariff free back to the United States. The only cost to the United States was a charge for the value added during Mexican production.

The major benefit of this system to Mexico is employment for people in relatively high-paying jobs. As many as 500,000 workers are employed in maquiladora plants. For the United States, the benefits include low labor costs (*see* **Outsourcing**) and the absence of import duties on finished goods.

There are some problems associated with this booming enterprise, however. In Mexico, floods of migrants have come to a region that does not have an adequate social **infrastructure** to sustain them. Housing shortages and poor sewage and sanitation systems plague many of the overcrowded settlements in the Mexican border towns. Serious outbreaks of such diseases as hepatitis and typhoid have frequently occurred. There has also been significant pollution of the Rio Grande from the casual disposal of industrial waste products. Both countries have agreed to continue intensive cleanup efforts to protect this valuable river. The United States has been criticized for allowing industries to set up operations in Mexico and deprive its own citizens of employment opportunities. In this regard, the maquiladora operation represents another example of the **globalization** of economic activity.

One of the provisions in the **North American Free Trade Agreement** (NAFTA) stipulates that the Mexican government gradually phase out the maquiladora program. Further, under NAFTA, products made in the maquiladora plants may also be marketed in Mexico.

Suggested Readings: J. M. Szekely, *Manufacturing across Borders and Oceans: Japan, the United States, and Mexico*, San Diego: Center for U.S.–Mexican Studies, University of California, 1991; Melissa W. Wright, "Crossing the Factory Frontier: Gender, Place and Power in the Mexican Maquiladora," *Antipode*, vol. 29 (1997).

Market gardening. The **intensive agriculture** practice of market gardening involves the production of vegetables and fruits primarily for sale in metropolitan areas. The term *market garden* comes from nineteenth-century England, and the concept has been used synonymously with truck gardening, the American version.

The production of perishable food products near the market is a key factor in **von Thunen's land use model,** developed in the early 1800s by German economist Johann Heinrich von Thunen. In von Thunen's time and now, location close to consumers is essential, given the perishable nature of the product. Lettuce, tomatoes, and asparagus, for example, must be shipped and marketed in the shortest possible time in order to maintain freshness.

A general rule in truck farming holds that the distances to market not exceed 24–36 hours. This rule has changed significantly in recent years with the refrigerated truck and railroad car. Now it is possible for agricultural fields in Florida and Texas to supply the eastern seaboard with fruits and vegetables in the winter when local operations are shut down for the season.

Market gardening has become specialized. For example, the Delmarva Peninsula, a productive agricultural region composed of parts of Delaware, Maryland, and Virginia, has farms that specialize only in potatoes. Farms in other regions specialize in citrus products and tree fruits. Specialization of product type in market gardens in another example of **agribusiness.** Vast fields of lettuce and tomatoes near Yuma, Arizona, for instance, provide these items to urban centers from Phoenix to Los Angeles to St. Louis. Depending on the crop grown, market gardens may require the hiring of migratory workers, most of whom travel from Mexico for employment in the fields during harvest season.

Market farms are found in Europe, where they provide such items as olives, fruits, and wine in addition to the standard vegetable products. Proximity to urban centers is the rule. In the United States, these operations are found in a number of regional concentrations stretching from southern California to the eastern seaboard. In California, an abundance of market gardens is located in the rich Central Valley and on the Pacific coastlands south of San Francisco. Others cluster in and near the Los Angeles Basin, serving that large metropolitan area. Another area of concentration is found along the Gulf of Mexico, from Texas through Louisiana, Mississippi, Alabama, and the Florida Panhandle. The market gardens in the South and the Southeast are growing rapidly in response to increasing demands for food locally and in the northern states.

By far the largest concentration of market gardens is found along the eastern seaboard, from Virginia to Long Island, New York. This is an ideal location because of its proximity to the millions of people in **Megalopolis** (the great cities of the Northeast), its productive alluvial soils, a relatively mild climate that allows farming for eight to nine months a year, and good transportation facilities. There are also extensive market garden activities along the southern shores of Lake Erie and Lake Ontario, which serve urban centers in the old North American Manufacturing Belt.

As urban centers continue to grow and population increases in the United States, market garden operations will expand to keep up with higher demands for their food products.

Suggested Readings: John Tarrant, "Farming and Food," in *The Illustrated Encyclopedia of World Geography*, New York: Oxford University Press, 1991; Iowa State University agricultural Web site, www.ag.iastate.edu.

Median-line principle. One of the provisions of the **United Nations Convention on the Law of the Sea** (UNCLOS) was the creation of an **exclusive economic zone** (EEZ) of up to 200 nautical miles from shore. Within this zone, countries have exclusive rights to explore, exploit, and manage all resources in both the seabed and the waters above. The EEZ may be extended up to 350 nautical miles if the continental shelf extends that far. Problems occur, however, when countries lie closer to each other and neither has the full 200-nautical-mile EEZ. In cases of this type, the median-line principle is invoked. For example, Australia and Indonesia are about 300 nautical miles from each other across the Timor Sea. A line 150 nautical miles from each, the median line, defines the limit of each EEZ. Cases like this one are fairly easily resolved.

For many countries with seacoast locations distant from other countries, the EEZ provision is positive for economic development. A continental shelf may contain mineral resources suitable for exploitation, including oil and gas reserves, and the waters above the relatively shallow continental shelf provide excellent fishing grounds.

Some regions of the world have extremely complex EEZ situations brought on by close proximity of countries one to another and claims to ownership of adjacent seas or parts of them. Perhaps the most complex region, and clearly the most contentious one in this sense, is the South China Sea, claimed in part or whole by eight countries. The areal extent of their claims in many cases overlap one another. To further complicate the matter, China, Taiwan, and Vietnam claim all of the South China Sea as their own, citing, for instance, 2,000-year-old historical evidence of ownership.

This multinational dispute only increases in intensity as time goes by, mainly because areas within the South China Sea contain reserves of oil and natural gas, two valuable fuels. Further, important sea lines of commerce for Middle East oil enter the South China Sea through the Strait of Malacca and proceed to Japan, a major fuel user. Any serious delays in the shipment of commodities through the South China Sea would be disruptive to the world economy.

There have been conflicts in the past. For example, China took the Paracel Islands by force in 1974 from South Vietnam. In 1995, China occupied Mischief Reef, a small atoll in the Spratly Island group, a place also claimed by the Philippines. Although the furor surrounding this incident seems to have cooled, there is high potential for further unrest in this key region.

Suggested Readings: Gerald H. Blake, *Maritime Boundaries*, vol. 5, World Boundaries Series, London: Routledge, 1994; Jerry Pitzl, "Mischief on Mischief Reef: Chinese Adventures in the Spratly Islands," Case 246, Institute for the Study of Diplomacy, 2001.

Megalopolis. The word *megalopolis* comes from the Greek *mega*, large or great, and *polis*, city. The eminent French geographer Jean Gottmann made specific reference to the highly urbanized U.S. coastal corridor from Boston, Massachusetts, to Washington, D.C., as Megalopolis. He had studied the eastern seaboard through the 1930s and 1940s and in the 1950s was named director of the Twentieth Century Fund's research project titled "A Study of Megalopolis."

Gottmann's initial study of Megalopolis in 1950 was based in large part on a **census** document titled *State Economic Areas*. This work used a statistical base for identifying counties as either metropolitan or nonmetropolitan. The map produced in the study clearly indicated an almost unbroken series of metropolitan counties stretching from the suburbs of Boson south to Washington, D.C., and its suburbs. It was clear from this map that a new urban form was emerging, one in which cities

Jean Gottmann. *Source:* Library of Congress.

within Megalopolis had continued to expand their boundaries until they reached the boundaries of those to the north and south. What was emerging was a single developed urban area stretching more than 400 miles along the eastern seaboard.

In his follow-up study in 1960, Gottmann found that Megalopolis had expanded even further. Several counties that were designated nonmetropolitan in 1950 had become metropolitan. It seemed clear as well to Gottmann that the northern and southern limits of Megalopolis would begin to reach farther. He suggested that Richmond and Norfolk, Virginia, would become part of Megalopolis in a short time. In 1960, Gottmann published his classic work, *Megalopolis: The Urbanized Northeastern Seaboard of the United States,* a detailed analysis of this growing concentration of people and socioeconomic activities.

Many of the major cities in Megalopolis were originally situated on the **fall line,** the point at which waterfalls presented a break in upstream travel, and along other rivers emptying into the Atlantic Ocean. Among them are New York City, on the Hudson River; Washington, D.C., on the Potomac; Hartford on the Connecticut; and Richmond on the James River. By 2000 it was clear that the boundaries of Megalopolis had reached north to Portland, Maine, and south to Virginia Beach, Virginia. Nonetheless, the region still retains its nickname, "Boswash" (Boston to Washington). The population of Megalopolis had increased to more than 50 million by the twentieth century's end and growth will certainly continue in the future.

There are two other large urban integrations in North America. One stretches along the St. Lawrence River from Quebec City through Montreal, Canada, and Chicago, Illinois, and includes a string of prominent cities on the south shore of the Great Lakes. The U.S. segment runs from Chicago to Pittsburgh, Pennsylvania, and has been nicknamed "Chipitts." Another can be found in a nearly unbroken sequence of built-up areas from San Francisco to San Diego. "Sansan" is its familiar name. Megalopolitan complexes are building as well in Latin America, Europe, and Asia as urbanization trends continue worldwide.

Suggested Readings: Jean Gottmann, *Megalopolis: The Urbanized Northeastern Seaboard of the United States*, Cambridge: MIT Press, 1961; Jean Gottmann, *Megalopolis Revisited: 25 Years Later*, College Park: University of Maryland, Institute for Urban Studies, 1987; Jean Gottmann and R. A. Harper, *Since Megalopolis*, Baltimore: Johns Hopkins University Press, 1990.

Melting pot. The notion of the melting pot, the merging of many ethnic characteristics to create a new identity, is particularly American in origin. It was born in the century of migration (1815–1915), during which millions of people from dozens of primarily European countries came to the United States and Canada to make a new life.

The melting pot idea is idealistic and reflects a somewhat naive although noble belief that after a period of time in the United States, individuals would leave their old cultural characteristics behind and become members of a unique American culture. The belief was that a transformation of this magnitude would occur through the full processes of **acculturation,** in which members of another culture group change in order to make their way in a new place, and **assimilation,** the shedding of all the old cultural attributes and the complete merging within the new society.

Is there an identifiable American culture? Particular attributes, such as language, dress, food preferences, and religion, show that Americans are exceptionally diverse. Even the common language, English, has strong regional differences and its use is far from uniform.

Pockets of strong ethnic identity mark the country: for example, Italian and Greek clusters in Chicago, Hispanic concentrations in the Southwest and in a number of major cities throughout the country, and Irish neighborhoods in Boston. In recent years, more migrants have arrived from Asian countries. Hmong, Vietnamese, and Chinese, to mention only a few ethnic groups, have established communities at a number of locations in the United States. Unlike the European groups before them, they have maintained virtually all aspects of their native culture and have not completely mixed with the local populace.

The retention of original cultural attributes and the clustering of like ethnic groups serves at least two important purposes: (1) there is strength in numbers, and it is always more comfortable to be with members of your own ethnic background; and (2) the established community in a new country provides a destination for recent arrivals from the country of origin.

Adoption of English has been suggested as the first step toward moving the melting process along. Clearly, a working knowledge of English is important in the United States. It is the language of commerce and business, and it is essential for daily living. Yet, many new arrivals learn English in order to make essential contacts for training and employment but use their native language at home. In public schools that host large numbers of new immigrant children, teachers and teachers' aides may be required to conduct classes in more than one language, or at least make the lessons understandable to non-English-speaking students. This is a practice that runs counter to the melting-pot idea.

Worldwide there is evidence of a resurgence of cultural identity and a strong insistence on retaining original ethnic identity. It would appear that the melting-pot notion has yet to take root in most regions. In fact, the most recent focus addresses the recognizable diversity within groups.

Suggested Readings: James P. Allen and Eugene Turner, *We the People: An Atlas of America's Ethnic Diversity*, New York: Macmillan, 1988; Allan G. Noble, *To Build in a New Land: Ethnic Landscapes in North America*, Baltimore: Johns Hopkins University Press, 1992.

Mental map. A mental map is a spatial image of a place that is carried in the mind. The place may be as small as a backyard or even a room. It may be as large as the entire world or, if one is interested in astronomy and the locations of the stars and planets, as large as the sky. The mental map represents an individual's personal perspective of a place. As such, the details recorded in the mind reflect those best known and favored.

It may be useful to think of a place with which one is familiar to get a sense of the notion of mental maps. For instance, a favorite shopping mall or one's own neighborhood. Particular features that stand out in this spatial image might include shops or neighborhood features that one is drawn to for particular reasons or that are favored over other features. In this sense, the mental map reflects individual knowledge of particular places and is also an indicator of attitudes toward aspects of a place.

Drawing a mental map of a place can also give an indication of how well a person knows the spatial arrangement of elements in that place. When tasked with drawing a map of the states in the United States from memory, people are likely to more accurately portray that part of the country in which they live. When an exercise of this type is expanded to the global scale, people may be supremely challenged. Just getting the continents and oceans correctly arranged would be difficult unless one had studied this topic.

Mental maps are useful in organizing information about places, remembering spatial features of areas visited, and as a reference for finding a place or giving someone else directions.

The use of mental maps was formalized in the early 1970s by British geographers Peter Gould and Rodney White in studies of the residential preferences of groups of people in particular locations. Interesting patterns emerged as the data was collected and mapped. For example, one study asked people in Pennsylvania to state the location in the United States where they would most like to live. The resulting map showed a high preference for the home state and those surrounding it and a very low preference for states in the South. When people in the South were asked the same question, the resulting map showed preference for their home region and low value for the northern tier of states. Residential preference studies represent a good example of research in the area of **environmental perception** and are reflective of one's knowledge of, and attitudes toward, places.

Suggested Readings: Peter Gould and Rodney White, *Mental Maps*, 2nd ed., Boston: Allen & Unwin, 1986; R. J. Johnston et al., *The Dictionary of Human Geography*, 2nd ed., Oxford, U.K.: Basil Blackwell, 1986.

Mercantilism. From the fourteenth century through the end of the eighteenth century, Europe was the center of monumental changes in economic systems and international expansion. Following the end of the feudal era, countries in Europe began extensive trading with one another. Profit and the accumulation of wealth were primary motives for this activity. During this period, the second **Agricultural Revolution** was well underway, and from 1650 to 1750 the **Commercial Revolution,** reflective of the advent of new and more powerful ocean-going ships, was opening markets throughout the known world. Spain and Portugal had established colonies in Latin America, and the British, Dutch, and French were developing business activities in Africa, Asia, and North America.

The guiding economic philosophy of this era was mercantilism, the insistence that state government use its power to manage the economy and increase national wealth by regulating foreign trade. This was accomplished by stressing the flow of exports over imports, the production and sale of manufactured goods as opposed to agricultural products or commodities, and the acquisition of precious metals. The Spanish were particularly successful in accessing large volumes of gold and silver in Latin America and shipping these riches home. It was an important aspect of mercantilism to stress foreign trade over domestic trade. The whole idea of mercantilism was the accumulation of wealth, and the primary measure of success in this regard was gaining relative advantage over other European countries.

This was an era of intense international rivalry as countries maneuvered to gain military and industrial supremacy. A number of key mercantile cities emerged as centers of commercial activity and the points of accumulation of great wealth. Amsterdam, London, Lisbon, and Madrid are all representative of these major centers of influence.

Mercantilism is one of a number of phases in the development of the international economic system. The next phase to follow mercantilism was the **Industrial Revolution** of the late eighteenth century, a time of unprecedented change in manufacturing, city growth, and international economic outreach. The conceptual base of mercantilism, the accumulation of wealth and intense country rivalry in the economic realm, helped to justify and further the acquisition of colonies in Africa and Asia. The era of **colonialism** ensured the supply of agricultural products not available in Europe and minerals needed in the burgeoning industrial processes.

Suggested Readings: P. T. Ellsworth and J. Clark Leith, *The International Economy*, New York: Macmillan, 1984; Paul R. Krugman, *Rethinking International Trade*, Cambridge, Mass.: MIT Press, 1990.

Metes and bounds system. The land survey system that uses visible landscape reference points to delineate a land holding is referred to as the metes and bounds system. This system invariably produces an irregularly shaped land holding, one that may be very difficult to resurvey if some of the features used in mapping have shifted or disappeared.

An example of a metes and bounds legal description would appear something like this:

> At the fork in Hemlock
>> Creek, from that
>> Southwesterly one-eighth mile to the
>> Lone oak tree, from that
>> East one-sixteenth mile to the footbridge
>> Over Hemlock Creek, from
>> That northerly along the
>> West bank of Hemlock
>> Creek to the first point.

It is easy to see that a legal description based on these points could be troublesome years later. To begin with, the creek may shift its location or dry up. The loan oak tree may die and be removed. The footbridge over Hemlock Creek could be removed as well; or it could be relocated along the creek. Any of these changes could lead to difficult interpretations should it be necessary at some point to prove ownership of the land, or at the time of sale. Legal litigation is not uncommon in situations involving lands surveyed under the metes and bounds system.

Areas of the United States surveyed under the metes and bounds system include a large segment of the eastern seaboard, stretching from Maine to coastal Georgia and extending inland to Kentucky and Tennessee. Another section is found along the lower Mississippi River, in Louisiana and Mississippi. A small portion of western Alabama near the coast of the Gulf of Mexico also has land surveyed by the metes and bounds system. The same is true in a large area of east Texas. Finally, sections of coastal California from San Francisco to the Los Angeles Basin include metes and bounds areas.

The metes and bounds system is reflected to a great extent in the shapes of counties within these areas. The same irregularity is apparent in county shapes.

A land ordinance of 1785 dictated a radically different land survey system for the remainder of the United States. The **township and range survey** was based on a rectangular grid. The new survey was first used in Ohio, at the eastern end of the Northwest Territory. All land north of the Ohio River and west of Pennsylvania was destined to be surveyed in the new manner.

Suggested Readings: John Fraser Hart, *The Rural Landscape*, Baltimore: Johns Hopkins University Press, 1998; Edward T. Price, *Dividing the Land: Early American Beginnings of Our Private Property Mosaic*, Chicago: University of Chicago Press, 1995.

Metropolitan statistical area. A metropolitan statistical area (MSA) is a metropolitan area (MA) that includes at least one city with 50,000 or more inhabitants, or an urbanized area with a total population of 100,000 or more. Before the era of suburbanization, data collected for individual towns and cities truly represented those places. But when settlement began spreading beyond the defined limits of municipalities, more people and activities began to occupy the new suburban settings, and data exclusive to the central city was no longer adequate to describe the emerging metropolitan area.

The term *metropolitan area* became an official designation of the U.S. Office of Management and Budget in 1990. Its conceptual base, however, reaches back to the mid-twentieth century. Generally, an MA consists of a core urban area with large population numbers and adjacent communities that have a high degree of economic and social integration with the core. Over time, the standards for identifying MAs have changed, but the general definition has held relatively constant.

In 1949, in response to the first formidable waves of suburbanization following the end of World War II, the standard metropolitan area (SMA) was designated. Data began to be collected at this time for the entire MA in addition to individual towns and cities. In 1959, a name change was made to standard metropolitan statistical area (SMSA), and in 1983, the designator became metropolitan statistical area.

For the New England region, the minimum population is 75,000. Another stipulation specifies the county that contains the largest city as the central county. Adjacent counties that have at least 50 percent of their population in the urbanized area of the largest city are part of the MSA if they are closely associated with the central county in terms of commuting to the central county and are urban in character. In New England, the MSAs are based in cities and towns.

If an MSA has a population of one million or more, it may be designated a consolidated MSA (CMSA) if the separate components meet the basic standard for an MSA and local opinion supports inclusion of the area. If these criteria are met, the component is designated a primary metropolitan statistical area (PMSA) within the CMSA.

Following are some examples of various MSAs as listed in the census. Population numbers are based on estimates as of July 1, 1992.

Orlando, FL MSA	1,305,000
Lake County	161,000

Orange County	715,000
Osceola County	119,000
Seminole County	310,000

Orlando is designated an MSA because the counties comprising the area meet the basic standards for designation as a PMSA. Note that the total population of the four counties equals that of the MSA.

In the next example, a CMSA is composed of several PMSAs.

Philadelphia–Wilmington–Atlantic City, PA–NJ–DE–MD CMSA	5,939,000
Atlantic–Cape May, NJ PMSA	326,000
Philadelphia, PA–NJ PMSA	4,944,000
Vineland–Millville–Bridgeton, NJ PMSA	138,000
Wilmington–Newark DE–MD PMSA	580,000

This CMSA includes PMSAs that have counties in four states. There are four PMSAs within the CMSA. Note that the Philadelphia–Wilmington–Atlantic City CMSA gets its name because these three PMSAs have the largest populations of all the components. Finally, each of the PMSAs in this example is composed of a number of counties, with Philadelphia having nine counties in its PMSA.

The MSA system of reporting data on populations and functions reflects the dynamic changes that have taken place in the settlement pattern of the United States in the twentieth century. The country has changed from an agricultural base to preeminence in industry and then to a dominant service-centered economy and high-technology giant. These changes in the economic structure occurred within a rapid shift of settlement patterns to urbanization and then suburbanization. The MSA system of reporting reflects these dynamic changes.

Canada defines a metropolitan area as a very large urban area that has a high degree of economic and social integration. The Canadian counterpart of the MSA is the census metropolitan area (CMA), with Toronto having the largest population (more than 3.5 million in the late 1990s).

Suggested Readings: *Canada Year Book*, Ottawa: Dominion Bureau of Statistics, annual; David T. Herbert and Colin J. Thomas, *Cities in Space, City as Place*, New York: John Wiley & Sons, 1997; U.S. Bureau of the Census, *Statistical Abstract of the United States*, Washington, D.C.: Author, annual.

Microclimates. The term *microclimate* has several applications in geography. Microclimate refers to the climate in a small area. Climate may change appreciably over a relatively short distance, depending on variations in landform, wind patterns, vegetation cover, and orientation to the sun. The narrow strip of land along an ocean coast may have a decidedly different climate from a place only a few miles inland.

One of the most striking examples of microclimate is the **urban heat island.** Building materials used in cities absorb more of the sun's shortwave radiation and transform that energy into long-wave radiation, or sensible heat. Thus, the average temperature of the city center is warmer than other areas of the city, the surrounding suburbs, and the rural areas beyond.

A microclimate can exist in an area as small as a few hundred square feet or extend to a lengthy coastline. The type of forest cover can make a difference in the climate of the forest floor. A pine forest, for example, cuts out about 30 percent of incoming sunlight. A birch forest, on the other hand, cuts out 60 percent of incoming sunlight. Everything else being equal, the microclimates of each of these forest floors are measurably different.

Agriculturists are aware of microclimatic differences. On rolling terrain, some fields are in partial shadow longer than others. Soil temperatures differ in these instances, and the keen agriculturist plans crop locations accordingly.

During the long period of an ecological succession, one of a series of distinct microclimates accompanies each plant community in the gradual transition from pioneer stage to the climax vegetative cover. Early plant communities are tolerant of high solar radiation and changeable soil temperatures. Once these pioneer-stage plants have set root and produced humus over a long enough period of time, bacteria and other insect life inhabit the place. Fallen and decaying leaves add to the nutrient level of the surface microclimate. At a suitable time, a successor plant community moves in and displaces the pioneer group. The new plants have a heavier branch and leaf configuration, which cool the air and soil, creating yet another microclimate at the surface.

Agricultural origins in prehistory can be traced to microclimates. In the mountain arc surrounding the valley of the Tigris and Euphrates Rivers in Southwest Asia, a series of varied microclimates are found. The many slopes and valleys, wind patterns, and soil types found within the region near the ancient city of Jarmo provided abundant opportunities for growing a wide variety of grains. Theory holds that early humans used this grain and eventually realized that the seeds could be used to grow a new crop the following growing season. There are, of course, a number of other theories of agricultural origin (for example, *see* **Carl Sauer**).

Suggested Readings: Wallace E. Akin, *Global Patterns: Climate, Vegetation, and Soil,* Norman: University of Oklahoma Press, 1991; Edward Linacre, *Climate Data and Resources,* New York: Routledge, 1992.

Migration. Theory holds that humans originated in East Africa. From this region, in time, groups of people migrated in all directions. Migration in its various forms has been occurring since that time. The mass movements of human groups have led to the development of distinct cultures throughout the inhabited world. Subsequent migrations out of established **culture hearth**s resulted in exchanges of ideas, goods, and processes. Migration and human encounter is a prime example of **spatial interaction.**

Migration takes place on all scales, from intercontinental to intraregional. The actual relocation of residence may be generated by so-called **push and pull**

factors. That is, a culture group may find it intolerable to stay at a location where the political regime has changed and the group is endangered. Nazi Germany in the 1930s was a clear threat to the Jewish population, and many Jews left for other regions. In this case, a compelling push factor existed. A pull factor is usually associated with the migration of young people from small towns and rural areas in search of employment in large cities. In this case, the pull of more-lucrative jobs is the key motivator.

Both push and pull factors may be in play in the same migration. Consider the mass migrations of African Americans from the South in the Reconstruction years following the American Civil War and continuing into the twentieth century. The push was a shortage of jobs in the South and the prejudicial social setting in which they lived, whereas the pull was provided by employment opportunities in northern and midwestern cities as the **Industrial Revolution** took hold in the United States and Canada.

Long-distance migrations have taken place in the past and are occurring today. The massive slave trade during the colonial period, from about 1500 to 1800, is a classic example of a forced migration. Millions of Africans were uprooted from their homes and forced to move to countries in the Western Hemisphere. They were sold as property and set to work on farms and plantations. Siberian labor camps were the destinations for thousands of people in Russia (and the Soviet Union) during periods of repression. The past several decades have seen millions of Asians from China, Vietnam, the Philippines, and other countries migrate to the United States and Canada in search of employment and a new life. This **cultural diffusion** is continuously occurring and bringing change to both the migrants and the regions in which they settle.

The century of migration, as it has been called, marked the period from 1815 to 1915. During that era, millions of people, primarily from European countries, migrated to the United States and Canada. This massive flow of people of various origins represented a transplantation of culture of unprecedented importance. The European immigrants changed the ethnic base of both the United States and Canada, and this influx of people led to the notion of the **melting pot,** the belief that all who entered the new society would leave behind their native cultures and become members of an American culture.

Migrations may happen when employment opportunities open in countries where the local supply of labor has diminished. Some western European countries that were first to complete the **demographic transition** now have lower numbers of people of working age. To fill this void, thousands have migrated to these countries from Spain, Greece, Turkey, and the North African region.

Conflicts have been the motivator for countless migrations through time. The 2001 war against terrorism in Afghanistan resulted in tens of thousands of Afghanis being forced to migrate from their homes. These people joined the growing legions of **refugees,** people forced to leave their home country. The United Nations estimated that in 2000 there were nearly 25 million refugees worldwide. All are victims of armed conflict, political upheavals, or a number of forms of social oppression.

During the period of **colonialism,** limits were placed on the number of indigenous people who could migrate into the **primate city.** When colonialism ended, these limitations were lifted and millions of new residents were added to already-crowded cities.

Environmental conditions have also been at the root of mass migrations. The Irish potato famine in 1840 forced thousands of people to leave the agricultural regions of Ireland and to migrate to the United States. Environmental situations can also be created from migration. In peninsular Florida, increased numbers of people have settled along both the Atlantic and Gulf Coasts. In addition, large-scale agricultural activities have been established south of Lake Okeechobee. People and agriculture both need water; the water is taken from Lake Okeechobee before it can flow south to maintain the Everglades. In order to save the Everglades from destruction and to satisfy the growing needs for water by growing populations, the South Florida Water Management District now monitors and manages a 1,800-mile system of canals and water-diversion pipes set in place to balance water flow.

Environmental disruptions during the 1930s in the United States forced thousands to leave the Dust Bowl in the Midwest for the greener pastures of California. Migration can have its genesis in economic, political, technological, and cultural factors. As such, it is certain that migrations of global and local dimensions will occur with frequency in the future.

Suggested Readings: Patricia Gober, "Americans on the Move," *Population Bulletin*, vol. 48, Population Reference Bureau, 1993; Vaughn Robinson, *Geography and Migration*, London: Edward Elgar, 1996; United Nations High Commission for Refugees Home Page, www.unhcr.ch.

Monsoon. The word *monsoon* comes from the Arabic *mausim*, meaning season. Monsoon is associated with weather and climate because of its relationship to wind patterns that reverse direction 180 degrees, or close to it, in a yearly cycle. Arab sailors used the word *mausim* to note the seasonal change in wind direction over the Indian Ocean.

Monsoons in the South Asian region are marked by winds from the southwest during the warm, moist summer and a reversal to northeast winds in the cool, dry winter. In the summer, a thermal low-pressure system is located over the Asian landmass. Moisture-laden warm air moves across the Indian Ocean toward this thermal low. The air mass passes over the Indian subcontinent, bringing rains for the upcoming agricultural season. India's west coast and the Ganges River Valley to the north receive more than 60 inches of rainfall per year. The amounts can vary widely. Cherrapungi is located in eastern India just north of Bangladesh, at the southern margin of the Himalayas. This place once received 31 feet of rain in one month and 87 feet in one year. Cherrapungi is the world leader in rainfall accumulation.

In the winter, the monsoon is a northeast wind blowing out of Asia and passing across the Indian subcontinent. The wind direction reversal occurs following the development of a thermal high-pressure system that forms over Asia in the region of eastern Siberia and Mongolia. During the winter monsoon, South Asia enters a decidedly dry season and remains in this pattern until the arrival of rains in the spring.

The South Asian farmer plans the beginning of the agricultural season around the arrival of the summer monsoon rain. The rainy season is remarkably predictable. Fields are readied, and all preparations are made in anticipation of the first rains. Occasionally, the monsoon arrives earlier or later than expected. As a result, the crop that year may be adversely affected. A summer may bring too little rain, and sometimes the rains are so torrential and of such long duration that severe flooding occurs, crops are lost, and homes ruined. Fortunately, the summer monsoon does not significantly vary from year to year in time of arrival and amount of precipitation.

Much of Indian literature and poetry is focused on the monsoon and the crucial part it plays in the livelihood of people in the nation. The first rains of the summer monsoon are anxiously awaited. When the rains finally come, they are called "the burst of the monsoon."

The same high-pressure system that sends cool, dry air over South Asia during the winter monsoon affects East Asia as well. Winds from this high-pressure system flow from the northwest over the deserts of Mongolia and pick up fine particulate matter and eventually deposit it in northern China. This material is the fertile **loess** that is the main constituent of the Loess Plateau near the Hwang He, China's Yellow River.

Suggested Readings: Edward Aguado and James E. Burt, *Understanding Weather and Climate*, Upper Saddle River, N.J.: Prentice Hall, 1999; P. J. Webster, "Monsoons," *Scientific American*, August 1981.

Multinational corporation. *See* **Transnational corporation.**

Multinational state. A country (state) that includes at least one ethnic minority is considered multinational in its composition. Nation refers to a cultural, or ethnic, group. By this definition, most countries of the world are multinational states. A multinational state may have reasonably good relations between the ethnic groups, or there may be discrimination of a minority group, a level of tension between groups, or worse.

In many cases, segregation of ethnic groups may result. The settlement of the French ethnic group in Canada came about over a long period of time. The French took root early in Canadian history and located along the St. Lawrence River in the current province of Quebec. Due in part to their concentration, the French maintained their cultural identity despite the presence of the majority English populace throughout the rest of Canada. Retention of their own language and way of life was the strongest element setting the

French Canadians apart. In recent years, feelings of strong nationalism and claims of unequal treatment by the Canadian national government prompted the French Canadians to demand secession from Canada. Although provincial voting returns on two occasions did not reach the levels needed to move toward secession, many in French Canada believe strongly that it will eventually happen.

Conflict within countries among ethnic groups can also result in segregation. The long-term fighting in Northern Ireland exemplifies this situation. Segregation of Turks and Cypriots in Cyprus is another example. Since 1974, Cyprus has been partitioned, and United Nations personnel have been on duty ensuring that fighting does not break out between the two ethnic groups.

The United Kingdom is an example of a multinational state. England, Scotland, Wales, and Northern Ireland are the constituents in this grouping of ethnic entities. The groups have coexisted in relatively calm conditions over time except, of course, for the turmoil in Northern Ireland.

The majority group in power can mandate multinational conflict. This occurred in South Africa during the twentieth-century era of **apartheid,** when black Africans were isolated to specified areas and given limited permission to travel outside these confines. In severe cases of multinational strife, groups may be expelled or even eliminated. Members of the Indian culture group were forced out of Uganda when Idi Amin was in power in the 1970s, and in 1984, Nigeria expelled people from neighboring Ghana.

Attempts at wholesale extermination have been rare but nonetheless wrenching. In the 1990s, many Kurds in Iraq were killed by poison gas allegedly at the order of the Iraqi leadership. During World War II, Nazi Germany attempted to exterminate its entire Jewish population. When the war ended, it was determined that six million Jewish people had been killed.

Atrocities such as these do not occur in all multinational states. Yet, discrimination and suppression is not uncommon. In the United States, American Indians were stripped of their land and placed in reservations. In the South, African Americans suffered great injustices, beginning with their subjugation under the practice of slavery.

By the end of the twentieth century, a rash of rising ethnic nationalistic movements were underway. With the demise of the Soviet Union in 1991, ethnic groups in that region demanded independence. Russia's long battle with Chechnya was waged in earnest to keep the Chechens from seceding. Had they been successful, the Russians feared that other ethnic groups, numerous in Russia, would attempt the same action.

The plight of the Kurds in Iraq is unusual in that they represent a culture group that is found in a region spanning three countries: Turkey, Iraq, and Iran. Until the 1920s, the Kurds had their own homeland in the country of Kurdistan. However, boundary changes proclaimed following World War II and assuring the Kurds of their own homeland were abrogated by Turkey in 1928. As a result, the Kurds are an ethnic group without a country of their own.

Suggested Readings: Liz Fawcett, *Religion, Ethnicity and Social Change*, New York: St. Martin's Press, 2000; Terance W. Haverluk, "The Changing Geography of U.S. Hispanics, 1850–1990," *Journal of Geography*, vol. 96 (1997).

Multiple-nuclei model. In 1945, American geographers Chauncey Harris and Edward Ullman created a model of urban structure that departed from the single **central business district** (CBD) type proposed in the **concentric zone model** and **sector model** developed earlier. The multiple-nuclei model suggested that large cities grow around a number of focal points, or nuclei. Harris and Ullman contended that the multiple-nuclei concept was especially true in cities that were rapidly expanding in area.

Harris and Ullman based their model on four principles:

1. A nucleus may develop around a specialized facility, such as a transportation hub or a shopping center. In these instances, there may be little or no stimulus from the CBD; the nuclei are growth points in and of themselves.

2. The clustering of industries for mutual locational advantage could produce a nucleus that attracts necessary supporting firms and services (*see* **Agglomeration**).

3. Some functions tend to repel one another in terms of location. That is, a concentration of heavy industry is not likely to be located next to high-cost residential housing or a municipal theme park.

4. Some functions avoid areas with high rent costs. Used car lots, for instance, are not likely to be found near the nuclei centers, where land costs are higher, nor will they be located next to a new shopping mall.

The multiple-nuclei model is far more complex than those that propose a single growth center at the CBD. As such, the multiple-nuclei model has been criticized by some experts, who said it attempts to replicate actual urban settings too closely and in doing so loses its potential for prediction. On the other hand, most urban geographers believe that the model is more reflective of the way cities have grown, the manner in which they function, and the complexity that marks urban structure.

The multiple-nuclei model suggests, for example, that as a city expands beyond its original areal limits, it may absorb a center that previously existed independently. Once absorbed into the larger city, the smaller center may well become another nucleus. Also, several nuclei may have been part of the city from the beginning and will continue to serve as growth points. The growth and persistence of any nucleus will depend on its ability to remain a viable focus of economic or social activity.

As cities grew to incorporate smaller centers and as suburbanization occurred following World War II, the emergence of new growth points was seen more frequently. In many metropolitan areas, large self-contained edge cities have grown along interstate beltways. These nuclei function essentially independent of an existing CBD or other nuclei.

Suggested Readings: Chauncy D. Harris, "The Nature of Cities and Urban Growth in the Last Half Century," *Urban Geography*, vol. 18 (1997); Philip Kivell, *Land and the City: Patterns and Processes of Urban Change*, London: Routledge, 1993; Web site for the Urban Morphology Research Group in the School of Geography, University of Birmingham, England, www.bham.ac.uk/geography.

Multiplier effect. When a new industry is successful, its presence will set in motion a series of economic events that eventually leads to greater growth within its region. The growth will take place not only in the new industry but also in the attraction of other comparable forms and in the **infrastructure** and service sector necessary to support industrial expansion. The term *multiplier effect* refers to the added growth that occurs when a successful operation acts as a generator for further widespread growth.

In the 1950s, Swedish economist Gunnar Myrdal used the phrase "circular and cumulative causation" to describe the sequence of events that unfolds when an economic system is positively stimulated by the addition of a successful new firm. The new industry adds more jobs, not only in the firm but also in construction and the building of infrastructure. In doing so, both the basic and nonbasic sectors benefit through expansion. As the firm grows, the pool of highly trained workers expands. With more workers added to the mix, the number of families expands. The added number of people necessitates shopping centers, schools, medical facilities, and a myriad of other functions and services. With added firm success and growth in the supporting activities, and increases in population, more income is available and the number of employment options increases. This leads to more buying power and a new impetus for growth in banking, education (both formal and vocational), and legal services. In time, with continued success and gains through invention and innovation, the business may well become a **growth pole,** a leader in its industry class. Achieving this status acts as a magnet for comparable and supportive industries to locate in proximity to the generating firm, to take advantage of the system that has been created (*see* **Agglomeration**).

Success stories of the type summarized here have not been rare. The economic history of the United States, Canada, western Europe, Japan, Australia, and other countries in the developed world is replete with examples of dynamic growth generating a multiplier effect.

The hope is held that comparable growth patterns will be realized in the developing world. In many regions of the developing world, a kind of reversal of Myrdal's circular and cumulative causation has been the rule. Instead of growth occurring on the heels of new industrial development, declines in economic activity or the inability of sound business ventures to take hold have resulted in a drain of qualified workers to other regions. This leads to a lower demand for infrastructural improvements and diminished income levels. Less income means less buying power and a shortage of essential services, including good medical delivery systems. Even safe water may become scarce. A negative sequence of outcomes is the antithesis of a multiplier effect, and its occurrence in the developing world is all too common.

Suggested Readings: J. W. Harrington and Barney Warf, *Industrial Location*, New York: Routledge, 1995; James O. Wheeler et al., *Economic Geography*, 3rd. ed., New York: John Wiley & Sons, 1998.

Nation-state. The term *nation-state* combines political and cultural aspects. In this sense, "nation" represents a cohesive grouping of people who share a single language and cultural background and are committed to common political goals. The "state" in nation-state refers to the political entity of the nation. The state has sovereignty over its territory. Therefore, a nation-state is a clearly delineated area that maintains its political sovereignty and contains a nation, or populace, held together by shared cultural attributes and the bonds of loyalty and allegiance to the state.

The criteria of loyalty and allegiance are crucial to the success and maintenance of the nation-state. They are more important than the common cultural attributes of the people. During the Vietnam War, the people of South Vietnam had a common cultural background and a single language. The economy of the country was primarily agricultural. The people clearly were representative of a nation. Yet, allegiance to the state and identification with it were lacking. The South Vietnamese people were hamlet oriented and inward looking. Attempts to rally them to take a more expansive political view and to identify with the state were unsuccessful. It was not uncommon for South Vietnamese soldiers to leave their military unit and return to their villages during the time of rice harvesting.

The nation-state provides a degree of order within its boundaries through the establishment of governmental controls and organization and with the sanctions and support provided by the people. The nation-state also provides protection for its people and institutions, both internally and from external threats, through the establishment of police and military forces. This aspect of nation-state activity is in place with the approval of the populace. Should the people not support military engagements contemplated by the nation-state, or if internal actions are viewed to be repressive, the people can voice their objections and seek remedies through the political processes in place. The nation-state establishes administrative, legislative, political, and legal systems that are in tune with the desires of the people.

Although the true nation-state is rare, a number of countries are recognized as having achieved a close approximation. Among them are France, Sweden, Greece, Iceland, Denmark, Germany, and Japan. Korea, before Japanese occupation and annexation early in the twentieth century and its split into two countries following World War II, would certainly have qualified as a nation-state. Should the long-sought reunification of North and South Korea come about, an opportunity for nation-state status may arise.

Since the fall of the Soviet Union and the end of the **cold war,** a number of new nation-states have arrived on the international scene. The severing of Czechoslovakia, a **multinational state,** resulted in two new nation-states: the Czech Republic and Slovakia.

During the 1930s, Nazi Germany insisted that German-speaking people in neighboring Austria and the Sudetenland of Czechoslovakia were the same nationality as people in Germany and belonged in a single state. In this example, the nation-state idea compelled Nazi Germany to invade and occupy those two regions.

In recent years, politicians and social scientists have expressed concern about the usefulness of the nation-state in the new era of **globalization.** Many experts believe that the nation-state is an anachronism and that it is not the best territorial organization for ensuring the rapid and unimpeded movement of goods and services in a fast-moving global economy. Some believe that the nation-state system should give way to the creation of larger and more logically conceived economic regions to ensure greater productivity and fewer delays in doing business. Ironically, these proclamations of consolidation are being made at the same time that **ethnicity** is becoming increasingly important, along with demands for greater recognition of existing nation-states and the creation of new nation-states.

Suggested Readings: George J. Demko and William B. Wood, *Reordering the World: Geopolitical Perspectives in the Twenty-first Century*, Boulder, Colo.: Westview Press, 1994; "The Rise of Europe's Little Nations," *Wilson Quarterly*, vol. 18 (1994).

Natural boundary. A boundary that follows a geological feature is considered to be a natural boundary. Boundaries of this type are found along rivers, lakes, deserts, and mountain ranges. River boundaries would seem to be ideal: they provide clear evidence of separation, and they are established and recognized physical features. In reality, however, river boundaries can change as rivers change course. Following flooding, a river's course may shift, altering the boundary between states or countries. Shifting of river course has occurred a number of times along the Mississippi River. The Rio Grande, separating the

United States and Mexico, has frequently shifted its course, causing problems in determining the exact location of the international boundary.

During the era of **colonialism,** the European occupiers of Africa, beginning in the late 1800s, chose rivers as boundaries. Doing so was a convenience for the Europeans but devastating to the indigenous African culture groups, which delineated their territory using the entire watershed. By using rivers as boundaries, the Europeans actually split African home territories down the middle. As a result, some of the home territory would be in a British colony, for instance, and some in a French colony. This practice has been disruptive to African culture groups since the colonial period, because the boundaries created at that time are still in force.

Deserts may also serve as boundaries. The great Sahara Desert in Africa separates a number of countries. Although boundaries in the desert are not as clearly identified as those marked by a river, there have been few territorial disputes, because the region is one of low population density.

Mountain ranges also serve as boundaries in a number of world regions. Along the western extent of South America, the Andes Mountains separate Chile and Argentina, and farther to the north, Ecuador and Peru. Disagreements have ensued over the specific line intended to be the mountain boundary between Chile and Argentina. Initial inability to decide between lines marked by mountaintops or watershed perplexed Chile and Argentina almost to the point of conflict before the issue was finally resolved. Similar disputes have occurred between China and India over their common mountain boundary.

Lake boundaries are common in East Africa, where Uganda, Kenya, Tanzania, Zambia, and Mozambique all have a boundary on one of three large lakes. When boundaries are formed on bodies of water, the midline between the countries is used to create the division. This procedure is usually effective. However, when there are competing claims of ownership of the body of water itself, problems can arise. A case in point is the South China Sea, the entirety of which is claimed by China, Taiwan, and Vietnam, whereas several other Southeast Asian countries lay claim to at least part of this strategically important body of water (*see* **Median-line principle**).

Suggested Readings: Gerald H. Blake, *Maritime Boundaries*, vol. 5, World Boundaries Series, London: Routledge, 1994; Herman Van der Wusten and John V. O'Loughlin, *A Political Geography of International Relations*, New York: Routledge, 1991.

Natural hazards. Flooding, hurricanes, cyclones, typhoons, earthquakes, volcanic eruptions, landslides, and droughts are all examples of natural hazards. There are few inhabited places in the world that are totally free of natural hazards of some type. People take risks when they choose to live, for instance, along the San Andreas fault in California, or in Tokyo, Japan, or along the Atlantic coast in Georgia or South Carolina, where the threat of earthquake, hurricane, or typhoon is ever present. Yet, people do choose to build homes and live in these places.

In 1906, an earthquake destroyed much of San Francisco, but the rebuilding of the city began immediately following this catastrophe. An earthquake in 1976 rocked China and claimed 242,000 lives; the rebuilding was begun soon after the devastation ended. Hurricanes have hit Bangladesh on a number of occasions. In 1970, some 500,000 people lost their lives in a devastating hurricane and the flooding that followed. Today, this region of Bangladesh is even more densely populated. Why do people continue to reside in places with known natural hazards? This question is best addressed in the context of **environmental perception.** People's perception of an area having natural hazards varies greatly. For those who choose to live in such places, the risk of experiencing a natural hazard is outweighed by the perceived positive attributes of the place. For example, millions of people live in earthquake-and-landslide-prone southern California. They know that the hazards are present, but for them the California lifestyle and the region's fine climate and scenic grandeur and its proximity to both the Pacific Ocean and mountain skiing outweigh the potential danger.

There are other reasons why people choose to live in areas of natural hazards. Research on this topic shows that the perception of danger is diminished because a serious earthquake, for example, is a rare incident. Also, earthquakes are hard to predict, and there may be differences of opinion among experts in their estimation of when a seismic event will take place. In the case of a hurricane or typhoon, prediction is much easier. Yet, residents of the disturbance may decide to stay in place until the storm passes, in hopes that the most destructive winds will be diverted away from them. Finally, owners of property in regions of natural hazards may be reluctant to leave because they have a large monetary investment in their property. It could also be true that an attempt to sell the property would fail simply because of its location. The perception by prospective buyers of living in a region of natural hazards could be quite different from that of the owner.

One of the most frequently occurring natural hazards is flooding. Humans have always favored living close to bodies of water. A glance at a world map of **population density** shows high concentrations along coastlines and in the floodplains of major rivers. Occupying a floodplain guarantees that high water will eventually cause damage.

The devastation from natural hazards is magnified when high concentrations of people live in their path. This is why Japan is so greatly affected by disastrous earthquakes and typhoons. There are more than 130 million people in Japan, and they live in an earthquake-prone land area roughly the size of Montana. The earthquake in the crowded city of Kobe in the mid-1990s was enormously destructive, even though buildings and freeway structures were engineered to be earthquake proof.

Suggested Readings: Natural Hazards Center, University of Colorado, Boulder, Web site, www.colorado.edu/hazards; Risa Palm, *Natural Hazards: An Integrated Framework for Research and Planning*, Baltimore: Johns Hopkins University Press, 1990; Graham A. Tobin and Burrell E. Montz, *Natural Hazards: Explanation and Integration*, New York: Guilford Press, 1997.

Neocolonialism. Neocolonialism, the "new colonialism," refers to the economic and political dependency remaining in former colonies despite gaining independence from their colonial rulers. Within 20 years after the end of World War II, the era of **colonialism** came to an end. Britain and France, the two leading colonial powers in Africa, began to relinquish control of their colonies. Former colonies became newly minted sovereign states. However, the trade relationships in place during the era of colonialism were, for the most part, retained. The inequitable levels of socioeconomic development that marked colonialism continued to plague the newly independent countries. Independence for the former colonies turned out to be a mixed blessing. On the positive side, they were politically independent and could, in theory, chart their own course. But along with independence, the new countries were left with the legacy of years of colonial rule.

The former colonies were poor and undeveloped. The colonial era saw little investment in the **infrastructure** necessary for a country to fully develop its resource base. Roads, railroad lines, communication systems, housing, and medical delivery systems were either missing or in need of repair, development, or expansion. Regions of potentially good agricultural land, if present, were not accessible because surface **transportation systems** had never been built. The colonies were left with the task of completing the internal regional development of their basic infrastructure, a task not undertaken during colonialism.

When Europeans left the colonies, they put in place leaders who, in large part, continued the political and economic practices used during colonialism. A small and privileged elite ruled the new countries and maintained trade relationships that held the previous colonies in the same economic situation they faced during colonialism. Although the European countries were no longer politically in power, they ruled through economic arrangements. The term used to describe this situation is *neocolonialism.*

The colonies were still linked to their former European rulers in a state of dependency. Although they were politically independent, **dependency theory** suggests that the former colonies still depended on the developed world as providers of raw material and commodities and as a market for goods produced in the developing world.

The status of the former colonies is well summarized in the **core-periphery model,** in which they represent the periphery, that region of the world that has suffered from low levels of socioeconomic development. The core-periphery theme is prominent in **Wallerstein's world-system analysis,** developed by social scientist Immanuel Wallerstein, which states, in part, that there must be a core and a periphery in the global capitalist economic system. There are neocolonialist overtones in Wallerstein's theory, which states that any gain in economic level by the periphery will be countered by a greater gain in the core.

Many development experts point to the presence in the developing world of **transnational corporation**s as another example of neocolonialism. These large and powerful enterprises, based in the core, become established in developing countries to take advantage of lower wage rates and the availability of raw materials. Although these organizations provide jobs and income to workers in the host country, the profits from the operation are exported to the home country in the core. This system has a striking resemblance to colonialism.

Suggested Readings: Rajesh Chandra, *Industrialization and Development in the Third World*, Introduction to Development Series, London: Routledge, 1992; International Bank for Reconstruction and Development, World Bank, *World Development Report,* annual; Web site of the U.S. Agency for International Development, www.info.usaid.gov, provides information on development programs worldwide.

Network. In geography, the term *network* initially referred to the multiple connections from point to point describing surface **transportation systems.** In this sense, the network is configured as an analog model of the system under analysis. Network modeling was developed to its fullest, complete with mathematical and statistical techniques, during the **Quantitative Revolution** in geography. In this process, the essential aspects of the transportation system were isolated for study and specific determinations were made, for instance, of **accessibility** between and among points.

Other quantitative measures, such as network completeness, were also developed. Measurements were made to determine the degree to which each point in the network was connected to all other points (*see* **Connectivity**). Another measure determined directional bias in the network. For instance, in the railroad system in the United States and Canada, the east–west lines are predominant in number and amount of traffic compared to the north–south lines.

Clearly, a great deal of attention has been devoted to studying transportation system development, operation, and change, because of the importance of this function in economic and social activities. Interest in studying networks has expanded in recent years. Geographers have created a body of literature on airline networks. Since the deregulation of the airlines in the 1980s, a number of changes have occurred in the industry. Most pertinent to the geographer is the growth of the hub system. Particular airline companies have established centers, or hubs, at selected terminals in major cities. Passengers are frequently required to fly from or to a hub in making connections for their ultimate destination. For instance, a passenger departing from Providence, Rhode Island, on Delta Airlines and heading for Albuquerque, New Mexico, will fly first to one of Delta's major hubs, probably Atlanta, Georgia, to board another plane for the final leg of the journey. One can speak generally of the Delta Airlines network that primarily serves the United States and several countries in Latin America but may also refer to the hub network, a limited set of routes within the Delta system.

Network analysis extends to the vast and growing realm of electronic communications. Radio, television, and the Internet are examples of networks that can be analyzed and studied in terms of their spatial extent, degree of connectivity, directorial bias, and regional concentration.

Suggested Readings: Stanley Brunn and Thomas Leinbach, *Collapsing Space and Time: Geographic Aspects of Communication and Information,* London: HarperCollins Academic, 1991; Nigel Thrift, *Spatial Formations,* Thousand Oaks, Calif.: Sage, 1996.

New industrial countries. The **new international division of labor** reflects basic changes in the global structuring of economic activity. The core has deemphasized the manufacture of tangible goods within its own borders. **Transnational corporation**s have been established in countries of the developing world to take advantage of low labor costs and other incentives (*see* **Core-periphery model**). In most cases, the host countries in the periphery remain economically dependent on the core and are unable to develop their own viable manufacturing and trade arrangements. They remain much as they were under **colonialism** (*see* **Dependency theory**). The exceptions to this situation are designated as new industrial countries (NICs).

Some areas have struggled upward on the economic ladder and have been successful in establishing a sound manufacturing base and a viable global trading position. Among these NICs are the **Asian Tigers** (South Korea, Taiwan, Singapore, and Hong Kong). Two of these entities are **city-state**s, Singapore and Hong Kong. Also considered NICs are Mexico, Brazil, and China, all of whom have developed an economic sector that is strong in manufacturing and trade.

Mexico is a member country of the **North American Free Trade Agreement** (NAFTA), along with Canada and the United States. NAFTA established a tariff-free trading arrangement to spur greater economic cooperation and exchanges of goods and commodities among the three countries. The phasing out of the **maquiladora** (factory) program between the United States and Mexico will allow the domestic marketing of manufactured goods produced in the many U.S.-owned border factories in Mexico.

Economic successes in South Korea and Taiwan were patterned on the Japanese model. Japan resumed its dynamic economic growth following its defeat in World War II. With monetary assistance from the United States, Japan rapidly rose to become one of the leading economic forces in the world. Taiwan, a refuge for the nationalist Chinese government following the 1949 takeover of China by Mao Tse Tung and the Chinese Communist Party, has also risen to prominence in manufacturing and global trade. Both of these NICs cater to a large local market purchasing manufactured goods.

Countries in the developing world, it is hoped, will follow a path similar to that of the current NICs. Manufacturing is increasing in these countries, known as the periphery, but much of it is still controlled by the transnational corporations based in the core.

Suggested Readings: A. Chowdhury and I. Islam, *The Newly Industrialized Economics of East Asia*, New York: Routledge, 1993; M. Freeman, *Atlas of the World Economy*, New York: Simon & Schuster, 1991.

New international division of labor. The new international division of labor (NIDL) reflects dramatic changes in the economic structure of the so-called old industrial countries (OICs) in the core (urban-industrial countries) and countries in the periphery, or the developing world. Toward the end of the twentieth century, the OICs entered a phase of **deindustrialization** coupled with rapid increases in service-sector and high-technology activities. The deindustrialization aspect of change saw a decline in the production of tangible goods within the OICs, but it did not mean that the OICs were significantly lessening their efforts in this sector. Instead of producing manufactured goods within their own borders, the OICs established assembly and production facilities in the developing world. In these settings, the OICs could take advantage of cheap labor, inexpensive land, tax breaks, and other incentives to ensure greater profits in their operation.

Giant **transnational corporation**s operated the new plants set up by the OICs. Although the advent of transnational corporations resulted in the transfer of some industrial technology to the developing world, the system was set up to favor the OICs and to essentially disallow host countries from further developing an industrial base for their own advantage. These arrangements were made by limiting host country operations to the production of components used in the manufacture of a product. Rarely was a fully integrated and complex manufacturing or industrial system established in a developing country. Consequently, the host country was not in a position to benefit in its own right through the attraction of comparable and supportive industries, an outcome reflective of growth in the OICs (*see* **Agglomeration** and **Multiplier effect**).

Limited in their ability to expand their economic systems, developing countries remain dependent on the transnational corporations in the wealthy core nations, just as they were during the era of **colonialism** (from about the late 1800s to the mid-twentieth century). Further, the presence of factories run by transnational corporations in the host countries has little, if any, connection to the local economy. Although the factories provide jobs to local workers and a market for some raw materials, virtually all of the profits are sent to the transnational corporate headquarters in the core. In this case, the similarity with operations under colonialism is evident (*see* **dependency theory**). Another similarity with colonialism is the lack of attention on the part of the transnational corporations to full regional development within the host countries.

The dependent status of the developing countries is also seen in their trade arrangements, which are almost exclusively with OICs. There is little economic activity between developing countries. The limited aspect of their involvement in the production process precludes their developing a more holistic and potentially profitable industrial base. Nearly all research and development on product lines is completed at facilities within the core.

One outcome of the NIDL that is promising is the success of the **Asian Tigers** (South Korea, Taiwan, Singapore, and Hong Kong) and countries such as Mexico, Brazil, and China, whose manufacturing and trade arrangements have made them important players on the world market. All of these countries have risen from low socioeconomic levels to the status identified as **new industrial countries.** They are no longer member countries in the developing world.

Suggested Readings: J. Allen and C. Hamnett, A *Shrinking World: Global Unevenness and Inequality*, Oxford, England: Oxford University Press, 1995; Doreen Massey, *Spatial Divisions of Labor: Social Structures and the Geography of Production*, 2nd ed., New York: Routledge, 1995.

Nodal (functional) region. *See* **Region.**

Nomadic herding. The practice of nomadic herding, a form of **pastoralism,** is complex and widespread. Nomadic herding is the controlled movement of livestock to areas with sufficient grasses and water for sustenance. This type of land use has been practiced for more than 10,000 years, predating the origins of agriculture. Nomadic herding is the most extensive of all land-use forms. In a yearly cycle, herders may move their animals hundreds of miles in search of plentiful forage and an adequate water supply.

Nomadic herding is found in the arctic regions of northern Canada and Eurasia, the arid lands from Southwest Asia east to Mongolia, the grasslands of the Sahel region of northern Africa, and in southwestern Africa. Herders with sheep, goats, camels, cattle, or yaks may be on the move throughout the year in search of forage for their animals. Some may travel periodically, moving to higher elevations in the summers and to valleys in winter. These herders are considered seminomadic (*see* **Transhumance**).

The activity of the nomadic herders is one of subsistence and normally involves no economic functions. Nomadic herders must be extremely knowledgeable about the physical environment. They must know precisely when to move their herds to locations that will provide adequate grass and water to keep the animals healthy. The animals provide the herders with food, skins for tents and shelters, and furs for clothing.

Nomadic herding is a land use that is in general decline for a number of reasons. Large areas of grazing land, especially in Africa, have been converted to agricultural fields in response to increased human populations. Many nomadic herders have given up the practice and taken jobs in the growing cities of Asia and Africa. Others have retained their herds but settled in one location rather than continuing the pattern of migration. Drought conditions in the Sahel in the last two decades of the twentieth century left previously rich grazing land parched and desolate. Changing environmental situations such as this have led to a further decline in nomadic herding.

Suggested Readings: Claudia Chang and Harold A. Kostner, *Pastoralists at the Periphery: Herders in a Capitalist World,* Tucson: University of Arizona Press, 1994; Harry M. Kaiser et al., *Agricultural Dimensions of Global Climatic Change,* Delray Beach, Fla.: St. Lucie's Press, 1993.

Nongovernmental organization. A major dilemma in developing countries is the inability to generate and sustain positive socioeconomic growth. Enormous inequities exist in the core-periphery relationship, in which wealthy developed countries represent the core and poorer developing nations the periphery (*see* **Core-periphery model**). Many of the socioeconomic disadvantages of countries in the periphery had their origins in the era of **colonialism,** from about the late 1800s to the mid-twentieth century.

In recent years a number of leading global organizations, such as the World Bank, the International Monetary Fund, and development offices within the United Nations, have called for greater cooperative efforts at every geographic level to reverse the downward spiral in the developing world. Due to either their inability or reluctance, national governments in developing countries have not created the economic setting necessary to ensure overall socioeconomic success. To assist these countries in overcoming their negative economic status, a cooperative effort involving organizations at all levels, from local to international, has been generated. Virtually all of these organizations are nongovernmental and nonprofit in nature.

These nongovernmental organizations (NGOs) number in the thousands globally and represent every aspect of concern in the developing world. There are NGOs devoted to human rights issues, women's rights, environmental concerns, and health issues. Most of the NGOs are found within individual countries, working with the people and the government to help solve problems.

NGOs devoted to generating positive economic development may provide technical assistance to a start-up firm manufacturing building materials. Another NGO may have established connections with medical equipment dealers in a developed country and is working to establish and equip a field hospital in the rural area of a developing country. Religious or professional organizations, research firms, or private organizations may support NGOs. One of the most notable NGOs, Doctors Without Borders, is based in the core and is found throughout the periphery, providing much-needed medical assistance. This organization organizes the visits of medical professions to countries that are extremely short of doctors and other health care professionals. Through this program, thousands of people in poor, developing countries have been given medical attention.

Some NGOs assist acquired immunodeficiency syndrome (AIDS) sufferers and their families throughout the developing world. The rapid spread of this insidious disease has overwhelmed local governments, especially in Sub-Saharan Africa. NGOs have been able to help in situations where the government cannot.

The NGO movement has steadily grown in importance and strength. For example, the Forum of African Voluntary Development Organizations is a regional organization of African countries established to provide assistance to one another on any and all development questions, to exchange ideas, and to share expertise on economic experiences and plans. The developing world needs more of these self-help efforts to enhance its collective opportunity for sound socioeconomic growth.

Suggested Readings: R. Bennett and R. Estall, *Global Change and Challenge: Geography for the 1990s*, New York: Routledge, 1991; Arthur Morris, *Geography and Development*, London: University College Press, 1998.

North American Free Trade Agreement. The United States, Canada, and Mexico entered into an agreement in 1993 to create a regional free-trade union. The North American Free Trade Agreement (NAFTA) grew out of an earlier pact between the United States and Canada, which aimed at reducing tariffs, stimulating more trade, and establishing true economic integration between the two countries. Even earlier (1965), Canada and the United States made initial strides along the course of economic cooperation and tariff reduction with the enactment of the Canadian–United States Automotive Agreement. In this pact, tariffs were eliminated on automobiles and automotive component sales. In addition, a strong cooperative relationship was forged between the two countries in the automotive industry.

NAFTA is patterned on the **European Union,** a powerful 16-country economic grouping. Unlike the European Union, however, NAFTA is not seeking to create a common currency. With more than 400 million people in the three member countries, NAFTA is second only to the European Union in population size.

NAFTA may be another step along the way to the creation of an even larger free-trade region. In time, the remainder of Latin America may join with the NAFTA countries to form the Free Trade Area of the Americas, a union that would include virtually every country in the Western Hemisphere.

The immediate aims of NAFTA are to eliminate tariffs on all agricultural goods and most manufactured products by the year 2010. In addition, NAFTA eases previous restrictions on the movement of executives and other professionals between the three countries.

Regional trade groupings like the European Union and NAFTA are representative of the **globalization** of economic activity. In this movement, countries in the developed world are setting up manufacturing plants in countries in the developing world to take advantage of lower wage rates. **Transnational corporations**, with headquarters located in countries in the developed world, manage many of these operations (*see* **Outsourcing**).

The United States and Mexico have a long history of economic cooperation, especially in the establishment of manufacturing plants along their common international border. The **maquiladora** program, for instance, was set up to produce U.S. manufactured goods in Mexican factories. These goods are then shipped back to the United States duty free. Under this arrangement, the United States profits from the lower Mexican wage rate, and Mexico gains thousands of jobs for its workers. Under NAFTA, the maquiladora program will be phased out, and goods produced in the border factories will be marketed in Mexico as well as in the United States.

Overall, regional trade groupings are economically successful. However, there are concerns about working conditions in the Mexican border factories, complaints of unsanitary housing developments in border towns, and problems with environmental degradation and the dumping of industrial refuse into the Rio Grande. In addition, workers in the United States claim that jobs are being lost as production moves across the border. There is also the general claim that regional trade groupings like NAFTA stimulate trade increases primarily among the developed countries.

Suggested Readings: Christopher D. Merrett, "Nation-States in Continental Markets: The Political Geography of Free Trade," *Journal of Geography*, vol. 96 (1997); "A Greener or Browner Mexico?" *The Economist*, 7 August 1999.

North Atlantic Treaty Organization. A new global balance of power evolved following the end of World War II, in 1945. The United States and the Soviet Union (USSR) emerged as dominant forces on the world scene, and their diametrically opposed political systems created an adversarial relationship between them. Within this tense political climate, the era of the **cold war** was about to begin. In response to concern about the expansion of Soviet influence in Western Europe, a military alliance called the North Atlantic Treaty Organization (NATO) was established in 1949 to counter any threats. NATO included the United States, Canada, and 14 countries in Western Europe (Belgium, Denmark, France, West Germany, Greece, Ireland, Italy, Luxembourg, the Netherlands, Norway, Portugal, Spain, Turkey, and the United Kingdom). All the NATO countries except France and Spain agreed to commit military personnel, should it become necessary. NATO headquarters was initially set up in France and was eventually relocated to Brussels, Belgium.

NATO was one of several multinational military organizations established in the post–World War II years to contain the spread of communism from the Soviet Union and China. Other military alliances included the Central Treaty Organization in western Asia and the Southeast Asia Treaty Organization.

The basic assumption guiding the operation of these agreements was that if any participating country was threatened or attacked by a belligerent state, all members were bound to engage in its defense. The bipolar nature of global **geopolitics** became even more pronounced in 1955, when Bulgaria, Czechoslovakia, East Germany, Hungary, Poland, Romania, and the Soviet Union formed the Warsaw Pact to counter the presence of NATO. The north–south tier of Eastern European countries provided the Soviet Union with a **buffer zone** to thwart further military invasions of its territory. The Soviet Union had been invaded by French emperor Napoleon Bonaparte's forces in the nineteenth century and by Nazi German leader Adolf Hitler's army during World War II. The Soviets vowed not to allow this kind of incursion to happen again.

When the Soviet Union was dissolved in 1991, the Warsaw Pact also became defunct, and the role of NATO changed considerably. The threat of Soviet expansion abruptly ended and geopolitical alignments were significantly altered. The role of NATO then shifted to protection of the newly emerging **European Union,** a supranational organization created in 1992 to form an economic union of European states, and to addressing rising ethnic disturbances in the Balkan states (Albania, Bosnia-Herzegovina, Bulgaria, Croatia, Macedonia, Romania, and Serbia). At the same time, a number of Eastern European countries, free following the demise of the Warsaw Pact, sought membership in both the European Union and NATO. In 1999, Poland, the Czech Republic, and Hungary were granted membership in NATO. Additional eastern European countries are also being considered for membership.

Discussions have taken place over the years on the subject of extending NATO membership to Russia. Hard-liners in Russia have opposed this prospect, citing that it would not be in the country's interest to be bound by military alliance to provide armed support in conflicts in which the Russians have no direct connection. On the positive side, it is argued that all countries in the developed world are vulnerable to the threat of conflict and terrorist activities from countries in the Middle East and Southwest Asia. In response to the changing geopolitical situation, Russia became a limited partner of NATO in 2002. Membership in the newly created NATO–Moscow Council allowed Russia to take part in discussions on antiterrorism initiatives, crisis management, peacekeeping, and military maneuvers. However, Russia does not have a binding vote in major NATO decisions. Also in 2002, NATO invited Bulgaria, Estonia, Latvia, Lithuania, Romania, Slovenia, and Slovakia to become members. It is expected that all seven countries will join NATO in 2004.

Suggested Readings: Brian B. Blouet, "The Political Geography of Europe: 1900–2000, A.D.," *Journal of Geography*, vol. 95 (1996); R. Muir, *Political Geography: A New Introduction*, New York: John Wiley & Sons, 1997.

North–South. The term *North–South* refers to the division of the world into rich and poor countries, the developed and underdeveloped worlds, and the core-periphery regional dichotomy (*see* **Core-periphery model**). The name derives from the title of a report submitted in 1980 to the United Nations: *North-South: A Programme of Survival*. The report represented a two-year effort on the part of members of the Independent Commission for Developmental Issues (the North-South Commission), a group of international experts headed by Willy Brandt, then chancellor of West Germany. The Brandt Report, as it came to be known, demanded that greater attention be paid to the developing countries in the South and that they be integrated more effectively into the global economic system. The Brandt Report included a map showing the boundary separating the North and the South. Even though Australia and New Zealand are in the Southern Hemisphere, they are both members of the North in a developmental context.

Brandt's message in the foreword of the report signaled the compelling nature of the socioeconomic disparity between the two regions:

> This report is based on the most simple of common interests—humanity wants to survive and, one can add, it has the moral duty to survive. This raises not only classical questions of war and peace, but also the questions how can one defeat hunger in the world, overcome mass misery, and meet the challenge of the inequality in living conditions between rich and poor. To express it in a few words: This report is about peace.

By the time of the submission of the Brandt Report, it was clear that the development gap separating the rich and poor countries was widening.

In an effort to reduce the great disparities, the North-South Commission in 1980 recommended a sharp increase in aid to developing countries. It was proposed that all countries in the North increase their development assistance to an amount equal to 0.7 percent of their **gross national product** (GNP) by 1985 and to 1 percent by 2000. Although some countries in the North met their obligations, most did not. By the mid-1990s the average contribution from the North was about 0.3 percent of GNP, and in 2000 the amount had dropped to 0.2 percent.

In February 2000, a conference organized by the cross-party, nonprofit Development and Peace Foundation and the Willy Brandt Foundation was held to determine what accomplishments had been made in efforts to assist the South. One of the outcomes of the conference was a realization that the knowledge needed to bring about change was certainly available but that the political willingness of the North was noticeably lacking. If their conclusions are correct, and the record seems to suggest that they are, socioeconomic conditions in the South will continue to lag behind the vastly more affluent North.

Suggested Readings: Independent Commission for International Developmental Issues, *North-South: A Programme for Survival*, Cambridge, Mass.: MIT Press, 1980; *Journal of Developing Areas* (focuses on issues of development in the periphery); United Nations Development Program, *Human Development Report*, New York: Oxford University Press, annual.

O

Optimum population. Theoretically, the optimum population is the number of people necessary for the full development of a country's resource base. Achievement of optimum population ensures maximum **gross national product** (GNP) and the highest possible standard of living. If the population is either too high (overpopulation) or too low (underpopulation) the GNP per capita and standard of living will be lower than those achieved with optimum population.

Optimum population varies depending on the quality of the resource base and the socioeconomic makeup of the population. A number of additional variables can also influence the determination of optimum population. American geographer Edward A. Ackerman developed a formula in the 1950s that measures a country's population against an extensive set of economic and social characteristics. Among them are the amount of resources in a country and a measure of resource quality, level of technology, efficiency of the country's governmental administration, resources acquired through trade, and determination of wastage of resources. Generally, Ackerman's formula derives a standard of living for a country that compares population with the natural-resource base and the technology available to effectively use the resources.

Optimum population varies with time and any change in the level of technology. For instance, breakthroughs in agricultural and industrial technologies result in greatly increased yields of food crops and a more efficient and productive manufacturing sector. These positive outcomes result in increases in overall population, expansion of the labor force, generally higher levels of productivity, a higher GNP per capita, and an elevated standard of living.

The process can also work in reverse. An aging population, typical of some western European countries in recent decades, results in fewer people in the workforce, a diminishment of productivity, and a lowered standard of living.

Bangladesh has been cited as an example of a country that is overpopulated. It has a population density of nearly 800 per square mile, a meager resource base, and a location within a **natural hazards** region. Its low levels of productivity, high population, and extremely low per capita GNP (less than $300 in 2000), mark Bangladesh as one of the poorest countries in the world.

Canada, on the other hand, is an example of a country experiencing underpopulation. With 27 million people in an area about the size of the conterminous United States and a considerable resource base, Canada's GNP per capita (over $20,000, in U.S. dollars, in 2000) would increase significantly if its total population were increased, even if it doubled. Canada's growth prospects are extremely positive; those of Bangladesh are negative.

Suggested Readings: John Bongaarts, "Population Pressure and the Food Supply System in the Developing World," *Population and Development Review*, vol. 22 (1996); Brian Goodall, *The Facts on File Dictionary of Human Geography*, New York: Facts on File, 1987.

Organization of Petroleum Exporting Countries. Several oil-exporting countries in the Middle East, along with Venezuela, formed the Organization of Petroleum Exporting Countries (OPEC) in 1960. At that time, crude oil was selling on the world market for about $2 per barrel, and this group wanted to use its collective efforts to increase the price. OPEC was unsuccessful in its bid to get higher payments for crude oil until 1973. That year, OPEC became a true cartel by controlling the production of oil within its countries and increasing the price from $3 per barrel to nearly $60 in 1980. Not only was a price increase instituted, the Arab members of OPEC boycotted oil shipments to the United States for one year because of its support of Israel in the 1973 Yom Kippur War. OPEC's moves beginning in 1973 proved for the first time its power in world politics.

OPEC's actions affected every region in the world. In the developed countries, the cost of energy shot upward, greatly increasing the cost of producing all manufactured goods. Shortages of gasoline forced prices upward; gasoline that cost 29 cents per gallon in 1972 rose to $1.40 in 1980. The developing countries were negatively impacted as well. These countries relied on low-cost energy to build their new industries and to provide much-needed fertilizers for use in agriculture.

The economic effects of OPEC's actions were reduced in the 1980s and 1990s. Non-OPEC oil producers (Canada, Mexico, Norway, the United Kingdom, Angola, and Colombia) increased their exports to the United States. Also, the United States and other developed countries began concerted efforts to conserve energy through the use of higher-gas-mileage automobiles and the installation of energy-efficient heating and cooling systems in homes and office buildings. All of these changes reduced the amount of oil purchased from

OPEC suppliers. As a result, oil prices dropped. In addition, the Iran-Iraq War in the 1980s, coupled with internal disagreements among its member countries, reduced OPEC's ability to effectively cooperate as a cartel.

Although the oil-price shocks of the 1970s are gone, OPEC is nonetheless a formidable influence on **geopolitics.** Throughout the era of the **cold war,** both the United States and the Soviet Union (USSR) competed for favor among the oil-producing countries of the Middle East. In the future, OPEC's influence will continue to be significant. The organization has 75 percent of the world's known reserves of crude oil, with more than two-thirds of the world total found in OPEC countries in the Middle East.

OPEC membership in 2000 included Algeria, Iran, Kuwait, Libya, Qatar, Saudi Arabia, the United Arab Emirates, Indonesia, Nigeria, and Venezuela. Former member countries include Ecuador and Gabon.

Suggested Readings: British Petroleum Company, *The BP Statistical Review of World Energy,* annual; Susan L. Cutter and William H. Renwick, *Exploration, Conservation, Preservation: A Geographical Perspective on Natural Resource Use,* 3rd ed., New York: John Wiley & Sons, 1999.

Outsourcing. A company may find it financially advantageous to have particular business functions completed outside the organization. For example, janitorial work, operation of the dining facility, and computer storage of archival records may be handled by outside firms instead of company personnel. Outsourcing, as this practice is called, has become a common occurrence in firms of all sizes.

Outsourcing allows a company to concentrate on its primary business objective. If the company is a manufacturer of automobile tires, for example, management may outsource the human resource function to a firm that specializes in that service. In this case, the outside firm would handle payroll, personnel record keeping, and all other facets of human resources. The company would then be restructured to more closely focus its attention on making tires.

Another form of outsourcing is seen in the relocation of manufacturing operations to other countries. In a move of this kind, companies are taking advantage of lower wage rates, less-expensive land, and other incentives found in the new location. Outsourcing of this type is associated in particular with **transnational corporation**s, large firms that are based in developed countries and have established factories in other countries (*see* **Core-periphery model**). The goods produced at these plants are then shipped back to the home country and marketed there. An example of this category of outsourcing is seen in the **maquiladoras,** manufacturing plants along Mexico's northern border. Other examples of outsourcing include the manufacture in other countries of computer parts, aircraft components, clothing, and athletic shoes for final product assembly or direct sale of the items in the home country. Outsourcing is an integral aspect of the **globalization** of economic activity and a factor in the **new international division of labor.**

Suggested Readings: Peter W. Daniels and W. F. Lever, eds., *The Global Economy in Transition,* Harlow, U.K.: Longman, 1996; Jeffrey Henderson, *The Globalization of High Technology,* New York: Routledge, 1991.

Overpopulation. The basic definition of overpopulation states that a country or region has too many people and is therefore incapable of achieving or maintaining a suitable standard of living. Overpopulation is a relative notion, and it generally refers to the relationship between the number of people and the capability of the environment to support them.

Overpopulation is one of two departures from the ideal status of **optimum population,** a condition in which the number of people in a country and its resource base and technology level are in balance, the **carrying capacity** of the land has not been exceeded, and an adequate standard of living has been established. The other departure is underpopulation, in which a country or region has a population of insufficient numbers to fully utilize the resource base at its disposal.

The English economist **Thomas Robert Malthus** was one of the first scholars to draw attention to the problem of overpopulation. Malthus concluded in his "Essay on the Principle of Populations As It Affects the Further Improvement of Society" (1798) that world population was growing faster than the food supply needed to support it. In this sense, Malthus was sounding an early warning of an impending **population explosion,** an idea that is frequently discussed and debated in the early twenty-first century.

Countering the Malthusian position was one put forth by Karl Marx (1818–83), German political philosopher and revolutionist, who denied the basic premise of overpopulation. To Marx, the major problem is not one of too many people but a distribution system that precludes the delivery of needed commodities to those unable to provide for themselves.

Another school of thought holds that the problem of overpopulation will be solved in time by new developments in technology. Exponents of this idea point to the impressive advancements in medical and agricultural technology in the past and the resulting ability to support greater numbers of people. Such countries as Japan provide support for the technology argument. Because of its technological superiority and the ability to use that asset to increase its industrial productivity, Japan can purchase those resources and commodities it cannot produce or acquire within its own borders (especially some foods and crude oil) and create an exceptionally high standard of living. Japan's population at the beginning of the twenty-first century was 130 million, and if the country were not so richly endowed with its positive attributes of productivity, it would certainly be classified as being overpopulated.

Overpopulation is commonly associated with countries in the developing world. In most of these countries, a large percentage of the people live at or near subsistence levels. Housing shortages, poor sanitation conditions, too few job opportunities, inadequate medical delivery systems, and a high **rate of nat-**

ural increase identify countries where the overpopulation label is correctly applied. The most seriously affected region in the world in this regard includes the countries of Sub-Saharan Africa. Development experts consider the task of ensuring socioeconomic improvements in this region to be one of the greatest challenges of the twenty-first century.

Suggested Readings: "Population," *National Geographic*, October 1998; United Nations Population Fund, *The State of the World Population*, New York: United Nations, annual.

P

Pacific Rim economic region. Fourteen countries spanning the eastern and western coasts of the vast Pacific Ocean basin represent a dynamically growing world economic region. Members of the Pacific Rim tier of countries are Japan, the **Asian Tigers** (the economic powers South Korea, Taiwan, Singapore, and Hong Kong), Thailand, Malaysia, Indonesia, the Philippines, China, Australia, New Zealand, the United States, and Canada.

This expansive region is experiencing rapid economic growth, and every country has developed significant worldwide trading connections. An important shift is underway on the global economic scene. Europe was the leading economic center in the nineteenth century during the heyday of the **Industrial Revolution.** Leadership passed to North America in the twentieth century as the U.S. economy grew rapidly. The twenty-first century may see the Pacific Rim emerge as the most affluent economic region in the world.

Japan was the first Asian country to gear its economy for world trade. Following the Meiji Restoration in 1868, Japan began to industrialize and broke out of its centuries-long isolation. The country's economy grew rapidly, and Japan exerted its influence throughout East and Southeast Asia. The annexation of Korea and the occupation of Taiwan and other areas in coastal China are examples of Japan's expansionist efforts in the early twentieth century. Following World War II, Japan's industrial base was severely shattered, but with the assistance of the United States, Japan quickly rebuilt its industrial structure and in a few decades became one of the leading economic powers in the world. By the end of the 1980s, Japan's **gross national product** was second in the world, behind that of the United States.

Japan's success was followed by the dynamic rise of the Asian Tigers (*see* **New industrial countries**), all of which prospered when Europe and North America were economically damaged by the oil price increases of the 1970s (*see* **Organization of Petroleum Exporting Countries**). The remaining countries in the Pacific Rim are recent contributors to regional growth. China, with its billion-plus population, has broken out of the isolation endured under the first five decades of communist rule and is developing a formidable world trade network. Australia and New Zealand, members of the developed world, are major suppliers of minerals, wood, and agricultural products, with primary markets in Japan and other Pacific Rim countries.

The United States and Canada are the only Pacific Rim countries in the Western Hemisphere. Now that Mexico is a member of the **North American Free Trade Agreement,** it may take a place as well within the Pacific Rim grouping. The United States and Canada have more trade with other Pacific Rim countries than with western Europe. By 2000, total U.S. and Canadian imports and exports with Asian countries in the region were 50 percent higher than those with their European trading partners. In that same year, the Asian countries in the Pacific Rim accounted for over 30 percent of world exports, an increase from 11 percent only 20 years earlier.

Trade patterns within the Pacific Rim countries are extensive. The United States and Canada are major importers of manufactured items from the other members. In turn, the United States and Canada supply other member countries with agricultural goods, timber, various industrial materials, and a great deal of capital and technology. Several Pacific Rim countries also host **transnational corporation**s based in the United States.

Continued economic growth of the Pacific Rim seems assured. Most of the emerging countries in Southeast Asia have lowered their population growth rates and are on their way to achieving economic success.

Suggested Readings: Mark Borthwick, *Pacific Century: The Emergence of Modern Pacific Asia*, 2nd ed., Boulder, Colo.: Westview Press, 1992; Godfrey Linge, *China's New Spatial Economy: Heading Toward 2020*, Hong Kong: Oxford University Press, 1997; Jonathan Riss, *Southeast Asia: The Human Landscape of Modernization and Development*, New York: Routledge, 1997.

Paddy rice farming. Rice cultivation in a small field, or paddy, is the dominant form of **subsistence agriculture** in many regions of Asia. The name *paddy* comes from the Malay language and means "wet rice." Over time, *paddy* has been used in Western literature to refer generally to wet-rice cultivation in all areas. Paddy rice farming is labor intensive, time consuming, and complex. The growing process begins by clearing the field to remove any plant debris from the previous crop, plowing the area and smoothing the surface, and adding the right amount of fertilizer. Water is then added to a depth of about 12 inches. Rice seedlings are then transplanted to the paddy from a seedbed, where they were sown earlier. Proper water level is maintained throughout the growing period. Weeding is accomplished when necessary and repairs made to any breaks in enclosing dikes that may be leaking. At a particular point in the process, the water is drained away and the final growth stage begins. The plants are now able to benefit from maximum sunlight important for grain maturation in the final growth period. The final step in the process involves cutting the mature plants and removing the rice grains from the chaff.

In some regions of India, Bangladesh, most of Southeast Asia, southern China, and southwestern Japan, the temperature and moisture regimes allow for **double-cropping** of paddy rice. In these regions, the sequence of steps begins in the early spring and the first harvest occurs in July. The fields are then cleared and prepared for the second planting in August and an eventual harvest in November.

Paddy rice farming requires flat land, an environmental feature that is at a premium in most Asian countries. For this reason, it is necessary to use hill slopes that have been modified to create narrow and flat expanses suitable for paddy fields. **Terracing,** as this adaptation is called, is commonly seen throughout the paddy rice growing regions in Asia, and its presence indicates both a shortage of flat land and a population base large enough to require expansion of the agricultural sector.

Rice is the primary grain in many parts of Asia, and this single food product may represent as much as 60–70 percent of an individual's daily caloric intake. Well over half of all the rice in the world is grown is Asia, and most of the crop is consumed within that region.

Suggested Readings: John Rutherford, *Rice Dominant Land Settlement in Japan,* Sydney, Australia: Department of Geography, University of Sydney, 1984; R. Suppiah, "Four Types of Relationships Between Rainfall and Paddy Production in Sri Lanca," *Geojournal,* vol. 10 (1985).

Pastoralism. The grazing of sheep and cattle on natural grasslands is referred to as pastoralism. This practice is found primarily in the semiarid midlatitude regions in North and South America, Africa, and Asia. An exception to the semiarid setting is the raising of sheep in the humid grassland of New Zealand. Pastoralism is an example of **extensive agriculture** and it can be a large-scale commercial venture (*see* **Agribusiness**) or a form of **subsistence agriculture.**

Pastoralism is normally practiced on land that is not ideally suited for agriculture and is generally found in sparsely populated areas that are steep and dry. Despite the fact that pastoralism is found in relatively remote areas, its commercial applications are quite lucrative. Livestock ranching in the Argentine pampas, the American West, and northern Australia is big business, and beef produced in those regions is marketed throughout the world. The same is true of commercial sheep farming in New Zealand, central Australia, and the Argentine region of Patagonia. Livestock raising was also practiced for a few years in the Amazon region of South America, where large expanses of tropical rain forest had been cleared and grasses planted. The practice began in earnest in the 1980s, and although it continues, it has been greatly diminished in favor of rain forest retention. Pastoralism in the western United States has been replaced to a great extent by the installation of **feedlot**s that are located near large metropolitan centers and on major surface transportation lines.

Another form of pastoralism is **nomadic herding,** a subsistence land use also found in the semiarid climatic regions, along the fringes of the Arctic Ocean in Eurasia, and on the northern Canadian mainland. Pastoralism was included in **von Thunen's land use model,** developed in the early 1800s by German economist Johann Heinrich von Thunen.

Suggested Readings: Jonathan B. Bascom, "Border Pastoralism in Eastern Sudan," *Geographical Review,* vol. 80 (1990); John G. Galaty and Douglas L. Johnson, *The World of Pastoralism: Herding Systems in Comparative Perspective,* New York: Guilford Press, 1990.

Pattern. Geography is a discipline that analyzes spatial interaction and the arrangement of objects in their spatial settings. The objects of study (for example, cities, farms, rock outcroppings, people on a beach, tanning parlors, or industrial sites) can be located and mapped. The resulting map shows a pattern of symbols representing the location of the objects and their arrangement.

Pattern is an important aspect of geographical analysis. For example, a map of the locations of automobile thefts in a city would show a pattern that could be used to assign more police surveillance in the affected neighborhoods. Economic development planners look at a number of map patterns (e.g., population density, access routes, residential areas) to help in determining the best location for a new retail center.

The **township and range survey** of 1789 created a rectilinear land pattern that is easily recognizable from the air and is seen on county maps of the midwestern and western United States. The east–west and north–south alignment of streets in areas surveyed under this system exhibits a familiar pattern in towns and cities throughout this region.

Pattern analysis can lead to the determination of conclusions about the way a particular arrangement of objects came about. For example, a linear series of points representing retail business establishments would be found along a transportation corridor that provides access to the places for potential customers. This is a familiar pattern throughout the world. A tight cluster of points on a map could represent customers at an ice cream stand on a hot summer day or industrial plants located close to each other for mutual economic advantage (*see* **Agglomeration**).

Work on pattern analysis has also been extended to determine a pattern's structure. That is, a pattern may be totally uniform, such as the regular spacing of fruit trees in an orchard or rows of corn on a flat agricultural field. Or, the arrangement may be completely random, with no observable order. "Uniform" and "random" represent the two extremes in a continuum of possible pattern structures. In the early 1950s, botanists interested in the arrangement of trees in forested areas wanted a precise measure of the tree pattern. The quantitative technique they developed is called "nearest-neighbor analysis," a numeric procedure that yields a single number within a set range across the continuum from random to uniform. The nearest-neighbor formula can be used to determine the structure of any pattern in terms of its uniformity or randomness.

Pattern is of great importance in **cartography.** Maps are a visual communication system, and the choice of symbol and graphic presentation is of fundamental importance in this process. Aspects of pattern are considered in the actual mapmaking process and in the interpretation of maps.

Suggested Readings: John Campbell, *Map Use and Analysis*, 3rd ed., Dubuque, Iowa: WCB/McGraw-Hill, 1998; Phillip C. Muehrcke and Julianna O. Muehrcke, *Map Use: Reading, Analysis, Interpretation*, Madison, Wis.: JP Publications, 1992.

Periodic market. Market centers have been important gathering places for personal interaction and the exchange of goods for centuries. In towns and cities, permanent market activities are found in abundance. In rural areas with small villages and low population densities, the demand for goods is present although the cumulative purchasing power may be too low to justify a permanent retail establishment. In these regions the periodic market is found. Periodic markets are mobile centers of activity. Groups of vendors travel from one village to another over a set period of time, offer their goods for sale for a day, and then move on to the next place.

Periodic markets are found throughout the developing world in areas of low population density. It is not uncommon for vendors in their weekly circuits to travel 50 miles or more on foot carrying heavy loads of merchandise. In West Africa, settlements have existed for thousands of years on the boundary of forest and grassland and along major trade routes. These small settlements became periodic market sites for the sale or exchange of goods and services. A great deal of bartering may go on between buyer and seller in these transactions as each one ties to gain the greatest advantage.

Periodic market activity has been studied within the context of **Christaller's central place theory,** developed by twentieth-century German geographer Walter Christaller. When placed within this functional model of urban places, periodic marketing can be graphically portrayed at multiple hierarchical levels.

Suggested Readings: Paul Cloke, *Rural Geography*, Oxford, U.K.: Basil Blackwell, 1997; Arthur Morris, *Geography and Development*, London: University College London Press, 1998.

Personal space. *See* **Territoriality.**

Physiological density. The number of people per unit area of cultivable or arable land is called its physiological density. The resulting number is invariably much higher than the overall **population density** of a country. Physiological density is an important measure because it relates population to the amount of land that can be used for agriculture. For example, the U.S. overall population density is just over 70 per square mile. Its physiological density is about 340 per square mile. Even though the density is higher when measured against arable land, the United States is a world leader in agricultural yield and variety of products. The wheat region of the United States and Canada provides an abundance of grain in any given year, enough to satisfy domestic needs, with millions of metric tons available for sale on the world market.

A much different picture is seen in Japan, a country about the size of Montana with a population of over 130 million. Japan's overall population density is 860 per square mile, but its physiological density is nearly 7,000 per square mile. This high figure results from Japan's relatively small size and the fact that only 16 percent of its land area is suitable for agriculture. Not only is there a paucity of flat land, but the land is slowly being taken over by the expansion of metropolitan areas.

There are four major plains areas in Japan, and the remainder of the four-island nation is mountainous. Clearly, Japan is not self-sufficient in food production, despite its leadership in developing innovative techniques in **intensive agriculture.** Japan is one of the leading economic countries in the world, and it has attained a position of affluence that allows for the purchase of necessary food items not produced on its own land.

China provides another interesting example. With a physiological density of 2,900 per square mile, about 10 times its overall population density, China claims to have achieved self-sufficiency in agricultural output. Very little data are available outside China, however, and it is difficult to verify this claim or to determine individual daily protein and caloric intake.

Physiological density does not provide insights into the agricultural production on arable land within individual countries. Actual outputs vary considerably, depending on the level of agricultural technology available within the country, the importance placed on agriculture, and the degree of **accessibility** to areas of arable land within the country. For example, Nigeria was not able to use its productive northern agricultural region until connecting transportation lines were installed.

Australia's population density is lower than 10 per square mile, and its physiological density is just over 90 per square mile. The difference in the figures shows that the amount of arable land in Australia is very limited. Yet, the country has achieved agricultural self-sufficiency because of its low total population and advanced agricultural system. Australia is an important exporter of wheat and meat products.

Suggested Readings: John Bongaarts, "Can the Growing Human Population Feed Itself?" *Scientific American*, vol. 270 (1944); Helen Ginn Daughert and Kenneth C. W. Kammeyer, *An Introduction to Population*, 2nd ed., New York: Guilford Press, 1995.

Place. The concept of place is basic to geographic thinking and practice. Geography has been characterized as a spatial discipline, and places within the spatial context are objects of interest to analysts. Cities, agricultural fields, countries, pizza parlors, and gold mines are all examples of places that geographers may choose to study. To the human geographer, a place may be characterized as an environment in which people live and work. It is important to note that a place has both cultural and physical components, and both are needed to fully understand and appreciate the place.

Places may be studied to reveal their similarities: Seattle and Dallas are both cities, but it is also true that these two cities, when closely observed, reveal significant differences in both their cultural components and physical settings. Recent geographical research suggests that places are beginning to lose their distinctiveness in some ways. The effects of modern culture, it is suggested, are creating a kind of spatial standardization that works to reduce the uniqueness of individual places. This phenomenon has been identified as a condition of "placelessness," in which places are becoming more like each other. Placelessness, the researchers suggest, is furthered by the presence of common features found in all places (franchise restaurants, the familiar string of billboards along highways, and national chain stores), the same music and entertainment forms, and rapid media communications through television, the Internet, and satellite transmissions.

Other researchers contend that people in the United States may be losing their **sense of place** over time. The close association with the physical and cultural attributes of the place in which they live seems to have diminished (*see* **environmental perception**). American naturalist Barry Lopez suggests that Americans are less aware of their immediate surroundings and are not as closely associated with their immediate surroundings as those of earlier generations.

The concept of place is a central theme in **humanistic geography.** Yi-Fu Tuan, a prominent American geographer, originally from China, and one of the principal architects of humanistic geography, considered place to represent a center of felt value. Viewed in this perspective, place has a strong emotional connotation, an orientation considerably distant from that of the more scientific and analytic geographer. Tuan used the term **topophilia,** love of place, which is a compelling reference to the affective domain.

Suggested Readings: Douglas K. Fleming and Richard Roth, "Place in Advertising," *Geographical Review*, vol. 81 (1991); Richard P. Horwitz, *The Strip: An American Place*, Lincoln: University of Nebraska Press, 1985; Leo Zinn, *Place Images in Media: Portrayal, Experience, and Meaning*, Savage, Md.: Roman & Littlefield, 1990.

Plantation agriculture. During the era of **colonialism** in the nineteenth and early twentieth centuries, the Europeans introduced large-scale agricultural operations in their colonies. These agricultural estates, or plantations, specialized in the production of one or two export crops that were in high demand in the European countries. Among the crops grown were sugarcane, tea, coffee, cocoa, bananas, pineapples, palms, and cotton. All of these crops continue to be grown in regions of tropical and subtropical climates.

Cotton was an important export crop during the era of slavery in the United States. The warm, moist climate of the South is ideal for cotton growing. Black Africans, who were brought to the United States against their will and put to work in the fields, provided labor for the cotton plantations. The plantation was home to the owners, managers, and their African slaves.

Cotton was grown extensively in the South, and much of the crop was exported to England. The invention of the cotton gin by American inventor Eli Whitney in 1793, one of hundreds of labor-saving devices developed during the **Industrial Revolution,** resulted in great increases in cotton production. When slavery was abolished in 1862, during the American Civil War, many of the plantations were broken up into smaller land holdings.

Plantations have continued to operate in many parts of the world. This form of agricultural land use is ideal for the cultivation of tree crops that take a number of years from the time of planting to produce their first crop. Modern plantations are a form of **agribusiness** with high capital inputs, the use of advanced agricultural technology, and sophisticated marketing techniques. The labor-intensive nature of the operation, however, has not changed. Many workers are needed in the fields, especially during the time of harvest. Because plantations are usually located in sparsely populated regions, workers in many cases must be brought to the sites.

Plantations are found primarily in the low-latitude regions of Latin America, Africa, and Asia. A location either on the coast or with good access to it is needed in order to expedite shipment of the product.

Suggested Readings: Percy P. Courtenay, *Plantation Agriculture,* 2nd ed., London: Bell & Hyman, 1980; Edgar Graham and Ingrid Floering, *The Modern Plantations in the Third World,* New York: St. Martin's Press, 1984.

Political geography. Geographers have long been interested in the political organization of space and the ways in which areas, large and small, have been modified through political action. Political geography is the oldest branch of the discipline. Evidence is abundant of decision making in past eras that has literally changed the map of the world. Wars, conquests, negotiations over boundaries, and territorial disputes are all part of human history, and they continue to command the attention of today's leaders. The breakup of Yugoslavia in the early 1990s and its reorganization into smaller successor countries is one example of political realignments in recent years. The continual turmoil in the Middle East and the demands made of Israel to give up land it conquered in past conflicts is another.

Political geography was originally concerned with the origins of sovereign states, the groupings of states into alliances, questions about **frontier**s and boundaries, the relations of states both friendly and adversarial, and the influence of state shape on its ability to maintain its sovereignty. Political geographers also study the operations of multinational organizations. During the **cold war,** political geographers closely watched and reported on the standoff between the **North Atlantic Treaty Organization** and its adversary the Warsaw Pact (*see* **Buffer state and buffer zone**).

Political geography was once greeted with some degree of disdain in the academic community. Before World War II, Nazi Germany used the work of geographer Karl Haushofer to justify its invasion of other European countries. For a number of years following World War II, political geography was not as popular as other branches of the discipline because of the manner in which Haushofer's brand of **geopolitics** was used to justify German expansionism.

Electoral geography is a branch of political geography dealing with the impact of the political process on the spatial system. For example, states that lose population between congressional elections may also lose seats in the House of Representatives. Conversely, states that gain in population may acquire additional membership. Gains or losses of representatives require the redistricting and remapping of the state to reflect the changes. On occasion, the redrawing of congressional districts has created some very unusual district shapes (*see* **Electoral geography**).

A number of ongoing boundary and territorial disputes have intrigued political geographers in recent years. One centers on the dispute between Japan and Russia over ownership of the four islands lying north of Hokkaido, Japan. The Soviets occupied the islands at the end of World War II and have held them since, claiming ownership as spoils of war. The Japanese, citing nineteenth-century treaties with the Russians, contend that the islands must be returned to them. There is also the ongoing debate about whether there are two Koreas or one. In the view of most countries in the world, the Republic of Korea (South Korea) and the Democratic People's Republic of Korea (North Korea) are legitimate sovereign states. China, on the other hand, recognizes only one Korea. Maps published in China do not show a boundary line separating the two countries.

Halford J. Mackinder (1861–1947), the prominent British geographer, proposed one of political geography's most famous theories. Mackinder put forward his heartland theory in his book *Demographic Ideas and Reality* (1919). It became one of the most influential summaries of the global geopolitical situation of that era.

Suggested Readings: Nurit Kliot and Stanley Waterman, *The Political Geography of Conflict and Peace*, London: Belhaven Press, 1991; Thomas F. Poulsen, *Nations and States: A Geographical Background to World Affairs*, Englewood Cliffs, N.J.: Prentice Hall, 1995.

Pollution. When more foreign material accumulates in a natural system than can be absorbed and reduced, the result is pollution. A classic case of pollution occurred in March 1988, when the oil supertanker the Exxon *Valdez* ran aground on an island off the coast of Alaska and discharged 11 million gallons of crude oil into the water. The oil gradually drifted onshore, causing extensive damage to vegetation and animal life. Billions of dollars were spent over many years in efforts to alleviate the destruction.

There are a number of forms of pollution, and the task of eradicating the associated problems is becoming more difficult every year. Air, water, and land surfaces worldwide are the repositories of excess waste materials that become pollution. Atmospheric pollution occurs in the form of **acid rain,** smog accumulations in metropolitan areas, and the introduction of greenhouse gases, which have been blamed for the onset of global warming (*see* **Greenhouse effect**). In the United States, the burning of coal in power plants in the Midwest causes acid rain. The particulate matter in the smoke is carried aloft by prevailing winds. The suspended solid material containing oxides of nitrogen and sulfur eventually combines with water vapor to form acidic compounds. The acids are contained in the precipitation that falls on upstate New York, portions of New England, and the Canadian Maritime Provinces. Acid rain damages forests, lakes, and agricultural land. A number of lakes in northern New York have been rendered lifeless from acid rain deposits. Eastern Germany and the Czech Republic are greatly affected by acid rain originating in the highly concentrated industrial centers to the west.

Air pollution has also been blamed for global warming, the gradual increase in the average temperature of the earth's atmosphere. Automobile exhaust fumes and industrial smoke containing carbon dioxide and other greenhouse gases accumulate in the atmosphere and prevent the natural dissipation of heat into space. The **Kyoto Protocol,** signed in 1997 by most of the world's countries, was the culmination of a decades-long program to legislate reductions in the production of greenhouse gases and reverse global warming. Although then–Vice President Al Gore signed for the United States, the proposal was not sent to the Senate for ratification. When George W. Bush became president, he proposed that large companies independently curtail polluting.

Smog in Los Angeles, Mexico City, and other major metropolitan centers is another form of air pollution. "Smog" is the name given to the accumulation of noxious gases and particulate matter in the air above a city. In Los Angeles, for example, the pollutants are generated from automobile exhausts and industrial smoke, which are held in place by the combination of overriding high-pressure air and a mountain barrier to the east.

The introduction of chlorofluorocarbons (CFCs) into the atmosphere is responsible for breaking down the earth's protective ozone layer. CFCs come from human-made gases such as freon, a substance used in refrigerators, freezers, and air-conditioning systems. The use of freon has been discontinued in the developed countries, and by 2010 the developing countries will also discontinue its use.

Lakes, rivers, and coastal waters have experienced pollution. By the 1960s, Lake Erie was severely polluted. Both the United States and Canada began successful cleanup campaigns, which lasted throughout the 1980s and 1990s. However, through the concerted efforts of governmental agencies, local industries, and environmental organizations, Lake Erie made a remarkable comeback, and its environmental condition is greatly improved. The Rio Grande in the vicinity of the Mexican **maquiladoras,** manufacturing plants along the border with the United States, was being polluted with industrial wastes. Both countries have vowed to reverse the process and clean up this important body of water.

The outlook for the Aral Sea in Russia and Kazakhstan, however, is not promising. Much of the water from the two rivers that replenish the Aral Sea was diverted for irrigation agriculture beginning in the 1970s. As a result of these diversions, the Aral Sea gradually began to disappear. Shorelines receded from the edges of fishing villages, and boats were stranded on land miles from the sea. All fish and plant life in the sea have long since died. Once the water disappeared and the seabed dried, fine particulate matter consisting of fertilizers and pesticides was picked up by the wind and broadcast over thousands of square miles of land. The result was a great increase in human and animal illnesses caused by toxic materials. The loss of the Aral Sea is an environmental tragedy of enormous proportions.

Lake Baikal in Siberia, the world's largest freshwater lake in volume, is also the site of serious pollution. For years, raw sewage and industrial wastes have been deposited in Lake Baikal. Because of its size, it was believed that the lake would always be able to break down the waste material and eliminate its toxicity. In time, however, the amount of wastes deposited in the lake increased to a point that exceeded the lake's tolerance levels. Lake Baikal is now experiencing high accumulations of pollutants.

Suggested Readings: Ross Gelbspan, "A Modest Proposal to Stop Global Warming," *Sierra*, May–June 2001; Andrew Goudie and Heather Viles, *The Earth Transformed: An Introduction to the Human Impact on the Environment*, Cambridge, Mass.: Basil Blackwell, 1997; "Restoring Life to the 'Dead Zone': How a Sound Farm Policy Could Save Our Oceans," *Environmental Defense Newsletter*, May 2000.

Population density. The relating of population totals to the area occupied defines the concept of population density. For example, Iceland occupies a land area of 39,790 square miles, and its total population in 2000 was approximately 300,000. Therefore, Iceland's population density is 7.5 per square mile. Considered alone, population density is not a very useful measure. Its value, however, is found in comparisons with other country values. For example, Pakistan has 307,376 square miles of territory and a population of 151 million. Its population density is 489 per square mile, over 65 times that of Iceland. Comparing the two population densities shows that, despite its larger territorial size, Pakistan is an overcrowded country. However, the population density comparison alone does not show whether either country has achieved **optimum population,** nor does it show whether Iceland is underpopulated or Pakistan is overpopulated. Without more information, one cannot tell whether either country has reached or surpassed its **carrying capacity.**

One might conclude, then, that population density is a measure of limited value and that its usefulness is increased when it is used to compare countries. Comparisons within a country make the measure even more useful. The population density of the United States is about 76 per square mile. The state of Minnesota has 4.4 million people in an area of 84,000 square miles. Minnesota's population density is 52 per square mile, below the country's average. A measure of the population density of the Twin Cities metropolitan area—

Minnesota's largest urban concentration, with 2.4 million people on 3,700 square miles of land—shows that it is 596 per square mile. This is a significant population concentration; half of Minnesota's population lives in this metropolitan area.

The country of Egypt provides a particularly interesting example. Egypt is located in the northern Sahara Desert, a vast desert region. Egypt's land area is 386,660 square miles, about one-tenth the size of the United States and 4.5 times as large as the area of Minnesota. Its population density is 177 per square mile. Again, overall population density values can be deceiving. In the case of Egypt this is especially true. First, the city of Cairo has over 13 percent of the country's population on a limited land area near the delta of the Nile River. The most startling fact, however, is that 98 percent of Egypt's population lives on only 3 percent of its land area. The location of this extraordinary concentration is the region composed of two narrow bands of land hugging both sides of the Nile River. There, the population density exceeds 8,000 per square mile. The Nile River is the lifeblood of the country, and it has supported civilizations from the time of the ancient pharaohs up to the present.

Suggested Readings: David A. Plane and Peter A. Rogerson, *The Geographical Analysis of Population,* New York: John Wiley & Sons, 1994; World Resources Institute, "Population and Human Development," in *World Resources 1996–97,* New York: Oxford University Press, 1996.

Population distribution. World population distribution is uneven. Some regions contain heavy concentrations of people, and others have a population density of less than one person per square mile. A few places in the world have no permanent settlements. Among them are Antarctica, the ice-capped interior of Greenland, and most of the Canadian archipelago.

A glance at a map of world population distribution reveals three major concentrations, a number of smaller ones, and extensive areas of very low populations. The single largest concentration of people is found in East Asia, which is composed of China, North and South Korea, and Japan. More than 1.5 billion people live in this region. This figure represents 25 percent of the total world population, which was 6.1 billion in 2000. China alone had 1.25 billion people in that year, the first country to pass the billion-persons mark. North and South Korea and Japan collectively have the remaining 250 million people. China's population is concentrated in the eastern one-third of the country along major rivers and near the seacoast. The largest concentration of people in China is found along the lower course of the Hwang He, the Yellow River, on the North China Plain. Twenty-five percent of China's population, or more than 310 million people, live in this highly productive agricultural region. China's 1.25 billion people represent 20 percent of total world population. Thus, one out of 5 people in the world live in China, and one of every 20 people in the world live in the region of the North China Plain. Population distributions in the two Koreas and Japan are primarily on plains near the coastlines and along river valleys. Expanses of flat land are rare in both of these mountainous countries. Consequently, population densities are decidedly high.

The second most populated region is South Asia, with 1.4 billion people. India is the most populated country in this region, followed by Pakistan and Bangladesh, both of which were part of India until the late 1940s. India's **rate of natural increase** is much higher than that of China, and it is estimated that India will surpass China in total population by 2030. The combined total population of East Asia and South Asia was 2.9 billion in 2000, nearly half the population of the world.

The third largest concentration is the European littoral (coastal regions), extending from the Atlantic coastline east to the Ural Mountains in Russia. Within this region were 750 million people in 2000, representing 12 percent of total world population.

The three major concentrations of population, in East Asia, South Asia, and Europe, account for roughly 60 percent of all people in the world. There are lesser concentrations in North America (300 million), Southeast Asia (500 million), Africa (743 million), and there are a number of smaller distributions in Latin America.

Vast areas of very low population exist in a number of world regions. In the Northern Hemisphere, Arctic North America, northern Siberia, and the Sahara Desert in Africa have very low numbers of people. The same is true of several regions in the Southern Hemisphere, including the Amazon River Basin, the desert areas of South America, the interior of Australia, and Antarctica.

Suggested Readings: Alene Gelbard et al., "World Population beyond Six Billion," *Population Bulletin*, vol. 54 (1999); Ma Jisen, "1.2 Billion: Retrospect and Prospect of Population in China," *International Social Science Journal*, vol. 48 (1996).

Population explosion. World population has grown dramatically in the last three centuries. At the beginning of the **Industrial Revolution** in the mid-eighteenth century, world population was estimated to be about 700 million. In just 250 years, the total had surpassed 6 billion. The term *population explosion* refers to the recent period of exponential population growth, a sustained and accelerating increase that is unprecedented in human history.

The population explosion got its start when significant declines occurred in **crude death rate**s. The lowering of death rates is attributed in part to improvements in medical delivery systems, improved sanitary conditions, and higher yields in agriculture. As death rates dropped, **crude birthrate**s remained high, resulting in higher **rates of natural increase.** The combination of these demographic factors drove total populations steadily upward (*see* **Demographic transition**).

The year 1820 was a watershed year in human history. That year, world population reached one billion. It had taken all of human history to achieve that total. By 1930, world population had doubled to two billion. The next doubling took only 45 years, and by 1970 the population of the world had reached four billion. Two billion more people were added by 2000, and estimates of future growth suggest that world population will reach nine billion by 2050 (*see* **Population projection**).

The population explosion is global, but immediate impacts are primarily regional. Countries in the developed world have completed the demographic transition and are experiencing low rates of increase. In fact, some countries in western Europe have begun to see decline in population. The developing world is another picture. Birthrates remain higher than death rates in these countries, and total population continues to grow. Although some countries in Asia have made great strides toward lowering population growth rates, most of the developing world has yet to fully accept and implement fertility controls. **Overpopulation** in particular regions of the developing world has dramatically slowed socioeconomic development.

Suggested Readings: Lester R. Brown et al., *Beyond Malthus: Nineteen Dimensions of the Population Challenge*, New York: W. W. Norton, 1999; Paul Ehrlich and Anne Ehrlich, *The Population Explosion*, New York: Simon & Schuster, 1990; Jennifer D. Mitchell, "Before the Next Doubling," *World Watch*, January–February, 1998.

Population geography. Population geography is concerned with spatial variation in the composition, distribution, migration, and growth of human groups. In addition, the population geographer studies changes in the characteristics of a population. For example, studies of **crude birthrate** and **crude death rate** and the manner in which they change over time yield valuable information about a country (*see* **Demographic transition**).

The work of the population geographer overlaps with that of the demographer. Both have conceptual concerns with birth and death rates, fertility rates, and **population projection.** However, the demographer does not as a rule consider **migration,** nor is the spatial variation theme taken into consideration.

Population geographers use two additional techniques to study population composition. One of these is the diagram of age and gender structure, the so-called **population pyramid,** a graphic that illustrates the percentages of males and females in the population by age group. The second is a simple expression called the population equation, which identifies the factors of change in a population:

$$P(f) = P(n) + (B - D) + (I - E)$$

Where P(f) is the population at some future time, P(n) is the population at the start of the measuring period, B – D is births minus deaths, and I – E is net migration (immigrants minus emigrants). This expression works for any region in the world, large and small, and over any time period for which data are available. Change in overall world population, however, requires information only on birth- and death rates of the current population.

Concepts in population geography are important components in **economic geography, social geography, urban geography, historical geography,** and, of course, **human geography.** This is so because all of these subdisciplines deal with human populations. The historical growth of population, globally and regionally, is an area of importance to the population geographer. Concern about **population growth** occurring since the time of the **Industrial Revolution** is of particular significance because it is in this period that the **population explosion** began. **Overpopulation** found in the developing world is of primary interest to population geographers and other scholars concerned about the socioeconomic development in this region.

Migration is another area of importance to the population geographer. Movements of people from region to region have occurred throughout history, and the study of this phenomenon exemplifies the dynamic nature of geography. Population geographers study the migration of diseases as well. In recent years, population geographers and epidemiologists have closely followed the migration of **HIV/AIDS.**

Suggested Readings: Gary L. Peters and Robert P. Larkin, *Population Geography: Problems, Concepts, and Prospects,* Dubuque, Iowa: Kendall/Hunt, 1993; Ian R. H. Rockett, "Population and Health: An Introduction to Epidemiology," *Population Bulletin,* vol. 54 (1999).

Population growth. The growth of world population from prehistoric times to the present is an important aspect of **population geography.** Archaeological and historical findings point to three important technological breakthroughs that had monumental influences on population growth. The first breakthrough in the distant past was the advent of toolmaking. With simple but effective hand tools, humans were able to manage their environment more effectively. Tools allowed them to build more-protective shelters, gather plant foods quicker, and more effectively acquire wild game. Life was precarious in these early times. Population growth rates were very slow, and in some periods death rates exceeded birthrates, resulting in population declines.

The second breakthrough occurred about 10,000 to 12,000 years ago, with the advent of agriculture. Human groups throughout the prehistoric period had operated as hunters and gatherers, continually on the move in search of edible grains and other plant foods and wild game. When agriculture was successfully established, it was no longer necessary to be continuously on the move to find food, and human groups were able to establish permanent settlements. Cities began to develop between 8,000 and 10,000 years ago as an outcome of the **Agricultural Revolution,** and populations began to grow more rapidly.

The third breakthrough was the **Industrial Revolution,** beginning in the late eighteenth century, a period of great advances in manufacturing and overall productivity. The Industrial Revolution impacted every aspect of Western society. The **population explosion,** a great surge in the **rate of natural increase,** accompanied and to a great extent was fostered by the Industrial Revolution. By 1820, world population is estimated to have reached one billion.

World population continued a steady upward climb throughout the remainder of the nineteenth century and the entire twentieth century. In 2000, world population had exceeded six billion, and **population projection**s estimate the number of people in the world will reach nine billion by 2050.

The high point in population growth rate in the United States was reached in the early 1960s, just as the post–World War II baby boom was nearing its end. At that time, the annual population increase in the United States was 2.1 percent. Since that time, the growth rate has declined to 0.6 percent, in 2000. This rate is less than half the world rate of 1.4 percent. Although neither of these growth rates appear to be exceptionally high, they confirm that population growth is continuing. For the United States, the 0.6 percent increase represents an additional 1.6 million people annually. Growth of this magnitude in the United States does not present a socioeconomic problem. However, world population, just over 6 billion in 2000, grew by an astounding 84 million, with a growth rate of 1.4 percent. Most of the increases were in the developing world, in countries already hard pressed to achieve positive levels of socioeconomic advancement. An increase of 84 million is significant. It is comparable to adding another country as large as Germany in only one year. Annual increases of this magnitude are responsible for the continued interest in the predictions of English economist **Thomas Robert Malthus** (1760–1834) and the ongoing concern about the population explosion.

Suggested Readings: Nathan Kayfitz and Wilhelm Flinger, *World Population Growth and Aging: Demographic Trends in the Late 20th Century,* Chicago: University of Chicago Press, 1991; Population Reference Bureau, "World Population Data Sheet," annual.

Population projection. The United Nations, the U.S. Census Bureau, and many other organizations are interested in determining best estimates for regional and global future population growth trends. Population projections are regularly completed and updated for every geographical area. Projections are categorized in terms of the number of years involved: short-term projections are normally for time periods of less than 15 years, medium-term for 15 to 50 years, and long-term for more than 50 years. The longer the term, the less accurate the projection. This is understandable: the higher the number of years involved, the greater is the probability for unpredictable events to occur, such as wars, famines, periods of unexpectedly high economic growth, and a myriad of other outcomes that could invalidate a projection.

The preparation of population projections for any country or region depends on three principal variables: fertility rates, mortality, and **migration.** The basic equation derived from these variables is:

$$\text{Projected population} = (\text{births} - \text{immigrants}) - (\text{deaths} + \text{emigrants})$$
$$\text{over the period of the projection.}$$

The same basic formulation can be used to project the change in population of an age cohort. For example, a U.S. Census Bureau study used this procedure to predict changes in the number of women in the 15–19 age group from 2000 to 2005. The projection, noted in O'Neill and Balk (*see* Suggested Readings for this entry), concluded that this group would increase from 9,672,000 women in 2000 to 9,902,000 in 2005. The cohort would then be a member of the 20–24 age group (*see* **Population pyramid**). This projection was based on a net gain of 345,000 women from migration and a loss of 115,000 from death. Similar cohort projections can be made for any other age groups of either men or women.

The United Nations has produced world population projections to the year 2100. Long-term projections such as these are, of course, the least reliable. For this reason the United Nations produced at least three growth scenarios in its projections: low, medium, and high. All three scenarios begin with the 2000 world population of just over six billion. The low scenario predicts that 7.5 billion people will be on the earth in 2050 and then a decline will occur until 2100,

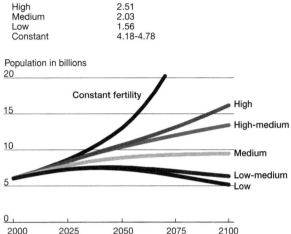

UN World Population Projections, 2000–2100

Assumed fertility rate (TFR) 2050–2100

Projection series	TFR (Average children per woman)
High	2.51
Medium	2.03
Low	1.56
Constant	4.18-4.78

Note: TFR (total fertility rate) is the average total number of children that would be born to a woman given current birth rates. These TFRs for the world are derived from the values assumed for geographic regions.

The TFR values for the high-medium and low-medium scenarios are between the high and medium, and medium and low values, respectively. The constant fertility scenario derives from holding constant the TFRs estimated for each region in 1995-2000.

Population Projection from the United Nations. *Source: Long Range World Population Projections: Based on the 1998 Revision,* ESA/P/WP 153 (1999). Used by permission of the United Nation.

when world population will be 5.1 billion. The medium scenario, the one that demographers believe to be most accurate, predicts 9.0 billion people in 2050 and 9.5 billion in 2100. Finally, the high scenario, clearly the least desirable, has 11 billion in 2050 and a further increase to 16 billion in 2100.

Each of these scenarios assumes a different **total fertility rate** for the 50-year period from 2050 to 2100. The low scenario fertility rate is 1.56, the medium is 2.03, and the high is 2.51. In 2000, the total fertility rate for the world was 2.9. All three growth scenarios assume a gradual drop in total fertility rate over the 100-year period. Predicting future global population numbers is a complex and difficult, but necessary, task.

Suggested Readings: John Bongaarts and Rodolpho A. Bulatao, *Beyond Six Billion: Forecasting the World's Population*, Washington, D.C.: National Academy Press, 2000; Wolfgang Lutz, *The Future Population of the World: What Can We Assume Today?*, London: Earthscan Publications, 1996; Brian O'Neill and Deborah Balk, "World Population Futures," *Population Bulletin*, vol. 56 (2001).

Population pyramid. The age and gender structure of a population is clearly presented in a useful graphic called the population pyramid. The graphic in-

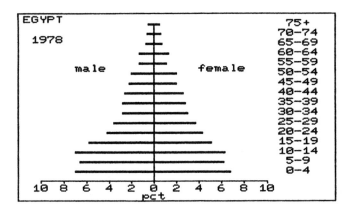

Population Pyramid. *Source:* Author's creation.

cludes data on female and male segments of the population plotted on either side of a vertical line in the center of the display. Numerical age groups, usually in 5-year cohorts, are plotted along the vertical line, with the youngest age group, 0–4 years, at the base of the graphic, and the oldest, 75 and above, at the top. The horizontal base line is plotted with either percentages of the population or actual numbers of females and males. The zero point on this line is located at the intersection of the vertical and horizontal lines.

The shape of the population pyramid provides an immediate visual indication of the country's age cohort structure and the potential for future growth. For example, a population pyramid that is wide at the bottom and narrow at the top identifies a population that is growing at a high rate of increase. The reasoning behind this conclusion is easy to see: the largest numbers of people are found in the youngest age cohorts (0–4, 5–9, 10–14) and in women in the childbearing years (15–45). Greater numbers of people in these age cohorts ensure high population growth rates in the future. There would be high population gains in this case even if all couples in the country could be convinced to adhere to the population replacement rate of 2.1 children per family.

A population pyramid with essentially equal representation of people across all the age cohorts, except for the oldest, indicates a stable population, one that has achieved or is near to achieving **zero population growth** (ZPG). Only a few countries in western Europe have reached this point. ZPG cannot occur until a country completes the **demographic transition,** in which **crude birthrate**s (CBRs) and **crude death rate**s (CDRs) are essentially even in value. Countries in the developing world all have high **rates of natural increase** (RNIs) because birth rates exceed death rates by significant margins. Continually high RNIs are behind what has been called the **population explosion.**

There are a few countries (Germany, Austria, and France, for instance) that have experienced negative RNIs and declines in population. A population pyramid for a country in this demographic situation would be narrow in the younger age cohorts and wider throughout the older ones.

Population pyramids can provide a kind of history lesson about a place. For example, the population pyramid for Russia in 1970 would illustrate the results of human losses in World War II (estimated at 20 million), the Stalinist purges of the 1930s (possibly another 20 million), and losses during the Russian Revolution at the end of World War I. These historical events appear on the population pyramid as a constriction, or narrowing, of the shape of the graphic. A population pyramid for the United States in 2000 would show a bulge in the 35–50 age cohorts, who are people born during the post–World War II baby boom.

Suggested Readings: C. Alison McIntosh and Jason L. Finkle, "The Cairo Conference on Population and Development: A New Paradigm?" *Population and Development Review,* vol. 21 (1995); United Nations, *Population and Women,* New York: United Nations, 1996.

Possibilism. Possibilism suggests that humans have choices in the way they interact with their physical setting; it is the antithesis of **environmental determinism.** A number of prominent European and American geographers working at the end of the nineteenth century furthered the idea that geography should become the science that studied the interface between nature and culture, the environment, and the human element. Among these disciplinary leaders were **Halford J. Mackinder, Friedrich Ratzel,** and **William Morris Davis.** These geographers were unanimous in the view that human–environment interaction should be the conceptual base of the discipline. However, they all believed that culture groups were reactive in their collective behavior to the more compelling physical environment.

At the end of the nineteenth century, some geographers modified this conceptual view and contended that the environment played a supremely dominant role by controlling and even determining the actions of the culture group living within that environment. The school of geography known as **environmental determinism** influenced thinking in the discipline over the opening two decades of the twentieth century. By the end of that period, geographers representing the school of **human geography** in France began to dispute the rigidity of the environmental determinist position. Through the work of **Paul Vidal de la Blache** and others, a more reasoned approach, called "possibilism," emerged.

Possibilists suggested that the environment provided its human occupants with a range of opportunities for action and with a set of choices to make in responding to their immediate physical setting. Possibilism, as proposed by French geographers, stressed that the environment exerted influences on the human occupiers but by no means controlled or determined their range of activities. Possibilism, then, proposed that the environment and its human occupants had essentially equal roles.

There is no argument among geographers about the fact that the environment influences human activity. People in the arctic regions respond in quite different ways to the environment than occupants of the tropical rain forest. It is equally true that countries equipped with advanced technological capabilities have far greater choice in their responses to the environment than do subsistence agriculturalists in West Africa. However, regardless of the technological level of a country, some extreme environmental episodes, such as flooding, drought, hurricanes, and other **natural hazards** can wreak havoc on countries, both rich and poor. Such severe environmental disruptions as the

San Francisco earthquake and Hurricane Hugo will dramatically limit the range of human choices, at least temporarily.

Suggested Readings: R. J. Johnston, *The Dictionary of Human Geography*, 2nd ed., Oxford, U.K.: Basil Blackwell, 2000; Paul Vidal de le Blache, "Meaning and Aim of Human Geography," in *Human Geography: An Essential Anthology*, ed. John Agnew et al., Cambridge, Mass.: Basil Blackwell, 1996.

Postindustrial economy. The United States, Germany, Japan, and a number of other countries in the developed world have experienced a significant change in economic structure in the last 50 years. Beginning in the 1950s, more jobs have shifted to the service sector, and goods-producing industries (agriculture, forestry, fishing, mining, construction, and manufacturing) have shown relative declines. In 1950, goods-producing industries represented 49 percent of total employment in the United States. By 1980 this sector had declined to 33 percent. The service sector, with 51 percent of total employment in 1950, jumped to 67 percent in 1980. The service sector in the United States reached 81 percent in 2000, and will most likely continue to grow.

The primary and secondary sectors of the U.S. economy have diminished in relative importance. The primary sector includes extractive industries, such as agriculture, fishing, and forestry. This sector has declined from 13 percent of the total workforce in 1950 to less than 3 percent in 2000. Agriculture alone represents about 2 percent of the U.S. workforce. Yet, despite its small number, yields of food products continue to increase. The high productivity levels in agriculture are due to technological advancements, mechanization, and the application of scientific methods in farming. Progress in this economic sector has allowed for the growth and development of expansive **agribusiness** organizations. The secondary sector, including manufacturing and processing activities, has also declined in relative representation as the overall economy shifted toward a strong service-sector orientation. However, the relative decline in the number of workers in the secondary sector is deceiving for two reasons: (1) the existing manufacturing workforce is much more productive than in earlier years due to greater technological inputs, advanced assembly techniques, and, in some industries, the use of robotics; and (2) thousands of manufacturing jobs have been "outsourced" to other countries in order to take advantage of lower labor costs. **Transnational corporation**s that are based in the leading industrialized countries manage these overseas operations.

The **tertiary sector,** the major provider of services directly to consumers, has increased dramatically in the postindustrial era. Retail clerks, maintenance workers, and janitorial services are a few of the occupations within the tertiary sector. The next level is the **quaternary sector,** in which medical services, research activities, higher education, and high-technology operations are found. This sector has experienced significant growth, especially since the introduction and refinement of the computer and its use in essentially every economic endeavor. Finally, the **quinary sector** has also emerged as a high-growth service component in the postindustrial economy. Workers in this sector are concerned with high-level investigations of new forms of social economic systems. Included in the quinary sector are decision makers at the highest level of business and government and chief executive officers of national and multinational corporations. These individuals are the so-called movers and shakers.

The postindustrial economy is marked by the emergence of high technology and information processing at its conceptual base. However, the goods-producing functions in the primary and secondary sectors of the economy have by no means been abandoned.

Suggested Readings: David Clark, *Post-Industrial America: A Geographical Perspective*, New York: Methuen, 1985; Peter Dicken and Peter E. Lloyd, *Location in Space: Theoretical Perspectives in Economic Geography*, 3rd ed., New York: Harper & Row, 1990.

Postmodernism. The Enlightenment in eighteenth-century Europe was a period in intellectual thought that stressed the power of reason and the progress of rationality. The Enlightenment signaled a move away from centuries of what was considered a traditional way of life and began the era of modernism. Postmodernism, introduced in the late twentieth century, is an assault on the basic building blocks of modernism, which emphasized order in social, economic, and political systems. Modernist thinkers sought theories and generalizations to explain the complexities of human life. Postmodernism, on the other hand, has been described as being postparadigm and refuting the necessity for theory building.

For example, modernists placed importance on the notion of systems theory, the contention that apparently random and seemingly disparate outcomes are, in reality, somehow connected to and integrated within larger systems. Modernists suggest that it is only necessary to find the ways in which the parts are connected to the whole. Postmodernist thinking disputes this approach, contending that that are no totalizing systems or universal truths.

Postmodernism first emerged in the fields of architecture and literary theory. Its incorporation in geography dates to the 1980s and its place within the discipline is still being negotiated. The postmodernist movement stimulated geographer Edward Soja to suggest that modernist thought accepted the theoretical primacy of history and time over geography and space. Soja and other geographers have worked to reassert space as an important social variable.

The postmodern urban geographer searches for the differences in each city rather than the similarities. Particularity, diversity, and uniqueness are the analytical goals of the postmodernist researcher. Justification for this approach lies in the belief that the world is simply too complex and disjointed and that the search for order is pointless. In fact, the postmodernist suggests that the search for disorder should be the goal.

Postmodernist geographers are opposed to the model-building and positivist thinking that supported the spatial-science approaches introduced during the

Quantitative Revolution. Postmodernism has also been called poststructuralism because it opposes the notions of some sociologists who suggest the presence of so-called deep structures that guide human behavior. Postmodernists extend their emphasis on difference to the entire realm of the social sciences. The term *disorganized capitalism* emphasizes the heterogeneity of economic activity, societal settings, and political functions. The heterogeneity implicit in the postmodernist perspective provided a conceptual context for the study of differences and diversity within regions instead of a search for order.

Suggested Readings: Derek Gregory, *Geographical Imaginations*, London: Blackwell, 1994; David Harvey, *The Condition of Postmodernity: An Enquiry into the Origins of Cultural Change*, Oxford, U.K.: Basil Blackwell, 1989; Edward W. Soja, *Postmodern Geographies: The Reassertion of Space in Critical Social Theory*, London: Verso, 1989.

Primary sector. Economic activities involved with agriculture, the extraction of minerals and fuels, lumbering, and the initial processing of the associated materials represents the primary sector. Industries in this category tend to be located close to the materials that are grown, extracted, or processed. For example, 98 percent of the ore containing copper is waste material. The first steps in the processing of this ore is accomplished at the mine site, because it would not be economically sensible to pay for the long-distance hauling of ore composed primarily of waste material. Processors of meat have, within the last few years, located their operations in **feedlot**s near metropolitan areas to be close to the market centers.

Primary extractive industries deal with both **renewable resources** and nonrenewable resources. Renewable resource industries include forestry, fishing, and agriculture. They are called renewable because the resource can be replaced. That is, new trees can be grown to replace those taken for lumber, fish populations continue to grow, and agricultural crops can be replanted the following year. However, care must be taken to ensure the continued availability of these resources. Overfishing of some oceanic fish and mammal species has greatly lowered their numbers. Also, the damming of rivers in the Pacific Northwest has disrupted the spawning runs of salmon and has resulted in a reduction in their numbers. Similar concerns have been raised about the clearcutting of forests. More than half of the original tropical rain forest has been eliminated, and if current rates of tree removal continue, the world's rain forests could be completely eliminated in a few decades.

The major nonrenewable resources are petroleum, natural gas, and coal. All three are important sources of power for industries and homes. Coal is the most plentiful of these three resources. China has reserves of coal that could last up to 500 years and the United States has reserves for 250 to 300 years, depending on usage rates. However, the known reserves of petroleum and natural gas are not nearly as plentiful. For instance, it is estimated that petroleum reserves in the Middle East will last for only another 100 years. Middle Eastern countries are the world's major suppliers of this precious commodity. Petroleum's importance to the global economy occasioned a group of suppliers to form a cartel in the 1960s called the **Organization of Petroleum Exporting Countries** (OPEC). This group decided to collectively raise the price of a barrel of crude oil from about $3 in 1973 to nearly $60 in 1980. The oil-price shocks that occurred in 1973 and 1980 were particularly devastating to the economy of North America and western Europe. This series of events is a classic example of the economic influence on **geopolitics.**

Countries that are engaged in primary industrial activities as their mainstay are called primary producers. Most of the countries in the developing world fall into this category. Chad, for instance, derives over 90 percent of its export income from the sale of raw cotton. Zambia is one of the world's major exporters of copper. Most of Sub-Saharan Africa is heavily invested the production of **plantation agriculture** goods for export. Dependence on one or two export crops to provide the majority of a country's income is not economically lucrative for three reasons: (1) the prices of commodities are low compared to their value when transformed into manufactured goods or processed into food products; (2) the price of commodities can swing widely depending on the supply of the item; and (3) a country may respond incorrectly to the lowering of prices on the world market because of overproduction by producing more of the item. Adding to an already saturated market has the effect of driving the price down even further.

Suggested Readings: John Tarrant, "Farming and Food," in *The Illustrated Encyclopedia of World Geography,* New York: Oxford University Press, 1991; John E. Young, *Mining the Earth,* Worldwatch Paper no. 109, Washington, D.C.: Worldwatch Institute, 1992.

Primate city. The term *primate city* has two different but related meanings. In 1939, American geographer Mark Jefferson published an article in the *Geographical Review* titled "The Law of the Primate City." In this article, Jefferson argued that a dominant city could be found in every major region, and that city was the foremost representative of the region's culture. The primate city in Jefferson's view was preeminent in the economic, social, and political life of the region. Jefferson also noted regularity in the size of the primate city relative to the second and third cities in the region. This ratio was expressed as 100:30:20, indicating that the population of the second-largest city was 30 percent of that of the first, and the population of the third-ranked city was 20 percent of that of the first. The primate city attained its commanding size because of its leadership in the region and its ability to attract economic enterprises and greater numbers of people. A simple numerical index has been devised to measure the degree of primacy of the leading center:

$$\text{Index of primacy} = P1/P2$$

Where P1 and P2 are the populations of the primate city and the second-largest city. In this formula, the higher the index the greater the primacy of the city. Obvious primate cities at the global level are New York, Paris, London, and Tokyo, all of them being economic, social, and political leaders in their countries.

Primate city has also been used to identify the largest urban place in developing countries. Fort example, Mexico City has a metropolitan population of 25 million, which is one-fourth the population of Mexico and more than 10 times that of Guadalajara, the second-largest city. In many cases, the explanation for the emergence of the primate city derives from its selection as the administrative headquarters during the era of **colonialism.** For example, Lagos, Nigeria, became the center of British activity in that era. Lagos was the administrative center and the major shipping point for the export of commodities destined for Britain and the import of manufactured goods and items needed in the colonial operation. Virtually all the functions of the colonial system focused on Lagos. Following Nigeria's independence in the 1960s, restrictions on indigenous **migration** into Lagos were lifted, and the city's population further increased. In 2000 the population of Lagos reached 11 million. To alleviate some of the population pressure on the city, a decision was reached to move the capital and some administrative functions to an inland city. Lagos, however, remains an extremely crowded city. Other primate cities around the world include Manila, Bangkok, and Nairobi, all of which are dominant centers of influence within their respective countries.

Suggested Readings: David Drakakis-Smith, *The Third World City*, New York: Methuen, 1987; Josef Gugler, *Cities in the Developing World: Issues, Theory, and Policy*, London: Oxford University Press, 1997.

Projection. The globe is the most accurate model of the earth. It is a replica of the earth in its spherical shape, and it graphically presents all of the land and water bodies in their correct locations, shapes, and distances from one another. Any area on the globe's surface is three-dimensional because of its curvature. A map, on the other hand, is a two-dimensional surface, and in the transformation from a curved surface a degree of distortion is introduced. The distortion is seen in one or more of four dimensions: size, shape, distance, and direction. A projection is the process used to transform the curved surface of the globe to the flat surface of a map.

Hundreds of map projections have been developed. Cartographers use a number of basic projection types related to the noted dimensions of distortion. If the cartographer wants a map that can be used to compare areas on the earth's surface as closely as possible, a projection in the equal-area family is used. With an equal-area projection, one may visually compare the areas, for example, of South America and Greenland or Montana and Mongolia.

The equidistant projection portrays areas accurately in term of the distances separating them. For the retention of correct directional relationships, the azimuthal projection is used. Geographers or map users must remember to choose the right map for the task at hand. If area comparison is important in a study, then an equal-area projection is required.

It is important for the map user to understand the nature of distortion in any map being considered. Knowledge of the globe's graticule, or latitude and longitude reference system, provides the needed insights to note the form of distortion on any map. On a globe, the lines of latitude (or parallels) are, as the name suggests, parallel to one another. Parallels are also evenly spaced: the surface distance between 10 degrees north and 25 degrees north is the same as that between 30 degrees south and 45 degrees south. Also, the parallels diminish in circumference toward the poles. The lines of longitude (or meridians) converge at the poles and the space between them diminishes toward the poles. Parallels and meridians create 90-degree angles wherever they cross. A glance at any map that has a graticule gives an immediate indication of the form and degree of distortion. For example, in a cylindrical projection the parallels remain parallel but the spacing between them increases toward the poles. Meridians on a cylindrical projection remain parallel and do not converge as they do on the globe. On maps of this type, areas in the high latitudes are greatly enlarged. For example, Greenland appears larger than South America, which of course is not the case. When in doubt about the true shapes or areas of places on a map, it is best to consult a globe.

Suggested Readings: American Cartographic Association, *Matching the Map Projection to the Need*, Special Publication no. 3, Falls Church, Va.: American Congress on Surveying and Mapping, 1991; John P. Snyder, *Flattening the Earth: Two Thousand Years of Map Projections*, Chicago: University of Chicago Press, 1993.

Ptolemy (ca. A.D. 100–ca. 170). Ptolemy (Claudius Ptolemaeus) was an extremely influential scholar whose conclusions about the dimensions of the earth and compilations of data on the celestial bodies became the guiding doctrine through the European Middle Ages (about A.D. 500–1500). Ptolemy worked at the famous library at Alexandria from A.D. 127 to 150. During that time he wrote the *Almagest*, a classic study of astronomy and the movements of the stars and planets. Ptolemy was in agreement with the ancient Greek philosopher Aristotle that the earth was the center of the universe and that all celestial bodies revolved around it. This theory was not proven false until the work of the Polish astronomer Copernicus in the sixteenth century.

Ptolemy wrote summaries of Greek knowledge of astronomy and a book listing places using the latitude and longitude system devised by an earlier Greek scholar, Hipparchus. He also produced a world map that showed the Indian Ocean enclosed on the south by a landmass named Terra Incognita (unknown land). The presence of this landmass was not finally refuted until the voyage of the English captain James Cook in 1768–71. Arabic sailors who were familiar with the region had reported long before Cook's voyage that Terra Incognita did not exist.

Ptolemy accepted the measurement of the earth's circumference calculated by Greek philosopher Posidonius in the second century B.C. This measurement was smaller than the remarkably accurate one completed a century earlier by

Greek astronomer and geographer **Eratosthenes.** When the Italian explorer Christopher Columbus planned his epoch-making voyage in the fifteenth century, he used the circumference measure accepted by Ptolemy. In doing so, Columbus figured that the distance to Asia was much shorter than it actually is. So, when Columbus landed in the New World he thought he had successfully reached Asia. He named the indigenous culture groups he encountered Indians, an inaccuracy that persists to the present time.

Ptolemy was the last great Greek scholar before the beginning of the Middle Ages, a 1,000-year period during which much of the literature of the Greek and Roman eras was lost. Through the Middle Ages, Ptolemaic thought dominated astronomy and astrology.

Suggested Readings: George Kish, *A Source Book in Geography,* Cambridge: Harvard University Press, 1978; Geoffrey J. Martin and Preston E. James, *All Possible Worlds: A History of Geographical Ideas,* 3rd ed., New York: John Wiley & Sons, 1993.

Purchasing power parity. The standard international measure of a country's affluence has been **gross national product** (GNP) and GNP per capita, reported in U.S. dollars. For a number of reasons, this measure provides an inaccurate picture of real buying power in developing countries. First, GNP per capita is a countrywide average, and it does not report the great differences in incomes within a country. Most developing countries have a dual societal structure in which a small percentage of wealthy people control most of the wealth and the majority of the population has very little. There are also great differences in the purchasing power of local currencies. For instance, an item in the United States or Canada that costs $5 might sell for $2 or $3 in a developing country. When the factor of increased purchasing power is taken into account, the economic level of a country is much higher than it is when reported by GNP alone. Another consideration invalidates GNP as an accurate measure of buying power in developing countries: only the formal sector of the economy is reported to the government and taken into account when total revenues are tabulated. Missing from the country's total income are the proceeds generated by the **informal sector,** a vast **network** of business activities that are not reported.

In 1993, the World Bank instituted a new reporting system called purchasing power parity (PPP). This new approach took into account the purchasing power in local currencies. GNP per capita in Sub-Saharan Africa is less than $750 in nearly every country in the region. When PPP is used as the measure, however, these same countries show per capita values ranging from less than $750 to over $4,000.

Although the PPP reporting system paints a more appealing picture of economic conditions in the developing world, it is true that general levels of affluence are behind those in the developed countries. The status of absolute poverty grips perhaps 30 to 35 percent of the population in developing countries. An income of $1 marks the level of absolute poverty. Using PPP increases the annual income from $365 to over $450, an improvement, but still a state of absolute poverty.

Despite the invocation of PPP, the plight of most people in the developing world is grim. Levels of absolute poverty are expected to climb as population continues to increase and economic growth stalls. Development experts are unanimous in their insistence that change in the developing countries requires an emphasis of improvements in education and more-efficient medical delivery systems. Of equal importance is the need to employ the large potential workforce in the developing world. In short, economic growth is the key to a better life in the developing world, and it takes time for viable economic systems to become established and to thrive. In the meantime, the bitterness of poverty persists.

Suggested Readings: International Bank for Reconstruction and Development/World Bank, *World Development Report*, New York: Oxford University Press, annual; George T. Kurian, *Atlas of the Third World*, New York: Facts on File, 1992.

Push and pull factors. Two primary generators of the **migration** of individuals and groups of people are push and pull factors. Basically, a push factor impels people to leave their present location because of political instability, adverse environmental conditions, or the lack of viable economic opportunities. For example, the Jewish population in Germany during the Nazi regime found the political climate of racial suppression unbearable, and millions left the country. Drought conditions over the last 20 years in the Sahel, the semiarid area on the southern margin of the Sahara Desert in Africa, forced thousands of people to leave that region. Many of them became **refugees** because they could not find suitable accommodations in other areas.

Following the end of the Vietnam War in 1975, many South Vietnamese fled the country as the North Vietnamese conquerors moved in to occupy the region. Another example of a push factor is seen in the exodus of people from East Germany as the Berlin Wall was under construction. The Berlin Wall, surrounding West Berlin, was built in 1961; it was torn down in 1989. Political repression in communist East Germany served as a compelling reason to leave the country.

Pull factors draw people to new places for economic, environmental, or cultural reasons. People are perennially drawn to large metropolitan areas because the prospects for employment are good. New York City, Chicago, and Los Angeles have an unending stream of newcomers arriving in search of jobs. The same is true of other major cities, such as Tokyo, London, and Paris. There is also the pull of an entire country. The United States has attracted millions of immigrants from all over the world seeking jobs and a better way of life. Western European countries have regularly drawn workers from countries in the Middle East and Southwest Asia as the younger age groups have diminished in numbers.

The Sunbelt in the United States—the tier of states from California east to Florida—has experienced dramatic growth in population in recent decades. Many companies in the northern states have chosen to either relocate or expand operations to the warmer climes of the Sunbelt. Movements of this kind bring employees to the new site. Individual retirees from northern states are choosing to retire in the Sunbelt and escape the long cold winters in the north. In both of these situations there are both push and pull factors in operation.

Suggested Readings: Phillip Martin and Elizabeth Midgley, "Immigration to the United States," *Population Bulletin,* vol. 54 (1999); Charles B. Nam et al., *International Handbook on Migration,* Westport, Conn.: Greenwood Press, 1990.

Q

Quantitative Revolution. American **geography** in the early twentieth century came out of a brief encounter with **environmental determinism** and then shifted to a regional focus. The regional approach came under attack in the 1950s by a group of geographers claiming that it had no sound theoretical underpinnings and that there were no attempts by regional geographers to develop higher-level generalizations that could lead to theory building in the discipline. For example, a study of a particular urban region in one part of the country was not undertaken with the aim of eventually being able to compare the research outcomes with an urban place somewhere else. The concern of the critics was that most geographical studies were particularistic and stressed the uniqueness of places. The work was ideographic in nature and not nomothetic, or law seeking. Against this disciplinary backdrop, geographers at a number of U.S. universities launched what has come to be called the Quantitative Revolution.

The view of these geographers was that the discipline of geography should become more robust and vital, and the way to accomplish this was to include statistical and quantitative techniques in geography research projects. Geography, it turns out, had always used quantitative techniques, but the advocates of a more scientific geography insisted on a great deal more of them. Physical geography had already incorporated a numerical analysis because of the nature of its work. What was new was the expansive inclusion of quantitative and statistical techniques within **human geography.** Especially significant was the use of the new techniques in **economic** and **urban geography.** Some areas of the discipline were little influenced by the wave of quantification that unfolded. Among them were **cultural geography** and **historical ge-**

ography, areas of the discipline that progressed without the need for added numerical analysis.

Within the discipline as a whole, there were many geographers who thought that the push for quantification was at best taking geography down the wrong road or at worst not geography at all. During the 1950s and 1960s, a number of spirited exchanges about the movement, both pro and con, appeared in *Professional Geographer,* one of the journals published by the Association of American Geographers.

The real goal of the advocates of quantification was to create added objectivity in geographical studies and to further the philosophical tenets of logical positivism in the discipline. This could be accomplished, the advocates contended, through the use of formal logic mathematics and empirical observation.

By the end of the 1960s, the Quantitative Revolution was challenged by geographers who insisted on a more humane approach in the discipline. Within the first few years of the 1970s, studies in **behavioral geography** and **humanistic geography** began to appear in the professional literature. Both of these philosophical streams were generated in reaction against what was perceived as the cold objectivity of quantification and its dehumanizing approaches to geographical study.

In time the initial fervor for the Quantitative Revolution abated, but many of the numerical techniques and a good share of the rationale for the approach remain in geography. For instance, the practice of sampling from a larger population, the use of correlation and regression techniques, and the analysis of **pattern** with statistics are all part of the geographer's methodological inventory.

Suggested Readings: W. K. D. Davies, *The Conceptual Revolution in Geography,* London: University of London Press, 1972; David Harvey, *Explanation in Geography,* London: Edward Arnold, 1969; Richard L. Morrill, "The Nature, Unity, and Value of Geography," *Professional Geographer,* vol. 35 (1983).

Quaternary sector. The quaternary sector is one of the fastest-growing industry groups in the **postindustrial economy.** Economic activities in the quaternary sector include accounting, finance, higher education, computer services, governmental operations, and the media. The quaternary sector is also known familiarly as the white-collar sector, a name that for years has identified middle and top management in business and industry.

A large and growing part of the quaternary sector involves the accumulation, processing, and transmission of information. In many ways, information has become the crucial element in coordinating the efforts of the **primary, secondary,** and **tertiary sector**s of the global economy.

The quaternary sector may be compared with the bridge and control center on a large naval vessel. The decision making engaged in is necessary to the smooth operation of the entire ship. Decisions made about the amount of crude steel to produce or to be imported in the next year, the number of automobiles to be manufactured, or the research directions to be taken by a pharmaceutical firm are examples of the kinds of tasks accomplished in the quaternary sector.

Employees in the quaternary sector are, for the most part, experts in their fields. They have developed the specialized knowledge and technical skills necessary to make difficult operational decisions and to anticipate and be proactive to changes in their particular industry. Many aspects of the decision-making process in the quaternary sector have become so specialized and complex that separate consulting firms have been created solely to handle these tasks. These firms make their services available to companies needing assistance in specific areas of their operation. For example, a manufacturer may want advice on establishing a robotics function in an assembly process and will seek the assistance of a consultant in that field. An accounting firm wanting to upgrade or change its business computer system may solicit help in choosing the right equipment from consultants knowledgeable in the latest computer systems. Even public school districts have employed educational consultants to help in the improvement of teaching and learning in their schools. In some cases, school districts have come under the management of private firms that run the schools on a contract basis.

Quaternary industries are located throughout every country in the developed world. Rapid communication and efficient **transportation systems** have allowed many activities to become footloose and to seek varied locales in which to set up operations. However, some quaternary industries are clustered in **high-tech corridor**s such as California's Silicon Valley, the Research Triangle Park in North Carolina, and Japan's high-density corridor reaching from Tokyo west to northern Kyushu.

Suggested Readings: Stanley D. Brunn and Thomas R. Leinbach, *Collapsing Space and Time: Geographical Aspects of Communications and Information,* London: HarperCollins Academic, 1991; Manuel Castels and Peter Hall, *Technopoles of the World: The Making of 21st Century Industrial Complexes,* London: Routledge, 1994; Mark E. Hepworth, *Geography of the Information Economy,* New York: Guilford Press, 1990.

Quinary sector. Decision making at the highest levels of the economy and national government occur within the quinary sector. In the United States, the work of the president, the presidential cabinet, and the two houses of Congress represent activities in the quinary sector. Certain forms of medical and scientific research are also found in the quinary sector. For example, the governmental decision to seek bids on a new military fighter plane or considerations of the efficacy of human cloning are quinary-sector activities.

It is in the quinary sector that research is conducted aimed at improving the existing socioeconomic system and taking it to new heights. The high-level decisions made in the quinary sector are meant to introduce new knowledge, information, and skills into the economy to bring about growth and improvement. For example, the governmental decision many years ago to create the Environmental Protection Agency (EPA) was made at the highest levels. The purpose of the decision was, of course, to create a federal agency to monitor and protect the environment. Taking this example a bit further, it is hoped that this quinary-sector decision will ultimately improve the socioeconomic setting for the entire country through sound management and protection of the environment.

International efforts to reduce the emissions of greenhouse gases into the atmosphere (*see* **Greenhouse effect**) resulted in a series of conferences over a two-decade period that culminated in the **Kyoto Protocol** of 1997. The United States signed the protocol, but the document was never submitted to the Senate for ratification. In time, the Kyoto Protocol was scrapped, but efforts continue to suppress greenhouse gas emissions. All of the decisions concerning atmospheric degradation and proposals to rectify the problems were made at the quinary level.

The quinary sector is increasing in size and importance in the same manner as the **quaternary sector.** In fact, all of the service sectors are on the increase and will continue to increase in the future. **Primary** and **secondary sector**s, although not as highly represented in numbers of workers since the transition to the **postindustrial society,** remain important in the overall economy. The number of workers in the primary and secondary sectors may be diminishing, but outputs remain high. This positive outcome is attributable in large part to the efficient coordinating efforts of the quaternary sector and the innovative and enhancing inputs from the quinary sector.

Suggested Readings: Maryanne Feldman and Richard Florida, "The Geographical Sources of Innovation: Technological Infrastructure and Product Innovation in the United States," *Annals of the Association of American Geographers*, vol. 84 (1994); Donald J. Porteus, *The Geography of Finance*, Aldershot, U.K.: Avebury Press, 1995.

R

Range. *See* **Christaller's central place theory.**

Rank-size rule. German geographer George K. Zipf (1902–50) developed a hypothesis published in 1949 for predicting the populations of urban places in a region based on the rank of any one urban place. His studies indicated that there was invariably a single largest urban place and that the populations of the other urban places were in a regular ratio to the first. This rank-size relationship can be stated in a simple expression:

$$Pr = P1/r$$

where Pr is the population of the urban place of rank r, P1 is the population of the first-ranked place, and r is the rank. For example, if City A has 900,000 people and is the first-ranked place, then according to the rank-size rule the population of City B, second to A, would be one-half that of A:

$$B = 900,000/2 = 450,000$$

The third-ranked city would be 300,000, and so forth. So, if it is known that the fourth-ranked city in a region has a population of one million, it is possible to predict the populations of the first, second, third, and other places in the region. The first-ranked city would have 4 million; the second, 2 million; the third, 1.33 million; and the fifth, 800,000.

When the rank-size values are graphed using arithmetic scales, the result is a J-shaped curve. The J-shaped curve illustrates the relationship very clearly, but it is difficult to use in determining adherence to the rank-size rule when actual values are plotted. To solve this problem, logarithmic scales are used on both the horizontal and vertical axes. The predicted values now connect with a straight line. When actual populations are plotted, it is easy to note variances from the predicted regularity of the rank-size rule.

When urban places in the developed world are plotted, there is a close adherence to the predicted regularity. Of course, no country exactly fits the relationship, but many are very close. Japan, Australia, Canada, and the United States, among others, have rank-size relationships that closely fit the predictions of the rank-size rule. In the case of the United States, the regularity is retained in every census year since the first in 1790. Since that year, when the population was a mere 4 million, the rank-size rule has held, even though total population increased to over 270 million by 2000. The rule holds through this period even though cities changed rank, some cities dropped out of the rankings, and new cities increased in population and joined the rankings as westward expansion unfolded.

An explanation for the regularity in the rank-size rule is that it applies primarily to the developed countries. But it applied to the United States when the country was engaged primarily in agriculture and into the industrial and postindustrial eras. The rule also works in the cities of China, a developing country throughout its history. The rank-size rule has never been explained to the satisfaction of all geographers. Yet, the regularity exists.

Developing countries, especially those that were former colonies, show a different rank-size relationship. In their case, the **primate city** is prevalent. During the era of **colonialism** in the nineteenth and early twentieth centuries, one urban place was chosen to be the administrative center. These places grew much faster than other urban places in the colony. Following independence, these primate cities retained their size advantage and continued to be the leading centers in the postcolonial period. Lagos, Nigeria, for example, the administrative center under British colonial rule, today is many times larger than the second city in the country. In fact, Lagos became so large and difficult to manage that a new administrative capital for the country was established in the interior. This has alleviated some of the pressure on Lagos, but it remains overcrowded.

Suggested Readings: John W. Marshall, "Beyond the Rank-Size Rule: A New Descriptive Model of City Sizes," *Urban Geography*, vol. 18 (1997); Clifton Pannell, "China's Urban Transition," *Journal of Geography*, vol. 94 (1995).

Rate of natural increase. The rate of natural increase (RNI) of a population is found by subtracting the **crude death rate** (CDR) from the **crude birthrate** (CBR) and transforming the result into a percentage. For example, the West African country Benin in 1998 had a CBR of 45 per thousand of total population and a CDR of 14 per thousand:

$$45 \text{ (per 1,000)} - 14 \text{ (per 1,000)} = 31 \text{ (per 1,000) or 3.1 per 100,}$$
$$\text{which is 3.1 percent}$$

Benin's RNI is considered high; world RNI is about 1.3 percent and the RNI for the developing world is about 1.6 percent. Benin's percentage is, of course, attributed to higher birthrates, a characteristic of countries in the developing world. Although birthrates have declined globally over the past few decades, their drop has not equaled that of death rates. Consequently, any country with an abnormally high birthrate invariably has a high RNI. Sub-Saharan Africa has the highest RNI values in the world. Within that vast region, West Africa and East Africa have RNI values near 3.0 percent, whereas the value for central Africa is over 3.0 percent.

In contrast, nearly every country in Europe has an RNI less than 1.0 percent, and some have experienced several years of negative RNI, a situation that occurs when the death rate exceeds the birthrate. A situation such as this may indicate a general lowering of total population in a country. However, an overall loss of population may not necessarily occur, because RNI does not consider the number of people gained or lost through **migration.** For example, in the 1980s, West Germany's RNI was negative for a number of years but its net migration into the country more than made up for natural decline. Unlike Benin, West Germany's CBR was very low and its average age was high. As a result, there were far fewer people in the childbearing years.

Suggested Readings: Arthur Haupt and Thomas Kane, *Population Handbook*, 4th ed., Washington, D.C.: Population Reference Bureau, 1997; several world population links are found at the Center for Disease Control Web site, www.cdc.gov/nchswww.

Ratzel, Friedrich (1844–1904). Friedrich Ratzel, with his contemporaries British geographer **Halford J. Mackinder** and American geographer **William Morris Davis,** was a pioneer in crafting late-nineteenth-century German geography. This period was crucial in the development of the discipline. The golden age of exploration had ended, and with it, as many historians of the discipline contend, the high point in the history of geography. It was also the dawn of a new era for geography as separate departments were opening in universities. Ratzel and other prominent geographers worked to make the case that geography should be granted a position in university curricula. The justification furthered by Ratzel and others was that no other discipline dealt with the spatial aspects of the interface between nature and culture, what is now referred to as human–environment interaction. Ratzel was one of the premier exponents of this conceptual view.

Ratzel's early education was in zoology, geology, and comparative anatomy. His doctoral thesis dealt with aspects of nineteenth-century English naturalist **Charles Darwin**'s theory of evolution. Ratzel was a prolific field worker in the style of **Alexander von Humboldt.** He studied German resettlement following the unification of the country in 1871. Ratzel visited the United States in

Friedrich Ratzel. *Source:* Geoffrey Martin.

1874–75 to do fieldwork on settlement **pattern** formation of different culture groups within a common region. His work in the United States convinced Ratzel to become a geographer.

In 1886, Ratzel was appointed professor of geography at Leipzig University. His major writing includes the two-volume work *Anthropogeographie*. In volume one, published in 1882, Ratzel discussed the effects of various physical features on the course of history. Later historians of geography used this work to link Ratzel to the concept of **environmental determinism,** an extreme stance on the pervasive dominance of the physical world on occupying culture groups. The second volume of *Anthropogeographie*, published in 1891, paid greater attention to the workings of culture groups and to **diffusion** and less to environmental influences. Ratzel also wrote an important book on **political geography** in 1897 in which he compared the earth to a living organism that must either grow or die and cannot remain constant. This notion was incorporated within **geopolitics** and later was adopted by the Nazi government in the 1930s to justify the German expansion into neighboring countries before World War II.

Suggested Readings: J. Anderson, C. Brook, and A. Cochrane, eds., *A Global World? Reordering Political Space*, Oxford: Oxford University Press, 1995; Brian W. Blouet, *Geopolitics and Globalization in the Twentieth Century*, North Kingstown, R.I.: Reaktion Books, 2001; Geoffrey J. Martin and Preston E. James, *All Possible Worlds: A History of Geographical Ideas*, 3rd ed., New York: John Wiley & Sons, 1993.

Refugees. The plight of refugees represents one of the most tragic situations in the world. In 1970 there were about three million refugees worldwide. By 2000, according to estimates by the U.S. Commission for Refugees, the number had increased to over 30 million. The United Nations High Commission for Refugees defines refugees as people who have been forced to leave their homes and are unable to return because of war, environmental disasters (*see* **Natural hazards**), famine, or repression based on race, religion, nationality, or membership in a social group not authorized by the present government.

Palestinians and Afghanis represent the two largest groups of refugees. There are more than five million Afghan refugees, most of whom fled their country during the Soviet military occupation from 1979 to 1989. Thousands more were displaced during the first few months of the war on terrorism in 2001. However, many of these Afghan refugees began returning to their homes in early 2002 as hostilities lessened. Palestinians were displaced when the country of Israel was created in 1948. Palestinians are spread throughout the Middle

East, with at least two-thirds of the population living in the Gaza Strip, Jordan, and the West Bank. Smaller groups are found in Syria, Lebanon, and Saudi Arabia. Continued conflict has plagued the Middle East since 1948, and one of the demands of the Palestinians is the creation of their own sovereign state, an outcome that has yet to be realized. In the meantime, tensions between the Palestinians and the Israelis remain high.

Iran is the leading country hosting refugees. More than two million refugees were living in Iran in 2000. Most of them were from Afghanistan and Iraq, countries where war has raged in recent decades.

Hundreds of thousands of Vietnamese refugees crossed into Thailand, Laos, and Cambodia during the Vietnam War, and thousands more left South Vietnam by boat, plane, and on foot in advance of the North Vietnamese occupation following the end of the war in 1975. A number of African countries have endured refugee problems in recent years. Among them are Somalia, Sudan, and Ethiopia. In Sudan, the southern highland region is predominantly Christian and the north is Muslim. Conflict between the two dissimilar culture groups over the years resulted in the displacement of more than two million Sudanese. A slave trade accompanied the conflict, and thousands of young people from Sudan's southern region were taken to the north in bondage.

Suggested Readings: John R. Rogge, *Refugees: A Third World Dilemma*, Totowa, N.J.: Rowman & Littlefield, 1987; United Nations High Commission for Refugees, *The State of the World's Refugees*, New York: Oxford University Press, annual; W. Wood, "Forced Migration," *Annals of the Association of American Geographers*, vol. 84 (1994).

Region. The region represents one way of classifying information about places. Every discipline has its own classification systems, and **geography** is no exception. Geography is a spatial discipline dealing with the physical and cultural content of areas. The region is a logical and convenient spatial form for organizing the significant contents of the areas under study.

The concept of region has a long and checkered history in geography. Both **Strabo** and **Ptolemy** made reference to regional studies in their writings. Ptolemy, in fact, proposed a three-level approach to the study of places in the known world. In this schema, geography was proposed as the focus for studying the entire world. Ptolemy also proposed that chorography (the art of describing or mapping a region) be the approach for studying large parts of the world. In Ptolemy's time, the known world extended from the Atlantic coast east through the Mediterranean Sea and its adjacent land areas and to the Indian subcontinent. South of the Indian subcontinent was the Indian Ocean, enclosed, Ptolemy claimed, by the landmass he called Terra Incognita (unknown land). Chorography, Ptolemy proposed, could be used to study parts of the whole world, such as North Africa or the Indian subcontinent.

Ptolemy's third level was called topography, and it dealt with the study of small areas in detail. Focus on the Nile River delta, for instance, would qualify as a topographical study in Ptolemy's schema. Two of the three levels of

Ptolemy's spatial hierarchy are still used and retain the same meaning: geography and topography. A **topographic map** covers a limited area in great detail. Chorography, however, was replaced in time by the concept of region. One part of the word, *choro*, is still in use in **choropleth map.**

Early in the twentieth century, American geography moved away from its prevailing focus on **environmental determinism** and took up the study of regions. A number of geographers found the regional approach to lack robustness and felt it was not suitably structured to develop a theoretical base in the discipline. The main criticism of the regional approach was that it focused on the unique aspects of the regions under study and that no possibility existed to compare research outcomes with work done on other regions. The ideographic or particularistic and unique approach, the critics stated, led to unscientific research outcomes. In the 1950s and 1960s, the **Quantitative Revolution** sent geography in new and unfamiliar conceptual directions and the longtime focus on the region was replaced by **systematic (thematic) geography.**

In contemporary geography the region remains a viable entity. In addition to its important role in providing a spatial classification system, there are three additional regional types used extensively in geography. One of these is the uniform, or formal, region, which is used to identify and delineate an area that has a predominant cultural or physical feature. The climatic classifications of tundra, tropical rain forest, and desert are examples of uniform regions. In like manner, maps showing such cultural attributes as Hinduism, the Sinitic languages, and the Inuit culture group are also examples of uniform regions.

Nodal, or functional, regions represent a second type. As the name implies, this regional form is based on the **range** of influence of a function. For example, a store owner may be interested in determining the extent of the store's customer base. A map could be compiled showing home addresses of all customers over the last year. A line on the map would then enclose the area that includes all customer locations. The delineated area identifies the nodal region of customers frequenting the store in the previous year. The function in this example is shopping activity and the attraction of customers to the store location. Another frequently used example of a nodal region is the range of Sunday newspaper circulation. Again, once the recipient addresses have been mapped, an enclosing line can be drawn around them to delineate the region.

A third form of region appears in a number of textbooks that discuss the geographical attributes of areas such as Latin America, East Asia, and Africa by dividing these large areas into logically based regions. For example, a regionalization of Africa would include discussion of the region of Sub-Saharan Africa and the regions within Sub-Saharan Africa: West Africa, central Africa, and southern Africa.

The United States and Canada are commonly divided into 15 distinct regions. Among them are **Megalopolis,** the Midwest, the South, the Great Plains and the prairies, and Maritime Canada. Again, the classification feature of the region is seen. Each of the regions mentioned was determined by the sum of the cultural and physical characteristics found within them. Clearly, the South is easily distinguished from the Arctic and the Pacific Northwest, just as Megalopolis is regionally quite distinct from the Arid Southwest.

Suggested Readings: John Allen, Doreen B. Massey, Allan Cochrane, and Julie Charlesworth, eds., *Rethinking the Region*, New York: Routledge, 1998; Paul Claval, "The Region as a Geographical, Economic, and Cultural Concept," *International Social Science Journal*, vol. 39 (1987); R. J. Johnstone and G. A. Koekveld, eds., *Regional Geography: Current Developments and Future Prospects*, New York: Routledge, 1990.

Regional geography. The branch of geography that uses the **region** as the primary focus of attention is regional geography. Textbooks in regional geography are organized around discussions of logically derived regional complexes within a larger areal setting. For example, a number of books deal with the regional geography of the United States and Canada, a region in itself and one of a dozen or so regions at the global level. Within the overall region of the United States and Canada there are 15 regions, each of which was determined by the sum of cultural and physical properties that make it distinct from other regions. Among the identified regions are **Megalopolis,** the urbanized eastern seaboard; the Pacific Northwest, home of the northern rain forest; the Midwest, traditionally a center of agricultural production and manufacturing; the arid Southwest, a region with a long history of settlement by American Indians, Hispanics, and Anglo-Americans; and the tundra, the northernmost region on the fringes of the Arctic Ocean. Note that some of the regional names are cultural and some reflect a physical or climatic basis.

The most interesting aspect of regional geography, and the factor that advocates of the regional focus suggest points to its strength, is the way in which it addresses both cultural and physical attributes of place. A study of the Pacific Northwest, for example, considers the salient **systematic (thematic) geography** of the place. Physical features, economic systems, the urban **network,** and the region's connections to other places in the world, all become components in a regional treatment. Regional geography, then, is an integrating and holistic analysis of a place. With this in mind, it is understandable that many geographers consider regional geography to be the most authentic approach in geographical analysis.

Regional geography also focuses on the areal extent of individual spatial attributes. The North American manufacturing belt, the Ruhr industrial district in Germany, and the productive agricultural region in the Ganges River Valley in northern India are all examples of this kind of focus. In studies of this type, the main intent is to derive the fullest possible explanation of the particular functions under analysis. In the case of the North American manufacturing belt, for example, the regional geographer explains how the region originated, its internal cultural and physical attributes, how it is connected with other regions, and the ways it has changed over time.

Regional geography is perhaps the most comprehensive approach to the study of places. It provides disciplinary proof that a full and comprehensive geographical treatment of any area on the earth's surface must include suitable inputs from both physical and **human geography.**

Suggested Readings: John C. Hudson, *Across the Land: A Regional Geography of the United States and Canada*, Baltimore: Johns Hopkins University Press, 2001; Kenichi Ohmae, "The Rise of the Region State," *Foreign Affairs*, spring 1993.

Relative location. Geographers may refer to the location of a place in relation to another place. To do so involves the concept of relative location. Locating places in this manner can be a very powerful tool for geographers because it invokes the dynamic character of the discipline. A reference to the Arcade Theater being six blocks north of the Cando, North Dakota, bus depot is an example of locating a place (the theater) relative to another place (the bus depot). On another **scale,** the location of Duluth, Minnesota, may be stated in this way: Duluth is located 150 miles north-northeast of the Twin Cities. It may also be stated that Chicago is 400 miles east-southeast of the Twin Cities. These three examples show how relative location can rise to a higher level of conceptual sophistication and robustness. In 2000 the population of the Twin Cities was about 2.2 million, Duluth had about 75,000 population, and Chicago had more than 5 million. It would not be surprising to learn that the number of nonstop scheduled airline flights between Chicago and the Twin Cities far exceeds the number of flights between the Twin Cities and Duluth. It may be concluded that Chicago, although it is farther from the Twin Cities in linear distance, is closer to the Twin Cities than Duluth if the measure of relative location is **accessibility** by scheduled airline flights.

Change the scale again and consider the location of the United States relative to the former Soviet Union as shown on a polar-centered map. During the **cold war,** it was readily apparent that intercontinental ballistic missiles, if launched, would be launched over the North Pole to reach their intended target. On a less-ominous note, consider the location of Los Angeles relative to the larger region of which it is a part: the highly urbanized corridor extending from San Francisco to San Diego. Familiarly named Sansan, this is the third-largest urban integration in the United States, and Los Angeles is strategically located within this fast-growing region, an advantage for economic growth.

At a truly global scale, note the location of Japan relative to its two major economic markets, North America and Europe. Both are essentially halfway around the world. This fact makes Japan's astounding economic success following its defeat in World War II even more remarkable.

In the discussion of **absolute location,** reference was made to Mischief Reef, a tiny atoll in the Spratly Islands in the South China Sea. The absolute location of the place is easily determined. However, it is in the relative location of Mischief Reef that its strategic importance is revealed. This seemingly insignificant island lies precisely along key sea-lanes that, among other things, are the delivery routes for virtually all of Japan's crude oil. Mischief Reef lies within the hotly contested South China Sea, a body of water claimed in total by both

Chinese governments and Vietnam to be their exclusive property. To add to the complexity of this geopolitical situation, the Philippines, located to the east of the Spratly Islands, claims ownership of that island complex, including Mischief Reef. Finally, there is strong evidence that petroleum and natural gas reserves are present in abundance in the seabed below the South China Sea. With all these factors in mind, it is clear that Mischief Reef, and the entirety of the South China Sea, is a very dynamic region. Applying the important concept of relative location helps to gain a sound perspective on this region and any other region under analysis.

Suggested Readings: William D. Pattison, "The Four Traditions of Geography," *Journal of Geography*, vol. 63 (1964); Tim F. Wood, "Thinking in Geography," *Geography*, vol. 72 (1987).

Relict boundary. A relict boundary is one that no longer delineates the separation between countries but remains visible because of existing features representing its previous function. The relict boundary is one of a number of **boundary** types that are recognized in **political geography.** It is testimony to the frequent changes that have taken place over time along the interfaces of sovereign states.

The many boundary changes that have taken place between Poland and Russia because of wars and political decisions made through history provide ample evidence of relict boundaries. Many of these discarded boundaries would be categorized as relict if there were features in the cultural landscape to attest to their presence in the past. A monument, the name of a town or city associated with the past boundary, or even a section of a wall that served as the physical boundary would classify the boundary as a relict.

The quick removal of the Berlin Wall following the shattering of the communist regimes in the Soviet Union and Eastern Europe resulted in a relict boundary. Any point along the line of the previous barricade where a remnant remains is evidence of a relict boundary. There is cultural evidence of the presence of the boundary separating North and South Vietnam before the end of the conflict in 1975. At these points a relict boundary exists.

Suggested Readings: M. D. Hancock and H. Welsh, *German Unification: Process and Outcomes*, 2nd ed., Boulder Colo.: Westview Press, 1993; J. R. R. Prescott, *Political Frontiers and Boundaries*, London: Allen & Unwin, 1987.

Relocation diffusion. The movement of a business organization to another location and the **migration** of people from one country to another are both examples of relocation diffusion. Relocation diffusion differs from **expansion diffusion** specifically in the vacating of the original location and moving to a new one. For example, companies relocate for a number of reasons. Wage rates and rental costs may be more attractive in another region. If the difference in costs is significant, a business may choose to relocate. Many companies in the crowded eastern seaboard of the United States have chosen to relocate to the Sunbelt and the fast-growing industrial states of Virginia and North Carolina.

People may migrate to other countries because of negative situations in their homeland, or they may perceive that more-positive conditions exist in another place. The basis for the move may be a combination of the two. In these situations, particular **push and pull factors** are closely associated with relocation diffusion.

Certainly the largest relocation diffusion in history was the migration of millions of people from the European and African countries during the two major phases of **colonialism.** The first colonial era began following the discovery of the Western Hemisphere in 1492 and continued into the twentieth century. The second colonial era occurred in the nineteenth and early twentieth centuries. Migration took place throughout these two eras. The migrants brought their religion, languages, social systems, and other cultural attributes to the New World and in doing so dramatically changed the world. In recent years, migrations have continued as people from Asian countries have migrated to North America and Europe to begin a new life.

The twentieth-century Swedish geographer **Torsten Hagerstrand** pioneered research in the process of diffusion. His statistical modeling of diffusion was influential in furthering this branch of geographical studies.

Relocation may be voluntary or forced. In the United States, families relocate to a new residence on average every five years. The move may be across town or from coast to coast. In either case, it is clear that Americans are mobile. Permanent changes of residence such as these are examples of relocation diffusion. A negative example was the forced migration of millions of African people during the era of slavery. The same is true of the expulsion of the Jewish population from Spain in 1492.

When groups relocate to new areas, they bring their culture with them. In turn, the new arrivals are exposed to the behaviors and traits of the host group. A certain degree of **acculturation** occurs following relocation when dissimilar groups of people live together in proximity.

Suggested Readings: Larry H. Long, *Migration and Residential Mobility in the United States*, New York: Russell Sage Foundation, 1988; Colin G. Pooley and Ian D. Whyte, *Migrants, Emigrants, and Immigrants: A Social History of Migration*, London: Routledge, 1991.

Renewable resources. The earth's natural resources are classified as being nonrenewable or renewable. Renewable resources, as the name suggests, can be regenerated, either naturally or by human action. Examples of renewable resources are forests, fish, agricultural products, livestock, grasses used for forage, and soils. All of these renewable resources are, however, subject to deterioration if usage rates exceed replenishment levels.

Some renewable resources have been greatly overused, and the chances are low for full replenishment in the future. The tropical rain forests that stretch across the equatorial belt have been decimated. Demands for tropical wood for furniture, the expansion of agricultural activities, and the growing of grasses for livestock have greatly decreased the area of tropical rain forest cover. At present rates of tree removal, it is estimated that the tropical rain forests could be completely eliminated within a few decades.

Another crisis is unfolding in the oceanic fishing industry. Fish species reduction through overfishing threatens to cripple the entire industry. The demise of the Atlantic cod is a case in point. There is a growing literature on the subject of **sustainable development,** an approach that stresses reasonable usage rates to ensure the preservation of the renewable resource base.

Naturally renewable resources represent a separate category and include the acquisition of power from solar, water, wind, and geothermal sources. Technology has been developed to harness the energy from these resources, and more attention will certainly be paid to advancing these prospects in the future. Increasing the amount of energy obtained from the naturally renewable resources will lessen our reliance on exhaustible fossil fuels, such as crude oil, natural gas, and coal. Exhaustible resources are nonrenewable. Some nonrenewable resources, such as metals and some petroleum products, however, are being recycled. This important process actually extends the life of a nonrenewable resource and delays the time of inevitable exhaustion.

Suggested Readings: James R. Coull, *World Fisheries Resources,* New York: Routledge, 1993; G. Tyler Miller Jr., *Resource Conservation and Management,* Belmont, Calif.: Wadsworth, 1990; Rainforest Action Network Web site, www.ran.org (organization devoted to the protection of the rain forests).

Resource. A resource may be an item of information or a material substance that a society wants or needs and is willing to absorb the cost for attaining. The resource may be ideas, information, or knowledge. This form of resource has increased in volume with the growth of the **postindustrial economy.** Material resources include valuable ores of copper, aluminum, and iron; fuel sources such as coal, natural gas, and petroleum; and the soils that support agricultural activities.

To be classified as a resource, the item must be perceived as having a value. For example, the nomadic herdsman would have no use for crude oil, even though he may travel the land directly over the underground source. The European industrialist in need of an uninterrupted supply of energy, however, pays top dollar for petroleum products. To the nomadic herdsman, petroleum is not a resource; to the European industrialist, it is a resource of the highest importance.

Material resources are classified as either renewable or nonrenewable. Renewable resources include forests, fish, agricultural products, plants used for forage, and soils. They are called renewable because they can be regenerated. Soils can be kept fertile and suitable for agriculture by the addition of nutrients. Forests can be managed so that trees taken for lumber or paper pulp are replaced. Livestock herds can be expanded to replace the animals taken for slaughter. The realities of renewal, however, are not always encouraging. Overfishing in the oceans has threatened the entire fishing industry, and clear-cutting of forests is rapidly decimating the acreage of remaining trees. Within a few decades, the remaining tropical rain forests in the world could be completely gone if present rates of clearing are not lowered.

When resources are depleted, the perception of other materials may change. For example, reserves of high-grade hematite and magnetite, the richest iron ores, began to diminish in the 1940s and 1950s. This valuable ore was used for decades in the steel mills of the North American manufacturing belt. When the supplies of these rich ores were exhausted, taconite, an ore containing less iron, was perceived for the first time as being of industrial value. Extraction of this ore and its formulation into pellets for shipment to steel mills marked a big change in the steelmaking industry.

The concept of resource is also applied to people. Human resources are needed in the economic systems worldwide. Capital resources—the machines, buildings, tools, railroads, airplanes, and office buildings that are essential components of business, industry, and government—also play a key role in the economy.

Suggested Readings: David Elliot, *Energy, Society, and Environment,* New York: Routledge, 1997; Judith Rees, *Natural Resources: Allocation, Economics, Policy,* 2nd ed., New York: Routledge, 1990; World Resources Institute and the International Institute for Environment and Development, *World Resources,* annual.

Rimland theory. *See* Mackinder, Halford J.

Ritter, Carl (1779–1859).

Carl Ritter, along with **Alexander von Humboldt,** was one of the greatest German geographers of the nineteenth century. Many geographers consider these two great scholars to be the founders of modern geography. They represent the end of one era in geography and the beginning of another.

Both Ritter and von Humboldt were universal scholars. That is, they studied and analyzed geographical aspects of a place in a holistic way. Geographers today tend to specialize in one area of the discipline. This is a necessary approach because of the vast accumulation of information that has been added to the geographic knowledge base over time. No longer can individual geographers, or any other disciplinarian, operate as a universal scholar in the manner of von Humboldt and Ritter. There is simply too much information available, and specialization is necessary.

It is interesting to note that both von Humboldt and Ritter died in 1859, the year in which English naturalist **Charles Darwin** published his revolutionary book on evolution. Because of Darwin, 1859 has been considered a watershed year in intellectual history.

Ritter was a professor at a number of schools in Germany. His initial research focused on the earth's influence on the course of history. Unlike a number of his contemporaries, Ritter stressed the importance of understanding the ways in which features on the earth are interconnected. This perspective on geographic analysis has endured and remains a basic premise in geography today. In 1811, Ritter published a two-volume textbook on the geography of Europe.

Ritter stressed direct observation in his field research, and he preferred to focus on **regional geography.** In taking the regional direction in his studies, Ritter differed from von Humboldt, who used **systematic (thematic) geography** in his work. Between 1817 and 1859, Ritter completed 11 volumes of his most prominent work, *Die Erdkunde*. The German word *erdkunde* means "earth science," and it is synonymous with the Greek word *geography*. In these volumes, Ritter detailed all aspects of the regions of Africa and parts of Europe. Following his death, some of his students continued work on the series with treatments of Australia and other regions in Europe. In his writing, Ritter stressed the importance of the earth as the home of man, a theme that American geographer Yi-Fu Tuan furthered in his work on **humanistic geography** in the early 1970s.

Carl Ritter. *Source:* Bettmann/CORBIS.

Ritter believed that the earth was created according to a master plan by a higher power. It was only necessary, Ritter contended, to continue investigations of the earth and its features to eventually reveal God's plan. For most of his career, Ritter compiled books based on the field observations of other geographers. He stated that his earlier fieldwork gave him the insights to use the observations of others and craft them into valid and useful written works.

Suggested Readings: Geoffrey J. Martin and Preston E. James, *All Possible Worlds: A History of Geographical Ideas*, 3rd ed., New York: John Wiley & Sons, 1993; George Kish, *A Source Book in Geography*, Cambridge: Harvard University Press, 1978.

Rostow, Walter W. (1916–2003). Walter W. Rostow, an American economic historian, in the 1950s proposed a five-stage model of economic growth. The model identified and detailed the stages that a country would complete in the development of its economic system. At the time Rostow wrote his book *The Stages of Economic Growth* (1960), many colonies had either received their independence or were close to it. Rostow's intention was to completely describe the succession of stages these countries would go though as their economic systems expanded.

The model was based on research Rostow completed of 15 European countries. The first stage he discussed was that of the traditional society, a hamlet or village generally inward looking, with a minimal economic system consisting of barter and trade in agricultural products and possibly some craft items. The culture group relies primarily on **subsistence agriculture,** the gathering of plants, hunting, and possibly fishing. There is little interaction with neighboring groups.

The second stage is identified as having the preconditions for take-off. In this stage, a big change has occurred. Possibly a leader has emerged whose charisma and drive stimulated a desire in the region to recognize and develop a **resource** and to generate a more viable economic system. The beginning may come in the harvesting and marketing of a tree crop, such as coconuts, or the extraction and sale of a mineral ore. Outside funding is usually required to begin such an enterprise. In any case, the business activity is set in motion and economic growth occurs.

The third stage is identified as take-off to sustained growth. Rostow estimated that 10–30 years are necessary to achieve this position. Sustained growth follows a period of continued economic progress, significant increases in business investment and savings, and the development of new industries. In addition, a viable manufacturing sector must be in place to handle previously unrecognized resources that are now exploited and brought into the production process. There are most likely some regions in the country that are not yet fully developed, although a few **growth poles** with dynamic activity are in place.

In the fourth stage, the drive to maturity, investments continue to rise, productivity increases and is sustained at high levels, and the economy expands. New industries are added to the matrix, and the latest technology is used throughout the economic system. **Agglomeration** of industrial activity occurs during this stage and the **multiplier effect** is operating to stimulate further growth. Economic diversification is in evidence, imports are minimized as domestic production expands to provide a wide range of new products, and exports increase as markets are found for manufactured goods. Full regional development is achieved in this stage.

The age of mass consumption is Rostow's fifth stage. This stage is marked by a significant increase in the production of consumer goods and an expansion of the service sector. Income per capita is high enough for most people to purchase a wide variety of personal goods. In the fifth stage, a welfare state begins to appear as excess revenues are directed toward remedying any social problems that persist.

Over the years since Rostow's book was published, a number of criticisms of the model have emerged. First, the model is considered to be descriptive because the underlying causes behind the generation of each stage are not explained. Second, critics have contended that economic growth is a continual process and not marked by distinct stages. Third, empirical evidence shows that many countries remain in Stages 1 or 2 despite input of financial assistance. Fourth, the model is seen as suspect because Rostow's only precedents for success were the 15 European countries that had already achieved Stage 5. With this in mind, critics suggest that there is no guarantee that developing countries will follow the same path to economic success.

Advocates of Rostow's stage model speculate on the emergence of a sixth stage in the form of the **postindustrial society** present in a number of developed countries. This claim is open to debate, because Rostow included a shift to the service sector in Stage 5. Despite its flaws, Rostow's stage model is useful for checking the development level of individual countries.

Suggested Readings: Gerald M. Meier and James E. Rauch, *Leading Issues in Economic Development*, 7th ed., New York: Oxford University Press, 2000; Arthur Morris, *Geography and Development*, London: UCL Press, 1998; Walter W. Rostow, *The Stages of Economic Growth*, London: Cambridge University Press, 1960.

S

Sahel. The Sahel is a narrow band of land on the southern edge of the Sahara Desert in Africa, extending from the country of Western Sahara east to the Sudan and northern Ethiopia. The word *sahel* comes from the Arabic and means "border" or "shore." Hence, the Sahel has been referred to as the "shore of the Sahara."

The Sahel is a semiarid region of steppe and savanna grasses and scrub forest. Normal annual precipitation ranges from 10 to 20 inches. However, beginning in the 1960s, rainfall amounts have been generally lower and unusually erratic. A number of years have brought drought and famine to the region. Soils in the Sahel, called aridosols, contain low levels of organic material due mainly to the continued drought conditions and perennial overuse by grazing animals. Since the mid-twentieth century, the populations of both humans and livestock have significantly increased, bringing greater pressure on the land. Soils have deteriorated, and the entire region is prone to erosion.

In 1977, the United Nations Conference on Desertification convened in Nairobi, Kenya. One of the key outcomes of the conference was the prediction that the Sahel was at high risk for **desertification** and that the region was becoming less productive because of the combination of drought and overuse. Per capita food production in recent decades has declined, and **nomadic herding** has all but ended in the region.

The Sahel has long been considered a marginal region for agriculture. With increases in human and livestock numbers and the persistent drought, the socioeconomic situation in the Sahel has worsened. Environmental conditions there are similar to those of the Dust Bowl era of the 1930s in the United States in parts of Kansas, Oklahoma, Texas, New Mexico, and Colorado. Years of drought and the expansion of agriculture onto semiarid lands resulted in serious land degradation and the mass exodus of thousands of farm families from the devastated area. The Soviets experienced a similar outcome in the 1950s following the failure of their Virgin Lands project, which involved the large-scale clearing of steppe vegetation in a semiarid region in order to expand wheat growing. In both of these instances, it was clear that cultivation of marginal lands is a precarious undertaking.

Initial conclusions reached in the 1970s about climatic change in the Sahel suggested that aridity was steadily increasing. However, satellite imagery gathered in subsequent years showed that the vegetation line fluctuated north and south depending on the amount of precipitation received in any given year. Nonetheless, environmental conditions in this fragile region are not improving, and **population growth** continues at a high rate.

Suggested Readings: Alan Grainger, *The Threatening Desert: Controlling Desertification*, London: Earthscan Publications, 1990; *Sub-Saharan Africa: From Crisis to Sustainable Growth*, Washington, D.C.: World Bank, 1989.

Salinization. Stream valleys, interior basins, and low-lying areas, especially in semiarid and desert environments, are subject to salinization from the application of excessive irrigation water. Irrigation water that is left to stand on the surface of an agricultural field quickly evaporates in a climate that is warm and dry. When the water evaporates, its salt is left in the exposed soil.

Salt accumulation in agricultural land reduces the amount of moisture that plants can absorb through their root systems. Excessive salt retards growth and could even kill the plants.

The problem of salinization is particularly serious in semiarid and desert soils because they are generally tightly compacted and do not drain freely. Ideally, irrigation water should be drained away from the fields and not be allowed to stand on the surface. Effective drainage systems, however, can be quite costly because they require the installation of tiles and pipes to collect and divert excess water to an outlet. However, even the best drainage system cannot completely eliminate all salt accumulations.

Israeli agriculturalists have devised an efficient irrigation system that both minimizes the amount of water used for crops and reduces the accumulation of salt in the soil. The system uses drip irrigation that is set to deliver the exact amount of water to each plant at the precise time it is needed. The Israeli drip irrigation system is costly but very efficient.

Salinization has adversely affected millions of acres of agricultural land in many parts of the world. It is especially prominent in the arid region from Egypt east to India. The southwestern United States has also experienced serious salinization problems. The agriculturally productive Central Valley in California has lost nearly 25 percent of its agricultural land to salinization from excess irrigation water. Even some northern regions in Saskatchewan and Ontario, Canada, have been aversely affected by salinization.

Suggested Readings: Malin Falkenmark and Carl Widstrand, "Population and Water Resources: A Delicate Balance," *Population Bulletin*, vol. 47 (1992); Sandra Postel, *Last Oasis: Facing Water Scarcity*, New York: W. W. Norton, 1992.

Sauer, Carl (1889–1975). Carl Sauer had a profound and lasting impact on American **geography.** His work in geography was diverse, and he wrote books and articles on a wide variety of geographical themes. Sauer was a tireless field-worker who believed that observation of the environment and talking with individuals knowledgeable about a place was important in gaining time in learning about the place and acquiring insightful information.

Sauer did his graduate work at the University of Chicago, in one of the most prestigious geography departments in the Midwest. He soon grew to appreciate the regional studies approach to geography introduced by French geographer **Paul Vidal de la Blache** (1845–1918) and others in France. Vidal published geographical works from 1891 to his death in 1918. His influential *Principles of Human Geography* was published in 1926, eight years after his death. Each region, Sauer contended, has its own distinctive landscape that reflected the social processes and physical changes to the area over time. One of Sauer's most prominent writings is titled "The Morphology of Landscape" (1925), in which he presented his model on the derivation of a cul-

Carl Sauer. *Source:* Library of Congress.

tural landscape. In this model, culture is the factor that begins the process. Every social group imparts its cultural imprint on the natural landscape. In time, this imprint produces what Sauer called a **cultural landscape,** which includes settlement patterns, distinctive structures, transportation systems, and all the attributes of a society. In Sauer's words, "The cultural landscape is fashioned from a natural landscape by a culture group."

"The Morphology of Landscape" is of great importance because it essentially ended the influence of **environmental determinism** in American geography.

Sauer spent 50 years in the geography department at the University of California at Berkeley. He was a prominent cultural geographer with a great concern for the environment. Among his many and varied projects and research endeavors was a compelling plea for a comprehensive land-classification system. He was concerned about the practice of clear-cutting in the forestry industry, and he wanted a system to identify resources and ensure their maintenance.

Sauer wrote important books and articles on the origins of agriculture. He believed strongly that Southeast Asia was a likely region for the development of agriculture because of its varied plant species. He also suggested that plant cultivation was invented in a number of different regions and that the notion of a single originating point was incorrect. He wrote about urban places and considered them to reflect the response of human society to the natural landscape. He even wrote an article about gerrymandering, which refers to a reapportionment process that greatly benefits the party in power, in which he drew attention to a particularly intriguing district of Missouri. In his article "The Education of a Geographer," Sauer included this statement reflecting his ideas about fieldwork: "Locomotion should be slow, the slower the better; and should be often interrupted by leisurely halts to sit on vantage points and stop at question marks."

Suggested Readings: Martin S. Kenzer, ed., *Carl O. Sauer: A Tribute*, Corvallis: Oregon State University, 1987; John Leighly, ed., *"Land and Life": A Selection from the Writings of Carl Ortwin Sauer*, Berkeley: University of California Press, 1969 (contains "The Morphology of Landscape," and "The Education of a Geographer").

Scale. The concept of scale is used in a number of ways in geography. For example, discussions may proceed on the topic of atmospheric pollution at the global scale, a surge of economic activity may be noted at the regional scale in Southeast Asia, or the devastation of a tornado hitting a small town in Nebraska might be reported at the local scale. These are all general references to particular levels of representation without numerical bases.

Scale in **cartography,** however, refers to a precise measuring system. Scale in this sense is a way of stating the relationship between a distance or area measurement on a map and the actual dimension in the real world. Scale tells to what degree that portion of the earth's surface has been reduced in order to create the map. Scale on a map may be stated in a number of ways. A simple graphic scale, for example, would state that "one inch = 10 miles" or "one centimeter = 50 kilometers." This information tells us a great deal about the relationship between the map and the area being represented. In the first example one inch on the map is equal to 10 miles on the earth's surface. Taking the example a step further reveals that one square inch on the map equals 100 square miles on the surface.

Another form of scale is called "representative fraction" or simply "rf." An rf of 1:63,360, or 1/63,360 in fractional form, is particularly useful because it represents exactly one inch to the mile. (One inch on the map is equal to 63,360 inches on the earth's surface, which is 12 inches/foot × 5280 feet/mile = 63,360.) If area were considered, one square inch on the map would equal one square mile on the surface. So, the rf of 1:63,360 would be understood to be 1:63,360 squared.

Maps are also identified as being large scale or small scale. The basis for this determination is found in the rf, which is a true fraction. For example, the

topographic map series produced by the U.S. Geological Survey comes in a number of scales and is devoted primarily to local area coverage. One of the topographic maps produced has a scale of 1:24,000, or 1/24,000 in fractional form. Consider a map of Asia, for instance, that has a scale of 1:2,000,000, or 1/2,000,000. Compare the numerical value of the two fractions. The topographical map has the larger fractional value, therefore it is considered a large-scale map, whereas the map of Asia is a small-scale map. A large-scale map shows a great deal of detail, but its disadvantage is that the area portrayed is limited. The small-scale map shows a much larger area but in doing so a great deal of detail is sacrificed. Both maps, however, generalize the areas portrayed. Generalization, along with scale and distortion, are the three attributes common to all maps.

Suggested Readings: Victor Miller and Mary Westerbrook, *Interpretation of Topographic Maps*, Columbus, Ohio: Charles E. Merrill, 1989; Judith Tyner, *Introduction to Thematic Cartography*, Englewood Cliffs, N.J.: Prentice Hall, 1992.

Secondary sector. The secondary sector in an economic system takes items from the **primary sector** and refines them through manufacturing or processing. Economists use the term *form utility* to describe the transformations that take place during these operations. Individual economic functions within the secondary sector include manufacturing, construction, public works, and utilities such as power companies.

Secondary-sector work is generated from items grown or extracted in the primary sector. For example, fish and agricultural products are processed and packaged for sale in the wholesale and retail marketplace. It is also common for one secondary-sector factory to provide another with items needed in the manufacture or processing of products. For example, fish processing and packaging requires plastic or metal containers for the processed fish and labels for identification. Other secondary-sector firms will most likely provide the containers and labels. An automobile assembly operation is very complex. Hundreds of secondary-sector suppliers provide all the needed components for the assembly of automobiles. Tires, windshields, seats and seat covers, dashboard instruments, batteries, cables, belts, and door locks must all be supplied by outside firms, and the components must be on hand at precisely the time they are needed in the assembly process.

With each step in processing or manufacturing, value is added to the product. The production of electronic parts that will be fashioned into subcomponents and finally assembled into handheld calculators involves a number of complex steps. Each step increases the value added in the process. The making of a basket from willow branches requires skill but only a few steps. The assembly of a new passenger airplane, however, is an incredibly complex process involving many assembly stages. The value added in each step of the process determines the ultimate selling price for the airplane. The basket may cost $10, but the airplane, perhaps $10 million.

Secondary-sector activities are found primarily in the developed countries in the Northern Hemisphere. The United States, Canada, Europe, Russia, Japan, Korea, Singapore, Taiwan, and Hong Kong have traditional strongholds of secondary activities. The **pattern** is changing, however, as **transnational corporation**s establish manufacturing centers in developing countries to take advantage of lower labor costs. In these operations, components of products are manufactured and then shipped to assembly points accessible to the ultimate markets for final sale. Some secondary-sector plants locate close to each other to gain the advantages of economic **agglomeration** and the **multiplier effect,** both of which can enhance the productivity of the clustered firms.

Primary and secondary activities have declined in the number of employees, in favor of the fast-rising service sectors (*see* **Tertiary, Quaternary,** and **Quinary sector**s) as the economic structure in developed countries shifts to the **postindustrial economy.** However, manufacturing and processing operations have by no means experienced real declines. On the contrary, their growth continues to increase, although growth in the service sectors, especially information processing, increases faster.

Suggested Readings: Ian Hamilton, ed., *Resources and Industry: The Illustrated Encyclopedia of World Geography,* New York: Oxford University Press, 1992; Frederick P. Stutz and Anthony R. de Souza, *The World Economy: Resources, Location, Trade, and Development,* 3rd ed., Upper Saddle River, N.J.: Prentice Hall, 1998.

Sector model. American economist Homer Hoyt is the author of one of three classic models of urban land use. His sector model, published in 1939, resulted from his study of the structure of more than 140 American cities and was in response to criticisms of the **concentric zone model** developed by R. E. Park, E. W. Burgess, and R. D. McKenzie, University of Chicago sociologists, two decades earlier.

Hoyt's research suggested that cities grow outward from the **central business district** (CBD) in wedge-shaped sectors that follow prominent roadways. The driving force in urban land use structure, according to Hoyt, is the high-income housing sector that is first established on the most attractive land near the CBD and in time grows outward toward open space to eventually join high-income residences in the suburban area. The high-income housing sector is built along scenic waterways, if present in the city, and on high ground. In addition, high-income housing follows the route of the fastest surface transportation corridor leading to the suburban fringe.

Adjacent to the high-income housing sector on both sides is middle-income housing. The low-income housing sector occupies the least-desirable land, usually adjacent to areas of industry, manufacturing, and transportation marshaling yards.

Hoyt's studies of American cities indicated that the Burgess concentric zone model was basically incorrect. Hoyt noted, for instance, that in many cases housing districts extended from the edge of the CBD to the city limits and that they were not found in concentric zones.

Hoyt and Burgess both used Chicago to illustrate their models. Burgess contended that the concentric zonation of Chicago was consistent except where it was broken in the east by Lake Michigan. Hoyt, on the other hand, pointed out that the high-income housing sector extended from the CBD north along Lake Michigan and that the industrial sector followed the railroad and highway lines south along Lake Michigan and extended to the steelmaking plants in Gary, Indiana.

Hoyt's model came 20 years after Burgess's and was more complex. Two decades after Hoyt's model was published, American geographers Chauncey Harris and Edward Ullman introduced an even more complex model. Their **multiple-nuclei model** of urban land use reflected changes in the post–World War II configuration of American cities and the decline in dominance of the CBD.

Suggested Readings: Phillip Kivell, *Land and the City; Patterns and Processes of Urban Change*, London: Routledge, 1993; Maurice Yeates, *The North American City*, 5th ed., New York: Longman, 1997.

Sense of place. There are at least two distinct meanings for the concept "sense of place." First, there is the immediate association that people make with prominent natural and human-made features. In the United States, Niagara Falls is a well-known setting for honeymooners, and it is known far and wide by individuals even they have not visited it. Mount Fuji in Japan evokes a high emotional response from the Japanese people. The same sense of awe is attached to Lake Baikal in Siberia, a place that is held in high reverence by people in Russia.

The Brooklyn Bridge, Saint Basil's Church in Moscow, and the Sydney Opera House are all universally identifiable human-made structures that evoke a compelling sense of place. Emotional responses ran high following the deliberate destruction of the World Trade Center twin towers in New York City on September 11, 2001. The loss of life in the attack was, of course, inordinately tragic, and the obliteration of the buildings, known worldwide, struck an emotional chord in millions of people.

Sense of place also applies to associations with places that have personal significance to people. The place may be a park or playground enjoyed as a child. Or it may be a particular room in one's home, a place of safety and solitude. Someone raised on a farm may have developed a strong sense of place for the entire expanse of agricultural fields, the barns and work sheds, and even an old windmill. Clearly, sense of place evokes a strong emotional connection that may arouse feelings about the place long after the individual has moved away. Sense of place implies an intimacy with the structures or physical features that occupy the setting. The prominent American cultural geographer Yi-Fu Tuan, published from the 1960s to the present, uses the term **topophilia,** suggesting an emotional tie with place, in his writings on **humanistic geography.**

Some writers on the subject, leading American nature writer Barry Lopez among them, express concern that Americans may be losing their sense of place because they are no longer as close to the physical environment as their ancestors were. Lopez suggests that intimacy with a local setting, a necessary aspect of developing a true sense of place, seems not to be as strong in Americans as it was in years past. If Lopez is correct, then it seems that people are, in some ways, looking away from their physical setting. For example, road trips using the interstate highways set us apart from the terrain we travel through. No longer are we coursing down narrow two-lane roads where we can almost reach out and touch the landscape. A trip on a scheduled airline at 37,000-foot altitudes distances us from the land below. Some features are recognizable, but there is a detachment that separates us from the physical features. This was not the case in decades past, when the old DC-3s would fly over the terrain at 7,000 to 10,000 feet; close enough to note physical and cultural features in detail.

Suggested Readings: R. J. Johnston et al., *The Dictionary of Human Geography*, 2nd ed., Oxford, U.K.: Basil Blackwell, 1986; Barry Lopez, "The American Geographies," *Orion Magazine*, autumn 1989; Yi-Fu Tuan, "Space and Place: Humanistic Perspective," in *Human Geography: An Essential Anthology*, ed. John Agnew et al., Cambridge, Mass.: Basil Blackwell, 1996.

Settlement. The term *settlement* has wide application in geography. In one sense it refers to the original occupation of a new area. For example, when the Russians built the Trans-Siberian Railroad from Moscow east to the Pacific Ocean, new settlements quickly began to grow up along the course of the great rail line. Settlement also refers to the places, large and small, in which people already live. A simple dwelling in a remote area of northwestern China is a settlement. By contrast, the booming metropolis of Seoul, South Korea, is also a settlement.

Urban settlements within a region vary in size from tiny villages to the **primate city.** There is regularity in the hierarchical nesting of urban places that became the basis for **Christaller's central place theory** and the derivation of the **rank-size rule.**

Some individual settlements are associated with a dominant function found there. Rochester, Minnesota, is world-famous because of the Mayo Clinic. San Jose, California, is one of the most prominent computer centers in the world. Las Vegas brings to mind casinos, nightclubs, posh hotels, and entertainment. New York City is the world headquarters for hundreds of corporations. **Megalopolis,** the term for the settlement stretching from Boston to Washington, D.C., is a dynamic and densely packed region whose single greatest export is decisions.

There are college towns, mining towns, and urban places where manufacturing predominates. Settlements of ethnic concentrations are found within towns and cities, and within regions of a country. All of these groupings are examples of settlements.

A number of settlement forms have been identified and classified. In the rural area, dispersed settlements are generally the rule. This settlement **pattern** shows individual farm sites spread out across the landscape. Dispersed settlements are contrasted with the nucleated settlement, which is identified by a tight clustering of residences in a small area within the larger rural setting.

A dry-point settlement is found on high ground within a region of ample precipitation. A wet-point settlement is found in an area that has a guaranteed water supply. A **squatter settlement** contains people who are occupying land they do not own. Many of the residents may be **refugees** from their own country, to which they cannot safely return. Squatter settlements, found mainly in the developing countries, collectively contain millions of people. Squatter settlements are a dominant factor in the **urbanization** of the developing world.

Suggested Readings: Allan G. Noble, ed., *To Build in a New Land: Ethnic Landscapes in North America*, Baltimore: Johns Hopkins University Press, 1992; Mathew J. Shumway and Richard H. Jackson, "Native American Population Patterns," *Geographical Review*, vol. 85 (1995).

Shatter belt. A country or group of countries strategically located within the spheres of influence of larger and competing countries has been referred to as a shatter belt. As a result of the pressures brought to bear on shatter belt countries, it is not uncommon to find economic development problems and political instability within their borders. There may well be boundary disputes within a shatter belt region as pressures for dominance is exerted by the larger competing states.

Poland was a shatter belt country during both World Wars by virtue of its location between the often-competing countries of Germany and Russia. There have been frequent **boundary** changes in Poland over the years as a result of these pressures. Southeast Asia has also been characterized as a shatter belt. The region is culturally diverse and is physically dissected. These conditions made it prone to takeover by European powers during the era of **colonialism** during the nineteenth and early twentieth centuries, associated with European occupation of parts of Southeast Asia.

During the 1970s and 1980s, the African country of Angola was the center of a struggle between Soviet and American forces battling for control of the country. Angola was subjected to external pressures as the two superpowers engaged in a proxy war to exert their influence and gain control in the region.

Perhaps the most serious and long-lasting shatter belt is the Middle East. For years the region has experienced strong political pressures from both internal and external origins. Iraq's invasion of Kuwait in 1991 brought a swift and decisive military response from the United States and its coalition forces. The struggle between Israel and the Palestinian Liberation Authority and other countries in the region has been ongoing since Israel was declared a sovereign state in 1948. Pressures from outside the region exacerbate the turmoil as such powerful countries as the United States and Russia exert their influence in Middle Eastern affairs.

The term *shatter belt* or *shatter zone* has often been applied to the Eastern European countries during the **cold war.** These countries, members of the Warsaw

Pact, comprised a **buffer zone** between the Soviet Union and the opposing forces of the **North Atlantic Treaty Organization**.

Suggested Readings: Kevin Hewison et al., eds., *Southeast Asia in the 1990s: Authoritarianism, Democracy and Capitalism,* St. Leonard's, NSW, Australia: Allen & Unwin, 1993; I. Griffiths, *The Atlas of African Affairs,* 2nd ed., Johannesburg, South Africa: Witwatersrand University Press, 1995.

Shifting cultivation. *See* **Extensive agriculture.**

Site. The physical features of a place that were important considerations in its initial selection as a **settlement** are called site factors. Before the era of railroads and highways, urban places were routinely sited on the banks of navigable rivers. The site factors of immediate importance is these instances were high ground to avoid flooding and a gentle slope to ensure **accessibility** to the river for transportation.

Site has been characterized as representing a vertical location factor. That is, the focus in site selection is limited to the physical terrain that supports the establishment of a viable settlement. Site is coupled with the concept of **situation,** in which consideration is made for the location of the place within its larger areal context. In the previous example, site factors were used to locate the place on a navigable river. A situational factor would identify, for instance, that the river location provides access to a local forest and to the possibility of establishing a lumber processing operation. The river also connects the place with other settlements.

A place may be sited near arable land that could provide the basis for agricultural activity. Situation, then, considers the location of a place in reference to other physical and cultural attributes within its area. For this reason, situation is identified as a horizontal location factor.

The site factors for St. Louis, Missouri, located on high ground near the confluence of the Missouri and Mississippi Rivers provides an ideal example of the way site and situation are simultaneously considered and how they work together. The site provides the physical base for the settlement, including access to the rivers. The situational factors link St. Louis to other settlements along the rivers and help to explain why the city became important as a port.

Site factors may change in time. As urban places grow in population and number of functions, more room may be needed to accommodate the additional activities. Such prominent metropolitan centers as New York City, Tokyo, Hiroshima, and Seoul, South Korea's port city of Inchon have for years reclaimed land from the sea in order to extend their physical limits. The borough of Manhattan in New York City has been extended to the south a number of times to gain more land. Battery Park City and the World Trade Center twin towers were built on reclaimed land. Tokyo Bay is fast being filled in as the demand for more land continues to increase in this bustling metropolitan center. Estimates of the rate of land reclamation in Tokyo Bay suggest that within a few decades only enough of the bay will remain to ensure ship navigation in and out of the important port facilities.

Suggested Readings: Edward L. Ayers et al., *All over the Map: Rethinking American Regions*, Baltimore: Johns Hopkins University Press, 1995; Arild Holt-Jensen, *Geography: Its History and Concepts*, 2nd ed., Totowa, N.J.: Barnes & Noble, 1988.

Situation. The concept of situation is used in geography to identify the physical and cultural attributes within close proximity to the location of a place. Situation has been characterized as the horizontal location factor, whereas its counterpart, **site,** is considered a vertical location factor. Site factors identify the immediate physical features that were important in the initial selection of the place as a **settlement.** The situation of a settlement identifies cultural and physical attributes within its local area. For example, the site factors for Chicago include the land on which it was built, close proximity to the southern end of Lake Michigan, and the presence of a river flowing through it. Chicago's situation reflects the potential economic gain from commerce on Lake Michigan, the city's access to rich agricultural land in Wisconsin and Illinois, and the city's **accessibility** to other settlements within its immediate region and beyond by long-distance **transportation systems.**

Site reflects the internal physical characteristics of the place. Situation reflects its external physical and cultural relationships of significance to the economic and social well-being of the settlement. Shanghai, China, was a sleepy little fishing village until the British chose the settlement for an administrative center in the nineteenth century. Since that time, Shanghai has grown to become a world-class metropolitan center. The site factor of importance to Shanghai is its location at the mouth of the Chang (Yangtze) River. Its situational setting locates it on China's only major river deep enough to allow oceangoing vessels to travel inland. Shanghai has become important as a shipping point and as China's foremost economic and technology development center. It also plays a key role in the expanding free-trade zone extending upriver to Chongqing. Economic development in this region of China is expanding rapidly and will continue to do so when the Three-Gorges Project is completed. This project will allow oceangoing vessels to move beyond the previous terminus at Wuhan, 600 miles from Shanghai, to Chongqing, another 600 miles to the west. The extension of navigation for ships will change the situational setting in a positive way for the economy of Shanghai.

Another example from China illustrates how situation can change. Before its reincorporation within China, Hong Kong was one of the economic powerhouses known as the **Asian Tigers** and operated as a successful economic center on the Pacific Coast. Only a few miles from Hong Kong, in China proper, is the city of Guangzhou. Over the years, this city benefited from its close proximity to Hong Kong, and its fortunes increased when Hong Kong reverted to Chinese control. In the case of Guangzhou, a situational change through a geopolitical action resulted in an economic boom for the city.

Situational changes occurred in the formative years on the East Coast of the United States. For a few years, Newport, Rhode Island, was a major port city. As settlements increased in number, Boston and then Philadelphia became the leading ports. However, once New York City established its port facility and developed its connections to the interior by way of the Hudson-Mohawk Depression, it became the dominant port on the East Coast, a position it holds to this day.

Suggested Readings: Michael P. Conzen, "The Progress of American Urbanization, 1860–1930," in *The Historical Geography of a Changing Continent*, ed. Robert T. Mitchell et al., Savage, Md.: Rowman & Littlefield, 1990; Truman A. Hartshorn, *Interpreting the City: An Urban Geography*, 2nd ed., New York: John Wiley & Sons, 1990.

Slash and burn agriculture. *See* **Extensive agriculture.**

Smog. Excessive amounts of automobile and truck exhausts combined with ultraviolet radiation from sunlight causes gaseous reactions that result in smog. The term *smog*, which derives from the words *smoke* and *fog*, is a misnomer. Nonetheless, it is used to refer to photochemical air pollution. Carbon monoxide and hydrocarbons from vehicular exhaust systems, when acted on by sunlight, produce nitrogen dioxide, nitric acid, and ozone, all of which are injurious to the health of humans and plant life.

A second form of smog comes from accumulations of sulfur dioxide, carbon dioxide, and particulate matter spewed into the atmosphere from industrial smoke. Both forms of smog are most prevalent in urban places because of the high concentrations of automobiles, trucks, and industrial plants.

Smog is particularly dangerous to people with any form of respiratory illness. If the concentration of smog is heavy enough for a long period of time it can cause serious injury and even death to those most susceptible to its ill effects. The Black Smog incident in Donora, Pennsylvania, in 1948 resulted in the death of 20 people and the hospitalization of hundreds more. Sulfur dioxide emitted over a five-day period from a zinc processing plant changed to sulfur trioxide, a substance that adversely affects the respiratory system. The severity of the Donora episode was increased by the presence of an atmospheric inversion caused by a cell of high-pressure air suspended over Donora. The inversion trapped the noxious fumes over the city, and the problem was not alleviated until the weather system changed and welcome rains came to clear the air.

Inversions are common over the Los Angeles basin. This is one reason why Los Angeles is called the smog capital of America. In addition to the cell of high-pressure air over Los Angeles, mountains to the east block the prevailing westerly winds from carrying the smog away from the basin. Even before Spanish and western European settlers came to the region, Los Angeles was known to the American Indian inhabitants as the valley of smoke.

Mexico City, Mexico, is another metropolitan area that has an enormous smog problem. The city frequently experiences smog accumulation because of atmospheric inversions and its location in a valley, the walls of which trap and hold the smog. The problem is so serious at times in the winter season that schools have been closed for from four to six weeks and people are told to stay at home rather than risk illness from the noxious air. *See also* **Pollution.**

Suggested Readings: Derek Elson, *Atmospheric Pollution: A Global Problem,* 2nd ed., Cambridge, Mass.: Basil Blackwell, 1992; Ian D. Whyte, *Climatic Change and Human Society,* New York: John Wiley & Sons, 1996.

Social geography. The subdiscipline of social geography centers on three areas of concern. First, consideration of the well-being of the poor and disenfranchised members of society has emerged, especially since the late 1960s and early 1970s. Second, there has been considerable criticism of the capitalist system because it allegedly breeds and maintains socioeconomic inequity, both at the country and global levels. Third, the ideas and thoughts of those in poverty have been largely ignored, and some social geographers contend that the views of the socially disadvantaged are just as valid as those of more-affluent members of society.

Social geography is a recent addition to the discipline and has been officially recognized since the mid-1950s. At times, the field of social geography has been synonymous with **urban geography** because the problems it deals with are most often found in cities. Its roots go back to the early years of the twentieth century and the successful challenge to **environmental determinism,** a charge led by French geographer **Paul Vidal de la Blache,** with his philosophy of **possibilism.** Environmental determinism held the view that the physical environment determined the actions of the culture group living in that setting. Possibilism contended that the environment was an influence on behavior but that humans could create their own lifestyle within their physical setting with the help of technology and their own ingenuity. The possibilist perspective was humane, and it opened the door to a balanced view of human–environment interactions. People were seen as having greater choice in managing their lives within the physical environment.

The modern era in social geography dates to the mid-1960s, a time of radical social change in the United States and other countries. Protests over U.S. involvement in the Vietnam War, President Lyndon Johnson's war on poverty and his expansive legislation on social justice, and the student revolts in Paris that toppled the French government were only a few of the key events in that momentous decade.

The year 1968 was particularly significant for both the country and geography. In that year, riots took place at the Democratic National Convention in Chicago. Police brutality was alleged, and the convention was disrupted. The following year, the annual meeting of the Association of American Geographers was scheduled to be held in Chicago but was moved to Ann Arbor, Michigan, in protest against the actions in Chicago one year earlier. At the Ann Arbor meeting, attendees were presented with studies of the social conditions in the city of Detroit. These revelations further inflamed many geographers, who demanded that the country and the discipline do more to address severe social problems and enhance human-welfare programs.

Social geography today focuses on (1) the patterns of social activity and problem areas, especially in cities, and (2) the processes that result in poverty and the decline of socioeconomic systems.

Suggested Readings: Peter Jackson, *Race and Racism: Essays in Social Geography,* London: Allen & Unwin, 1987; Paul A. Jargowsky, "Beyond the Street Corner: The Hidden Diversity of High Poverty Neighborhoods," *Urban Geography,* vol. 17 (1996); R. J. Johnston et al., eds., *The Dictionary of Human Geography,* 2nd ed., Oxford, U.K.: Basil Blackwell, 1986.

Soil. Soil is a complex and dynamic mixture of rock debris, organic material, inorganic minerals, living organisms (worms and insects), air, and water. Soil is dynamic in nature because it is continually being formed as rock material disintegrates from physical and chemical weathering and organic material decays and decomposes into what is called humus. A balance must be maintained between the amount of new soil being formed and losses from **soil erosion.** Every year, tons of rich topsoil are eroded from agricultural fields by rainfall and wind. In some regions, the amount of soil lost from erosion exceeds that gained from replacement. This is especially true of regions undergoing long-term drought conditions, such as the **Sahel,** in Africa. During periods of drought, not as much plant growth occurs and less organic material is made available for the formation of new soil. Also, dry and parched soil is prone to be carried away by winds. If these conditions persist in a semiarid region for a long enough time, **desertification** may occur.

In most soils, a distinct vertical zonation is present. There are three basic zones in soil. The first is called the "A" horizon. It is the zone that contains the largest amount of organic material and is the richest for plant growth. "A" horizon soils are dark in color and vary in thickness from several inches to as much as a few feet. The "A" horizon has also been called the organic horizon because it clearly is the most active and fertile layer. The "B" horizon is lighter in color and consists of clay, minerals, and some organic material. It is much less productive for plant growth. The "C" horizon is the upper surface of the underlying bedrock; it consists of broken rock mixed with clay and contains very little organic material.

Soil composition in any given area is reflective of the climate. For example, desert climates are not conducive to lush plant growth. The soil in desert climates is called aridisol; it is sandy and light in color and contains little, if any, organic material. On the other hand, the rich and productive agricultural soils of the midwestern United States and the Fertile Triangle in Russia and Ukraine are dark in color and abundant in the nutrients necessary for large-scale farming. These soils are called molisols; they have formed naturally over the years beneath extensive grass cover.

In recent years, large sections of the tropical rain forest have been cleared for a variety of economic purposes. In addition to the demand for exotic tropical woods, there were schemes to use the cleared land for grazing livestock and for farming. The soils in the tropical rain forests do not lend themselves to the growing of grass or to other agricultural pursuits. The primary reason for this lies in the makeup of the soil. There is no real "A" horizon present, and the soil itself is essentially infertile. The natural vegetation in the tropical rain forest is the towering trees that have root systems that capture decaying material at ground level. Consequently, the soil does not develop a layer of rich nutrients that new grasses or other agricultural plants can use. In order to make these soils productive once the giant trees have been cleared, a big investment in fertilizers, pesticides, and machine tilling is required. Without these expensive additions, the soil of the cleared rain forest is essentially useless.

Suggested Readings: Robert W. Christopherson, *Geosystems: An Introduction to Physical Geography*, 3rd ed., Upper Saddle River, N.J.: Prentice Hall, 1997; Steve Ellis and Tony Mellor, *Soils and Environment,* New York: Routledge, 1995; U.S. Department of Agriculture, *Soil Taxonomy*, Agricultural Handbook no. 436, Washington, D.C.: U.S. Government Printing Office, 1975.

Soil erosion. The loss of valuable topsoil through erosion processes has been called the quiet crisis, and it is an environmental problem of global proportions. Wind, rainfall, snowmelt, and any number of human disruptions to the earth's surface can result in the loss of topsoil. It is true that new topsoil forms from decaying plant material and its absorption within the surface layer. However, the rate of loss of topsoil generally exceeds that of natural regeneration. Some estimates of soil loss indicate that the earth is losing up to 7 percent of its rich topsoil every 10 years, and this rate has been on the rise in recent years.

Soil erosion is a natural process; it occurs even if humans are not present. However, soil erosion increases dramatically when the natural vegetative cover is removed and the land is readied for agriculture. When land is cleared, wind and rainfall remove more of the soil than they would if the natural vegetation were still in place. It is perhaps ironic that the land-use practice of agriculture that is reliant on soil actually hastens the loss of that precious resource.

Another human-induced cause of soil erosion is overgrazing by cattle. Not only is erosion increased, but the following year less grass cover will be present. This is another example of the way eliminating vegetative cover increases the degree of soil erosion.

Soil erosion in the agricultural sector can lead to lower yields of crops and increased silting in streams and rivers. Some U.S. agricultural regions have lost up to 70 percent of their topsoil to erosion. Yet, there is increased pressure on farmers to produce more food.

Because of a global population increase and the need for more food, farmers are moving agricultural production onto steeper slopes on previously avoided marginal land (*see* **Terracing**). In some instances, the soil regenerative practice of allowing a field to renew itself by keeping it out of crops for a year or more is being abandoned under the pressure for increased food production.

A pointed example of severe soil erosion is seen in the tragedy of the topical rain forests of South America. Vast expanses of rain forest were cleared for agriculture and grazing only to find that the thin topsoil was essentially infertile without the addition of expensive fertilizers and pesticides. An added bit of irony was revealed when areas cleared for agriculture and grazing were abandoned and the rain forest vegetation would not regenerate in the areas where lush trees once stood. Soil erosion is unquestionably one of the modern world's most serious problems.

Suggested Readings: Lester R. Brown and Edward C. Wolf, *Soil Erosion: Quiet Crisis in the World Economy*, Worldwatch Paper no. 60, Washington, D.C.: Worldwatch Institute, 1984; Judith Getis, *You CAN Make a Difference: Help Protect the Earth*, 2nd ed., Dubuque, Iowa: WCB/McGraw-Hill, 1999.

Space. Geographers use the term *space* in an absolute manner. That is, reference may be made to the space occupied by any physical entity: an automobile, a person, a metropolitan center, an agricultural field, or an aircraft carrier. Space used in this way is objective; it is used to define the physical dimensions of objects. Relative space, on the other hand, is not objective but is constantly changing. Relative space is reflective of the actions and intentions of the person operating within it. For example, people have their own **activity space,** the area within which their normal daily activities take place. In addition, each person has a personal space around the body, an area that if penetrated causes discomfort.

Geography has often been described as a spatial science (*see* **Quantitative Revolution**). Geographers have contended for decades that the discipline is unique in its emphasis on the spatial aspects of human activities. From an early point in the history of modern geography, prominent scholars saw geography as the discipline that studied the spatial aspects of the interface between nature and culture (*see* **Geography**).

The eighteenth-century German philosopher Immanuel Kant considered space to be represented by geography and time by history. Kant taught at the university in Konigsburg from 1755 to 1797. Among his courses was one on physical geography, which he taught for 41 years, and his views on geography, space, and time influenced the formation of the discipline.

Geography is a dynamic discipline. It deals with entities that change and interact. **Spatial interaction** is a key theme in geography. No place exists in and of itself. Places are affected by events occurring in other settings. For example, advancements in transportation technology have resulted in a kind of compression of time and space. Places have been brought closer together, so to speak, and the degree of **accessibility** between places has increased significantly. When the fifteenth-century Italian explorer Christopher Columbus sailed to the Western Hemisphere, his first voyage took 38 days. Years later, the American aviation pioneer Charles Lindbergh flew a single-engine airplane from the East Coast of the United States to Paris in about 33 hours. Today, a scheduled airline flight from London to New York City takes only a few hours. Our ability to negotiate space in shorter time frames seems commonplace.

The twentieth-century American geographer Yi-Fu Tuan makes a distinction between space and place in his writings on **humanistic geography.** According to Tuan, space is undifferentiated, whereas place has a familiarity gained from personal experiences within it. Space is timeless, but place has a history.

Suggested Readings: Stanley Brunn and Thomas Leinbach, *Collapsing Space and Time: Geographic Aspects of Communication and Information,* Winchester, Mass.: Unwin Hyman, 1991; R. J. Johnston et al., eds., *The Dictionary of Human Geography,* 2nd ed., Oxford, U.K.: Basil Blackwell, 1986; Yi-Fu Tuan, *Space and Place: The Perspective of Experience,* Minneapolis: University of Minnesota Press, 1977.

Spatial interaction. Places and regions are interdependent; they do not function alone. The geographic term that reflects this interdependence is spatial interaction, a concept introduced in the 1950s by the eminent American geographer Edward Ullman. In an important article that detailed aspects of spatial interaction (*see* **Intervening opportunity**), Ullman contended that the concept was comparable in importance to the theme of human–environment interaction.

Spatial interaction assumes a system of places and regions within which a degree of **connectivity** exists. Goods are shipped from one place to another, people travel to places near and far, and ideas are sent by mail, fax, telephone, and computer. All of these activities further assume that a degree of **accessibility** exists. That is, goods cannot be shipped if there is no way to transport them, and people cannot travel to a place that will not accept them for political reasons.

These examples suggest the presence of barriers to spatial interaction, and there are a number of them. Distance can be a barrier, especially to the physical movement of people and goods. Generally there is a greater degree of spatial interaction if the distance to negotiate is shorter (*see* **Distance decay**). Physical impediments may reduce the degree of spatial interaction between places. For several decades during the colonial period, settlement in the United States was limited to the eastern seaboard because the Appalachian Mountains blocked further westward movement. However, with advances in technology and new **transportation systems,** physical barriers are no longer as imposing.

Political barriers can impede spatial interaction. Some countries have established rigid restrictions on entry, and others have discouraged the importation of certain goods by setting high tariffs. Language can also be a barrier to spatial interaction. If two parties cannot communicate, there is little likelihood that business can be conducted. Along a number of international borders, a **lingua franca** that incorporates words and phrases from two or more languages has been established to break the communications barrier.

During the **Quantitative Revolution** in American geography during the late 1950s through mid-1960s, models and quantitative techniques were developed to precisely measure the spatial interaction between urban places.

The so-called **gravity model** used a simple formula to predict the degree of interaction that would occur between urban places of various sizes within a region.

A great body of literature has accumulated in the last 50 years on the concept of **diffusion** in its many forms. Pioneered by twentieth-century Swedish geographer Torsten Hagerstrand, the diffusion concept is perhaps the single most prominent and widely applied aspect of spatial interaction.

Suggested Readings: Reginald G. Golledge and Robert J. Stimson, *Decision Making and Spatial Behavior: A Geographic Perspective*, New York: Guilford Press, 1966; Nigel Thrift, *Spatial Formations*, Thousand Oaks, Calif.: Sage, 1996.

Sprawl. *See* **Urban sprawl.**

Squatter settlement. High **rates of natural increase** and steady rural-to-urban **migration** in Africa, Asia, and Latin America continues to overwhelm the host cities. People are arriving in urban areas in numbers that far exceed available housing to accommodate them. The result of this mass movement has been the creation of squatter settlements on the fringes of the cities. Migrants occupy unused private or governmentally owned property as a last resort.

Squatter settlements normally have no services, such as electricity, potable water, sewage systems, health care facilities, or schools. If the residents persist in staying in a settlement and the officials do not evict them, improvements may be added and makeshift huts replaced by more substantial structures. In time, more services may be added.

The presence of squatter settlements in great numbers throughout the developing world is another indication of the low levels of socioeconomic development and inadequate **infrastructure** that marks this region. United Nations studies indicate that in 2000 nearly 40 percent of all urban residents in the world lived in squatter settlements. If this estimate is correct, more than one billion people, 18 percent of the world's population, live in squatter settlements. This is an astounding figure, and the number certainly will increase as more people leave the desolation of rural areas in hopes of finding a better life in the cities.

During the Vietnam War, millions of hamlet-dwelling South Vietnamese people were uprooted from the rural areas and relocated in the cities of Saigon and Danang for safety reasons. The people were very poor, and most could not afford to rent existing housing. Squatter settlements began to appear on the fringes of Danang, with structures made from discarded pieces of wood, cardboard, and corrugated metal. The main road leading out of Danang to the north included a one-mile segment that became known as garbage road. Displaced Vietnamese could be found daily rummaging through the debris dropped on both sides of the road. They sought out anything that could be useful in building or repairing a dwelling. Even scraps of food would be taken if they could be found. The refuse piles, some reaching 12 feet in height, were the deposits of garbage and trash primarily from the military bases in the Danang area, transported there by Vietnamese trash collectors.

Squatter settlements have different names in each region. They are called *favellas* in Brazil, *barriadas* in Peru, *bustees* in India, and *kampongs* in Malaysia.

Suggested Readings: Alan Gilbert and Josef Gugler, *Cities, Poverty and Development: Urbanization in the Third World*, 2nd ed., New York: Oxford University Press, 1992; United Nations Center for Human Settlements, *An Urbanizing World: Global Report on Human Settlements*, New York: Oxford University Press, 1996.

Stimulus diffusion. *See* **Expansion diffusion.**

Strabo (ca. 64 B.C.–ca. A.D. 25). The Greek geographer Strabo's *Geographica*, his only extant writing, is a valuable collection of geographical knowledge because of its breadth of coverage and its mention of Greek sources no longer available. Strabo was a great chronicler who summarized the works of other scholars. His work mentions other prominent researchers and writers from the Greek poet Homer onward, and he provides a detailed description of the **ecumene,** the habitable world as known to the Greeks.

Strabo accepted **Aristotle**'s zones of habitability as summarized by **Eratosthenes.** However, he did not agree with Eratosthenes on his determination of the circumference of the earth, a measurement that proved to be remarkably accurate. Instead he followed Posidonius, whose circumferential measurement was incorrect. Strabo correctly concluded that flooding of the Nile River resulted from the maximum summer rainfall in Ethiopia. Earlier, **Herodotus** theorized that the changing levels of water on the Nile were due to winds that blew the sun southward in the winter, drawing the river waters with it. When the winds abated in the spring, the sun could again travel northward, and the Nile water followed. This was, of course, a false theory. But it did reflect the important approach of process analysis, the consideration of actions and events through time.

Strabo's *Geographica* was not used extensively when it was first made available. Its value was realized centuries later when interest in the classical world revived. Strabo could be called a field geographer because he traveled widely in the known world, he gathered information about the places he visited, and he wrote accurate descriptions of his observations. *Geographica* is composed of 17 volumes. Strabo also completed written reports for military commanders and government officials. He has been called a writer of practical geography because his work was used in ongoing administrative activities.

In *Geographica*, Strabo discussed the general aspects of geography and referred to it as a science that was of concern to philosophers. He discussed the ecumene at length and wrote of changes on the earth's surface, a good example of process investigation. Strabo explained volcanoes and discussed the mathematical and physical principles of geography. Like other scholars in classical times, he speculated on the extent of the habitable world and on the climatic zones: the so-called torrid, temperate, and frigid zones.

Strabo also used the regional approach in his writing. He detailed the geographical features of India, the Alps, the Iberian Peninsula, the Dead Sea, Arabia, and Egypt. He also completed an extensive historical work that was lost.

Suggested Readings: Geoffrey J. Martin and Preston E. James, *All Possible Worlds: A History of Geographical Ideas*, 3rd ed., New York: John Wiley & Sons, 1993; George Sarton, *A History of Science: Hellenistic Science and Culture in the Last Three Centuries* B.C., Cambridge: Harvard University Press, 1959; George Kish, *A Source Book in Geography* Cambridge: Harvard University Press, 1978.

Subsistence agriculture. Individual farm families, extended families, and entire settlements engage in subsistence agriculture when the producers consume most or all of the food that is produced. Subsistence agriculture is a common practice in countries of the developing world. Pure subsistence agriculture means that no surplus remains and all the food produced is consumed by the growers. Usually, a small surplus of food is available for barter or sale in a **periodic market.**

Subsistence agriculture has regional variations. Extensive subsistence agriculture is found in the Americas, Sub-Saharan Africa, and to a lesser extent in Southeast Asia (*see* **Extensive agriculture**). This form of subsistence agriculture includes **nomadic herding** and shifting cultivation. In both cases, large areas of land are used in the production process. Intensive subsistence agriculture is found primarily in South, East, and Southeast Asia (*see* **Intensive agriculture**). In these places, farming is geared toward maximizing the amount of food produced on a limited area of land. In climates where the growing season is long, **double-cropping** of plants is possible. Two crops of rice can be produced in one year in warm, moist regions, or as an alternative, one planting of rice followed by a vegetable.

The amount of surplus food produced in a subsistence agricultural system varies from year to year, depending on environmental changes and the number of people that must be fed. In recent decades, **population growth** in the developing countries has been significantly high in a number of world regions. With the increased numbers has come the need for more food. Many regions have reached their environmental **carrying capacity** and have been unable to produce sufficient quantities of food for their growing numbers.

Subsistence agriculture has been practiced for hundreds of years throughout the developing world. The practice has successfully maintained the fertility of the soil through countless generations. However, in recent decades the ability of this agricultural system to provide all the food needed has been limited by drought, **soil erosion,** and population growth. Africa south of the Sahara Desert is a worst-case example: although total food production has increased significantly in the last several decades, food production per capita has declined.

Subsistence agriculture does not normally involve large numbers of livestock (except, of course, for nomadic herding). In a number of large cities in the developing world, urban agriculture is being practiced. Individuals or groups of agriculturalists intensively cultivate unused land within cities for their own consumption and for sale or exchange in local markets.

Suggested Readings: Tim Dyson, *Population and Food: Global Trends and Future Prospects,* New York: Routledge, 1996; Uma Lele, *Population Pressure, the Environment, and Agricultural Intensification,* Washington, D.C.: Worldwatch Institute, 1989.

Suburbia. The suburbs are separate governmental units within an urban area, and they are usually contiguous with the central city. Suburban development represents a transfer of land over a several-year period from rural to urban. Suburbs originally developed as residential areas within commuting distance to employment, retail activity, and entertainment within the city. The major burst in suburban growth took place following World War II, when members of the military services returned home and a civilian consumer economy was reinstated. Within a year following the end of the war, the so-called baby boom began, and with it came a surge in new home construction in the emerging suburbs. Adequate **transportation systems** allowed suburban dwellers to live on the urban fringes and have **accessibility** to workplaces in the city.

As the number of suburbanites increased, retailers began to relocate their businesses to the suburbs to be close to their customers. Manufacturing plants also began to relocate to the suburbs, where both lower-cost land and the opportunity for expansion could be found. The 1960 census pointed out that by the end of the 1950s employment in manufacturing was evenly split between locations in central cities and suburbs.

Rapid growth of suburbia in many regions has led to **urban sprawl,** the physical expansion of the developed area of urban centers far beyond the **central business district** (CBD). Such metropolitan centers in the United States as Atlanta, Houston, the Twin Cities (Minneapolis and St. Paul), and, of course, Los Angeles have experienced extraordinary suburban growth. Some urban places can boast of a first ring of suburbs, a second, and even a third, as growth continues outward from the center. Many large metropolitan areas now have settlements expanding beyond suburbia to the exurban ring, a zone beyond the built-up area and marking the rural–urban fringe. Like the suburban expansion decades earlier, the exurbs are commuter zones made possible by improvements in surface transportation systems, which have greatly increased accessibility within the greater metropolitan area and allowed it to expand. It is not uncommon in the early twenty-first century to see suburbanites commuting from one suburb to another for work and shopping. **Edge cities** have grown up along the interstate beltways encircling metropolitan centers. Edge cites contain virtually all of the functions needed by suburban residents.

The continued growth of suburbia has drawn business activity away from the original CBD and has reduced the tax base in the central cites of many metropolitan areas. It is estimated that in the 1990s twice as many people moved from central cities to suburbs than from suburbs to central cities. This imbalance is true despite the recent **gentrification** of some neighborhoods close to the CBD.

The attraction of people to the suburbs seems not to be lessening. Although commuting distances in suburbia are usually greater than in the central cities, the lower population densities, larger residential lot sizes, plentiful job opportunities, newness of the areas, and the presence of expansive shopping and entertainment centers continue to draw new residents.

Suggested Readings: Paul L. Knox, *Urbanization: An Introduction to Urban Geography*, Englewood Cliffs, N.J.: Prentice Hall, 1994; John C. Teaford, *Post-Suburbia: Government and Politics in the Edge Cities*, Baltimore: Johns Hopkins University Press, 1996; Joseph S. Wood, "Suburbanization of the Center City," *Geographical Review*, vol. 78 (1988).

Suitcase farmer. The suitcase farmer is an agricultural manager who owns several farms but does not have a residence on any of them. According to one definition, the suitcase farmer lives at least 30 miles from the closest landholding. A variation on the term is sidewalk farmer, one who lives within an urban place. The suitcase farmer owns several agricultural holdings for two important reasons. First, owning several farms in different regions is a hedge against losses due to inclement weather or problems associated with **natural hazards** that may impact one of the farms but not all of them. Second, the suitcase farmer's diversification lessens the affects of negative market fluctuations in the pricing of individual crops.

A suitcase farmer may own apple orchards in northern New Mexico, alfalfa fields in Oregon, and wheat fields in Kansas. Travel is necessary at key times in the growing season to ensure the efficient operation of each farm. During plowing, fertilizing, harvesting, and any other time that human labor is involved, the suitcase farmer or a foreman in his employ may visit the farms to supervise the activities.

Suitcase farming started in the wheat-growing regions of the northern Great Plains after World War II. Over the years, the number of farms in this category has increased. The major wheat belt in the United States and Canada is aligned north and south, and crews of workers start in the south and travel northward from farm to farm to plant, fertilize, and harvest the grain. Except for the periodic visits of the suitcase farmer and his workers, the farms are usually uninhabited. For that reason, the suitcase farmer is not considered to be an absentee landlord.

As farm size has increased in the United States and Canada, the suitcase farmer has become more closely associated with **agribusiness.**

Suggested Readings: John Fraser Hart, *The Rural Landscape*, Baltimore: Johns Hopkins University Press, 1998; Leslie Hewes, *The Suitcase Farming Frontier: A Study in the Historical Geography of the Central Great Plains*, Lincoln: University of Nebraska Press, 1973.

Superimposed boundary. A **boundary** that is drawn after the close of settlement and the development of a **cultural landscape** is called a superimposed boundary. The boundary may be the result of a conquering power imposing its will on the region, or it may be a demarcation line set up to divide the administrative duties of two occupying groups. For example, the boundary set at the 38th parallel in Korea after World War II was established as an administrative line. The Soviet Union was to administer the Korean territory north of the line and the United States that to the south. The division was to remain in place only long enough for preparations to be made for democratic elections to take place. The planned elections were never held, and in time two separate countries were formed, each politically antithetical to the other.

In 1947, Pakistan was separated from India when Great Britain left the South Asian region. The two countries shared a superimposed boundary. Within a short time, Muslims in India fled to Pakistan from the predominantly Hindi India.

In 1945, following the defeat of the French in Vietnam, the country was divided by a superimposed boundary along the 17th parallel. This division remained until 1975, when the two countries, North Vietnam and South Vietnam, were united following the end of the Vietnam War and the departure of U.S. military forces. The newly reunified country was named the Socialist Republic of Vietnam.

The most expansive example of superimposed boundary creation occurred during the era of **colonialism** in Africa. Boundaries set in place by the European occupiers invariably cut through and separated the home territories of distinct African culture groups, causing widespread dislocation. Following the end of colonialism, the superimposed boundaries established in Africa during that period became permanent.

Suggested Readings: Clive H. Scholfield, ed., *Global Boundaries*, vol. 1, World Boundaries Series, London: Routledge, 1994; P. J. Taylor, ed., *Political Geography of the Twentieth Century: A Global Analysis*, New York: Halstead Press, 1993.

Supranationlism. Supranationalism identifies the growing movement of alliance formation including three or more countries for economic, cultural, or military reasons. Supranational alliances are entered into for mutual benefit and protection and the expression of shared goals. There were more than 100 supranational organizations in 2000.

Following World War I, the League of Nations was formed with the goal of preventing future conflicts. The United States chose not to join the League, and without U.S. support, it soon collapsed.

In 1948, the United Nations (UN) was formed to ensure that no future global conflict would occur. The UN has maintained its existence into the twenty-first century, and it is the most extensive supranational organization in history, with nearly 200 member countries. During the **cold war,** the **North Atlantic Treaty Organization** (NATO) was formed to counter any aggressive moves made against Western Europe by the Soviet Union and its Eastern European **buffer zone** of countries. NATO's opposing forces also formed a supranational group called the Warsaw Pact.

In Southeast Asia, the Association of Southeast Asian Nations (ASEAN), founded in 1967, functions as both a political and economic supranational organization. Originally formed to counter any threatening moves by China, the group has worked to achieve regional cooperation and the peaceful settlement of any boundary disputes that may arise. The organization initiated the ASEAN Free Trade Association, which is patterned after two other economically based alliances, the **European Union** and the **North American Free Trade Agreement.**

It is anticipated that the number of supranational organizations in the world will increase. The major factor underlying this projected growth is the **globalization** of political and economic activity and the relatively diminished role of national governments in the new world order.

Suggested Readings: Thomas M. Poulsen, *Nations and States: A Geographical Background to World Affairs*, Englewood Cliffs, N.J.: Prentice Hall, 1995; Colin H. Williams, *The Political Geography of the New World Order*, London: Belhaven Press, 1993.

Sustainable development. The basic premise of sustainable development is the continued survival of land-use practices and the maintenance of the environmental base. Ideally, the use of the environmental base will not be lost through degradation or **resource** exhaustion. In short, a balance will be achieved between development and the environment that supports it.

Subsistence agriculture has long been identified as a successful form of sustainable development. For millennia, farmers throughout the developing world have maintained the proper balance between the growing of food crops and preservation of the **soil.** One form of subsistence agriculture, shifting cultivation, has been particularly successful in this regard. Shifting cultivation, farming a plot of ground for a number of years and then moving cultivation to another field, allows the vacated field to lie fallow for a number of years and regain full soil fertility (*see* **Extensive agriculture**). However, in recent decades population increase and drought conditions in many regions of Sub-Saharan Africa have put added pressure on existing farmland in the developing countries. As a result of these added pressures, fields used in shifting cultivation are farmed for an increased number of years before being rested, and this decreases their soil fertility and level of productivity.

The concept of sustainable development has at least two interpretations: (1) the environmentalist's view of the long term—to ensure that the land is used frugally and without environmental degradation so it will remain equally productive for future generations; and (2) the economist's view, which holds that resources are created to meet new demands. From the economist's perspective, technology will provide enhancements to the productive process as new needs are realized.

In 1992, the United Nations Commission on Sustainable Development convened a conference in Rio de Janeiro, Brazil. The conference drew attention to the need for conservation and the diligent use of resources. Particular attention was devoted to the topic of soil care, proper use of forest reserves, the avoidance of overfishing, species decline, and the reduction of air pollution from gaseous emissions (*see* **Deforestation, Pollution,** and **Renewable resources**). Additionally, attention was drawn to the need for increased recycling efforts and the substitution of energy sources wherever possible. For instance, coal and oil shale were seen as suitable substitutes for the fast-depleting supplies of crude oil. Emphasis was also placed on developing such renewable energy sources as geothermal, wind, and solar.

Suggested Readings: *The Agricultural Link: How Environmental Deterioration Could Disrupt Economic Progress*, Washington, D.C.: Worldwatch Institute, 1997; Timothy O'Riordan, "From Environmentalism to Sustainability," *Scottish Geographical Journal*, vol. 115 (1999).

Systematic (thematic) geography. Most geographic research is either systematic (thematic) or regional. Systematic geography limits itself to a particular subdiscipline. For example, an agricultural geographer studies and conducts research on particular farming techniques or some other aspect of agricultural processing. A medical geographer conducts research on the spread of a particular disease, such as the spatial diffusion of an influenza outbreak.

There are dozens of systematic specialties in geography. The Association of American Geographers, the primary professional organization for the discipline, lists more than 50 specialty groups that members of the association may select when they join. Such diversity is not uncommon in academic disciplines. Individuals in all areas of academia and research must choose a rather narrow subfield within their discipline because of the enormous increase in accumulated information and data. It is no longer possible to be a universal scholar in the mode of **Alexander von Humboldt** or **Carl Ritter.** Specialization has become an attribute of all disciplines.

The table of contents in an introductory **human geography** textbook arranged systematically will identify the major subfields. For example, *Human Geography: Landscapes of Human Activities*, by Fellmann, Getis, and Getis (*see* bibliography), lists the following chapter topics: roots and meanings of culture; spatial interaction and spatial behavior; populations, language, and religion; ethnic geography; folk and popular culture; economic geography; urban systems and urban structures; the political ordering of space; and human impact on the environment. All of these topics are systematic, or thematic, as is the main theme of the book, human geography.

Systematic geography gained prominence during the post–World War II era as a result of disciplinary disenchantment with the form of regional geography being practiced. Systematic geography also received a boost from the **Quantitative Revolution,** a movement that began in the 1950s.

Suggested Readings: Peter Haggett, *The Geographical Art*, Cambridge, Mass.: Basil Blackwell, 1995; Carville Earle et al., eds., *Concepts in Human Geography*, Lanham, Md.: Rowman & Littlefield, 1996.

Systems theory. Thinking of the earth, the economy, a person, and even a single leaf as a system is commonplace in the sciences, and geography is no exception. A system may be described as a set of parts that are linked through interdependence. A system has inputs and outputs. In short, a system is dynamic. For example, an automobile has inputs in the form of gasoline, oil, and antifreeze, among others. Its outputs include exhaust gases, heat, worn tires, and other parts too numerous to mention. The inputs are necessary for the operation of the system (the automobile), and the outputs reflect the conversion of energy and materials into waste products as the automobile is used.

Systems also have feedback of information. If a car is driven in winter from Miami, Florida, to Minot, North Dakota, a considerable temperature change takes place along the way. The climate-control system in the car, if set to operate automatically, will sense the temperature changes and regulate the climate within the car. As the journey north continues and colder weather is experienced, the engine will work a bit harder to maintain ideal operating conditions, which will require an increase in the amount of gasoline used per mile, another example of feedback to the system and its response.

Geographers use systems theory with regularity. In fact, geography is supremely organized to operate in a systems mode. Historians of American geography Preston James and Geoffrey Martin, in their book *All Possible Worlds: A History of Geographical Ideas,* contend that "geography has always had a holistic tradition so that it comes as no intellectual shock to study systems of interconnected and interdependent parts of diverse origin" (p. 9). Systems theory began in earnest with the publication of Ludwig von Bertalanffy's book *General Systems Theory: Foundations, Development, Applications* in 1968. Von Bertalanffy, one of the most important theoretical biologists of the first half of the twentieth century, insisted that a holistic approach was necessary in scientific studies to understand ecological problems and find ways to solve them.

The Club of Rome, a group of prominent industrialists and scientists located in Hamburg, Germany, undertook one of the most important applications of systems theory in the 1970s. The group used systems theory to study such major global problems as resource depletion, pollution, and population growth. Its program of study was titled the "Project on the Predicament of Mankind." The computer programs the group used were aimed at determining how the key variables of population, resource use, pollution, industrial production, and food availability worked together in a systematic way through time. Initial conclusions from the study suggested that **sustainable development** to the year 2100 was possible only if industrial production was significantly reduced.

Geographers today work with urban systems, economic systems, political systems, and atmospheric circulation systems, among others. It is generally accepted that occurrences in one part of the world can have an effect someplace else. One example of this interdependence is the El Niño phenomenon, in which a change in the water temperature in the eastern Pacific Ocean impacts the atmospheric circulation system, causing unusual and abnormal weather outcomes as far away as North America and Europe.

Suggested Readings: Robert W. Christopherson, *Geosystems: An Introduction to Physical Geography*, 3rd ed., Upper Saddle River, N.J.: Prentice Hall, 1997; Geoffrey J. Martin and Preston E. James, *All Possible Worlds: A History of Geographical Ideas*, 3rd ed., New York: John Wiley & Sons, 1993; Donella H. Meadows et al., *The Limits to Growth*, New York: Universe Books, 1972.

T

Telecommuting. Increasing numbers of workers who once commuted from home to their place of employment now complete job assignments at home or in local work centers. They are still employed by the same company but rarely commute to the office. These workers are engaged in telecommuting. Increased efficiency in communications technology and the need to reduce the amount of vehicular traffic on busy urban thoroughfares has resulted in a boom in telecommuting.

Workers at home are connected to the main office by computer, telephone, and fax. Assignments are sent to them electronically or by mail; they complete their tasks and return completed work to the office. If the worker does not operate from home, there is most likely an established work center nearby that can be used for the same purpose. Work centers have communications equipment, photocopiers, word processors, and other items necessary for accomplishing the work. Work centers are established either by the telecommuter's place of employment or outside firms that specialize in that service (*see* **Outsourcing**). Telecommuting is a reflection of the decided increase in the size of the **tertiary sector** in advanced economies. It is also suggestive of a changed relationship between employer and employee. There is a conceptual parallel between telecommuting employees and **footloose industries.**

One of the earliest and most successful efforts to encourage telecommuting occurred in Los Angeles in the 1980s. The Los Angeles Basin suffers from serious **smog** accumulation, and efforts have been underway since the 1950s to address the problem and alleviate the health hazards associated with the noxious gases. In 1988, a plan was proposed to improve air quality and relieve congestion on the roadways in the region. Because the materials in vehicular exhaust systems are the major cause of smog, plans were proposed to cut back on these emissions.

Telecommuting was one of the major components in the proposal. Others included highway improvements, the expansion of the multilane road system in the region; expansion of mass transit, which in turn would require more traffic lanes; using more high-occupancy vehicles to transport people to work; creating alternative work schedules to ease congestion during normal rush-hour times; and reorganizing the physical structure of the metropolitan area to have jobs and homes closer to each other. The last item is, of course, gigantic in scope and would take trillions of dollars and several decades to complete. The other components were considered worthy of considering in a plan that would span 20 years.

It was clear that telecommuting would be an important part of the overall plan. In surveys of companies that were involved primarily in information processing, it was determined that workers directly involved in that aspect of the operation represented up to 60 percent of the company's workforce. Allowing these employees to telecommute eliminated thousands of miles traveled by automobile and also reduced smog levels.

Telecommuting, a somewhat novel idea in the mid-1950s, is widely used in today's economy, and it is anticipated that this efficient business practice will continue to grow. Telecommuting is another feature of the **postindustrial economy**.

Suggested Readings: James M. Lents and William J. Kelly, "Cleaning the Air in Los Angeles," *Scientific American,* October 1993; Esther Scott, "Cleaner Air and Clearer Roads: A Plan for the Los Angeles Region," case number C16–93–1170.0, Cambridge, Mass.: John F. Kennedy School of Government, Harvard University, 1992; Office of Technology Assessment, *The Technological Reshaping of Metropolitan America,* Washington, D.C.: Congress of the United States, 1995.

Teleology. The word *teleology* literally interpreted from its Greek origins means "complete discourse." Teleology is a theory stating that events can be explained only as stages in a preordained outcome that is either planned by people or externally determined. **Carl Ritter**'s **geography** was teleological because he insisted that God designed the earth for the benefit of humans. Ritter influenced other geographers with his teleological views. One of his advocates, Arnold Guyot, wrote this about the association of a higher power and the earth: "All is in order, all is harmony in the universe, because the whole universe is a thought of God" (Livingstone, p. 151).

Teleology contends that explanation comes only through the understanding of a design or plan and not by mechanical causation. In short, a divine purpose, the teleologist suggests, explains the earth and all within it. Evidence of teleological thinking is found in early Egyptian documents. The ancient Greek philosophers Socrates and Plato spoke of ordered creation. But **Aristotle** departed from other classical thinkers in his belief that an internal logic existed in nature and that no predetermined outcomes existed. Teleology, then, is a theory in opposition to causal analysis. For example, **Charles Darwin,** in his theory of natural selection, used causal analysis to explain the evolution of species: particular causes brought about subsequent effects on plant and animal life, resulting in changes. The teleologist, on the other hand, would discount this form of explanation and state that the end itself is the means to understand the cause. For the teleologist, the explanation of a pine cone is that it will become a pine tree.

Teleologists, invoking a literal interpretation of Judeo-Christian biblical statements, conclude that God created earth for the benefit of humans and that humans are to take over the earth and modify it. In doing so, they would be completing the act of creation. This philosophical tenet resulted in the separation of humanity and nature. In this philosophy, humans and the environment are separate, and this view identifies one of the most pervasive dichotomies that geographers have contended with for centuries.

Suggested Readings: David Livingstone, *The Geographical Tradition: Episodes in the History of a Contested Enterprise*, Cambridge, Mass.: Basil Blackwell, 1992; Carl Ritter, "What Geography as a Science Has Yet to Consider," in *A Source Book in Geography*, ed. George Kish, Cambridge, Mass.: Harvard University Press, 1978.

Terracing. Agricultural activity practiced on mountainsides and hill slopes is done with terracing. The slopes are notched into level steplike terraces, or benches, which are enclosed and sectioned with retaining walls. The walls retain the irrigation water needed for plant growth and prevent **soil erosion.** Terracing is used in regions that lack extensive areas of flat land and where population numbers require maximum efforts to provide ample food.

Terracing is a labor-intensive practice from the original installation of terraces to the planting, growing, and harvesting of the crops. The use of labor-saving machinery is not possible because of slope

Terracing near Taegu, South Korea, in the Fall. *Source:* Author's photo.

steepness, and water in most cases must be manually carried uphill. Clearing the narrow terraces, cultivating the land, planting, weeding, harvesting, and maintaining the enclosing retaining walls are all accomplished by human labor. Despite these difficulties, terracing is practiced throughout South, East, and Southeast Asia and in some areas in the Mediterranean region.

Terracing is a special form of **intensive agriculture,** because maximum yields of a crop are produced on a limited amount of land. Rice is a commonly grown crop in terracing agriculture.

Suggested Readings: Bruce Koppel et al., *Development or Deterioration: Work in Rural Asia*, Boulder, Colo.: Lynne Reiner, 1994; Barbara Weightman, *Geography of Asia: Of Dragons and Tigers*, New York: John Wiley & Sons, 2000.

Territoriality. The act of establishing control over a defined space and applying to it a condition of ownership is called territoriality. The space can be as large as a sovereign state or as small as the personal space surrounding an individual. Territoriality is an eminently viable geographical concept, because space, area, and territory are all directly involved. Therefore, the concept lies at the heart of the discipline.

The system of dividing the earth into clearly demarcated countries is based on territoriality. A country may open its borders to outsiders for business activities, recreation, or personal visits, but any attempts at taking over the state or parts of it will invite an aggressive response. The same emotional reaction may occur if the return of land once accessed by a country through conquest is demanded. For example, the Soviet Union has occupied four islands north of Hokkaido, Japan, since the end of World War II. Discussions have been held over the years between the two countries, but the issue has not been resolved. In the early 1990s, the nationalist leadership in Russia made it clear that it would strenuously oppose the return of even one square inch of the territory claimed by Japan.

In the 1960s, anthropologist Robert Ardrey (1908–80) published an influential book titled *The Territorial Imperative,* in which he claimed that human territoriality is analogous to the animal instinct to control spaces they have marked. Two decades later, American geographer Robert Sack suggested that Ardrey's animal-instinct analogy was not suitable. Human territoriality, Sack contended, is far more complex and its manifestations can differ greatly in time and place. For instance, attitudes toward land vary from culture to culture. In some countries, land may be used in common by a number of families for farming. But in other countries, the sanctity of private land is strong enough to preclude similar practices.

Territoriality at the level of sovereign states reflects the practice of organizing space into either spheres of influence or state territory with clearly marked boundaries. The demarcated areas are legally bounded spaces and are exclusive to the occupants. The sovereign state system was set up to ensure political identity and the security of its citizens.

The notion of personal space also applies on the level of the individual. Personal space is the invisible area proximate to a person's body into which others may not enter. If someone gets too close, especially to one's face, an immediate feeling of discomfort arises. Yet, one may tolerate invasions of personal space if caught in a crowd and jostled around. Of course, one sacrifices personal space completely by diving into a packed mosh pit! Normally, however, personal space is an emotionally charged zone.

Suggested Readings: Robert Ardrey, *The Territorial Imperative*, New York: Atheneum, 1966; A. B. Murphy, "The Sovereign State as Political-Territorial Ideal: Historical and Contemporary Considerations," in *State Sovereignty as Social Construct*, ed. T. Biersteker and C. Weber, Cambridge: Cambridge University Press, 1966.

Tertiary sector. The tertiary sector in an economic system is entirely devoted to services. The tangible products grown or extracted in the **primary sector** that are subsequently processed or manufactured in the **secondary sector** are transported, wholesaled, and retailed in the tertiary sector.

Some of the hundreds of industries in the tertiary sector include restaurants, hotels, barber and beauty shops, repair facilities, commercial and distribution centers, wholesale and retail operations, and clerical services. The business of the tertiary sector is to provide a wide array of services directly to consumers. The consumer may be the end user of the service, such as the purchaser of a new suit of clothes from a retailer, or the consumer may be another service organization. In the **postindustrial economy,** specialization of economic effort is the rule. For example, an office equipment retailing firm may contract with another service firm to provide all human resources work (*see* **Outsourcing**). Business arrangements of this type are commonplace in today's economy.

Since the 1950s, the service sector in developed-world economies has grown significantly in prominence. Tertiary-sector employment in 2000 exceeded 75 percent of all nonfarm workers in the United States. In 2002, tertiary-sector employment exceeded 80 percent of all nonfarm workers in the United States. Other developed countries reported comparable advances in service jobs. Increases in the tertiary sector are expected to continue in the future.

Most service organizations are clustered in urban places, where potential customers are most plentiful. In the United States and Canada, the **central business district** (CBD) of cities traditionally served as the center for services to the community. Following World War II, suburban growth brought about a shift of service providers outward from the city center. As **suburbia** grew in population size and areal extent, **edge cities** began to develop along interstate beltways. These centers provide virtually all of the same services found in the CBD.

Suggested Readings: Peter W. Daniels, *Service Industries in the World Economy*, Institute of British Geographers, Studies in Geography, Cambridge, Mass.: Basil Blackwell, 1993; J. N. Marshall, *Services and Space: Aspects of Urban and Regional Development*, White Plains, N.Y.: Longman, 1995.

Threshold. *See* **Christaller's central place theory.**

Time-space convergence. Time-space convergence reflects changes in transportation technologies that have resulted in places becoming closer to each other in terms of travel time and **accessibility.** For example, in the 1830s a trip from New York City to San Francisco by the fastest surface transportation would take at least two months. Today, the trip could be made in a matter of hours by scheduled airline or in a few days by train or automobile. Increases in accessibility such as these suggest a decrease in the significance of distance.

With each refinement in transportation technology, the friction of distance is reduced (*see* **Distance decay**). However, time-space convergence in surface transportation contexts applies most directly to people and places that have access to transportation systems that have significantly reduced travel time. Not all places in the world are effectively connected to such modern systems, nor do many people and locations, especially in the developing world, have easy access to them. For places not so connected, it is possible that a time-space divergence has occurred.

Another aspect of time-space convergence has even greater potential for impacting accessibility. Revolutionary changes in communications technology in recent years has brought about virtually instantaneous global connections. Telephones, fax machines, and computer connections through electronic mail and the Internet allow this instant communication to take place among people who have the technology. In the current era of information processing and the importance of that activity in global economies, a significant transformation is underway in the way business is conducted. Again, those without the means to access this technology cannot benefit directly.

The importance of the communications revolution cannot be overemphasized. Some experts are convinced that the world of electronic communications and information processing will lead to the death of distance. Time-space convergence implies two simultaneous outcomes: (1) an expansion of the potential for interaction over space; and (2) the contraction of space over time. The notion of death of distance states that both interaction over space and contraction over time are maximized. In short, any place can be reached from any other place instantaneously. Again, however, the technology must be available to potential users, and the idea applies only to the communications realm. The transport of crude oil from the Middle East, bananas from Costa Rica, a loaf of bread to the local convenience store, or a family driving from Missoula, Montana, to Seattle on vacation are all limited by the time it takes to travel across the surface.

Suggested Readings: J. Allen and C. Hamnett, eds., *A Shrinking World? Global Unevenness and Inequity,* Oxford: Oxford University Press, 1995; Frances Cairncross, *The Death of Distance; How the Communications Revolution Will Change Our Lives,* Boston: Harvard Business School Press, 1997.

Topographic map. The topographic map, produced by the U.S. Geologic Survey, is a large-scale map that accurately depicts detailed physical and cultural features within a limited area. Topographic maps are produced in a range of sizes in the form of quadrangles based on latitude and longitude. Topographic maps range in scale from 1:250,000, representing an area measuring one degree of latitude by two degrees of longitude, to the largest of topographic map scales, 1:24,000, depicting a 7.5-minute by 7.5-minute quadrangular area. This topographic map is commonly called a 7.5-minute quad. There are also 15-minute quads (1:62,500), 30-minute quads (1:125,000), and the 30-minute by one-degree topographic map (1:1,000,000). By the mid-1990s, mapping of the entire conterminous United States was completed with 7.5-minute quads. Coverage of Alaska is completed with 15-minute quads.

The topographic map holds a wealth of valuable information. Because of its large scale and coverage of a limited area, a great deal of detail can be included on any given map. A representative topographic map may include symbolized information on transportation corridors, city street grids, individual buildings, cemeteries, mine sites, race tracks, and airports to name only a few. The U.S. Geologic Survey publishes a detailed symbol sheet to assist the map reader in interpreting the information on each map.

Topographic maps also provide information on the degree of surface relief and elevations above mean sea level in the mapped area. Elevations are reported with a series of enclosed contour lines, each of which connects points of equal elevation (*see* **Cartography**). The contour lines are plotted in series of elevation values based on the selected contour interval. For example, an elevation range from 900 feet to 1,200 feet could be mapped with contour lines representing every 20-foot change in elevation.

The **pattern** of contour lines on the map provides a clear indication of the degree of change in elevation anywhere in the area. If the contour lines are closely spaced, a steep slope is present. If the lines are widely spaced, the slope is gentler. Mountains, valleys, and ridgelines, as well as relatively flat alluvial plains, are easily distinguished through an analysis of the contour-line pattern.

The topographic map is an excellent tool for introducing the cartographic principles of **scale** and generalization, two of three attributes common to all maps. Because a topographic map shows individual buildings, bridges, and orchards, for example, the student of map reading can be taken to the actual site of a feature to see it directly and then note how the feature is symbolized on the topographic map. This activity introduces the idea of generalization. The third attribute common to all maps, distortion, is not easily perceived with topographic maps because the area portrayed is too small. However, referring to a small-scale map will clearly illustrate the effects of map distortion.

Suggested Readings: Victor Miller and Mary Westerbrook, *Interpretation of Topographic Maps*, Columbus, Ohio: Charles E. Merrill, 1989; John Noble Wilford, "Revolutions in Mapping," *National Geographic*, vol. 193 (1998).

Toponym. A toponym is a place name, and toponymy is the study of place names. Place names are an important part of the **cultural geography** of a region. They can reveal the attitudes of the people who chose the names and may reveal important information about the nature of the place. For example, the word *winter* is found in a number of Florida place names, a state not usually associated with the perception of winter as a cold season. In this case, it is a promotional association: Winter Haven, one of the places in Florida, is an invitation to northerners to seek refuge in its relative warmth when the chill northern winds blow.

George Washington is commemorated in place names more than any other American leader. He is the only president to have a state named for him, and the U.S. capital bears his name, as do 31 counties. Place names often have ancient roots, such as Troy, New York, named for the city made famous in the ancient Greek epic poet Homer's *Iliad*. Truth or Consequences, New Mexico, was named for a successful radio quiz show of the 1940s and 1950s.

Sometimes a controversy serves as the basis for a place name. Cando, North Dakota, got its name after county officials proclaimed they could name the town anything they chose. Others in the community did not think that way. In time, the officials got their way and chose to use the combined words *can* and *do* in the name, reflective of their claim.

Louis Agassiz (1807–73) was a famous nineteenth-century Swiss biologist and geologist. His name is used to identify a number of physical settings, including Agassiz Glacier, Alaska, and Agassiz Peak, Arizona. The word *enterprise* was chosen for the enterprising people in three communities, including Enterprise, Alabama. This town's economic history was marked by decades of relatively unsuccessful cotton growing. When the boll weevil entered the southern states and ravaged the cotton crop, the people of Enterprise were elated. They quickly shifted their efforts to peanut growing and erected a statue to honor the boll weevil for relieving them of their economic woes.

Los Angeles, California, "the city of angels," was founded in 1769 and was originally named El Pueblo de la Reine, de los Angeles de la Porciuncula. In time, and probably to most people's relief, the name was shortened to Los Angeles. Hollywood was not named for the wood of the holly tree, but for the wife of the developer of the settlement. Pancake Range, Nevada, was not named after a chuck wagon breakfast favorite but the flat rock formations in the region.

Thousands of toponyms in the United States and Canada derive from American Indian words. One is Chanhassen, a Twin Cities suburb in Minnesota. In the Sioux language, this word refers to the sugar maple tree. The place name translates to "the tree with sweet juice." Sometimes the reference is not so pleasant. Stinkingwater Peak, Wyoming, takes its unflattering name from a nearby river.

Ranger, Texas, commemorates the actions of the Texas Rangers who protected the settlement during the building of the Texas and Pacific Railroad. Many toponyms begin with the word *new*. New York City, New Mexico, and New Trier are examples. Another is New Bern, North Carolina, county seat of

Craven County, named after Bern, Switzerland, and famous as a longtime refuge for the infamous pirate Bluebeard. Travelers between Colorado and New Mexico on Interstate 25 will pass through Raton, New Mexico, and the Raton Pass on the border of the two states. In Spanish, *raton* means "mouse." In Raton, the word is used to identify a particular breed of local ground squirrel. This is an example of a misinterpretation that remains in the place name. To further confound the matter, many people in the region believe that Raton refers to rat. So, a mouse became a ground squirrel and is believed to be a rat!

In some cases, the toponym can be straightforward. An example is Midway Island, named for its location in the Pacific Ocean exactly halfway between North America and Asia. Before the advent of the Boeing 747 and other long-range jet airplanes that can fly across the Pacific Ocean without the need for a refueling stop, Midway Island was regularly visited. In 1942, the famous Battle of Midway was fought between the naval forces of the United States and Japan. The U.S. victory proved to be a turning point in World War II.

Place names can change over time. The town of St. Petersburg, Russia, was founded and named in 1703 by Czar Peter the Great. Beginning in 1712, the fast-growing city became the capital of the Russian Empire, a position it held for more than 200 years. In 1917, at the time of the Russian Revolution, the name was changed to Petrograd, and in 1924 it became Leningrad in commemoration of the Russian communist leader Vladimir Lenin. The city held that name until the fall of the Soviet Union in 1991; today it is again called St. Petersburg.

Suggested Readings: Harold E. Gulley, "British and Irish Toponyms in the South Atlantic States," *Names*, vol. 43 (1995); Kelsie B. Harder, ed., *Illustrated Dictionary of Place Names: United States and Canada*, New York: Facts on File, 1976; George Stewart, *Names on the Globe*, New York: Oxford University Press, 1975.

Topophilia. This word *topophilia* was coined by cultural geographer Yi-Fu Tuan and means "love of place." Tuan is a renowned exponent of **humanistic geography,** a concept he developed in the 1970s and one of the approaches in the discipline that followed and took issue with the scientific bent of the **Quantitative Revolution.** Topophilia is about the affective domain in human experiences. The concept is especially applied to, and aims to uncover emotional ties with, the physical environment. Centered in the affective domain, topophilia is not concerned with the cognitive or objective analyses of **place.** Therefore, the intellectual camp of topophilia is in the humanities, as opposed to much of geography, which is housed in the social sciences. Irish geographer Anne Buttimer contends that the humanistic perspective is important in geography and in many ways it lies at the heart of the discipline.

The ties that humans have with their environmental setting run the gamut from aesthetic to tactile, to the strong emotional attachment associated with home and expressed in warm memories and even nostalgia for places once lived in long ago.

The feelings people have for particular places vary in intensity. A fleeting memory of a lake resort visited on a recent vacation trip may capture one's attention for a moment and then fade away. But the intensity of feeling for a favorite corner in the home of one's childhood can be enormously compelling and filled with powerful recollections.

Topophilia is conceptually related to **environmental perception** in a positive way. A place with strong emotional ties is not only perceived but is revered and held in high esteem. Yi-Fu Tuan believes that topophilia can be related even to places not actually seen but vividly imagined. How many children have read with great feeling and a near personal association with the landscapes in L. Frank Baum's *The Wonderful Wizard of Oz* (1900), perhaps even imagining they are in that place with Dorothy and the other characters? Topophilia can be related to utopian landscapes clearly imagined and the object of great longing.

Not all landscapes and places are the object of love and endearment. Most are, in fact, considered casually if at all. Some are the object of topophobia, the antithesis of topophilia. A place may evoke feelings of depression, fear, and even suffering. For instance, a survivor of the brutality of a World War II concentration camp revisiting the place years later would most certainly recoil in anguish at the prospect of the experience.

Suggested Readings: Anne Buttimer, *Geography and the Human Spirit*, Baltimore: Johns Hopkins University Press, 1993; J. Douglas Porteous, *Landscapes of the Mind: Worlds of Sense and Metaphor*, Toronto: University of Toronto Press, 1990; Edward Relph, *Place and Placelessness*, London: Methuen, 1976; Yi-Fu Tuan, *Topophilia: A Study of Environmental Perception, Attitudes, and Values*, Englewood Cliffs, N.J.: Prentice Hall, 1974.

Total fertility rate. The total fertility rate (TFR) represents the average number of children a woman will have throughout her childbearing years, which is taken to be ages 15 through 45. TFRs in all regions of the world have declined over the last several decades. Nonetheless, the world TFR still exceeds three children per woman. To put this number into context it is necessary to know that replacement rate, the average number of children born during the childbearing years, is 2.1. This is the rate at which **zero population growth** would eventually be achieved.

In 2000, all countries in the developed world and China had TFRs that were below 2.1. Some European countries had TFRs that were 1.5 and below, the lowest overall rates of any major region in the world. Not surprisingly the highest rates are found in Africa. The TFRs in most African countries exceed 4.0, and some Sub-Saharan countries have rates over 6.0.

It would seem clear from this brief regional summary that global population growth will continue well into the twenty-first century. Even if every country in the world immediately achieved the 2.1 children replacement rate, significant population increase would still occur for many years into the future. This is understood when the age composition of the developing countries is taken into account. Because the **population pyramid** of any of the developing countries shows high numbers of people in the young age groups, there is certainty that high population growth will persist even if the 2.1 replacement rate were to be immediately accepted.

Whereas many countries are experiencing high population increases (and high TFRs), the European region has actually experienced declines in total population. The explanation lies in early completion of the **demographic transition,** a steadily increasing average age in most countries, a lower percentage of the population in the childbearing years, and consequently much lower TFRs.

The United Nations is continually monitoring TFRs and other demographic measures in an attempt to arrive at accurate predictions of future population trends. The TFR is a key factor in these formulations. In a recent demographic study, the United Nations predicted that total world population in 2100 would range from a high of 16 billion to a low of 5 billion. The median prediction, based on a TFR of 2.03, would result in a total world population in 2100 of more than nine billion people, a 50 percent increase over the 2000 total.

Suggested Readings: Brian O'Neill and Deborah Balk, "World Population Futures," *Population Bulletin,* vol. 56 (2001); Bryant Robie et al., "The Fertility Decline in Developing Countries," *Scientific American,* vol. 269 (1993).

Township and range system. Federal legislation in the 1790s produced a land survey system for the United States and its continental territories not already settled. The township and range survey is a rectangular division of the land into nearly square parcels of various sizes. This system eased the identification of specific blocks of land and served as an aid in the sale of land as westward expansion began to build momentum.

The township and range system of land division proceeded from a number of base lines set along parallels of latitude and principal meridians. The basic grid system was composed of square areas called townships, each measuring six miles on each side. Townships were further divided into 36 one-mile square (640 acres) sections, which in turn were divided into quarter sections (160 acres) and the so-called 40s, a 40-acre square of land. A unique addressing system was devised to identify each township and its subdivisions and was based on their location relative to the nearest base line and principal meridian. Canada also uses a rectangular land survey system; it is evident especially in the landscape of the prairie provinces.

The township and range system had a profound visual impact on the land. Anyone who has traveled by airplane over the midwestern United States cannot escape seeing the stark grid pattern of agricultural fields that mark the landscape. The grid pattern with its adherence to cardinal directions (north, south, east, and west) was used in town planning as well. In most urban places, cardinal directions were used to lay out the street **network.** This is generally true even in places that were originally sited along a river not flowing along a cardinal direction. The original plat paralleled the river at that point, but as

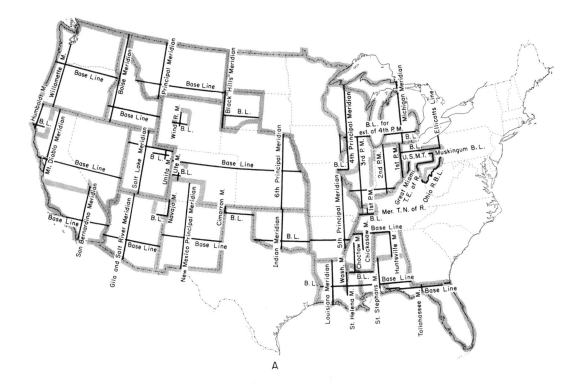

Township 3 North, Range 2 West of the Principal Meridian abbreviated T.3N., R.2W.

Section 9 Township 3 North, Range 2 West of the Principal Meridian abbreviated Sec. 9, T.3N., R.2W.

A

6	5	4	3	2	1
7	8	9	10	11	12
18	17	16	15	14	13
19	20	21	22	23	-24-
30	29	28	27	26	25
31	32	33	34	35	36

Northeast quarter of section 24, abbreviated NE ¼ sec. 24

Sections 1 through 6 on the north side and 7, 18, 19, 30, and 31 on the west side are fractional sections.

B   C

U.S. Rectangular Surveys. *Source:* U.S. Department of Agriculture.

the place grew in size, subsequent plats were aligned east–west and north–south.

The township and range system dictated the form of the original road network. Roads were set along township and section borders, following cardinal directions. The system, for all its simplicity and ease of application, was not without problems. The square grid was ideally suited to flat expanses of land, but for highly dissected landscapes it was not nearly as effective.

Suggested Readings: Hildegard Binder Johnson, *Order upon the Land: The U.S. Rectangular Land Survey and the Upper Mississippi Country*, New York: Oxford University Press, 1976; Chris Thomas, *Rural Geography*, London: Routledge, 1997.

Transhumance. The seasonal moving of domesticated animals (i.e., cattle, sheep, and goats) between regions of dissimilar climates in order to find adequate grassland for grazing is called transhumance. The word derives from two Latin stem words, *trans* (across) and *humus* (land). Thus, "traveling across the land."

Transhumance is a practice associated with permanent pastoralists as opposed to nomadic herders, who move continuously between grazing lands and do not own permanent dwellings. Transhumance is practiced in the European Alps and to a lesser extent in the American Rocky Mountain region. The periodic movement occurs on a regular basis: animals and people tending them move to meadows at high elevations in summer to take advantage of lush grasses that have regenerated following the spring snow melt. The pastoralists occupy small houses in the mountains during the summer period. In the fall, another periodic movement occurs as animals and tenders return to the lower elevations for the winter season.

The practice of transhumance remains viable in the European Alps but is declining somewhat in the United States. In recent years, range grazing of cattle has given way to the **feedlot** system, in which animals are kept in locations close to major urban markets. In the feedlots, animals are fattened for slaughter, and the meat products are quickly transported to wholesalers in the cities for immediate sale. Transhumance involving sheep, goats, and dairy cows is still in evidence throughout the western mountains and the intermontane regions in the United States.

Suggested Readings: John G. Galaty and Douglas L. Johnson, *The World of Pastoralism: Herding Systems in Comparative Perspective*, New York: Guilford Press, 1990; Terry G. Jordan, *North American Cattle-Ranching Frontiers: Origins, Diffusions, and Differentiation*, Albuquerque: University of New Mexico Press, 1993.

Transnational corporation. A transnational corporation (TNC), also known as multinational enterprise or a global industry, is a large firm with headquarters in one country and production facilities in one or more other countries. The advent of the TNC is without doubt the major source of change in the global economy. By 2000 there were more than 40,000 TNCs operating worldwide. TNCs set up operations in other countries to take advantage of inexpensive labor, available land, low energy costs, and other incentives. The operation usually involves the manufacture of components for computers, electronic equipment, automobiles, aircraft, and consumer durable goods, among other industries. The manufactured components are then shipped to locations near the market for sale. Profits made in the operation remain with the TNC.

The TNC movement has grown to gigantic proportions. Total sales revenues in many TNCs exceed the **gross national product** of entire countries. Their large size allows them to exert considerable influence on the economic and political situation in the host country. One of the major factors underlying the phenomenal growth of TNCs is the ease with which foreign investment funding can be accomplished. In years past, monetary exchanges between countries were cumbersome and time consuming. This is no longer true. Electronic transfers of foreign investment funds are now handled effortlessly. Another factor in the rise of TNCs is the greater **accessibility** afforded by improved **transportation systems.** The ease of moving both manufacturing components and money has allowed TNCs to become **footloose industries** on a global scale.

The home countries of TNCs are, of course, in the developed world. The United States, Canada, France, Germany, the United Kingdom, and Japan are the leading countries in this regard. Recently, the economic powerhouses known as the **Asian Tigers** (South Korea, Taiwan, Singapore, and Hong Kong) have also become the home base for TNCs. Japanese companies have established manufacturing and assembly plants in the United States, among other places, to produce automobiles and textile products.

TNCs are representative of the significant economic and political changes that are taking place in the era of **globalization** and the development of the **new international division of labor.** It is now standard practice for a TNC based in one country to have employees in perhaps dozens of other countries producing components for finished goods that reach markets worldwide.

Suggested Readings: Peter Dicken, *Global Shift: The Internationalization of Economic Activity,* 3rd ed., New York: Guilford Press, 1998; John Mills, *Managing the World Economy,* New York: St. Martin's Press, 2000; Patrick O'Sullivan and Alasdair McNeely, "World Trade in the 1990s," *Geography,* vol. 81 (1996); Michael Storper, *The Regional World: Territorial Development in a Global Economy,* New York: Guilford Press, 1997.

Transportation systems. The movement of people and goods via surface and air transportation systems is the essence of one of geography's basic attributes: **spatial interaction.** Transportation systems provide the **connectivity** that unites distant places and allows them to work together. The revolution in transportation development from the time of horse-drawn carts and sailing ships to railroads and steamships through jet aircraft and high-speed interstate highway systems is considered by many geographers and other scholars to be as important as the **Agricultural Revolution** and the **Industrial Revolution.** Indeed, without essential transportation systems in place, neither of these world-changing revolutions could have taken place.

Transportation is essential to sound economic growth. Its role in the economy is especially prominent in the **tertiary sector,** but it is equally important in both the **primary** and **secondary sector**s as well. Transportation is a key factor in the location of industrial activities. A firm must consider its **accessibility** to other firms with which it works and to its market. Transportation systems make these forms of spatial interaction possible.

Improvements in transportation systems have the effect of bringing places closer together and reducing the impact of friction of distance (*see* **Distance decay**). Geographers have noted that the properties of time and space are changed with each improvement and refinement in transportation technology. A trip by covered wagon from St. Louis to San Francisco in the early nineteenth century was long and arduous. Travel between the same two places by automobile on the interstate system, however, can be a nearly effortless experience taking no more than a few days. Changes of this type are suggestive of the notion of **time-space convergence** and the virtual shrinking of the world in terms of access times between places.

Another indicator of the importance of transportation is its inclusion in some of the most important theories and models used in geography. For example, **von Thunen's land use model** bases the types of agriculture in the isolated state on distance from the market center and the associated transportation costs. **Christaller's central place theory** includes discussion of transportation within the urban system. **Weber's least cost theory** of economic activity aims at selecting the ideal location for an industrial plant while minimizing the cost of transportation.

Transportation systems are essential to the development and growth of the urban system within a region. In the United States, urban places were initially sited on navigable rivers and along existing roads to be connected with one another. With the introduction of the railroad, cities were provided with access to every other urban center within range of this new form of transportation. The **central business district** (CBD) was the base for a major railroad transfer point for both passengers and cargo. The rail lines served the downtown area of cities and the adjacent manufacturing, warehousing, and industrial districts. Following World War II, the move to **suburbia** was underway, and this shift took place in large part because of efficient transportation systems that provided access to the CBD and to points within the greater region.

Some of the outcomes of the transportation revolution have not been positive. The move to suburbia has continued, and in many metropolitan areas **urban sprawl** has been the outcome. In nearly every metropolitan area, the problem of rush-hour gridlock occurs on a daily basis. In a few cities, such as Los Angeles, the problem of **smog** combines with gridlock to plague the city with noxious air and extended commuting delays.

Suggested Readings: Susan Hanson, ed., *The Geography of Urban Transportation*, 2nd ed., New York: Guilford Press, 1995; Brian S. Hoyle and Richard D. Knowles, eds., *Modern Transport Geography*, New York: Halstead Press, 1992; John A. Jakle and Keith A. Sculle, *The Gas Station in America*, Baltimore: Johns Hopkins University Press, 1994; Edward Taafe et al., eds., *Geography of Transportation*, 2nd ed., Upper Saddle River, N.J.: Prentice Hall, 1996.

Truck farming. See **Market gardening.**

U

United Nations Convention on the Law of the Sea. Sixty countries ratified the international agreement of the United Nations Convention on the Law of the Sea (UNCLOS), establishing offshore zones in oceanic waters and regulations for operating on the high seas, in 1994. Establishment of UNCLOS reflected a desire to create a legal order for the ocean areas to establish communications among all sovereign states and to ensure the peaceful use of the oceans. The United States did not sign the agreement in the early 1980s because of concerns about potentially adverse outcomes with the Soviet Union and disagreements over the claims of developing countries to mineral resources on the ocean floor.

UNCLOS contained four major provisions aimed at settling years of disagreements and challenges by countries around the world: (1) establishment of a 12-nautical-mile territorial sea within which a country would have sovereignty and exclusive fishing rights; (2) establishment of a contiguous zone extending 24 nautical miles for the enforcement of customs, immigration, and sanitation laws; (3) establishment of an **exclusive economic zone** (EEZ) extending 200 nautical miles from shore, allowing the country to explore, exploit, conserve, and manage all natural resources on the seabeds and in the waters; and (4) provision that the high seas be open to all countries, whether coastally located or landlocked. According to the UNCLOS agreement, if the continental shelf goes beyond 200 nautical miles, the EEZ could be extended up to a maximum distance of 350 nautical miles.

The 200-nautical-mile EEZ is problematical. Countries that are less than 200 nautical miles from one another would not enjoy the full 200-nautical-mile privileges. In these cases, UNCLOS provided for a solution in the **median-line**

principle, which gave each country one-half the distance between them for their EEZ. However, more serious problems are found in the South China Sea, where there are not only median-line arrangements in place but multiple and overlapping claims to sovereignty over the waters of the sea. China, Taiwan, and Vietnam, for example, claim all of the South China Sea as their own.

The second problem concerns ownership of rich mineral resources on the seabeds of the open oceans. UNCLOS declared that these mineral resources are the common heritage of all humankind, to be managed for the benefit of all people on earth. This declaration clearly favored the developing countries that were either landlocked or did not have the technology to extract the resources, or both. The specific resource in question at the time of negotiations was prized manganese nodules, large clusters of highly valuable metals lying on the seabed. Only a handful of countries, the United States included, have the technical capability to harvest the manganese nodules.

Suggested Readings: Albert R. Cole, *Should the Reagan Administration Have Signed the U.N. Convention on the Law of the Sea?* Pew Case Studies in International Affairs, Case 403, Washington, D.C.: Institute for the Study of Diplomacy, Georgetown University, 1988; J. M. Van Dyke et al., *Freedom for the Seas in the 21st Century: Ocean Government and Environmental Harmony,* Washington, D.C.: Island Press, 1993.

Universalizing/ethnic religions. Major religions in the world exhibit a number of geographic characteristics. Each has a place of origin from which the **diffusion** of that religion began. Also, each religion eventually established itself in an identifiable region in which it is the most highly represented. Universalizing religions make a conscious effort to attract converts. The major universalizing religions are Christianity, Islam, and Buddhism. Christianity began in the region of present-day Israel and spread to areas of East Africa, Europe, the Western Hemisphere, and eventually to Australia and New Zealand. Islam began in Saudi Arabia and diffused to North Africa, Southwest Asia, and parts of Southeast Asia. Buddhism originated in Nepal and northern India and eventually spread to Southwest, Central, East, and Southeast Asia.

Christianity has the greatest number of adherents of any religion, with more than two billion followers. Islam is second in number with nearly 1.5 billion. Buddhism has about 350 million followers.

Ethnic religions are not expansionistic and do not actively attract others to join their membership. By far the largest ethnic religion is Hinduism, with more than 900 million members, nearly all of them living in India. Other ethnic religions include Confucianism, Daoism (Taoism), Shintoism, and Judaism. All of these are of Asian origin except Judaism, which emerged in the Middle East. Judaism claims to have 15 million members, two-thirds of them living in the United States and Israel.

Suggested Readings: Adrian Cooper, "New Directions in the Geography of Religion," *Area,* vol. 24 (1992); Michael Paccione, "The Relevance of Religion for a Relevant Human Geography," *Scottish Geographical Journal*, vol. 115 (1999); Ninian Smart, ed., *Atlas of the World's Religions*, New York: Oxford University Press, 1999.

Urban geography. Urban geography, the study of urban places, emerged as a separate branch of **geography** in the 1950s and 1960s and quickly rose to prominence in the discipline. By the late 1970s, urban geography was the leading specialty group in membership numbers in the Association of American Geographers, the discipline's primary professional organization. Urban geography held that position until the late 1990s, when the fast-rising field of **geographic information systems** (GIS) enrolled larger numbers in its specialty group.

Urban geography has two major research directions. The first focuses on the **patterns** of urban settlements and their interactions. **Christaller's central place theory** considers urban places in this way. In central place theory, urban places are studied to determine their relationships to each other within a hierarchically arranged system.

The second research direction looks at patterns within urban settlements. Analysis centers on the form of the urban place and its internal functions. Three models of urban structure exemplify this research direction in urban geography: the **concentric zone model,** the **sector model,** and the **multiple-nuclei model.** All three of these models identify in different ways the internal structure of urban places.

During the 1950s and 1960s, urban geographic studies were closely linked with the emerging field of location theory, and it became an important venue for the statistical and mathematical models coming out of the **Quantitative Revolution** at that time.

Suggested Readings: Harold Carter, *The Study of Urban Geography*, 4th ed., New York: John Wiley & Sons, 1996; Truman Hartshorn, *Interpreting the City: An Urban Geography*, 3rd ed., New York: John Wiley & Sons, 1992; Helga A. Leitner, "Urban Geography: Responding to New Challenges," *Progress in Human Geography*, vol. 16 (1992).

Urban heat island. Urban areas are generally 10–15 degrees warmer than the surrounding rural countryside. A number of factors explain this phenomenon. The materials used in the construction of urban areas are metals, glass, stone, concrete, and asphalt. All of these materials, except glass, have a lower albedo (reflective power) than the open fields, grasses, and trees in rural areas. As such, incoming shortwave solar radiation is readily absorbed in these building materials. Absorbed shortwave radiation is quickly transformed into long-wave radiation, or sensible heat. Glass adds to the heating of urban areas in a somewhat different way. Glass allows shortwave radiation to easily pass through it. Once inside a building, the shortwave energy is transformed into long-wave energy, and heat is generated. This process has commonly been referred to as the greenhouse effect. It explains why an automobile parked in the sun on a warm day with the windows closed builds up an exceedingly high interior temperature.

Asphalt, widely used on streets in urban areas, has a very low albedo, and virtually all the sun's shortwave radiation is absorbed and changed to sensible heat. The old saying that asphalt can get so hot an egg can be fried on its surface is, in fact, true.

Another factor explaining the urban heat island is **pollution.** Concentrations of **smog** and carbon dioxide trapped in a dome of air over an urban area can block reflected shortwave radiation and hold it in the air. Also, winds are generally less intense in built-up areas because they are lowered and diverted by tall buildings. Solar inputs become trapped in the narrow spaces between buildings, and the reduced air flow cannot move the warm air out of the area.

Urban areas burn great amounts of fossil fuels to heat buildings in winter and to cool them in summer. Heat generated from the burning of these fuels also becomes trapped in the urban area. Finally, automobiles, trucks, and buses add greatly to the heat accumulation in urban areas, and their exhaust gases contribute to pollution levels in the atmosphere, another element in the development of the urban heat island.

Suggested Readings: Eldon D. Enger and Bradley F. Smith, *Environmental Science: A Study of Interrelationships*, 7th ed., Dubuque, Iowa: WCB/McGraw-Hill, 2000; Andrew Goudie and Heather Viles, *The Earth Transformed: An Introduction to the Human Impact on the Environment*, Cambridge, Mass.: Basil Blackwell, 1997.

Urban landscapes. Urban places have a distinctive landscape. Closely packed residences, businesses, manufacturing and industrial buildings, and a complex street and road **network** set them off from the surrounding rural area. An urban landscape also reflects distinctive features within the place. For example, the **central business district** (CBD) is usually identified by an array of tall office buildings, theaters, restaurants, and a transportation system linking the CBD to other parts of the city. By contrast, residential areas vary from high-rise apartment complexes to low-density, high-income housing districts. An urban place may also include manufacturing, industrial, and transportation sectors, each with its particular combination of structures. All of these varied scenes are landscapes in themselves, and collectively they make up the larger landscape of an urban place.

All urban places share these attributes in varying degrees. The term *urban landscape* is a generalization. Yet, every urban place is unique in the specific arrangement of its landscape features. For example, both St. Louis, Missouri, and Paris, France, have an urban landscape, and in a general sense they are comparable. But they are also unique. St. Louis has its arch and Paris the Eiffel Tower. The comparison, of course, could be extended to include hundreds of features unique to each of these major urban places. New York City has the Statue of Liberty, the Empire State Building, and, until the tragic events of September 11, 2001, it had the twin towers of the World Trade Center. The loss of a prominent urban landscape feature changes not only the look of the place but its emotional impact as well. When the loss results from a purposeful act of destruction, strong emotional responses are evoked.

The urban landscape is always changing. The growth of suburban developments following World War II and the emergence of **edge cities** on the fringes of the developed area change the visual impact of the place and create a modified urban landscape. Even the presence of **smog** hanging over a city becomes part of the urban landscape.

The concept of urban landscape applies at the regional level as well. Coalesced urban areas such as **Megalopolis,** a nearly continuous series of urban places along the U.S. eastern seaboard between Boston and Washington, D.C. may validly be considered a single urban landscape.

Suggested Readings: Truman A. Hartsorn and Peter O. Muller, "Suburban Downtowns and the Transformation of Metropolitan Atlanta's Business Landscape," *Urban Geography,* vol. 10 (1989); Edward Relph, *The Modern Urban Landscape: 1880 to the Present,* Baltimore: Johns Hopkins University Press, 1987.

Urban planning. The aim of urban planning is to regulate and control the growth and modification of cities. Specifically, planning may focus on changes to the transportation systems within the city to ensure optimum **accessibility** to all internal areas. Planning may also be devoted to improving neighborhood structures and to remedying urban blight (*see* **Gentrification**).

One of the biggest concerns of planners in fast-growing metropolitan areas is the avoidance or containment of **urban sprawl.** Some American metropolitan areas like Atlanta, Houston, Minneapolis–St. Paul, and Los Angeles have grown outward, displacing extensive areas of rural land. If the sprawl cannot be stopped, then planning must be invoked to determine how best to manage the expanded area. British cities have largely avoided sprawl by legislating the inclusion of **green belt**s on the edges of existing cities. Growth outside the cities must take place in designated areas beyond the green-belt zone. One American city, Portland, Oregon, has instituted a similar plan. Portland established a no-growth line beyond which urban development cannot proceed.

Another concern of planners is addressing the problems of **smog** and other forms of atmospheric **pollution** that occur in some urban areas. Los Angeles is an example of a major metropolitan area that has been adjusting to a smog problem since the 1950s. Mexico City, Mexico, is another. Serious smog conditions in the past have caused Mexico City officials to close schools for extended periods because of the high levels of toxic fumes.

Tokyo experienced high rates of growth following World War II, and its planned green belt was quickly overrun. The postwar return to a commercial economy and the rebuilding of the war-ravaged city were far too compelling to yield to building restrictions in the planned green-belt areas. Planners in Tokyo are now tasked with finding ways to keep the giant metropolitan area operating efficiently despite its size and crowded conditions.

Suggested Readings: Gordon O. Ewing, "The Bases of Differences between American and Canadian Cities," *Canadian Geographer,* vol. 36 (1992); Brian J. Godfrey, "Restructuring and Decentralization in a World City," *Geographical Review,* vol. 85 (1995).

Urban sprawl. Urban sprawl is the unplanned expansion of urban and suburban development (structures and activities) onto adjacent rural land. The expansion may be in the form of residential developments, office complexes, business parks, or industrial centers. Regardless of the form of expansion, urban sprawl implies minimal control over growth and the absence of viable **urban planning.**

Urban sprawl occurs in three basic forms: ribbon development, low-density housing development, and leapfrog growth. Ribbon development is found along new or existing surface-transportation corridors leading away from urban areas. If the land adjacent to the corridor is available for commercial development, it may become developed with small businesses, restaurants, gasoline stations, and light industrial firms. Location along a well-traveled corridor is ideal for doing business, and strip developments are found along corridors in nearly every world region. The question is, was the growth planned or did it happen haphazardly? If the latter is true, then the result is urban sprawl.

Another form of urban sprawl is the building of expansive low-density housing developments on previously rural, and possibly agricultural, land. Once a housing development is in place, service businesses quickly follow. Continued growth of the new development may serve as an impetus for further growth, and the phenomenon of urban sprawl is underway.

Sprawl often occurs as a result of leapfrog development. For example, a manufacturing firm may build a new plant on inexpensive rural land a mile from an urban area. The factory is located in a transportation corridor leading into the city. Ribbon development may soon follow along the corridor, and if the plant continues to grow, housing developments may begin to fill the empty area between the plant and the urban center.

Suggested Readings: Mark Goodwin, *Reshaping the City,* London: Edward Arnold, 1998; James E. Vance, *The Continuing City: Urban Morphology in Western Civilization,* 2nd ed., Baltimore: Johns Hopkins University Press, 1990.

Urbanization. Urbanization is the general term that refers to city building. The forms that urbanization may take have varied greatly through time. Urbanization is the process of a location's initially becoming urban, with an increased concentration of people and functions in cities. Urbanization in the United States began during the colonial period of the 1700s with a handful of towns and cities located on the eastern seaboard. In time, urbanization marched hand in hand with the westward movement as the great interior was inhabited and settlements were established on the Pacific Coast.

The traditional urban place in the United States included a well-defined **central business district** (CBD), wholesaling and manufacturing districts, a range of residential areas, and surface transportation networks to provide **connectivity** within the place.

Following World War II, a radical change took place in the urbanization process: the growth of suburban developments. **Suburbia** brought great changes to urban areas. Growth away from the center city and outward to the surrounding rural areas marked this new era. As suburban residential areas increased in population size, service providers began to relocate to be closer to their customers. In addition, manufacturing and industrial firms also began to relocate to the suburbs, where rural land was less expensive and efficient **transportation systems** ensured **accessibility** to destinations near and far. As suburbia continued to grow, greater concentrations of commercial activities found their way there. **Edge cities** emerged along interstate beltways surrounding the metropolitan area, providing all of the services found in the CBD.

Suburban growth occurred to a large extent at the expense of the central city. Tax base was lost as people moved out of the city to suburbia, and the earlier importance of the CBD dissipated. However, in recent decades the process of **gentrification,** or restoring older homes and apartment buildings in the inner cities, helped to increase the attractiveness of the inner city and draw people back. Some metropolitan areas have grown at such high rates that **urban planning** efforts have simply not been effective. The result has been **urban sprawl,** the virtually unplanned and uncontrolled expansion of the metropolitan area into the adjacent rural areas.

Globally, the process of urbanization has steadily increased. In 2000, 45 percent of the world's population lived in urban areas. The developed countries have the highest urban resident percentages, averaging about 75 percent. However, growth rates in the developing countries are steadily increasing. The United Nations estimates that by 2025 no major region in the world will have less than one-half of its population living in urban places. It is also certain that metropolitan areas in the developing world will have the highest population concentrations in the world. Places like Shanghai, São Paulo, Mexico City, Bombay, Lagos, Karachi, and Calcutta will all have populations exceeding 20 million by 2025.

Suggested Readings: David Clark, *Urban World/Global City*, New York, Routledge, 1996; Alexander Garvin, *The American City: What Works, What Doesn't*, New York: McGraw-Hill, 1996; Paul L. Knox, *Urbanization: An Introduction to Urban Geography*, Englewood Cliffs, N.J.: Prentice Hall, 1994.

Vernacular cultural regions. Vernacular regions reflect the cultural identities of individuals or groups and are derived from a strong **sense of place.** These regions derive from the feelings and images about a place, and they are also called popular or perceptual regions. Because the vernacular region has an emotional and perceptual origin, it is distinct from the formal and functional **region,** which is widely used in **geography** and is based on the results of objective and possibly statistical analysis. For example, the American South is a vernacular region. The association that people in the South hold for the region is based on their cultural identity and emotional attachment to the place.

The vernacular region occurs on every **scale,** from the city neighborhood to large parts of a continent. Studies have been conducted on people's perception of the extent of the Midwest. Researchers have attempted to determine the extent of the South by noting the frequency of use of the term *Dixie* in the classified section of telephone directories. At a different scale, residents of the North Shore of Lake Superior refer to the area as simply "the shore," and this reflects their personal connection with the place and the pride they have for the region. Lake Superior has a south shore as well, but for North Shore residents, there is really only one shore of consequence.

The Chinese psyche holds that China occupies the Middle Kingdom, a location of superiority in the world. This perception has existed for centuries, and it may be abating for the first time as China strives to reach out to other regions in the world and take part in the global economy.

Vernacular regions are about **place,** and place, as Yi-Fu Tuan (cultural geographer who developed the concept of humanistic geography in the 1970s) contends, have a history. Part of that history include a love of the place (*see* **Topophilia**) and a sense of belonging to the place.

Suggested Readings: George O. Carney, ed., *The Sounds of People and Places: Readings in the Geography of American Folk and Popular Music*, 3rd ed., Lanham, Md.: Rowman & Littlefield, 1994; Wilbur Zelinsky, *The Cultural Geography of the United States*, 2nd ed., Englewood Cliffs, N.J.: Prentice Hall, 1992.

Vidal de la Blache, Paul (1845–1918). Considered to be the father of French geography in the modern era (post-1859), Paul Vidal de la Blache was comparable in stature to the British geographer **Halford J. Mackinder** and the American geographer **William Morris Davis.** Throughout his career he advocated the study of human relationships with their immediate environmental surrounds (*milieu*). This particular relationship, human–environment interaction, continues to lie at the heart of geographical studies today. Vidal insisted that the significance of these studies was best approached by analyzing small "regions" (*pays*) and noting the assemblage of distinct physical characteristics (e.g., soils, water, drainage patterns, surface formations) with human settlement patterns and agricultural land use.

Paul Vidal de la Blache. *Source:* Geoffrey Martin.

Vidal invoked the notion of **possibilism** to counter the accepted theory of **environmental determinism** as expressed in the first decade of the twentieth century by geographer Ellsworth Huntington in the United States. Possibilism suggested that humans have a wide range of potential actions within an environment, and they respond depending on their value systems, attitudes, and behavior patterns—in short, their cultural attributes determine their possible responses to the environment and the limits it imposes. According to Vidal, humans have choices in how they respond to their environment. The overall outcome of the interaction between humans and their physical surroundings identifies their "way of living" (*genre de vie*).

Not all occupying groups respond in the same way to a similar environment. For example, if an East Asian culture group had occupied the southeastern United States during the colonial period, the resulting land-use patterns would differ from those created by the European immigrants.

Vidal was appointed chair of geography at the Sorbonne in Paris in 1898. His book *Principles of Human Geography*, completed by others following his death in 1918, became a classic in the field. Over the next several decades,

Vidal's followers continued the work of this important geographer. The outline of Vidal's book contained three major divisions of geographical knowledge: (1) global population distributions; (2) patterns of civilization (including human relationships with their *milieu*); and (3) circulation systems (roads, railroads, and sea-lanes).

Vidal's thrusts toward integrating human actions within *milieu* to create a *genre de vie* is important not only for understanding the key theme of human–environment interaction but in appreciating the clear tie between **human geography** and physical geography. There was no conflict between the two as had been seen in other countries; they were viewed as working together. The separation of physical and human geography and the resulting tensions associated with the split has never affected French geography. Physical geography was seen as being both inseparable from and indispensable to human geography.

Suggested Readings: Geoffrey J. Martin and Preston E. James, *All Possible Worlds: A History of Geographical Ideas*, 3rd ed., New York: John Wiley & Sons, 1993; Paul Vidal de la Blache, "Meaning and Aim of Human Geography," in *Human Geography: An Essential Anthology*, ed. John Agnew et al., Cambridge, Mass.: Blackwell, 1996.

Von Humboldt, Alexander (1769–1859). Along with his contemporary, German geographer Carl Ritter, German geographer Alexander von Humboldt is considered one of the founders of modern **geography.** He and Ritter were the last prominent advocates of the age of universal knowledge. Their work in geography and their perspective on science were both exceptionally broad. For example, when von Humboldt conducted field investigations in northern South America, he considered all aspects of the environment. He collected plant specimens and minerals, and he observed and recorded the activities of the culture groups he encountered. Von Humboldt's instrument kit included sextants, timepieces, and other astronomical devices for observing and documenting the movements of celestial bodies and to accurately determine the longitude of places he visited.

Alexander von Humboldt. *Source:* National Library of Medicine.

Von Humboldt had a natural curiosity about the physical environment. Early in his career he was greatly influenced by the German traveler and writer Georg Forster, a naturalist who had accompanied the English captain James Cook on his voyage around the world (1772–75). Von Humboldt learned from Forster the importance of keen observation and detailed recording of noted physical features.

Following his journeys through South America and the Caribbean, von Humboldt wrote a 30-volume series documenting his field studies. During this expedition, he collected 60,000 plant specimens, which were shipped back to Germany and laboriously catalogued. Von Humboldt visited the United States for a short time and was welcomed by American statesman Thomas Jefferson; the two became good friends.

In 1829, von Humboldt visited Russia. He traveled by coach from St. Petersburg to Siberia, as far as the border with China. He convinced the Russian authorities to install weather stations from St. Petersburg east to the islands near Alaska. Data from these weather stations were later used to make the first world map of average temperatures. During his Siberian sojourn, he observed and commented on the presence of permafrost (a permanently frozen layer of earth beneath the surface) in the region.

Von Humboldt also noted and recorded the changes of vegetation with increases in altitude, a transition similar to one found in moving from lower to higher latitudes.

In his last few years, von Humboldt wrote a five-volume work titled *Kosmos*, considered to be the most important scientific book of its time. These volumes deal with all aspects of existence, from speculation on the universe and astronomy to plant communities and physical geography. He considered that humans were an integral part of the environment and that they could influence and change their environmental settings.

Unlike Ritter, von Humboldt was not an exponent of **teleology,** the belief that events are preordained. He believed that nature had an internal logic and that the physical world could be explained through understanding causal connections.

Suggested Readings: Geoffrey J. Martin and Preston E. James, *All Possible Worlds: A History of Geographical Ideas,* 3rd ed., New York: John Wiley & Sons, 1993; George Kish, *A Sourcebook in Geography,* Cambridge, Mass.: Howard University Press, 1978.

Von Thunen's land use model. Johann Heinrich von Thunen (1783–1850) was a wealthy landowner in Germany and a scholar of economics as it applied to agricultural activities. His primary interest was to determine the ideal location of specific agricultural activities to maximize his profits. Long before the publication of his most important work, *The Isolated State* (1826), von Thunen had worked with an idea that later would become the conceptual basis for **Christaller's central place theory.** He imagined a uniform plain within which all environmental factors (e.g., soil fertility, relief, and climate) were the same throughout. In addition, all farmers working the land were assumed to be similar in their aim to maximize profits. Transportation on the plain was by horse-drawn wagon. The isolated state measured 40 miles in diameter, and in its center was the only urban place. The purpose of the urban place was to accept and market agricultural products produced on the plain and to provide all equipment and services needed by the farmers working the land.

Von Thunen then proposed that specific agricultural land uses would organize around the single urban place in a logical manner. That is, activities that were essential in serving the daily needs of the urban residents (e.g., dairy products and other perishables) or derive the highest value of product per unit area of land would locate closest to the urban place. These activities would be able to pay the higher land cost closer to the center. Because of the uniformity of the plain, all activity zones outward from the center would be arranged in concentric rings. Moving away from the center, the activities generally changed from **intensive agriculture** to **extensive agriculture.** The activity in the farthest zone outward from the center was grazing, the most extensive land use. Grazing

Johann Heinrich von Thunen. *Source:* The Warren J. Samuels Portrait Collection at Duke University.

also had the lowest monetary return of all the land uses on the plain. As such, it occupied the concentric zone with the lowest "land rent" (von Thunen's term).

The single variable in the model was transportation cost, a direct function of distance from the center. The basic concentric zone model allowed von Thunen to determine which agricultural activities would be ideally placed in each of the concentric zones. Realizing that real-world agricultural regions are not isolated and do not have the degree of uniformity he included in the model, von Thunen introduced two modifications. First, he placed a smaller urban place onto the plain and concluded that the new center would develop its own set of land use zones. The second modification was the introduction of a river that ran from the urban place at the center of the plain to the edge of the isolated state. The river provided a transportation corridor of far superior speed to that of the horse and wagon.

The concentric zones present in the original model were radically changed because activities with **accessibility** to the river could take place farther away from the center and still provide the center with its goods in essentially the same amount of time. Von Thunen's work was not used extensively in the United States until the mid-twentieth century. Since that time, his ideas have been widely accepted within the mainstream of geographical thinking.

Suggested Readings: Michael Chisholm, *Rural Settlement and Land Use,* London: Hutchins, 1962; Hildegard Binder Johnson, "A Note on von Thunen's Circles," *Annals of the Association of American Geographers,* vol. 52 (1962).

W

Wallerstein's world-system analysis. The prominent American social scientist Immanuel Wallerstein theorized in the 1960s and 1970s that the world is a single economic entity. He further stated that the world economic system operates in a capitalistic mode of production. In the capitalist world economy, as Wallerstein called it, meaningful change comes only through alterations in the world system and not by addressing the problems of a single country. In this regard, Wallerstein disagreed with twentieth-century American economic historian **Walter W. Rostow** and his stage theory of economic development.

The capitalist world economy, Wallerstein contended, has three basic features: (1) a single integrated world market that operates in a capitalistic mode of ceaseless capital accumulation; (2) a multiple-state system in which no single country can dominate the entire system; and (3) a capitalist world system with three regional components—the core, the periphery, and the semiperiphery. The core consists of the affluent and urban-industrialized developed countries. The economic system in each of these countries continues to be successful in the accumulation of capital. These countries are the generators of the capitalist world economy.

The periphery is composed of countries in the developing world. Most of these countries were under the control of a core country during the era of **colonialism** from the last quarter of the nineteenth century to the 1960s, and in many cases their economic system is little changed (*see* **Neocolonialism**). Although the developing countries have seen improvements in their socioeconomic situation, the gap between the core and the periphery continues to widen. Wallerstein pointed out that in the capitalist world economy there must be both a core and a periphery, and any gain made in the periphery will be matched and usually surpassed in the core. For example, **transnational corporations** (TNCs) operate in many developing countries. These plants provide jobs and other economic advantages to the host country, but the major gain in profits from the operation remains with the TNC, whose headquarters is in a country in the developed world. Inequity in regional economic development is a basic tenet of the capitalist world economy.

Wallerstein included the semiperiphery as a third region in the world system. Within this region, a dynamic struggle is underway as countries attempt to move from the periphery into the core. Over time, the individual countries in each of the three regions may change positions. Also, over extended cycles, the core may experience periods of dynamic growth and paralyzing stagnation.

Suggested Readings: R. J. Johnston et al., eds., *The Dictionary of Human Geography*, 2nd ed., Oxford, U.K.: Basil Blackwell, 1986; Immanuel Wallerstein, *The Capitalist World-Economy*, Cambridge: Cambridge University Press, 1979.

Weber's least cost theory. Alfred Weber (1868–1958), a German location economist, was a pioneer in the field of industrial location. He received his

doctorate at the University of Berlin in 1897. Ten years later, he became chairman of the Social Sciences and Political Economy department at Heidelberg University, a position he held throughout his illustrious career. Weber's 1909 book, *Theory of the Location of Industry,* is a classic in the field, and his work has been referred to and expounded on since its publication. Weber greatly influenced Soviet economic geographers in the 1930s as they worked on full regional economic development and the establishment of territorial production complexes. He also influenced German economic geographer Walter Christaller in his work on **Christaller's central place theory.** In the 1950s and 1960s, Weber's ideas became part of the **Quantitative Revolution** in American geography.

Weber's primary research motive was to find ways to reduce production costs in industrial operations. He focused on the development of three least-cost theories addressing transportation, labor, and **agglomeration.** His approach to the problem used a model similar to the one used by German economist Johann Heinrich von Thunen in his studies of agricultural systems in the 1800s. Weber assumed the following: (1) a uniform country with equal transportation rates throughout; (2) known locations for acquiring raw materials, with equal transportation rates from any one of them to the point of production; (3) known points of consumption; (4) a fixed labor

Alfred Weber. *Source:* Library of Congress.

supply in known locations, with no wage differentials; and (5) production costs that would not vary at any manufacturing point. Weber constructed a flat table complete with weights, pulleys, and lines to mechanically determine the ideal location for a manufacturing plant. Each raw material required in the manufacturing process and the location of the market was weighted to reflect its influence on the location process. The equilibrium point resulting from the pull of all the variables determined the ideal plant location.

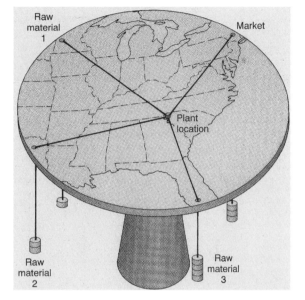

One factor in weighting the raw materials was whether or not each was a "weight-gaining" or a "weight-losing" material. For example, copper ore contains up to 98 percent impurities. Therefore, initial processing must take place at or near the mine site. It would not be economically sound to ship the ore without first removing the impurities. Copper represents a weight-losing product. Beverage bottling, on the other hand, is a weight-gaining product. Bottling plants are located near the market because of the weight added in the process.

A plane table using weights to show the point of least transport cost where there are several sources of raw materials. *Source:* Jerome D. Fellmann, Arthur Getis, and Judith Getis, *Human Geography: Landscapes of Human Activities*, updated 6th ed., Boston: McGraw-Hill, 2001. Reproduced by permission of The McGraw-Hill Companies.

This particular approach was based primarily on determining the location with the least transportation costs. Weber was also concerned about the affects of **agglomeration** on overall costs. Agglomeration, the clustering of industrial plants for mutual advantage, has obvious positive advantages. However, if agglomeration becomes too great in any one location, negative outcomes such as rising labor costs and land rents and overcrowding can occur.

Suggested Readings: Dean M. Hanink, *Principles and Applications of Economic Geography*, New York: John Wiley & Sons, 1997; Alfred Weber, *Theory of the Location of Industries*, trans. Carl J. Freidrich, Chicago: University of Chicago Press, 1929; reissued, New York: Russell & Russell, 1971.

Weight-gaining/weight-losing products. *See* **Weber's least cost theory.**

Z

Zero population growth. The achievement of zero population growth (ZPG) has been a goal of demographers and economic development experts for decades. Steadily increasing population, both globally and in a number of major regions, has in many ways outstripped the earth's capacity to adequately support the burgeoning numbers. Although there has been a slight decline in the global **rate of natural increase** (RNI) in recent decades, total population is still increasing by 80–90 million people each year. Most of the increase is occurring in the developing world, a region that can ill afford to support more people.

ZPG is seen to be the long-term goal for alleviating the pressure of higher population totals. For ZPG to become a reality, the **total fertility rate** (TFR), or replacement rate, must reach and be maintained at 2.1 or lower. This number represents the average number of children born to a woman during her childbearing years, ages 15–45. The average TFR for the developed world in 2000 was 1.6. Most of the countries in the world, however, have much higher TFRs. For instance, in 2000, world TFR was 2.9, and the TFR for the developing world, excluding China, was 3.8.

A regional TFR of 3.8 indicates that the countries in the region have not completed the **demographic transition** and will continue to experience population increase. The problem of continued growth is understood when it is noted that large percentages of the population in developing countries are found in the youngest age group (0–4). As long as this age group remains high in numbers, there is a guarantee that population increase will continue.

United Nations **population projection**s suggest that ZPG will be in place in all major regions within the twenty-first century. ZPG is expected to be achieved in Europe by 2020, in North America (Canada and the United

States) by 2030, China by 2070, Southeast Asia and Latin America by 2090, and Africa by 2100.

Suggested Readings: Anne Boyd et al., *The World's Youth: 2000*, Washington, D.C.: Population Reference Bureau, 2001; Wolfgang Lutz et al., eds., "Frontiers of Population Forecasting," *Population and Development Review*, vol. 24 (1998).

Selected Bibliography

GENERAL REFERENCES

Bergman, Edward F. *Human Geography: Cultures, Connections, and Landscapes*. Englewood Cliffs, N.J.: Prentice Hall, 1995.

de Blij, H. J., and Alexander B. Murphy. *Human Geography: Culture, Society, and Space*. 6th ed. New York: John Wiley & Sons, 1999.

Earle, Carville, Kent Mathewson, and Martin S. Kenzer, eds. *Concepts in Human Geography*. Lanham, Md.: Rowman & Littlefield, 1996.

Fellmann, Jerome D., Arthur Getis, and Judith Getis. *Human Geography: Landscapes of Human Activities*. Updated 6th ed. Boston: McGraw-Hill, 2001.

Johnston, R. J., ed. *The Dictionary of Human Geography*, 2nd ed., Oxford: Basil Blackwell Ltd., 1986.

Kish, George, ed. *A Source Book in Geography*. Cambridge, Mass.: Harvard University Press, 1978.

Knox, P., and S. Marston. *Human Geography: Places and Regions in a Global Context*. Upper Saddle River, N.J.: Prentice Hall, 1998.

Martin, Geoffrey J., and Preston E. James. *All Possible Worlds: A History of Geographical Ideas*. 3rd ed. New York: John Wiley & Sons, 1993.

Nelson, Ronald E., Robert E. Gabler, and James W. Vining. *Human Geography: People, Cultures, and Landscapes*. Fort Worth, Tx.: Saunders, Harcourt Brace College Publishers, 1995.

Norton, William. *Human Geography*. 3rd ed. Toronto: Oxford University Press, 1998.

Pattison, William D. "The Four Traditions of Geography." *Journal of Geography*, vol. 63 (1964): 211–16.

Rubenstein, James M. *The Cultural Landscape: An Introduction to Human Geography*. Upper Saddle River, N.J.: Prentice Hall, 2002.

Shelley, Fred M., and Audrey E. Clarke. *Human and Cultural Geography: A Global Perspective*. Dubuque, Iowa: William C. Brown, 1994.

CULTURAL GEOGRAPHY

Anderson, K., and F. Gale. *Cultural Geographies*. Melbourne: Longman, 1999.

Boal, Frederick W., and Stephen A. Royle. *North America: A Geographical Mosaic*. London: Arnold, 1999.

Foote, K., et al., eds. *Rereading Cultural Geography*. Austin: University of Texas Press, 1994.

Jackson, W. A. Douglas, *The Shaping of Our World: A Human and Cultural Geography*. New York: John Wiley & Sons, 1985.

Jordan-Bychkov, Terry G., and Mona Domosh. *The Human Mosaic: A Thematic Introduction to Cultural Geography*. 8th ed. New York: W. H. Freeman, 1999.

Mitchell, D. *Cultural Geography: A Critical Introduction*. Malden, Mass.: Blackwell, 2000.

Tuan, Yi-Fu. *Space and Place: The Perspective of Experience*. Minneapolis: University of Minnesota Press, 1977.

Zelinsky, Wilbur. *The Cultural Geography of the United States*. Englewood Cliffs, N.J.: Prentice Hall, 1992.

ECONOMIC DEVELOPMENT

Black, Jan Knippers. *Development in Theory and Practice: Paradigms and Paradoxes*. 2nd ed. Boulder, Colo.: Westview Press, 1999.

Dickerson, John. *Geography of the Third World*. 2nd ed. New York: Routledge, 1996.

Griffith, Keith. *Studies in Development Strategy and Systematic Transformation*. New York: St. Martin's Press, 2000.

Meier, Gerald M., and James E. Rauch. *Leading Issues in Economic Development*. 7th ed. New York: Oxford University Press, 2000.

Morris, Arthur. *Geography and Development*. London: University College London Press, 1998.

Ros, Jaime. *Development Theory and the Economics of Growth*. Ann Arbor: University of Michigan Press, 2000.

Simpson, Edward S. *The Developing World: An Introduction*. 2nd ed. New York: Longman, 1994.

ECONOMIC GEOGRAPHY

Berry, Brian J. L., Edgar G. Conkling, and Michael Ray. *The Global Economy in Transition*. Upper Saddle River, N.J.: Prentice Hall, 1997.

Bryson, John, et al. *The Economic Geography Reader: Producing and Consuming Global Capitalism*. New York: John Wiley & Sons, 1999.

Dicken, Peter. *Global Shift: Transforming the World Economy*. 3rd ed. New York: Guilford Press, 1998.

Grigg, David. *An Introduction to Agricultural Geography*. New York: Routledge, 1995.

Hanink, Dean M. *Principles and Applications of Economic Geography: Economy, Policy, Environment*. New York: John Wiley & Sons, 1997.

Harrington, J. W., and Barney Warf. *Industrial Location*. New York: Routledge, 1995.

Lee, Roger, and Jane Wills. *Geographies of Economies*. New York: Arnold, 1997.

Mills, John. *Managing the World Economy*. New York: St. Martin's Press, 2000.

Wheeler, James O., et al. *Economic Geography*. 3rd ed. New York: John Wiley & Sons, 1998.

MAPS AND CARTOGRAPHY

Campbell, John. *Map Use and Analysis*. 3rd ed. Dubuque, Iowa: WCB/McGraw-Hill, 1998.

Dent, Borden C. *Cartography: Thematic Map Design*. 4th ed. Dubuque, Iowa: Wm. C. Brown Publishers, 1996.

MacEachran, Alan M. *How Maps Work*. New York: Guilford Press, 1995.

Monmonier, Mark. *Drawing the Line: Tales of Maps and Cartocontroversy*. New York: Henry Holt, 1995.

Muehrcke, Phillip C., and Julianna O. Muehrcke. *Map Use: Reading, Analysis, Interpretation*. Madison, Wis.: JP Publications, 1992.

Robinson, Arthur H., et al. *Elements of Cartography*. 6th ed. New York: John Wiley & Sons, 1995.

Thrower, Norman J. W. *Maps and Civilization: Cartography in Culture and Society*. Chicago: University of Chicago Press, 1996.

Tyner, Judith. *Introduction to Thematic Cartography*. Englewood Cliffs, N.J.: Prentice Hall, 1992.

Wood, Dennis. *The Power of Maps*. New York: Guilford Press, 1992.

POLITICAL GEOGRAPHY

Agnew, John A., ed. *Political Geography: A Reader*. London: Arnold, 1997.

Demko, George J., and William B. Woods. *Reordering the World: Geopolitical Perspectives on the Twenty-first Century*. Boulder, Colo.: Westview Press, 1994.

Glassner, Martin I. *Political Geography*. New York: John Wiley & Sons, 1993.

Hooson, David, ed. *Geography and National Identity*. Oxford, U.K.: Blackwell, 1994.

Kliot, Nurit, and Stanley Waterman. *The Political Geography of Conflict and Peace*. London: Belhaven Press, 1991.

Muir, Richard. *Political Geography: A New Introduction*. New York: John Wiley & Sons, 1997.

Poulsen, Thomas M. *Nations and States: A Geographical Background to World Affairs*. Englewood Cliffs, N.J.: Prentice Hall, 1995.

Short, John R. *An Introduction to Political Geography*. London: Routledge, 1994.

Slowe, Peter M. *Geography and Political Power: The Geography of Nations and States*. London: Routledge, 1990.

Taylor, Peter J. *Political Geography: World-Economy, Nation-State, and Locality*. 3rd ed. New York: John Wiley & Sons, 1993.

Taylor, Peter J., ed. *Political Geography of the Twentieth Century: A Global Analysis*. New York: Halstead Press, 1993.

POPULATION GEOGRAPHY

Castles, Stephen, and Mark J. Miller. *The Age of Migration: International Population Movements in the Modern World*. New York: Guilford Press, 1998.

Cohen, Joel E. *How Many People Can the Earth Support?* New York: Norton, 1995.

Ehrlich, Paul, and Anne Ehrlich. *The Population Explosion*. New York: Simon & Schuster, 1990.

Daugherty, Helen Ginn, and Kenneth C. W. Kammeyer. *An Introduction to Population.* 2nd ed. New York: Guilford Press, 1995.

Hornby, William F., and Melvyn Jones. *An Introduction to Population Geography.* Cambridge: Cambridge University Press, 1993.

Jones, Huw. *Population Geography.* 2nd ed. New York: Guilford Press, 1990.

Keyfitz, Nathan, and William Flinger. *World Population Growth and Aging: Demographic Trends in the Late 20th Century.* Chicago: University of Chicago Press, 1991.

Parnell, Mike. *Population Movements and the Third World.* New York: Routledge, 1993.

Peters, Gary L., and Robert P. Larkin. *Population Geography: Problems, Concepts, and Prospects.* Dubuque, Iowa: Kendall/Hunt, 1993.

Plane, David A., and Peter A, Rogerson. *The Geographical Analysis of Population.* New York: John Wiley & Sons, 1994.

Robert, Godfrey. *Population Policy, Contemporary Issues.* New York: Praeger, 1990.

Robinson, Vaughn, ed. *Geography and Migration.* London: Edward Elgar, 1996.

REGIONAL GEOGRAPHY

Aryeety-Attoh, Samuel, ed. *Geography of Sub-Saharan Africa.* Upper Saddle River, N.J.: Prentice Hall, 1997.

Blouet, Brian W., and Olwyn M. Blouet. *Latin America and the Caribbean: A Systematic and Regional Survey.* New York: John Wiley & Sons, 1993.

Bradshaw, Michael. *World Regional Geography: The New Global Order.* Updated 2nd ed. New York: McGraw-Hill, 2002.

Clawson, David L., ed. *World Regional Geography: A Developmental Approach.* 7th ed. Upper Saddle River, N.J.: Prentice Hall, 2001.

Getis, Arthur, and Judith Getis, eds. *The United States and Canada.* Dubuque, Iowa: Wm. C. Brown, 1995.

Heffernan, Michael. *The Meaning of Europe: Geography and Geopolitics.* New York: Oxford University Press, 1998.

Leeming, F. *The Changing Geography of China.* Cambridge, Mass.: Blackwell, 1993.

McLoud, D. G. *Southeast Asia: Tradition and Modernity in the Contemporary World.* Boulder, Colo.: Westview Press, 1995.

Pulsipher, Lydia Mihelic, and Alex A. Pulsipher. *World Regional Geography: Global Patterns, Local Lives.* 2nd ed. New York: W. H. Freeman, 2002.

Rigg, Jonathan. *Southeast Asia: The Human Landscape of Modernization and Development.* New York: Routledge, 1997.

Shaw, Dennis J. B. *Russia in the Modern World: A New Geography.* Malden, Mass.: Blackwell, 1999.

Stock, R. *Africa South of the Sahara: A Geographical Interpretation.* New York: Guilford Press, 1995.

Unwin, Tim, ed. *A European Geography.* Harlow, U.K.: Addison Wesley Longman, 1998.

Weightman, Barbara. *Geography of Asia: Of Dragons and Tigers.* New York: John Wiley & Sons, 2000.

URBAN GEOGRAPHY

Brunn, Stanley D., and Jack F. Williams. *Cities of the World: World Regional Urban Development.* 2nd ed. New York: HarperCollins, 1993.

Carter, Harold. *The Study of Urban Geography.* 4th ed. New York: John Wiley & Sons, 1996.

Ford, Larry R. *Cities and Buildings: Skyscrapers, Skid Rows, and Suburbs.* Baltimore: Johns Hopkins University Press, 1994.

Garreau, Joel. *Edge Cities: Life on the New Frontier.* New York: Doubleday, 1991.

Garvin, Alexander. *The American City: What Works, What Doesn't.* New York: McGraw-Hill, 1996.

Gilbert, Alan, and Josef Gugler. *Cities, Poverty, and Development: Urbanization in the Third World.* 2nd ed. New York: Oxford University Press, 1992.

Herbert, David T., and Colin J. Thomas. *Cities in Space: Cities as Place.* New York: John Wiley & Sons, 1997.

Knox, Paul L. *Urbanization: An Introduction to Urban Geography.* Englewood Cliffs, N.J.: Prentice Hall, 1994.

Knox, Paul L., ed. *The Restless Urban Landscape.* Englewood Cliffs, N.J.: Prentice Hall, 1993.

Vance, James E. *The Continuing City: Urban Morphology in Western Civilization.* 2nd ed. Baltimore: Johns Hopkins University Press, 1990.

Wilson, David, ed. *Globalization and the Changing U.S. City.* Thousand Oaks, Calif.: Sage, 1997.

Yeates, Maurice. *The North American City.* 5th ed. New York: Longman, 1997.

Index

About the Author

GERALD R. PITZL is Professor Emeritus of Geography, Macalester College, St. Paul, Minnesota. He now lives in Santa Fe, New Mexico.